IFIP Advances in Information and Communication Technology

532

Editor-in-Chief

Kai Rannenberg, Goethe University Frankfurt, Germany

Editorial Board

IFIP – The International Federation for Information Processing

IFIP was founded in 1960 under the auspices of UNESCO, following the first World Computer Congress held in Paris the previous year. A federation for societies working in information processing, IFIP's aim is two-fold: to support information processing in the countries of its members and to encourage technology transfer to developing nations. As its mission statement clearly states:

> *IFIP is the global non-profit federation of societies of ICT professionals that aims at achieving a worldwide professional and socially responsible development and application of information and communication technologies.*

IFIP is a non-profit-making organization, run almost solely by 2500 volunteers. It operates through a number of technical committees and working groups, which organize events and publications. IFIP's events range from large international open conferences to working conferences and local seminars.

The flagship event is the IFIP World Computer Congress, at which both invited and contributed papers are presented. Contributed papers are rigorously refereed and the rejection rate is high.

As with the Congress, participation in the open conferences is open to all and papers may be invited or submitted. Again, submitted papers are stringently refereed.

The working conferences are structured differently. They are usually run by a working group and attendance is generally smaller and occasionally by invitation only. Their purpose is to create an atmosphere conducive to innovation and development. Refereeing is also rigorous and papers are subjected to extensive group discussion.

Publications arising from IFIP events vary. The papers presented at the IFIP World Computer Congress and at open conferences are published as conference proceedings, while the results of the working conferences are often published as collections of selected and edited papers.

IFIP distinguishes three types of institutional membership: Country Representative Members, Members at Large, and Associate Members. The type of organization that can apply for membership is a wide variety and includes national or international societies of individual computer scientists/ICT professionals, associations or federations of such societies, government institutions/government related organizations, national or international research institutes or consortia, universities, academies of sciences, companies, national or international associations or federations of companies.

More information about this series at http://www.springer.com/series/6102

Gilbert Peterson · Sujeet Shenoi (Eds.)

Advances in Digital Forensics XIV

14th IFIP WG 11.9 International Conference
New Delhi, India, January 3–5, 2018
Revised Selected Papers

 Springer

Editors
Gilbert Peterson
Department of Electrical and Computer
  Engineering
Air Force Institute of Technology
Wright-Patterson AFB, OH
USA

Sujeet Shenoi
Tandy School of Computer Science
University of Tulsa
Tulsa, OK
USA

ISSN 1868-4238   ISSN 1868-422X (electronic)
IFIP Advances in Information and Communication Technology
ISBN 978-3-030-07584-2   ISBN 978-3-319-99277-8 (eBook)
https://doi.org/10.1007/978-3-319-99277-8

This Springer imprint is published by the registered company Springer Nature Switzerland AG
The registered company address is: Gewerbestrasse 11, 6330 Cham, Switzerland

Contents

PART V   MOBILE AND EMBEDDED DEVICE FORENSICS

Contributing Authors

Gail-Joon Ahn is a Professor of Computer Science and Engineering, and Director of the Center for Cybersecurity and Digital Forensics at Arizona State University, Tempe, Arizona. His research interests include security analytics and big-data-driven security intelligence, vulnerability and risk management, access control and security architectures for distributed systems, identity and privacy management, cyber crime analysis, security-enhanced computing platforms and formal models for computer security devices.

Saad Alabdulsalam is a Ph.D. student in Computer Science at University College Dublin, Dublin, Ireland. His research interests include Internet of Things security and forensics.

Harald Baier is a Professor of Internet Security at Darmstadt University of Applied Sciences, Darmstadt, Germany; and a Principal Investigator at the Center for Research in Security and Privacy, Darmstadt, Germany. His research interests include digital forensics, network-based anomaly detection and security protocols.

Chun-Fai Chan is a Ph.D. student in Computer Science at the University of Hong Kong, Hong Kong, China. His research interests include penetration testing, digital forensics and Internet of Things security.

Wenhao Chen is a Ph.D. student in Computer Engineering at Iowa State University, Ames, Iowa. His research interests include program analysis and digital forensics.

Saheb Chhabra is a Ph.D. student in Computer Science and Engineering at Indraprastha Institute of Information Technology, New Delhi, India. His research interests include image processing and computer vision, and their applications to document fraud detection.

Kam-Pui Chow is an Associate Professor of Computer Science at the University of Hong Kong, Hong Kong, China. His research interests include information security, digital forensics, live system forensics and digital surveillance.

Spyridon Dosis is a Security Engineer at NetEnt, Stockholm, Sweden. His research interests include network security, digital forensics, cloud computing and semantic web technologies.

Adam Doupé is an Assistant Professor of Computer Science and Engineering, and Associate Director of the Center for Cybersecurity and Digital Forensics at Arizona State University, Tempe, Arizona. His research interests include vulnerability analysis, web security, mobile security, network security and ethical hacking.

Binxing Fang is a Member of the Chinese Academy of Engineering, Beijing, China; and a Professor of Information Engineering at the University of Electronic Science and Technology, Guangdong, China. His research interests are in the area of cyber security.

Thomas Göbel is a Ph.D. student in Computer Science at Darmstadt University of Applied Sciences, Darmstadt, Germany; and a Researcher at the Center for Research in Security and Privacy, Darmstadt, Germany. His research interests include digital forensics, anti-forensics and network forensics.

Mahesh Govil is a Professor of Computer Science and Engineering at Malaviya National Institute of Technology, Jaipur, India; and Director of National Institute of Technology Sikkim, Ravangla, India. His research interests include real-time systems, parallel and distributed systems, fault-tolerant systems and cloud computing.

Yong Guan is a Professor of Electrical and Computer Engineering at Iowa State University, Ames, Iowa. His research interests include digital forensics and information security.

Garima Gupta is a Postdoctoral Researcher in Computer Science and Engineering at Indraprastha Institute of Information Technology, New Delhi, India. Her research interests include image processing and computer vision, and their applications to document fraud detection.

Gaurav Gupta is a Scientist D in the Ministry of Information Technology, New Delhi, India. His research interests include mobile device security, digital forensics, web application security, Internet of Things security and security in emerging technologies.

Monika Gupta recently received her Ph.D. degree in Physics from National Institute of Technology Kurukshetra, Kurukshetra, India. Her research interests include image processing and computer vision, and their applications to document fraud detection.

Irvin Homem is a Ph.D. student in Computer and Systems Sciences at Stockholm University, Stockholm, Sweden; and a Threat Intelligence Analyst with IBM, Stockholm, Sweden. His research interests include network security, digital forensics, mobile forensics, machine learning, virtualization and cloud computing.

Tahar Kechadi is a Professor of Computer Science at University College Dublin, Dublin, Ireland. His research interests include data extraction and analysis, and data mining in digital forensics and cyber crime investigations.

Nhien-An Le-Khac is a Lecturer of Computer Science, and Director of the Forensic Computing and Cybercrime Investigation Program at University College Dublin, Dublin, Ireland. His research interests include digital forensics, cyber security and big data analytics.

Xiang Li is a Researcher at the Bank of China, Beijing, China. Her research interests include web application security and digital forensics.

Ondrej Lichtner is a Ph.D. student in Information Technology at Brno University of Technology, Brno, Czech Republic. His research interests include network architecture design and secure network architectures.

Li Lin is a Ph.D. student in Applied Mathematics at Iowa State University, Ames, Iowa. His research interests include digital image forensics and statistical machine learning.

Changwei Liu is a Postdoctoral Researcher in the Department of Computer Science at George Mason University, Fairfax, Virginia. Her research interests include network security, cloud security and digital forensics.

Danjun Liu is an M.S. student in Computer Science and Technology at the National University of Defense Technology, Changsha, China. His research interests include cyber security and software reliability.

Qingyun Liu is a Professor of Information Engineering at the Institute of Information Engineering, Chinese Academy of Sciences, Beijing, China. His research interests include information security and network security.

Mike Mabey recently received his Ph.D. in Computer Science from Arizona State University, Tempe, Arizona. His research interests include digital forensics, threat intelligence sharing and security in emerging technologies.

Anand Kumar Mishra is a Ph.D. student in Computer Science and Engineering at Malaviya National Institute of Technology, Jaipur, India; and a Guest Researcher in the Information Technology Laboratory at the National Institute of Standards and Technology, Gaithersburg, Maryland. His research interests include digital forensics and cyber security, especially related to cloud computing and container technology.

Nour Moustafa is a Postdoctoral Research Fellow at the Australian Centre for Cyber Security, University of New South Wales, Canberra, Australia. His research interests include cyber security, intrusion detection and machine learning.

Rajender Nath is a Professor of Computer Science and Engineering at Kurukshetra University, Kurukshetra, India. His research interests include computer architecture, parallel processing, object-oriented modeling and aspect-oriented programming.

Jijnasa Nayak is a B.Tech. student in Computer Science and Engineering at National Institute of Technology Rourkela, Rourkela, India. Her research interests include computer vision, image processing, natural language processing and their applications to document fraud detection.

Jennifer Newman is an Associate Professor of Mathematics at Iowa State University, Ames, Iowa. Her research interests include digital image forensics and image processing.

Richard Overill is a Senior Lecturer of Computer Science at King's College London, London, United Kingdom. His research interests include digital forensics and cyber crime analysis.

Panagiotis Papapetrou is a Professor of Computer and Systems Sciences at Stockholm University, Stockholm, Sweden; and an Adjunct Professor of Computer Science at Aalto University, Helsinki, Finland. His research interests include algorithmic data mining with a focus on mining and indexing sequential data, complex metric and non-metric spaces, biological sequences, time series and sequences of temporal intervals.

Slobodan Petrovic is a Professor of Information Security at the Norwegian University of Science and Technology, Gjovik, Norway. His research interests include cryptology, intrusion detection and digital forensics.

Emmanuel Pilli is an Associate Professor of Computer Science and Engineering at Malaviya National Institute of Technology, Jaipur, India. His research interests include cyber security, privacy and forensics, computer networks, cloud computing, big data and the Internet of Things.

Jan Pluskal is a Ph.D. student in Information Technology at Brno University of Technology, Brno, Czech Republic. His research interests include network forensics, machine learning and distributed computing.

Kyle Porter is a Ph.D. student in Information Security and Communications Technology at the Norwegian University of Science and Technology, Gjovik, Norway. His research interests include approximate string matching algorithms, and applications of machine learning and data reduction mechanisms in digital forensics.

Stephanie Reinders is a Ph.D. student in Applied Mathematics at Iowa State University, Ames, Iowa. Her research interests include steganalysis and machine learning.

Ondrej Rysavy is an Associate Professor of Information Systems at Brno University of Technology, Brno, Czech Republic. His research interests are in the area of computer networks, especially, network monitoring, network security, network forensics and network architectures.

Mark Scanlon is an Assistant Professor of Computer Science, and Co-Director of the Forensic Computing and Cybercrime Investigation Program at University College Dublin, Dublin, Ireland. His research interests include artificial-intelligence-based digital evidence processing, digital forensics as a service and remote evidence processing.

Kevin Schaefer is an Information Technology and Forensics Investigator at the Land Office of Criminal Investigation Baden-Wuerttemberg in Stuttgart, Germany. His research interests include mobile phone and smartwatch forensics.

Pankaj Sharma is an Assistant Professor of Computer Science and Engineering at Chitkara University, Punjab, India. His research interests include digital forensics, security and privacy.

Ambika Shrestha Chitrakar is a Ph.D. student in Information Security and Communications Technology at the Norwegian University of Science and Technology, Gjovik, Norway. Her research interests include approximate search algorithms, intrusion detection and prevention, big data, machine learning and digital forensics.

Bhupendra Singh is a Ph.D. student in Computer Science and Engineering at the Defence Institute of Advanced Technology, Pune, India. His research interests include digital forensics, filesystem analysis and user activity analysis in Windows and Linux systems.

Shweta Singh is a B.Tech. student in Computer Science at Maharishi Dayanand University, Rohtak, India. Her research interests include machine learning and their applications to digitized document fraud.

Upasna Singh is an Assistant Professor of Computer Science and Engineering at the Defence Institute of Advanced Technology, Pune, India. Her research interests include data mining and knowledge discovery, machine intelligence, soft computing, digital forensics, social network analysis and big data analytics.

Anoop Singhal is a Senior Computer Scientist, and Program Manager in the Computer Security Division at the National Institute of Standards and Technology, Gaithersburg, Maryland. His research interests include network security, network forensics, cloud security and data mining.

Jill Slay is the La Trobe Optus Chair of Cyber Security at La Trobe University, Melbourne, Australia. Her research interests include digital forensics, cyber intelligence and cyber skilling.

Yong Sun is a Professor of Information Engineering at the Institute of Information Engineering, Chinese Academy of Sciences, Beijing, China. His research interests include information security and network security.

Yong Tang is an Associate Researcher in the Network Research Institute at the National University of Defense Technology, Changsha, China. His research interests include cyber security and software reliability.

Erwin van de Wiel is a Digital Forensic Investigator with the Dutch Police in Breda, The Netherlands. His research interests are in the area of digital forensics.

Baosheng Wang is a Researcher in the Network Research Institute at the National University of Defense Technology, Changsha, China. His research interests include computer networks and software reliability.

Yangxiao Wang recently received his B.S. degree in Computer Engineering from Iowa State University, Ames, Iowa. His research interests include digital forensics and information security.

Duminda Wijesekera is a Professor of Computer Science at George Mason University, Fairfax, Virginia. His research interests include systems security, digital forensics and transportation systems.

Wei Xie is an Assistant Researcher in the Network Research Institute at the National University of Defense Technology, Changsha, China. His research interests include cyber security and software reliability.

Ken Yau is a Ph.D. student in Computer Science at the University of Hong Kong, Hong Kong, China. His research interests are in the area of digital forensics, with an emphasis on industrial control system forensics.

Siu-Ming Yiu is an Associate Professor of Computer Science at the University of Hong Kong, Hong Kong, China. His research interests include security, cryptography, digital forensics and bioinformatics.

Bo Yu is an Assistant Researcher in the Network Research Institute at the National University of Defense Technology, Changsha, China. His research interests include cyber security and software reliability.

Ziming Zhao is an Assistant Research Professor in the School of Computing, Informatics and Decision Systems Engineering at Arizona State University, Tempe, Arizona. His research interests include system and network security.

Chao Zheng is an Associate Professor of Information Engineering at the Institute of Information Engineering, Chinese Academy of Sciences, Beijing, China. His research interests include deep packet inspection, digital forensics, protocols and network security.

Preface

Digital forensics deals with the acquisition, preservation, examination, analysis and presentation of electronic evidence. Computer networks, cloud computing, smartphones, embedded devices and the Internet of Things have expanded the role of digital forensics beyond traditional computer crime investigations. Practically every crime now involves some aspect of digital evidence; digital forensics provides the techniques and tools to articulate this evidence in legal proceedings. Digital forensics also has myriad intelligence applications; furthermore, it has a vital role in information assurance – investigations of security breaches yield valuable information that can be used to design more secure and resilient systems.

This book, *Advances in Digital Forensics XIV*, is the fourteenth volume in the annual series produced by the IFIP Working Group 11.9 on Digital Forensics, an international community of scientists, engineers and practitioners dedicated to advancing the state of the art of research and practice in digital forensics. The book presents original research results and innovative applications in digital forensics. Also, it highlights some of the major technical and legal issues related to digital evidence and electronic crime investigations.

This volume contains nineteen revised and edited chapters based on papers presented at the Fourteenth IFIP WG 11.9 International Conference on Digital Forensics, held in New Delhi, India on January 3-5, 2018. The papers were refereed by members of IFIP Working Group 11.9 and other internationally-recognized experts in digital forensics. The post-conference manuscripts submitted by the authors were rewritten to accommodate the suggestions provided by the conference attendees. They were subsequently revised by the editors to produce the final chapters published in this volume.

The chapters are organized into five sections: Themes and Issues, Forensic Techniques, Network Forensics, Cloud Forensics, and Mobile and Embedded Device Forensics. The coverage of topics highlights the richness and vitality of the discipline, and offers promising avenues for future research in digital forensics.

This book is the result of the combined efforts of several individuals. In particular, we thank Gaurav Gupta and Robin Verma for their tireless work on behalf of IFIP Working Group 11.9 on Digital Forensics. We also acknowledge the conference sponsors, Cellebrite, Magnet Forensics and Lab Systems, as well as the support provided by the Department of Electronics and Information Technology (Ministry of Communications and Information Technology, Government of India), U.S. National Science Foundation, U.S. National Security Agency and U.S. Secret Service.

GILBERT PETERSON AND SUJEET SHENOI

I

THEMES AND ISSUES

Chapter 1

MEASURING EVIDENTIAL WEIGHT IN DIGITAL FORENSIC INVESTIGATIONS

Richard Overill and Kam-Pui Chow

Abstract   This chapter describes a method for obtaining a quantitative measure of the relative weight of each individual item of evidence in a digital forensic investigation using a Bayesian network. The resulting evidential weights can then be used to determine a near-optimal, cost-effective triage scheme for the investigation in question.

Keywords: Bayesian network, evidential weight, triage, digital crime templates

1.   Introduction

An inability to reliably quantify the relative plausibility of alternative hypotheses purporting to explain the existence of the totality of the digital evidence recovered in criminal investigations has hindered the transformation of digital forensics into a mature scientific and engineering discipline from the qualitative craft that originated in the mid 1980s [3]. A rigorous science-and-engineering-oriented approach can provide numerical results and also quantify the confidence limits, sensitivities and uncertainties associated with the results. However, there is a dearth of research literature focused on developing rigorous approaches to digital forensic investigations.

Posterior probabilities, likelihood ratios and odds generated using technical approaches such as Bayesian networks can provide digital forensic investigators, law enforcement officers and legal professionals with a quantitative scale or metric against which to assess the plausibility of an investigative hypothesis, which may be linked to the likelihood of successful prosecution or indeed the merit of a not-guilty plea. This approach is sometimes referred to as digital meta-forensics, some examples of which can be found in [4, 5].

© IFIP International Federation for Information Processing 2018
Published by Springer Nature Switzerland AG 2018. All Rights Reserved
G. Peterson and S. Shenoi (Eds.): Advances in Digital Forensics XIV, IFIP AICT 532, pp. 3–10, 2018.
https://doi.org/10.1007/978-3-319-99277-8_1

A second and closely related issue involves the reliable quantification of the relative weight (also known as the probative value) of each of the individual items of digital evidence recovered during a criminal investigation. This is particularly important from the perspective of digital forensic triage – a prioritization strategy for searching for digital evidence in order to cope with the ever-increasing volumes of data and varieties of devices that are routinely seized for examination. The economics of digital forensics, also known as digital forensonomics [8], provides for the possibility of a quantitative basis for prioritizing the search for digital evidence during criminal investigations. This is accomplished by leveraging well-known concepts from economics such as the return-on-investment, or equivalently, the cost-benefit ratio.

In this approach, a list of all the expected items of digital evidence for the hypothesis being investigated is drawn up. For each item of digital evidence, two attributes are required: (i) cost, which is, in principle, relatively straightforward to quantify because it is usually measured in terms of the resources required to locate, recover and analyze the item of digital evidence (typically investigator hours plus any specialized equipment hire-time needed); and (ii) relative weight, which measures the contribution that the presence of the item of digital evidence makes in supporting the hypothesis (usually based on the informal opinions or consensus of experienced digital forensic investigators) [9].

The principal goals of this research are to: (i) demonstrate that a quantitative measure of the relative weight of each item of digital evidence in a particular investigation can be obtained in a straightforward manner from a Bayesian network representing the hypothesis underpinning the investigation; and (ii) demonstrate that the evidential weights can be employed to create a near-optimal, cost-effective evidence search list for the triage phase of the digital forensic investigation process.

It has been observed that a substantial proportion of digital crimes recorded in a particular jurisdiction at a particular epoch can be represented by a relatively small number of digital crime templates. It follows that, if each of these commonly-occurring digital crimes can be investigated more efficiently with the aid of its template, then the overall throughput of investigations may be improved with corresponding benefits to the criminal justice system as a whole.

2.   Methodology

Bayesian networks were first proposed by Pearl [11] based on the concept of conditional probability originated by Bayes [2] in the eighteenth century. A Bayesian network is a directed acyclic graph (DAG) representation of the conditional dependency relationships between entities such as events, observations and outcomes. Visually, a Bayesian network typically resembles an inverted tree.

In the context of a digital forensic investigation, the root node of a Bayesian network represents the overall hypothesis underpinning the investigation, the child nodes of the root node represent the sub-hypotheses that contribute to the overall hypothesis and the leaf nodes represent the items of digital evidence associated with each of the sub-hypotheses. After populating the interior nodes with conditional probabilities (likelihoods) and assigning prior probabilities to the root node, the Bayesian network propagates the probabilities using Bayesian inference rules to produce a posterior probability for the root hypothesis. However, it is the architecture of the Bayesian network together with the definition of each sub-hypothesis and its associated evidential traces that together define the hypothesis characterizing the specific investigation.

The first application of a Bayesian network to a specific digital forensic investigation appeared in 2008 [4]. Figure 1 presents a Bayesian network associated with a BitTorrent investigation, which will be employed later in this chapter.

The posterior probability produced by a Bayesian network when all the expected items of digital evidence are present is compared against the posterior probability of the Bayesian network when item i of the digital evidence is absent (but all the other expected evidential items are present). The difference between, and the ratio of, these two quantities provide direct measures of the relative weight of item i of the digital evidence in the context of the investigative hypothesis represented by the Bayesian network.

The relative weight RW_i of evidential item i satisfies the following proportionality equation:

$$RW_i \propto PP - PP_i \tag{1}$$

where PP is the posterior probability of the Bayesian network and PP_i is the posterior probability of the Bayesian network when evidential item i is absent.

This equation can be written in normalized form as:

$$RW_i \propto 1 - \frac{PP_i}{PP} \tag{2}$$

or, alternatively as:

$$RW_i \propto \frac{PP}{PP_i} \tag{3}$$

From a ranking perspective, any of Equations (1), (2) or (3) could be used because, in each case, the relative weight of evidential item i

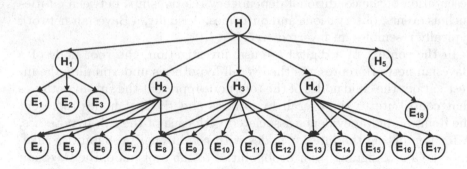

HYPOTHESES:

H   The seized computer was used as the initial seeder to share the pirated file on a
      BitTorrent network
H_1 The pirated file was copied from the seized optical disk to the seized computer
H_2 A torrent file was created from the copied file
H_3 The torrent file was sent to newsgroups for publishing
H_4 The torrent file was activated, which caused the seized computer to connect to
      the tracker server
H_5 The connection between the seized computer and the tracker was maintained

EVIDENCE:

E_1 Modification time of the destination file equals that of the source file
E_2 Creation time of the destination file is after its own modification time
E_3 Hash value of the destination file matches that of the source file
E_4 BitTorrent client software is installed on the seized computer
E_5 File link for the shared file is created
E_6 Shared file exists on the hard disk
E_7 Torrent file creation record is found
E_8 Torrent file exists on the hard disk
E_9 Peer connection information is found
E_{10} Tracker server login record is found
E_{11} Torrent file activation time is corroborated by its MAC time and link file
E_{12} Internet history record about publishing website is found
E_{13} Internet connection is available
E_{14} Cookie of the publishing website is found
E_{15} URL of the publishing website is stored in the web browser
E_{16} Web browser software is available
E_{17} Internet cache record about the publishing of the torrent file is found
E_{18} Internet history record about the tracker server connection is found

Figure 1.   Bayesian network for a BitTorrent investigation [4].

increases monotonically with the difference between the posterior probabilities. The remainder of this work will continue to employ Equation (1).

For a Bayesian network incorporating n items of digital evidence, it
is necessary to perform $n + 1$ executions of the network. After all the
relative evidential weights have been obtained in this manner using any
of Equations (1), (2) or (3), the return on investment (RoI) and cost-
benefit ratio (CBR) for item i of the expected digital evidence in the
hypothesis satisfy the following proportionality equations [8]:

$$RoI_i \propto \frac{RW_i}{(EH_i \times HC) + EC_i} \tag{4}$$

$$CBR_i \propto \frac{(EH_i \times HC) + EC_i}{RW_i} \tag{5}$$

where EH_i is the examiner hours spent on evidential item i, HC is the
hourly cost and EC_i is the equipment cost associated with evidential
item i.

3.   Results and Discussion

The real-world criminal case involving the illegal uploading of copy-
righted material via the BitTorrent peer-to-peer network [4, 6] is used to
illustrate the application of the proposed approach. The freely-available
Bayesian network simulator MSBNx from Microsoft Research [7] was
used to perform all the computations. The results were subsequently
verified independently using the freeware version of AgenaRisk [1]. A
previous sensitivity analysis performed on the Bayesian network for the
BitTorrent case [10] demonstrated that the posterior probabilities and,
hence, the relative evidential weights derived from them, are stable to
within ±0.5%.

The ranked evidential weights of the eighteen items of digital evidence shown in Figure 1 are listed in Table 1 along with their estimated relative costs [9] and their associated return-on-investment and
cost-benefit-ratio values computed using Equations (4) and (5), respectively. The relative evidential recovery costs for the Bayesian network
are taken from [9]; they were estimated by experienced digital forensic
investigators from the Hong Kong Customs and Excise Department IPR
Protection Group, taking into account the typical forensic examiner time
required along with the use of any specialized equipment. The proposed
approach assumes that the typical cost of locating, recovering and analyzing each individual item of digital evidence is fixed. However, it is
possible that the cost could be variable under certain circumstances; for
example, when evidence recovery requires the invocation of a mutual

Table 1. Attribute values of digital evidential items in the BitTorrent investigation.

Posterior Probability	Evidential Item	Relative Weight	Relative Cost	RoI	CBR
0.9255	–	–	–	–	–
0.8623	E_{18}	0.0632	1.5	4.214	0.237
0.8990	E_{13}	0.0265	1.5	1.767	0.566
0.9109	E_3	0.0146	1.0	1.459	0.685
0.9158	E_1	0.0097	1.0	0.968	1.033
0.9158	E_2	0.0097	1.0	0.968	1.033
0.9239	E_{11}	0.0016	2.0	0.082	12.20
0.9240	E_6	0.0015	1.0	0.151	6.622
0.9242	E_{16}	0.0013	1.0	0.127	7.874
0.9247	E_{12}	0.0008	1.5	0.050	20.00
0.9248	E_9	0.0007	2.0	0.036	27.78
0.9248	E_{10}	0.0007	1.5	0.047	21.28
0.9249	E_8	0.0006	1.0	0.062	16.13
0.9251	E_{15}	0.0004	1.0	0.040	25.00
0.9251	E_{17}	0.0004	1.5	0.027	37.04
0.9252	E_{14}	0.0003	1.5	0.021	47.62
0.9252	E_4	0.0003	2.0	0.013	76.92
0.9253	E_5	0.0002	1.0	0.015	66.67
0.9254	E_7	0.0001	1.5	0.007	142.90

legal assistance treaty with a law enforcement organization in another jurisdiction.

The relative evidential weights in Table 1 can be used to create an evidence search list, with the evidential items ordered first by decreasing relative weight and, second, by decreasing return-on-investment or, equivalently, by increasing cost-benefit ratio. This search list can be used to guide the course of the triage phase of the digital forensic investigation in a near-optimal, cost-effective manner. Specifically, it would ensure that evidential "quick wins" (or "low-hanging fruit") are processed early in the investigation. Evidential items with low relative weights that are costly to obtain are relegated until later in the investigation, when it may become clearer whether or not these items are crucial to the overall support of the investigative hypothesis.

An advantage of this approach is that, if an item of evidence of high relative weight is not recovered, then this fact is detected early in the investigation; the investigation could be de-prioritized or even abandoned before valuable resources (time, effort, equipment, etc.) are expended unnecessarily. In addition, it may be possible to terminate the investigation without having to search for an item of evidence of low relative weight with a high recovery cost (e.g., having to use a scanning electron microscope to detect whether or not a solid state memory latch or gate is charged) as a direct consequence of the law of diminishing returns.

In the BitTorrent example, if evidential item E_{18} cannot be recovered, the impact on the investigation would probably be serious and may well lead to the immediate de-prioritization or even abandonment of the investigation. On the other hand, the absence of evidential items E_5 or E_7 would make very little difference to the overall support for the digital forensic investigation hypothesis.

The approach can be refined further by considering the roles of potentially exculpatory (i.e., exonerating) items of evidence in the investigative context. Such evidence might be, for example, CCTV footage that reliably places the suspect far from the presumed scene of the digital crime at the material time. The existence of any such evidence would, by definition, place the investigative hypothesis in jeopardy. Therefore, if any potentially exculpatory evidence could be identified in advance, then a search for the evidence could be undertaken before or in parallel with the search for evidential items in the triage schedule. However, since, by definition, the Bayesian network for the investigative hypothesis does not contain any exculpatory evidential items, the network cannot be used directly to obtain the relative weights of any items of exculpatory evidence. Therefore, it is not possible to formulate a cost-effective search strategy for exculpatory items of evidence on the basis of the Bayesian network itself.

4. Conclusions

This chapter has described a method for obtaining numerical estimates of the relative weights of items of digital evidence in digital forensic investigations. By considering the corresponding return-on-investment and cost-benefit ratio estimates of the evidential items, near-optimal, cost-effective digital forensic triage search strategies for the investigations can be constructed, eliminating unnecessary utilization of scarce time, effort and equipment resources in today's overstretched and under-resourced digital forensic investigation laboratories. The application of the method to evidence in a real case involving the illegal uploading of copyright protected material using the BitTorrent peer-to-peer network demonstrates its utility and intuitive appeal.

References

[1] Agena, AgenaRisk 7.0, Bayesian Network and Simulation Software for Risk Analysis and Decision Support, Cambridge, United Kingdom (www.agenarisk.com/products), 2018.

[2] T. Bayes, An essay towards solving a problem in the doctrine of chances. By the late Rev. Mr. Bayes, F.R.S. communicated by Mr. Price, in a letter to John Canton, A.M.F.R.S., *Philosophical Transactions (1683-1775)*, vol. 53, pp. 370–418, 1763.

[3] F. Cohen, *Digital Forensic Evidence Examination*, ASP Press, Livermore, California, 2010.

[4] M. Kwan, K. Chow, F. Law and P. Lai, Reasoning about evidence using Bayesian networks, in *Advances in Digital Forensics IV*, I. Ray and S. Shenoi (Eds.), Springer, Boston, Massachusetts, pp. 275–289, 2008.

[5] M. Kwan, R. Overill, K. Chow, J. Silomon, H. Tse, F. Law and P. Lai, Evaluation of evidence in Internet auction fraud investigations, in *Advances in Digital Forensics VI*, K. Chow and S. Shenoi (Eds.), Springer, Heildelberg, Germany, pp. 121–132, 2010.

[6] Magistrates' Court at Tuen Mun, Hong Kong Special Administrative Region v. Chan Nai Ming, TMCC 1268/2005, Hong Kong, China (www.hklii.hk/hk/jud/en/hksc/2005/TMCC001268A_2005.html), 2005.

[7] Microsoft Research, MSBNx: Bayesian Network Editor and Tool Kit, Microsoft Corporation, Redmond, Washington (msbnx.azurewebsites.net), 2001.

[8] R. Overill, Digital forensonomics – The economics of digital forensics, *Proceedings of the Second International Workshop on Cyberpatterns*, 2013.

[9] R. Overill, M. Kwan, K. Chow, P. Lai and F. Law, A cost-effective model for digital forensic investigations, in *Advances in Digital Forensics V*, G. Peterson and S. Shenoi (Eds.), Springer, Heidelberg, Germany, pp. 231–240, 2009.

[10] R. Overill, J. Silomon, M. Kwan, K. Chow, F. Law and P. Lai, Sensitivity analysis of a Bayesian network for reasoning about digital forensic evidence, *Proceedings of the Third International Conference on Human-Centric Computing*, 2010.

[11] J. Pearl, *Probabilistic Reasoning in Intelligent Systems: Networks of Plausible Inference*, Morgan Kaufman, San Mateo, California, 1988.

Chapter 2

CHALLENGES, OPPORTUNITIES AND A FRAMEWORK FOR WEB ENVIRONMENT FORENSICS

Mike Mabey, Adam Doupé, Ziming Zhao and Gail-Joon Ahn

Abstract   The web has evolved into a robust and ubiquitous platform, changing almost every aspect of people's lives. The unique characteristics of the web pose new challenges to digital forensic investigators. For example, it is much more difficult to gain access to data that is stored online than it is to access data on the hard drive of a laptop. Despite the fact that data from the web is more challenging for forensic investigators to acquire and analyze, web environments continue to store more data than ever on behalf of users.

   This chapter discusses five critical challenges related to forensic investigations of web environments and explains their significance from a research perspective. It presents a framework for web environment forensics comprising four components: (i) evidence discovery and acquisition; (ii) analysis space reduction; (iii) timeline reconstruction; and (iv) structured formats. The framework components are non-sequential in nature, enabling forensic investigators to readily incorporate the framework in existing workflows. Each component is discussed in terms of how an investigator might use the component, the challenges that remain for the component, approaches related to the component and opportunities for researchers to enhance the component.

Keywords: Web environments, forensic framework, timelines, storage formats

1.   Introduction

   The web has transformed how people around the globe interact with each other, conduct business, access information, enjoy entertainment and perform many other activities. Web environments, which include all types of web services and cloud services with web interfaces, now offer mature feature sets that, just a few years ago, could only have been

© IFIP International Federation for Information Processing 2018
Published by Springer Nature Switzerland AG 2018. All Rights Reserved
G. Peterson and S. Shenoi (Eds.): Advances in Digital Forensics XIV, IFIP AICT 532, pp. 11–33, 2018.
https://doi.org/10.1007/978-3-319-99277-8_2

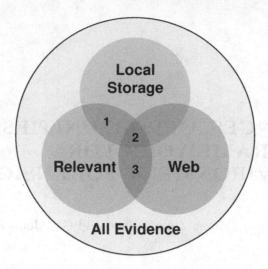

Figure 1. Types of evidence acquired during investigations.

provided by software running on a desktop computer. As such, the web provides users with new levels of convenience and accessibility, which have resulted in a phenomenon that critically impacts digital forensic investigations – people are storing less and less data on their local devices in favor of web-based solutions.

Current digital forensic techniques are good at answering questions about the evidence stored on devices involved in an incident. However, the techniques struggle to breach this boundary to handle evidentiary data that is stored remotely on the web. As Figure 1 illustrates, if forensic investigators depend only on the storage of the devices they seize as evidence, they will miss relevant and potentially vital information. Region 1 and 2 in the figure correspond to what a digital forensic investigator typically seeks – relevant artifacts that reside on the seized devices originating from: (i) programs and services running on the local devices; and (ii) the web, such as files cached by a web browser or email client. Region 3 corresponds to relevant data that the suspect has stored on the web, but the data cannot be retrieved directly from the seized devices. Everything outside the top and right circles represents non-digital evidence.

Modern cyber crimes present challenges that traditional digital forensic techniques are unable to address. This chapter identifies five unique challenges that web environments pose to digital forensic investigations: (i) complying with the rule of completeness (C0); (ii) associating a suspect with online personas (C1); (iii) gaining access to the evidence stored

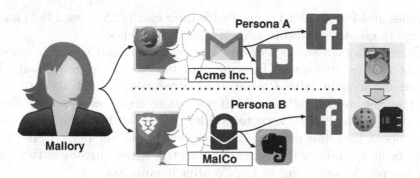

Figure 2. Motivating scenario.

online (C2); (iv) giving the evidence relevant context in terms of content and time (C3); and (v) integrating forensic tools to perform advanced analyses (C4). Currently, forensic investigators have no strategy or framework to guide them in their analysis of cases involving devices and users, where the evidentiary data is dispersed on local devices and on the web.

This chapter proposes a framework designed for conducting analyses in web environments that addresses challenges C0 through C4. The framework, which is readily integrated into existing workflows, enables a digital forensic investigator to obtain and give relevant context to previously-unknown data while adhering to the rules of evidence.

2.   Motivating Scenario

Figure 2 presents a motivating scenario. Mallory, an employee at Acme Inc., is using company resources to start a new business, MalCo. This action is a violation of Acme's waste, fraud and abuse policies, as well as the non-compete agreement that she has signed. Mallory knows that eventually her computer may be analyzed by the IT department for evidence of her actions to provide grounds for Acme claiming ownership of MalCo after it is launched. Therefore, she uses various web services whenever she works on her new company to minimize the evidence left on her computer at Acme.

Mallory conscientiously segregates her web browsing between the work she does for Acme and what she does for MalCo, even using different web browsers. This segregation effectively creates two personas: (i) Persona A (Acme); and (ii) Persona B (MalCo).

When Mallory takes on Persona A, she uses Firefox as her web browser. Because Acme uses Google's G Suite, her work email is essentially a Gmail address. Mallory's team at Acme uses Trello to coordinate their activities and Facebook to engage with their clients. She used the Gmail address to create her accounts on Trello and Facebook.

When Mallory assumes Persona B to work on MalCo, she is careful to only use the Brave web browser. For her MalCo-related email, she created an account with Proton Mail because of its extra encryption features. She used her Proton Mail address to create accounts on Evernote and Facebook. In Evernote, Mallory stores all her MalCo business plans, client lists and product information. Using her Persona B Facebook account, Mallory has secretly contacted Acme customers to gauge their interest in switching to MalCo after it launches.

3.   Unique Forensic Challenges

This section discusses the five principal challenges that web environments pose to digital forensic investigations. For convenience, the five challenges are numbered C0 through C4.

3.1   Rule of Completeness (C0)

The rules of evidence protect victims and suspects by helping ensure that the conclusions drawn from the evidence by forensic investigators are accurate. The completeness rule states that evidence must provide a complete narrative of a set of circumstances, setting the context for the events being examined to avoid "any confusion or wrongful impression" [14]. Under this rule, if an adverse party feels that the evidence lacks completeness, it may require the introduction of additional evidence "to be considered contemporaneously with the [evidence] originally introduced" [14].

The rule of completeness relates closely to the other challenges discussed in this section, which is why it is numbered C0. By attempting to associate a suspect with an online persona (C1), an investigator increases the completeness of the evidence. The same is true when an investigator gains access to evidence stored on the web (C2).

The rule of completeness can be viewed as the counterpart to relevant context (C3). By properly giving context to evidence, an investigator can ensure that the evidence provides the "complete narrative" that is required. However, during the process of giving the evidence context, the investigator must take care not to omit evidence that would prevent confusion or wrongful impression.

3.2   Associating Online Personas (C1)

When an individual signs up for an account with an online service provider, a new persona is created that, to some degree, represents who the individual is in the real world. The degree to which the persona accurately represents the account owner depends on a number of factors. Some attributes captured by the service provider (e.g., customer identification number) may not correlate with real-world attributes. Also, a user may provide fraudulent personal information, or may create parody, prank, evil-twin, shill, bot or Sybil accounts.

The challenge faced by a forensic investigator is to associate a persona with an individual in order to assign responsibility to the individual for the actions known to have been performed by the persona. If an investigator is unable to establish this link, then the perpetrator effectively remains anonymous.

In addition to being difficult to make an explicit link to an individual, it is also difficult to discover personas in the first place, especially if the forensic investigator only (at least initially) has access to data from the devices that were in the suspect's possession. This difficulty arises because web environments tend to store very little (if any) data on a user's local devices that may reveal a persona.

In Mallory's case, the data left behind that could reveal her personas resides in browser cookies and her password vault. After determining the online services associated with these credentials, the investigator still must find a way to show that it was actually Mallory who created and used the accounts. This is a more difficult task when many users share the same computer.

3.3   Evidence Access (C2)

An investigator could determine that a service provider would be likely to have additional data created or stored by the suspect. In this case, the typical course of action is to subpoena the service provider for the data. However, this option is available only to law enforcement and government agencies. If an investigation does not merit civil or criminal proceedings, corporate and non-government entities are essentially left to collect whatever evidence they can on their own.

While many web services provide APIs for programs to access data, no unified API is available to access data from multiple web services nor should such an API exist. Since web services are so disparate, a unique acquisition approach has to be developed for each web service. Moreover, because there is no guarantee that APIs will remain constant, it may be necessary to revise an approach every time the service or its API change.

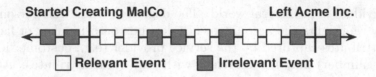

Figure 3. Timeline of Mallory's actions.

3.4 Relevant Context (C3)

The objective of a digital forensic investigator is to distill evidence down to the artifacts that tell the story of what happened during an incident by increasing the relevance of the contexts of artifacts. A context comes in two forms, both of which are critical to an investigation.

The first form is thematic context, which effectively places labels on artifacts that indicate their subjects or themes. An investigator uses the labels to filter out artifacts that are not relevant to the investigation, thereby focusing on artifacts that help prove or disprove the suspect's involvement in the incident. A common tool for thematic context is a keyword search, in which the investigator enters some keywords and the tool searches the file content and returns instances that match the provided text or related text (if the tool uses a fuzzy-matching algorithm).

The second form of context is temporal context, which places an artifact in a timeline to indicate its chronological ordering relative to events in the non-digital world as well as other digital artifacts. Creating a timeline provides an investigator with a perspective of what happened and when, which may be critical to the outcome of the investigation.

Although these forms of context have always been important objectives for digital forensic investigators, web environments make it much more difficult to create contexts because web users can generate artifacts and events at a higher pace than traditional evidence. Furthermore, the web has diverse types of data, such as multimedia, many of which require human effort or very sophisticated software to assign subjects to the data before any thematic context can be determined.

Figure 3 shows Mallory's actions in creating MalCo. Identifying the relevant events from the irrelevant events provides thematic context. Temporal context is provided to events by placing them in chronological order and creating a window of interest by determining the points at which Mallory engaged in inappropriate behavior.

3.5 Tool Integration (C4)

Researchers have long decried the shortcomings of the two types of tools that are available to digital forensic investigators. The first type,

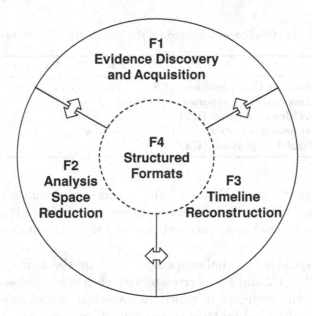

Figure 4. Web environment forensics framework.

one-off tools, are usually designed to perform very specific actions or analyses; they may not have very good technical support or may be outdated, poorly documented or have other issues. The second type, monolithic tools, seek to cover as many use cases as possible in a single package. While these tools often enjoy the benefits of commercial software, their vendors have an obvious interest in keeping the details about the tools and underlying techniques proprietary to maintain a competitive edge. Also, monolithic tools often do not support scripting, automation and importing/exporting data from/to other tools [5, 12, 33].

Given the complexity of the situation, it is unreasonable to expect a single tool or technique to address the challenges that hinder web environment forensics. Therefore, it is clear that forensic tools designed to properly accommodate evidence from web environments will have to overcome the status quo and integrate with other tools to accomplish their work.

4.   Web Environment Forensics Framework

Figure 4 presents the proposed web environment forensics framework. It incorporates four components that are designed to directly address the challenges discussed in Section 3. The four components are: (i) evidence discovery and acquisition (F1); (ii) analysis space reduction (F2); (iii)

Table 1.　Challenges addressed by the framework components.

	F1	F2	F3	F4
Rule of Completeness (CO)	✓	✓	✓	–
Associating Personas (C1)	✓	–	–	–
Evidence Access (C2)	✓	–	–	–
Relevant Context (C3)	–	✓	✓	–
Tool Integration (C4)	–	–	–	✓

timeline reconstruction (F3); and (iv) structured formats (F4). The components provide a digital forensic investigator with: (i) previously-unknown data related to an incident; and (ii) the relevant context of the incident.

Table 1 identifies the challenges addressed by the four components. Components F1, F2 and F3 interrelate with each other non-sequentially, meaning that the sequence in which an investigator could use the components is not dictated by the components themselves, but by the flow of the investigation and the investigator's needs. In fact, after an investigator completes one component, he may subsequently need one, both or neither of the other two components. However, as will be discussed later, component F4 relates to the components F1, F2 and F3 in a special way.

The non-sequential relationships between components F1, F2 and F3 enable an investigator to incorporate the components into an existing workflow as needed and in a manner that befits the investigation. For example, after acquiring new evidence from the web, it may be necessary to narrow the focus of the investigation, which, in turn, may tell the investigator where to find new, previously-inaccessible evidence, thus creating the sequence $F1 \rightarrow F2 \rightarrow F1$. Similarly, an investigator may use acquired data to reconstruct a timeline of events, which may be most useful after it is reduced to the periods of heightened activity. With a focus on these events, it may then become necessary to create a timeline of even finer granularity or to acquire new evidence specific to the period of interest. The sequence of these steps is $F1 \rightarrow F3 \rightarrow F2 \rightarrow F3$.

The remainder of this section describes the objectives of each component in the framework, the investigator's process for fulfilling the component, the research challenges that impede progress on the component, related approaches and key research opportunities for the component.

4.1　Evidence Discovery and Acquisition (F1)

The objective of framework component F1 is to overcome the challenges involved in: (i) establishing associations between a suspect and online personas (C1); and (ii) gaining access to the evidence stored in web services by the personas (C2). It is important to note that component F1 does not attempt to discern whether or not the data is relevant to the investigation. Instead, the focus is to discover and acquire web-based evidence created by the suspect, but not stored on the seized devices; this is evidence that would not otherwise be accessible to the investigator. Of course, component F1 also helps an investigator comply with the rule of completeness (C0).

Investigator Process (F1). The investigator's process for fulfilling component F1 comprises two actions: (i) discovery; and (ii) acquisition.

- **Discovery:** In order to discover previously-inaccessible evidence, an investigator has to analyze the storage of the devices in custody for clues that connect the user to evidence stored on the web. Example clues include web session cookies, authentication credentials and program-specific artifacts such as those collected by the community and posted at `ForensicArtifacts.com`. Finding and identifying these artifacts requires a sound understanding of their critical characteristics and, in some cases, a database of artifact samples to facilitate efficient comparison.

  In the case of authentication artifacts with certain formats, the process of discovery can be automated, relieving an investigator from attempting manual discovery, which does not scale well. However, even with automated discovery, it may be necessary for the investigator to manually determine the service to which a credential gives access. For example, if a user stores the username and password in a text file, even if the artifact has the structure that enables a program to accurately extract the credentials, it may require a human to consider the context of the file (name of the directory or file) in order to derive the corresponding service.

- **Acquisition:** After the investigator discovers an authentication artifact and identifies the corresponding service, it is necessary to devise a means to acquire data from the service. Given the variety of web services, an approach for acquiring data from one source may not apply directly to other sources. Investigators and tool developers need to understand which principles are transferable and design their workflows and tools to be as general-purpose as possible [26]. They should also leverage structured storage formats (F4) for the acquired evidence.

Challenges (F1). The discovery and acquisition actions of component F1 face unique challenges:

- **Discovery:** The task of discovering evidence in the web has some challenges. First, the volume of data a suspect can store on the web is nearly unlimited. Not only does this present a challenge in terms of storage requirements for holding the evidence, but it also makes the task of analyzing it more complex.

  Second, the boundaries of the data set are nebulous in a geographical sense as well as in terms of the service that maintains the data. In contrast, the boundaries of hard drive storage (e.g., total number of sectors) are well-defined and an investigator can identify the boundaries easily via simple analysis of the disk media. However, it is difficult for an investigator to find a starting point for discovering evidence in a web environment. In contrast, any investigator knows that the best place to start analyzing a desktop computer is its hard drive. The best analog for evidence in the web is for the investigator to start with what can be accessed, which, in most instances, is a device with storage, such as a smart phone, computer, laptop, GPS device or DVR. However, it is also possible that the devices possessed by a suspect contain no information about where their data is stored on the web.

  A third challenge occurs when a suspect has many accounts on the web – accounts with multiple web services and multiple accounts with a single service. While it is possible that all the user accounts are active and accessible, it is more likely that some accounts have been suspended or deactivated due to inactivity, intentional lockout, unsuccessful authentication attempts or other circumstances. Furthermore, with so many web services and accounts, it is not uncommon for an individual to forget that an account was created with a particular web service months or years after the fact. It is unlikely that the data from an inactive or forgotten account would play a critical role in an investigation, but this illustrates the challenge of discovering all the data created by a user on the web. The existence of a large number of user accounts also makes it more difficult to evaluate their relevance, although this challenge relates more directly to component F2.

- **Acquisition:** Acquiring data presents its own set of challenges. First, the data stored by web services changes continually. This is especially true when the data is automatically generated on behalf of a user. With the continued proliferation of Internet of Things devices, forensic investigators are likely to see an ever-increasing amount of automatically generated data for the foreseeable future. Such data is not dissimilar to evidence that requires live acquisition, but it may be more fragile and require special care and handling.

The other key challenge to acquiring data from a service provider involves actually accessing the data (discussed in Section 3.3). Since a unified API is not available for acquiring data from web services, considerable manual effort is required on the part of an investigator to understand and interface with each service.

Related Approaches (F1). Very few approaches are currently available to an investigator to complete component F1 of the framework, and even fewer are automated [22]. Dykstra and Sherman [11] have evaluated the efficacy of forensic tools in acquiring evidence from an Amazon EC2 instance. In general, the tools did well considering they were not designed for this type of evidence acquisition. However, the approach only works for instances under the control of the investigator at the guest operating system, virtualization and host operating system layers, not at the web application layer.

Research Opportunities (F1). Artifact repositories such as `Foren-sicArtifacts.com` and `ForensicsWiki.org` are valuable resources for forensic investigators. However, a critical shortcoming is that the information they contain is only suitable for human consumption, meaning that it is not currently possible for automated tools to leverage the data hosted on these sites. Future research should focus on converting the information to a structured format (F4) with the necessary semantics to facilitate automation.

Although each web service has its own set of APIs, it may be possible, through a rigorous study of a wide range of services, to create an abstraction of the various calls and create a generic and reusable method that facilitates acquisition.

4.2   Analysis Space Reduction (F2)

Not every evidence artifact is equally important to an investigation. Investigators would greatly benefit from assistance in identifying and focusing on the most relevant artifacts (C3). When irrelevant data is filtered in a triaging process, an investigator can save time and effort in completing the analysis – this is the motivation and the objective of component F2.

Although component F2 removes evidence from view, the process helps an investigator comply with the rule of completeness (C0). This is because the narrative of the evidence is unfettered by irrelevant artifacts.

While analysis space reduction through improved thematic context can benefit forensic analyses of digital evidence of all types, due to the virtually limitless storage capacity, analyses of evidence from web environments stand to gain particular performance improvements from the incorporation of component F2.

Investigator Process (F2).   There are two general approaches to reducing the analysis space of evidence: (i) classification; and (ii) identification.

- **Classification:** This approach involves the categorization of evidentiary data and indicating the types of data that are of interest and are not of interest. Classification is the more common form of thematic context and aligns well with the example provided in Section 3.4. Forensic investigators may also wish to classify or separate artifacts according to when they were created, modified or last accessed, in which case, techniques from component F3 would be helpful.

- **Identification:** This approach reduces the analysis space by determining what exactly comprises the evidence; this is especially important when evidence is encrypted or otherwise unreadable directly from device storage. The primary task is more about identifying the data rather than classifying it or determining its relevance. Nevertheless, identification is still a method for providing thematic context because it enables an investigator to determine if the data is relevant to the investigation or not. The main difference is that, instead of identifying the subject of the data directly, the investigator determines the subject from the identity of the data.

  One method to reduce the analysis space via identification is to use information about data (i.e., metadata) to eliminate what the data cannot be, incrementally approaching an identification via true negatives. This approach is applicable only when the set of possibilities is limited (i.e., the approach does not apply to arbitrary files created by a user).

Because the ultimate goal of component F2 is to end up with less (but more relevant) evidence than the original data set, F2 tools may export their results in the same format as the data input to the tools. This provides the benefit that F2 tools can be incorporated in existing workflows without having to change how other tools process data. However, even in cases where the reduction of the analysis space yields data of a different type than the input (e.g., via the identification approach), tools should still use structured formats for the reasons discussed in Section 4.4.

Challenges (F2). Reducing the analysis space in an automated manner requires the careful consideration of a number of factors. First, the implication here is that an algorithm is given the responsibility to understand the nature of the evidence and make a judgment (albeit a preliminary one) concerning its bearing on an individual's guilt or innocence. While false positives reduce the analysis space in a sub-optimal manner, a false negative obscures a relevant artifact from the investigator's view and could alter the outcome of the investigation, which is, of course, unacceptable.

Exculpatory evidence, which suggests innocence, is particularly sensitive to false negatives because it is inherently more difficult to identify than inculpatory evidence, which, by definition, tends to suggest guilt. In other words, evidence that exonerates a suspect is more difficult to interpret in an automated fashion because it may not directly relate to the incident under investigation, it may require correlation with evidence from other sources or it may be the absence of evidence that is of significance.

In addition to the challenges related to the accuracy of the tools that reduce the analysis space, it is also important to consider the fact that the volume of data stored by a suspect on the web may be very large. Even after an accurate reduction to relevant data, the size of the resulting data set may still be quite large and time-consuming for analysis by a human investigator.

Related Approaches (F2). Researchers have developed several data classification techniques such as object recognition in images and topic identification of documents [16]. Another classification example is the National Software Reference Library (NSRL) [20], which lists known files from benign programs and operating systems. By leveraging the National Software Reference Library to classify evidence that is not of interest, an investigator can reduce the analysis space by eliminating from consideration files that were not created by the user and, thus, do not pertain to the investigation.

Research Opportunities (F2). Perhaps the most important potential research topic related to reducing analysis space is developing methods to minimize false positives without risking false negatives. Such an undertaking would clearly benefit from advances in natural language processing, computer vision and other artificial intelligence domains. The better a tool can understand the meaning of digital evidence, the more likely it would accurately minimize false negatives.

Because people regularly use multiple devices on a typical day, the evidence they leave behind is not contained on a single device. Forensic investigators would benefit greatly from improved cross-analytic techniques that combine the evidence from multiple sources to help correlate artifacts and identify themes that otherwise would have been obscured if each source had been analyzed individually.

Researchers have already demonstrated that it is possible to identify encrypted data without decrypting it [15, 24]. Although such approaches may not be well-suited to every investigation involving encrypted data, the fact that it is possible under the proper circumstances demonstrates there are research opportunities in this area.

4.3   Timeline Reconstruction (F3)

The objective of framework component F3 is to improve the temporal context of the evidence by reconstructing the incident timeline, giving the artifacts a chronological ordering relative to other events. This timeline, in turn, helps tell a more complete story of user activities and the incident under investigation. The additional information also contributes to a more complete narrative, helping satisfy the rule of completeness (C0).

Investigator Process (F3). The first step in reconstructing a timeline from web environment data is to collect all available evidence that records values of time in connection with other data. This task requires F1 tools and methods. Accordingly, all the challenges and approaches discussed in Section 4.1 apply here as well.

All the collected timeline information should be combined into a single archive or database, which would require a unified storage format (F4) that accommodates the various fields and types of data included in the original information. However, because the information originates from several sources, the compiled timeline may include entries that are not relevant to the investigation. In this case, it would be beneficial to leverage component F2 approaches to remove entries that do not provide meaningful or relevant information, thereby improving the thematic context of the evidence. Similarly, if a particular time frame is of significance to an investigation, removing events that fall outside the window would improve the temporal context of the evidence.

After the timeline information has been compiled and filtered, it is necessary to establish the relationships between entries. Establishing the sequence of events is a simple matter if everything is ordered chronologically. Other types of relationships that may prove insightful include event correlations (e.g., event a always precedes events b and c) and clustering (e.g., event x always occurs close to the time that events y and z occur). Finally, an investigator may leverage existing analysis and visualization tools on the timeline data, assuming, of course, that they are compatible with the chosen storage format.

Challenges (F3). The analysis of traditional digital evidence for timeline information is well-researched [3, 8, 19, 28]. However, current approaches may not be directly applicable to web environments due to the inherent differences. For example, timeline reconstruction typically incorporates file metadata as a source of time data and previous work has demonstrated that web service providers regularly store custom metadata fields [26]. These metadata fields are typically a superset of the well-known modification, access and creation (MAC) times, and include cryptographic hashes, email addresses of users with access to the file, revision history, etc. Clearly, these fields would be valuable to investigators, but they are not accommodated by current timeline tools.

For forensic tool developers to incorporate these fields into their tools, they would have to overcome some additional challenges. Since web service providers use different sets of metadata fields, it would be critical to devise a method that supports diverse sets of fields. One approach is to create a structured storage format (F4) with the flexibility to store arbitrary metadata fields. Another approach is to unify the sets of metadata fields using an ontology such that the metadata semantics are preserved when combining them with fields from other sources.

Another challenge to incorporating metadata from web environments in timeline reconstruction is that the variety of log types and formats grows as new devices emerge (e.g., Internet of Things devices). Many of these devices perform actions on behalf of their users and may interface with arbitrary web services via the addition of user-created "skills" or apps. Forensic researchers have only recently begun to evaluate the forensic data stored on these devices [13, 23].

Finally, as with any attempt to reconcile time information from different sources, it is critical to handle differences in time zones. While it is a common practice for web services to store all time information in the UTC mode, investigators and tools cannot assume that this will always be the case. Reitz [25] has shown that correlating data from different time zones can be a complicated task.

Related Approaches (F3). As mentioned above, it is uncertain if current approaches to timeline reconstruction would assist investigators with regard to evidence from web environments; in fact, the research literature does not yet contain any approaches designed for this purpose. However, because the first step in timeline reconstruction is to collect data with time information, some cloud log forensic approaches may provide good starting points.

Marty [17] presents a logging framework for cloud applications. This framework provides guidelines for what is to be logged and when, but it requires application developers to be responsible for the implementations. As such, this approach may complement other logging methods, but it may not be directly applicable to web environments.

Research Opportunities (F3). The visualization of timeline data is an active research area [8, 21, 29, 31] and there will always be new and better ways to visualize timeline data. For example, virtual and augmented reality technologies may help forensic investigators to better understand data by presenting three-dimensional views of timelines.

One unexplored aspect of timeline reconstruction is the standardization of the storage format (F4) of the data that represents timelines. Separating the data from the tool would facilitate objective comparisons of visualization tools and enable investigators to change tools without having to restart the timeline reconstruction process from scratch.

When reconstructing a timeline from multiple sources, there is always the chance that a subset of the time data will correspond to an unspecified time zone. A worthwhile research topic is to develop an approach that elegantly resolves such ambiguities.

4.4   Structured Formats (F4)

Structured formats provide a means for storing information that is not specific to a single tool or process, thereby facilitating interoperability and integration (C4). Structured formats also enable comparisons of the outputs of similar tools to measure their consistency and accuracy, which are key measurements of the suitability of forensic tools with regard to evidence processing.

Component F4 is positioned at the center of the framework because components F1, F2 and F3 all leverage some type of storage format, even if the format itself is not a part of each component. For example, after discovering and acquiring new evidence, a tool must store the evidence in some manner; clearly, the format in which the evidence is stored should have a generic, yet well-defined, structure. The structure used by the acquisition tool does not change how it performs its principal task, but it is a peripheral aspect of its operation.

Structured formats are critical to the proper functioning of the proposed framework. In order for a tool that provides one component to communicate with another tool that provides a different component, the two tools must be able to exchange data that they can both understand. Defining a structured format for the data is what makes this possible.

Investigator Process (F4). Structured formats are intended to facilitate tool interoperability and integration. Therefore, a forensic investigator should rarely, if ever, have to work directly with structured formats.

Challenges (F4). In order to realize the benefits, a structured format must satisfy three conditions. First, it must precisely represent the original evidence without any loss of information during conversion. Second, there must be a way to verify that the data conforms to the format specifications. This leads to the third condition, which requires that the specifications must be published and accessible to tool developers.

While many storage formats exist, none of them is perfect or covers every use case. As in the case of software engineering projects, format designers are constantly faced with the need to compromise or make trade-offs; this, in turn, makes them less suitable for certain circumstances. For example, some storage formats fully accommodate the file metadata fields used by Windows filesystems, but not Unix filesystems. This illustrates how difficult it can be to incorporate the correct level of detail in a format specification [6]. In this regard, open-source formats have an advantage in that the community can help make improvements or suggest ways to minimize the negative effects of trade-offs.

It is critical to the proposed framework and to the principle of composability that analysis tools use structured formats to store their results in addition to the evidence itself. This is the only way to support advanced analyses that can handle large evidence datasets, such as those originating from the web.

Related Approaches (F4). Several structured formats have been proposed for digital forensic applications over the years, most of them designed to store hard disk images [10, 32]. This section summarizes some of principal structured formats.

The Advanced Forensic Format (AFF) [9] provides a flexible means for storing multiple types of digital forensic evidence. The developers, Cohen et al., note in their paper that "[unlike the Expert Witness Forensic (EWF) file format], AFF [employs] a system to store arbitrary name/value pairs for metadata, using the same system for both user-specified metadata and for system metadata, such as sector size and device serial number."

The Cyber Observable Expression (CybOX) [18] language was designed "for specifying, capturing, characterizing or communicating ... cyber observables." Casey et al. [6] mention in their work on the Digital Forensic Analysis Expression (DFAX) that CybOX can be extended to represent additional data related to digital forensic investigations. The CybOX Project has since been folded into version 2.0 of the Structured Threat Information Expression (STIX) specification [1].

The Cyber-Investigation Analysis Standard Expression (CASE) [7], which is a profile of the Unified Cybersecurity Ontology (UCO) [30], is a structured format that has evolved from CybOX and DFAX. CASE describes the relationships between digital evidence artifacts; it is an ontology and, therefore, facilitates reasoning. Because CASE is extensible, it is a strong candidate for representing evidence from web environments.

Digital Forensics XML (DFXML) [12] is designed to store file metadata, the idea being that a concise representation of metadata would enable investigators to perform evidence analyses while facilitating remote collaboration by virtue of DFXML's smaller size. Because it is written in XML, other schemas can extend DFXML to suit various scenarios.

Email Forensics XML (EFXML) [22] was designed to store email evidence in a manner similar to DFXML. Instead of storing email in its entirety, EFXML only stores the metadata (i.e., headers) of all the email in a dataset. EFXML was designed to accommodate email evidence originating from traditional devices as well as from the web.

The Matching Extension Ranking List (MERL) [15] is more specialized than the formats discussed above. Instead of storing evidence, MERL files store the analysis results from identifying extensions installed on an encrypted web thin client such as a Chromebook. MERL does not have the flexibility to store other kinds of data. However, unlike many of the other formats, it was created specifically for web-based evidence.

Of course, none of the formats were created to capture the diverse types of evidence in the web. However, some formats, such as AFF4, the latest version of AFF, may provide enough flexibility to store arbitrary types of web-based evidence.

Research Opportunities (F4).   Buchholz and Spafford [4] have evaluated the role of filesystem metadata in digital forensics and have proposed new metadata fields that would assist in forensic examinations. A similar study conducted for web-based evidence would be of great use to the digital forensics community. As discussed above, each web service has its own custom metadata that serves its purposes, but it is important to understand how the metadata differ from service to service, which ones have value to investigators, how to unify (or at least reconcile the semantics of) the various fields and which fields would be useful if digital forensic investigators were able to make suggestions.

5.   Related Work

The previous sections have discussed many approaches related to the individual components of the proposed framework. This section examines key approaches that relate to the framework as a whole.

Paglierani et al. [22] have developed a framework for automatically discovering, identifying and reusing credentials for web email to facilitate the acquisition of email evidence. Although their approach directly addresses the objectives of discovering and acquiring web evidence (F1) and provides a concise, structured format for storing email evidence (F4), their framework is tailored too closely to web email to be applied to web environments in general.

Ruan et al. [27] have enumerated several forensic challenges and opportunities related to cloud computing in a manner similar to what has been done in this research in the context of web environments. However, Ruan et al. do not provide a guide that could assist investigators in using the cloud for forensic examinations; instead, they only highlight the potential benefits of doing so. Additionally, although much of the modern web is built on cloud computing, the two are not synonymous. As such, many of the challenges listed by Ruan and colleagues, such as data collection difficulties, services depending on other services and blurred jurisdictions, apply to web environments, but the opportunities, such as providing forensics as a service, apply mainly to implementing forensic services in the cloud.

Birk and Wegener [2] provide recommendations for cloud forensics, separated by the type of cloud service provider, infrastructure as a service (IaaS), platform as a service (PaaS) and software as a service (SaaS). Of these the most applicable to web environments is, of course, software as a service. However, Birk and Wegener place the responsibility for providing the means of forensic acquisition on cloud service providers. In contrast, the framework proposed in this chapter assists digital forensic investigators in understanding what they can accomplish even with uncooperative cloud service providers.

6.   Conclusions

Conducting digital forensic analyses of web environments is difficult for investigators because of the need to comply with the rule of completeness, associate suspects with online personas, gain access to evidence, give the evidence relevant contexts and integrate tools. The framework presented in this chapter mitigates these challenges, guiding digital forensic investigators in processing web-based evidence using their existing workflows. Web environments provide exciting challenges to digital forensics and the area is ripe for research and innovation.

Acknowledgement

This research was partially supported by the DoD Information Assurance Scholarship Program and by the Center for Cybersecurity and Digital Forensics at Arizona State University.

References

[1] S. Barnum, Standardizing Cyber Threat Intelligence Information with the Structured Threat Information Expression (STIX), Technical Report, MITRE Corporation, Bedford, Massachusetts, 2014.

[2] D. Birk and C. Wegener, Technical issues of forensic investigations in cloud computing environments, *Proceedings of the Sixth IEEE International Workshop on Systematic Approaches to Digital Forensic Engineering*, 2011.

[3] F. Buchholz and C. Falk, Design and implementation of Zeitline: A forensic timeline editor, *Proceedings of the Digital Forensics Research Workshop*, 2005.

[4] F. Buchholz and E. Spafford, On the role of file system metadata in digital forensics, *Digital Investigation*, vol. 1(4), pp. 298–309, 2004.

[5] A. Case, A. Cristina, L. Marziale, G. Richard and V. Roussev, FACE: Automated digital evidence discovery and correlation, *Digital Investigation*, vol. 5(S), pp. S65–S75, 2008.

[6] E. Casey, G. Back and S. Barnum, Leveraging CybOX to standardize representation and exchange of digital forensic information, *Digital Investigation*, vol. 12(S1), pp. S102–S110, 2015.

[7] E. Casey, S. Barnum, R. Griffith, J. Snyder, H. van Beek and A. Nelson, Advancing coordinated cyber-investigations and tool interoperability using a community developed specification language, *Digital Investigation*, vol. 22, pp. 14–45, 2017.

[8] Y. Chabot, A. Bertaux, C. Nicolle and T. Kechadi, A complete formalized knowledge representation model for advanced digital forensics timeline analysis, *Digital Investigation*, vol. 11(S2), pp. S95–S105, 2014.

[9] M. Cohen, S. Garfinkel and B. Schatz, Extending the advanced forensic format to accommodate multiple data sources, logical evidence, arbitrary information and forensic workflow, *Digital Investigation*, vol. 6(S), pp. S57–S68, 2009.

[10] Common Digital Evidence Storage Format Working Group, Survey of Disk Image Storage Formats, Version 1.0, Digital Forensic Research Workshop (`www.dfrws.org/sites/default/files/survey-dfrws-cdesf-diskimg-01.pdf`), 2006.

[11] J. Dykstra and A. Sherman, Acquiring forensic evidence from infrastructure-as-a-service cloud computing: Exploring and evaluating tools, trust and techniques, *Digital Investigation*, vol. 9(S), pp. S90–S98, 2012.

[12] S. Garfinkel, Digital forensics XML and the DFXML toolset, *Digital Investigation*, vol. 8(3-4), pp. 161–174, 2012.

[13] J. Hyde and B. Moran, Alexa, are you Skynet? presented at the *SANS Digital Forensics and Incident Response Summit*, 2017.

[14] Legal Information Institute, Doctrine of completeness, in *Wex Legal Dictionary/Encyclopedia*, Cornell University Law School, Ithaca, New York, 2018.

[15] M. Mabey, A. Doupé, Z. Zhao and G. Ahn, `dbling`: Identifying extensions installed on encrypted web thin clients, *Digital Investigation*, vol. 18(S), pp. S55–S65, 2016.

[16] F. Marturana and S. Tacconi, A machine-learning-based triage methodology for automated categorization of digital media, *Digital Investigation*, vol. 10(2), pp. 193–204, 2013.

[17] R. Marty, Cloud application logging for forensics, *Proceedings of the ACM Symposium on Applied Computing*, pp. 178–184, 2011.

[18] MITRE Corporation, Cyber Observable Expression (CybOX) Archive Website, Bedford, Massachusetts (`cybox.mitre.org`), 2017.

[19] S. Murtuza, R. Verma, J. Govindaraj and G. Gupta, A tool for extracting static and volatile forensic artifacts of Windows 8.x apps, in *Advances in Digital Forensics XI*, G. Peterson and S. Shenoi (Eds.), Springer, Heidelberg, Germany, pp. 305–320, 2015.

[20] National Institute of Standards and Technology, National Software Reference Library (NSRL), Gaithersburg, Maryland (`www.nist.gov/software-quality-group/national-software-reference-library-nsrl`), 2018.

[21] J. Olsson and M. Boldt, Computer forensic timeline visualization tool, *Digital Investigation*, vol. 6(S), pp. S78–S87, 2009.

[22] J. Paglierani, M. Mabey and G. Ahn, Towards comprehensive and collaborative forensics on email evidence, *Proceedings of the Ninth International Conference on Collaborative Computing: Networking, Applications and Worksharing*, pp. 11–20, 2013.

[23] J. Rajewski, Internet of Things forensics, presented at the *Endpoint Security, Forensics and eDiscovery Conference*, 2017.

[24] A. Reed and M. Kranch, Identifying HTTPS-protected Netflix videos in real-time, *Proceedings of the Seventh ACM Conference on Data and Application Security and Privacy*, pp. 361–368, 2017.

[25] K. Reitz, Maya: Datetimes for Humans (`github.com/kenneth reitz/maya`), 2018.

[26] V. Roussev, A. Barreto and I. Ahmed, API-based forensic acquisition of cloud drives, in *Advances in Digital Forensics XII*, G. Peterson and S. Shenoi (Eds.), Springer, Heidelberg, Germany, pp. 213–235, 2016.

[27] K. Ruan, J. Carthy, T. Kechadi and M. Crosbie, Cloud forensics, in *Advances in Digital Forensics VII*, G. Peterson and S. Shenoi (Eds.), Springer, Heidelberg, Germany, pp. 35–46, 2011.

[28] B. Schneier and J. Kelsey, Secure audit logs to support computer forensics, *ACM Transactions on Information and System Security*, vol. 2(2), pp. 159–176, 1999.

[29] J. Stadlinger and A. Dewald, Email Communication Visualization in (Forensic) Incident Analysis, ENRW Whitepaper 59, Enno Rey Netzwerke, Heidelberg, Germany, 2017.

[30] Z. Syed, A. Padia, T. Finin, L. Mathews and A. Joshi, UCO: A unified cybersecurity ontology, *Proceedings of the Workshop on Artificial Intelligence for Cyber Security at the Thirtieth AAAI Conference on Artificial Intelligence*, pp. 195–202, 2016.

[31] C. Tassone, B. Martini and K. Choo, Forensic visualization: Survey and future research directions, in *Contemporary Digital Forensic Investigations of Cloud and Mobile Applications*, K. Choo and A. Dehghantanha (Eds.), Elsevier, Cambridge, Massachusetts, pp. 163–184, 2017.

[32] S. Vandeven, Forensic Images: For Your Viewing Pleasure, InfoSec Reading Room, SANS Institute, Bethesda, Maryland, 2014.

[33] O. Vermaas, J. Simons and R. Meijer, Open computer forensic architecture as a way to process terabytes of forensic disk images, in *Open Source Software for Digital Forensics*, E. Huebner and S. Zanero (Eds.), Springer, Boston, Massachusetts, pp. 45–67, 2010.

Chapter 3

INTERNET OF THINGS FORENSICS – CHALLENGES AND A CASE STUDY

Saad Alabdulsalam, Kevin Schaefer, Tahar Kechadi and Nhien-An Le-Khac

Abstract   During this era of the Internet of Things, millions of devices such as automobiles, smoke detectors, watches, glasses and webcams are being connected to the Internet. The number of devices with the ability of monitor and collect data is continuously increasing. The Internet of Things enhances human comfort and convenience, but it raises serious questions related to security and privacy. It also creates significant challenges for digital investigators when they encounter Internet of Things devices in criminal scenes. In fact, current research focuses on security and privacy in Internet of Things environments as opposed to forensic acquisition and analysis techniques for Internet of Things devices. This chapter focuses on the major challenges with regard to Internet of Things forensics. A forensic approach for Internet of Things devices is presented using a smartwatch as a case study. Forensic artifacts retrieved from the smartwatch are analyzed and the evidence found is discussed with respect to the challenges facing Internet of Things forensics.

Keywords: Internet of Things, smartwatch forensics, acquisition, analysis

1.   Introduction

The Internet of Things (IoT) is a revolutionary technology that enables small devices to act as smart objects. The Internet of Things is intended to make human life more comfortable and convenient. For example, an automobile that drives itself, a smart light that switches itself off when nobody is in the room and an air conditioner that turns itself on when the room temperature goes above a certain value. Internet of Things devices are connected to each other by various network media types, and they exchange data and commands between themselves

© IFIP International Federation for Information Processing 2018
Published by Springer Nature Switzerland AG 2018. All Rights Reserved
G. Peterson and S. Shenoi (Eds.): Advances in Digital Forensics XIV, IFIP AICT 532, pp. 35–48, 2018.
https://doi.org/10.1007/978-3-319-99277-8_3

to provide convenient services. For example, a smart player selects and plays a particular song based on the blood pressure of the user measured by his/her smartwatch. Internet of Things technology crosses diverse industry areas such as smart homes, medical care, social domains and smart cities [16].

However, Internet of Things technology creates more opportunities for cyber crimes that directly impact users. As with most consumer devices, Internet of Things devices were not designed with security in mind, the focus being on providing novel features while minimizing device cost and size. As a result, the devices have limited hardware resources. The lack of resources means that security tools cannot be installed in Internet of Things devices [22]. This makes them easy targets for cyber crimes.

A single Internet of Things device can be used to compromise other connected devices; the collection of compromised devices may then be used to attack computing assets and services [3]. Cyber crimes that leverage the power of Internet of Things technology can cross the virtual cyber world and threaten the physical world and human life. In January 2017, the U.S. Food and Drug Administration [21] warned that certain pacemakers are vulnerable to hacking. This means that a hacker who compromises a vulnerable pacemaker could potentially use it as a murder weapon.

Digital evidence pertaining to Internet of Things devices is a rich and relatively unexplored domain. Vendors provide a wealth of information about the functionality and features of their devices, but little, if any, details about exactly how the functionality and features are realized by their device implementations. For example, an LG smart vacuum cleaner is designed to clean a room by itself; it appears that its sensors measure the size, shape and other characteristics of the room and pass this information on to the decision system that controls device movements and cleaning operations. However, security researchers discovered a vulnerability in the LG portal login process that enabled them to take control of a vacuum cleaner, even gaining access to live-streaming video from inside the home [18]. This incident raises some important questions. Does the LG portal continuously record information about the cleaning process when the vacuum cleaner is running? Where is the information stored? Where does the cleaning process execute? Locally or in the cloud?

From the forensic perspective, Internet of Things devices contain important artifacts that could help investigations. Some of these artifacts have not been publicly disclosed by vendors, which means that investigators should consider what artifacts are available on devices, where they reside and how they can be acquired. In addition to serving as rich sources of evidence, Internet of Things forensics is complicated by the reliance on diverse operating systems and communications standards [17]. Current research primarily focuses on security and privacy; important aspects such as incident response and forensic investigations of Internet of Things devices have not been covered in adequate detail. This chapter discusses the major challenges related to Internet of Things forensics. A forensic approach for Internet of Things devices is presented using a smartwatch as a case study. Forensic artifacts retrieved from the smartwatch are analyzed and the evidence found is discussed with respect to the challenges facing Internet of Things forensics.

2. Internet of Things Forensics

Digital forensics involves identifying digital evidence in its most original form and then performing a structured investigation to collect, examine and analyze the evidence. Traditional digital forensics and Internet of Things forensics have similarities and differences. In terms of evidence sources, traditional digital evidence resides on computers, mobile devices, servers and gateways. Evidence sources for Internet of Things forensics include home appliances, automobiles, tag readers, sensor nodes, medical implants and a multitude of other smart devices.

Traditional digital forensics and Internet of Things forensics are essentially similar with regard to jurisdictional and ownership issues (ownership could be individuals, groups, companies, governments, etc.). However, unlike traditional forensics where the evidence is mostly in standard file formats, Internet of Things evidence exists in diverse formats, including proprietary vendor formats. Internet of Things devices employ diverse network protocols compared with traditional computing devices; additionally, the network boundaries may not be as well defined as in the case of traditional computer networks. Indeed, the blurry network boundaries render Internet of Things forensics extremely challenging. Oriwoh et al. [14] discuss this issue along with techniques for identifying evidence sources in Internet of Things forensics.

The Internet of Things covers three technology zones: (i) Internet of Things zone; (ii) network zone; and (iii) cloud zone. These three zones constitute the evidence sources in Internet of Things forensics. For example, evidence may reside on a smart Internet of Things device or sensor, or in an internal network device such as a firewall or router, or externally in an application or in the cloud. Thus, Internet of Things forensics has three aspects: (i) device forensics; (ii) network forensics; and (iii) cloud forensics.

Device forensics focuses on the potential digital evidence that can be collected from Internet of Things devices (e.g., video, graphic images and audio) [4, 13]. Videos and graphics from CCTV cameras and audio from Amazon Echo are good examples of digital evidence residing at the device level.

Network forensics in the Internet of Things domain covers all the different kinds of networks that devices use to send and receive data and commands. These include home networks, industrial networks, local area networks, metropolitan area networks and wide area networks. In Internet of Things forensics, the logs of all the devices through which traffic has flowed should be examined for evidence [10].

Most Internet of Things devices cross the Internet (via direct or indirect connections) through applications to share their resources in the cloud. Due to the valuable data that resides in the cloud, it has become a target of great interest to attackers. In traditional digital forensics, an investigator gains physical possession of a digital device and extracts evidence from the device. However, in cloud forensics, evidence is distributed over multiple locations, which significantly complicates the task of evidence acquisition [19]. Additionally, an investigator has limited access to and control of digital equipment in the cloud; even identifying the locations where evidence may reside is a challenge [1]. Dykstra and Sherman [6] discuss how this challenge could be addressed in a case study involving a child pornography website – the warrant provided by an investigator to a cloud provider should specify the name of the data owner or specify the locations of the data items that are sought. Because cloud services use virtual machines as servers, volatile data such as registry entries and temporary Internet files in the servers could be erased if they not synchronized with storage devices. For instance, the data could be erased when the servers are shut down and restarted.

2.1   Forensic Challenges

This section discusses the major challenges facing Internet of Things forensics.

Distributed Data. Internet of Things data is distributed over many locations, the vast majority of which are outside user control. The data could reside on a device or mobile phone, in the cloud or at a third-party's site. Therefore, the identification of the locations where evidence resides is a major challenge. Internet of Things data may be located in multiple countries and mixed with data belonging to multiple users, which means that different regulations would be applicable [12]. In August 2014, Microsoft refused to comply with a search warrant issued in the United States that sought data stored outside the country [7]. The jurisdictional and regulatory differences prevented the case from being resolved for a long period of time.

Digital Media Lifespan. Due to device storage limitations, the lifespans of data in Internet of Things devices are short; data items are overwritten easily and often. This increases the likelihood of evidence loss [9]. Transferring the data to another device such as a local hub or to the cloud are easy solutions. However, they present new challenges related to securing the chain of evidence and proving that the evidence has not been changed or modified [9].

Cloud Service Requirements. Cloud accounts are often associated with anonymous users because service providers do not require users to provide accurate information when signing up. This can make it impossible to identify criminal entities [15]. For example, although an investigator may find evidence in the cloud that proves that a particular device was involved in a crime, it may not be possible to identify the real user or owner of the device.

Lack of Security Mechanisms. Evidence in Internet of Things devices can be changed or deleted due to the lack of security mechanisms; this could negatively affect the quality of evidence and even render it inadmissible in court [11, 20]. Vendors may not update their devices regularly or not at all, and they often stop supporting older devices when they release new products with new infrastructures. As a result, newly-discovered vulnerabilities in Internet of Things devices can be exploited by hackers.

Device Types. During the identification phase of forensics, an investigator needs to identify and acquire evidence at a digital crime scene. In traditional forensic investigations, the evidence sources are workstations, laptops, routers and mobile phones. However, in Internet of Things forensic investigations, the evidence sources could be objects such as smart refrigerators, thermostats and coffee makers [14].

One challenge is to identify all the Internet of Things devices, many of them small, innocuous and possibly powered off, that are present at a crime scene. Additionally, extracting evidence from these devices is a major challenge due to the diversity of devices and vendors – different platforms, operating systems and hardware. An example is CCTV device forensics [2], which is complicated by the fact that each device manufacturer has a different filesystem format. Retrieving evidence from

CCTV storage is a difficult task. Interested readers are referred to [8] for an approach for carving the deleted video footprint in a proprietary CCTV filesystem.

Data Formats. The formats of data generated by Internet of Things devices do not match the formats of data saved in the cloud. In addition, users do not have direct access to their data and the formats of stored data are different from the formats of data presented to users. Moreover, data could have been processed via analytic functions in different locations before being stored in the cloud. In order to be admissible in court, the retrieved data should be returned to the original format before performing any analysis [14].

2.2   Forensic Tool Limitations

Current digital forensic tools are not designed to cope with the heterogeneity in an Internet of Things environment. The massive amounts of diverse and distributed evidence generated by Internet of Things devices encountered in crime scenes significantly increase the complexity of forensic investigations. Since most Internet of Things data is stored in the cloud, forensic investigators face challenges because current digital forensic techniques and tools typically assume physical access to evidence sources. Knowing exactly where potential evidence resides in the cloud is very difficult [1]. Moreover, cloud servers often house virtual machines belonging to multiple users. All these challenges have to be addressed in order to develop Internet of Things forensic techniques and tools that can support investigations and yield evidence that is admissible in court [4].

3.   Smartwatch Forensics Case Study

This section presents a case study involving an Internet of Things device, specifically an Apple smartwatch. The case study demonstrates that forensic acquisition and analysis in an Internet of Things environment is heavily device-oriented.

A smartwatch is a digital wristwatch and a wearable computing device. A smartwatch is used like a smartphone and has similar functions. It shows the date and time, counts steps and provides various types of information, including news, weather reports, flight information, traffic updates. It can be used to send and receive text messages, email, social media messages, tweets, etc. Smartwatch connectivity plays an important role in the retrieval of information from the Internet. A full-featured smartwatch must have good connectivity to enable it to communicate with other devices (e.g., a smartphone) and it should also be able to work independently.

The Apple Watch Series 2 used in the case study has the following technical specifications:

- Network-accessible smartwatch with no cellular connectivity.

- Dual-core Apple S2 chip.

- Non-removable, built-in rechargeable lithium-ion battery.

- WatchOS 2.3, WatchOS 3.0, upgradable to WatchOS 3.2.

- Wi-Fi 802.11 b/g/n 2.4 GHz, Bluetooth 4.0, built-in GPS, NFC chip, service port.

- AMOLED capacitive touchscreen, Force Touch, 272×340 pixels (38 mm), 312×390 pixels (42 mm), sapphire crystal or Ion-X glass.

- Sensors: Accelerometer, gyroscope, heartrate sensor, ambient light sensor.

- Messaging: iMessage, SMS (tethered), email.

- Sound: Vibration, ringtones, loudspeaker.

The Apple Watch Series 2 has a hidden diagnostic port [5]. An official cable was not available for the diagnostic port. Therefore, the Apple Watch was synchronized with an Apple iPhone, and Cellebrite UFED was used to perform a logical acquisition that extracted relevant data from the iPhone. Additionally, a manual acquisition was performed by swiping the Apple Watch to view and record information on the screen. The artifacts of interest included GPS data, heartrate data, timestamps, MAC address, paired device information, text messages and email, call logs and contacts.

3.1   Logical Acquisition

The following results related to the Apple Watch were obtained from the iPhone after multiple logical extractions were performed in order to clarify the attempts and changes.

The first hint of the Apple Watch was discovered in the database: `com.apple.MobileBluetooth.ledevices.paired.db`. This database is accessed via the path `/SysSharedContainer Domain-systemgroup.com.apple.bluetooth/Library/Database` in the iPhone filesystem.

The database contained the UUID, name, address, resolved address, LastSeenTime and LastConnectionTime. Since the Apple Watch does

healthdb.sqlite

Datenbankansicht   Hex-Ansicht   Dateiinfo

	authorization	(32)
	datatype_source_order	(57)
	key_value	(19)
	nano_pairing	(1)
	source_devices	(20)
	sources	(14)
	sqlite_sequence	(10)
	subscription	(3)
	subscription_app_launch	(0)
	subscription_data_anchors	(17)
	sync_anchors	(20)
	sync_stores	(1)

	ROWID	name	manufacturer	model	hardware	firmware	software	localidentifier
✓	1	iPhone	Apple	iPhone	iPhone8,1		9.0.1	
✓	2	_NONE_						_NONE_
✓	3	iPhone	Apple	iPhone	iPhone8,1		9.0.2	
✓	4	iPhone	Apple	iPhone	iPhone8,1		9.1	
✓	5	iPhone	Apple	iPhone	iPhone8,1		9.2	
✓	6	iPhone	Apple	iPhone	iPhone8,1		9.2.1	
✓	7	iPhone	Apple	iPhone	iPhone8,1		9.3	
✓	8	iPhone	Apple	iPhone	iPhone8,1		9.3.1	
✓	9	iPhone	Apple	iPhone	iPhone8,1		9.3.2	
✓	10	iPhone	Apple	iPhone	iPhone8,1		9.3.3	
✓	11	iPhone	Apple	iPhone	iPhone8,1		9.3.4	
✓	12	iPhone	Apple	iPhone	iPhone8,1		9.3.5	
✓	13	iPhone	Apple	iPhone	iPhone8,1		10.0.1	
✓	14	iPhone	Apple	iPhone	iPhone8,1		10.0.2	
✓	15	iPhone	Apple	iPhone	iPhone8,1		10.1.1	
✓	16	iPhone	Apple	iPhone	iPhone8,1		10.2	
✓	17	Apple Watch	Apple	Watch	Watch2,4		3.1	
✓	18	_NONE_						_NONE_
✓	19	iPhone	Apple	iPhone	iPhone8,1		10.2.1	
✓	20	iPhone	Apple	iPhone	iPhone8,1		10.3.1	

Figure 1. Screenshot of the `healthdb.sqlite` database.

not have a separate filesystem on the iPhone, Apple Watch data had to be searched for within the application data on the iPhone. In the case study, the Apple Watch was used with five applications: (i) Health app; (ii) Nike+ GPS app; (iii) Heartbeat app; (iv) Messages app; and (v) Maps app. The artifacts retrieved from these applications are discussed in this section.

Health App. The `healthdb.sqlite` database with path `/var/mobile` `/Library/Health` indicated the Apple Watch as a source device for health data (Figure 1).

Nike+ GPS App. The Nike+ GPS app contained the folder named `com.apple.watchconnectivity` with path `/Applications/com.nike.` `nikeplus-gps/Documents/inbox/`. Data in a contained folder named `71F6BCC0-56BD-4B4s-A74A-C1BA900719FB` indicated the use of the Apple Watch.

The main database in the Nike+ GPS app is `activityStore.db` with the path `/Applications/com.nike.nikeplus-gps/Documents/`. `Activity Store.db` contained an activity overview, lastContiguosActivity, metrics, summaryMetrics and tags, all of which would be highly relevant in an investigation.

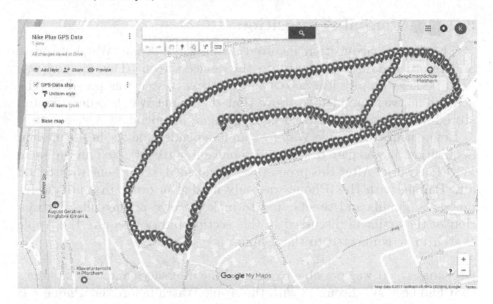

Figure 2. GPS data.

GPS Data. GPS data was found in the metrics and tags tables. Latitudes and longitudes generated by the Nike+ GPS app were saved in the tables with timestamps. The GPS data was input to Google maps to create the map shown in Figure 2.

Analysis. The logical acquisition employed the Cellebrite UFED and UFED 4PC software. Information about the paired Apple Watch (UUID and name) was found in the iPhone filesystem; information pertaining to the last connection was also found.

After retrieving information about the Apple Watch, the iPhone filesystem was examined for information about the applications used with the Apple Watch. Some applications contained information about the paired Apple Watch as a source device. Considerable information on the iPhone was generated by the Apple Watch. This included information about workouts that were manually started by the user while wearing the Apple Watch. Heartrate data, steps data and sleep data were recorded when the user wore the Apple Watch even when no applications were manually started. All this data was stored with timestamps, but in different formats.

Discussions with law enforcement have revealed that GPS data has never been found on a smartwatch. However, GPS data generated by the Nike+ GPS app on the Apple Watch was found on the paired iPhone.

3.2   Manual Acquisition

The manual acquisition involved swiping the Apple Watch to view and record the data displayed on the device screen. This method was used because no physical access to the Apple Watch was possible. The acquisition was intended to prove that the Apple Watch generated and stored data, and that it could be used as an independent device.

Before using the Apple Watch as an independent device in the manual acquisition, it was paired with an iPhone and authenticated on the same Wi-Fi network. After this process was performed, the iPhone was turned off. Pairing with the iPhone was only needed in order to send/receive messages, emails and tweets, and to make/receive phone calls. Extraction of the artifacts discussed in this section did not require the Apple Watch to be connected to the iPhone.

Messages.   It was possible to view all the iMessages and text messages that had been synchronized with the Apple Watch before the iPhone was turned off. These could be read even after the watch was placed in the flight mode.

Attempts were made to write and send iMessages and text messages directly from the watch to recipients with the flight mode off. It was possible to send iMessages directly from the watch to recipients. Text messages could be written on the Apple Watch. However, the text messages were not sent after the send button was tapped; instead, they were saved on the watch. The saved text messages were sent to the recipients after the iPhone was turned on.

Pictures.   Pictures were also synchronized with the Apple Watch before the iPhone was turned off. The watch was placed in the flight mode in order to determine whether copies of the pictures were on the watch (instead of in the cloud). The examination indicated that the pictures were, indeed, still on the watch.

Apps.   The HeartRate, HeartWatch, Activity, Maps, Workout, Nike+ Run, Twitter and Instagram apps on the Apple Watch were browsed. The HeartRate app only maintained data about the last and current heartrate measurements. HeartWatch, a third-party app, contained a little more data, including pulse, daily average, training data and sleep tracking data.

The Workout app maintained a little data about the last workout performed and recorded; specifically, the type, length and date of the workout. The Nike+ Run app also contained little data – only the distance ran during the last workout.

Twitter and Instagram could only be used when the Apple Watch was connected to the iPhone. When the iPhone was turned off, the Apple Watch displayed the icon that indicated that no phone was connected.

Email. Email could be read on the Apple Watch in the same manner as iMessages and text messages. The Apple Watch could receive, open and send email independently of the iPhone. After the Apple Watch was placed in the flight mode, the standard icon was displayed and email could be read, but not sent or received.

Calendar. The Calendar app displayed user entries starting from the day before the manual acquisition was performed and ending seven days in the future. The entries could be read when the Apple Watch was placed in the flight mode.

Contacts and Phone. Contacts were saved on the Apple Watch independent of the status of the iPhone. The contacts remained on the Apple Watch after the iPhone was turned off and the watch was disconnected from all networks. The contact details were the same as those displayed on the iPhone.

The Phone app contained a call log and favorites list. Voicemail could be seen and listened to even after the iPhone was powered off and the Apple Watch was placed in the flight mode. Additionally, the originating phone numbers, dates and times of voicemail were displayed.

Analysis. Since physical access to the Apple Watch was not possible, a manual acquisition by swiping the screen is currently the only method for determining the artifacts stored on the Apple Watch. This research reveals that the Apple Watch can be used as a standalone device independent of the iPhone. Furthermore, many artifacts that are important in an investigation can be found on the Apple Watch. These include information pertaining to iMessages, text messages, pictures, heartrate data, workout data, email, calendar entries, contacts, call logs and voicemail. However, logical and manual acquisitions can be performed only when the Apple Watch is not pin-locked.

4.   Conclusions

This chapter has discussed various aspects related to Internet of Things forensics along with the challenges involved in acquiring and analyzing evidence from Internet of Things devices. Most research in the area of Internet of Things forensics focuses on extending traditional forensic techniques and tools to Internet of Things devices. While the case study involving the Apple Watch demonstrates that current digital forensic tools can be used to perform some tasks, efficient Internet of Things forensic models and processes are needed to cope with the challenges encountered in Internet of Things environments. Future research will focus on developing such forensic models and processes.

References

[1] M. Alex and R. Kishore, Forensics framework for cloud computing, *Computers and Electrical Engineering*, vol. 60, pp. 193–205, 2017.

[2] A. Ariffin, J. Slay and K. Choo, Data recovery from proprietary formatted CCTV hard disks, in *Advances in Digital Forensics IX*, G. Peterson and S. Shenoi (Eds.), Springer, Heidelberg, Germany, pp. 213–223, 2013.

[3] E. Blumenthal and E. Weise, Hacked home devices caused massive Internet outage, *USA Today*, October 21, 2016.

[4] E. Casey, Network traffic as a source of evidence: Tool strengths, weaknesses and future needs, *Digital Investigation*, vol. 1(1), pp. 28–43, 2004.

[5] J. Clover, Apple watches shipping to customers confirmed to have covered diagnostic port, *MacRumors*, April 23, 2015.

[6] J. Dykstra and A. Sherman, Understanding issues in cloud forensics: Two hypothetical case studies, *Proceedings of the ADSL Conference on Digital Forensics, Security and Law*, pp. 45–54, 2011.

[7] E. Edwards, U.S. Supreme Court to hear appeal in Microsoft warrant case, *The Irish Times*, October 16, 2017.

[8] R. Gomm, N. Le-Khac, M. Scanlon and M. Kechadi, An analytical approach to the recovery of data from third-party proprietary CCTV file systems, *Proceedings of the Fifteenth European Conference on Cyber Warfare and Security*, 2016.

[9] R. Hegarty, D. Lamb and A. Attwood, Digital evidence challenges in the Internet of Things, *Proceedings of the Tenth International Network Conference*, pp. 163–172, 2014.

[10] R. Joshi and E. Pilli, *Fundamentals of Network Forensics: A Research Perspective*, Springer-Verlag, London, United Kingdom, 2016.

[11] D. Lillis, B. Becker, T. O'Sullivan and M. Scanlon, Current challenges and future research areas for digital forensic investigations, *Proceedings of the ADFSL Conference on Digital Forensics, Security and Law*, 2016.

[12] C. Liu, A. Singhal and D. Wijesekera, Identifying evidence for cloud forensic analysis, in *Advances in Digital Forensics XIII*, G. Peterson and S. Shenoi (Eds.), Springer, Heidelberg, Germany, pp. 111-130, 2017.

[13] L. Morrison, H. Read, K. Xynos and I. Sutherland, Forensic evaluation of an Amazon Fire TV Stick, in *Advances in Digital Forensics XIII*, G. Peterson and S. Shenoi (Eds.), Springer, Heidelberg, Germany, pp. 63–79, 2017.

[14] E. Oriwoh, D. Jazani, G. Epiphaniou and P. Sant, Internet of Things forensics: Challenges and approaches, *Proceedings of the Ninth IEEE International Conference on Collaborative Computing: Networking, Applications and Worksharing*, pp. 608–615, 2013.

[15] S. O'Shaughnessy and A. Keane, Impact of cloud computing on digital forensic investigations, in *Advances in Digital Forensics IX*, G. Peterson and S. Shenoi (Eds.), Springer, Heidelberg, Germany, pp. 291–303, 2013.

[16] H. Pajouh, R. Javidan, R. Khayami, D. Ali and K. Choo, A two-layer dimension reduction and two-tier classification model for anomaly-based intrusion detection in IoT backbone networks, *IEEE Transactions on Emerging Topics in Computing*, vol. PP(99), 2016.

[17] S. Perumal, N. Norwawi and V. Raman, Internet of Things (IoT) digital forensic investigation model: Top-down forensic approach methodology, *Proceedings of the Fifth International Conference on Digital Information Processing and Communications*, pp. 19–23, 2015.

[18] B. Popken, Hacked home devices can spy on you, *NBC News*, October 26, 2017.

[19] K. Ruan, J. Carthy, T. Kechadi and M. Crosbie, Cloud forensics, in *Advances in Digital Forensics VII*, G. Peterson and S. Shenoi (Eds.), Springer, Heidelberg, Germany, pp. 35–46, 2011.

[20] S. Ryder and N. Le-Khac, The end of effective law enforcement in the cloud? To encrypt or not to encrypt, *Proceedings of the Ninth IEEE International Conference on Cloud Computing*, pp. 904–907, 2016.

[21] U.S. Food and Drug Administration, Cybersecurity Vulnerabilities Identified in St. Jude Medical's Implantable Cardiac Devices and Merlin@home Transmitter: FDA Safety Communication, Silver Spring, Maryland (`www.fda.gov/MedicalDevices/Safety/Alerts andNotices/ucm535843.htm`), January 9, 2017.

[22] Z. Zhang, M. Cho, C. Wang, C. Hsu, C. Chen and S. Shieh, IoT security: Ongoing challenges and research opportunities, *Proceedings of the Seventh IEEE International Conference on Service-Oriented Computing and Applications*, pp. 230–234, 2014.

II

FORENSIC TECHNIQUES

Chapter 4

RECOVERY OF FORENSIC ARTIFACTS FROM DELETED JUMP LISTS

Bhupendra Singh, Upasna Singh, Pankaj Sharma and Rajender Nath

Abstract   Jump lists, which were introduced in the Windows 7 desktop operating system, have attracted the interest of researchers and practitioners in the digital forensics community. The structure and forensic implications of jump lists have been explored widely. However, little attention has focused on anti-forensic activities such as jump list evidence modification and deletion. This chapter proposes a new methodology for identifying deleted entries in the Windows 10 AutoDest type of jump list files and recovering the deleted entries. The proposed methodology is best suited to scenarios where users intentionally delete jump list entries to hide evidence related to their activities. The chapter also examines how jump lists are impacted when software applications are installed and when the associated files are accessed by external storage devices. In particular, artifacts related to file access, such as the lists of most recently used and most frequently used files, file modification, access and creation timestamps, names of applications used to access files, file paths, volume names and serial numbers from where the files were accessed, can be recovered even after entries are removed from the jump lists and the software applications are uninstalled. The results demonstrate that the analysis of jump lists is immensely helpful in constructing the timelines of user activities on Windows 10 systems.

Keywords: Windows forensics, Windows 10, deleted jump lists, recovery

1.   Introduction

Microsoft launched the Windows 10 operating system on July 29, 2015. As of November 2017, Windows 10 was the second most popular desktop operating system with a market share 31.85%, after Windows 7 with a market share 43.12% [8]. Forensic investigators are encountering large numbers of Windows 10 workstations for evidence recovery and analysis. The initial version of Windows 10 (v1511) was shipped

© IFIP International Federation for Information Processing 2018
Published by Springer Nature Switzerland AG 2018. All Rights Reserved
G. Peterson and S. Shenoi (Eds.): Advances in Digital Forensics XIV, IFIP AICT 532, pp. 51–65, 2018.
https://doi.org/10.1007/978-3-319-99277-8_4

with many new features, including Cortana, Edge Browser, Action (or Notification) Center, Universal App Platform, OneDrive, Continuum, Windows Hello and Quick Access. These features have direct implications on digital forensic investigations [11]. Windows 10 File Explorer opens up the Quick Access view by default to ease access to frequently used folders and recent files. These files and folders are stored in the *C:\Users\UserName\AppData\Roaming\Microsoft\Windows\Recent* directory in the form of Windows shortcut (LNK) files. The LNK file format has not changed in the Windows 10 operating system, but Microsoft has modified the structure of Windows 10 jump lists, especially the DestList stream [10]. Also, the number of items to be displayed in a list is now hard coded.

Microsoft introduced the jump list feature in the Windows 7 desktop operating system to improve user experience by providing the lists of recently opened files and directories. Before the introduction of jump lists, forensic investigators were dependent on the Windows registry to identify the most recently used (MRU) and most frequently used (MFU) items. Compared with the Windows registry, jump list data files provide more valuable artifacts related to user activity history. For instance, it is possible to extract useful information about file accesses, including MRU and MFU lists for users and applications, file names, full file paths, modified, accessed and created (MAC) timestamp values, volume names and volume serial numbers from where files were accessed, unique file volumes and object IDs. These artifacts appear to persist even after the files and the software applications that accessed them have been removed. Jump list information is maintained on a per application basis. However, not all applications create jump lists; these include host-based applications such as Regedit, Command Prompt and Run [12].

This chapter presents a methodology for recovering deleted jump list entries in Windows 10 systems. The open-source JumpListExt tool was used to parse and view information in jump list data files. Several experiments were conducted to detect and recover deleted jump lists and carve their artifacts, such as the applications used to access files, MRU and MFU lists, volume names and serial numbers used for access and files accessed during specific boot sessions. These artifacts appear to persist even after files have been deleted and their target software applications have been uninstalled.

2.   Jump Lists in Digital Forensics

The structure and applications of jump list files have been widely discussed in the forensics community since the release of Windows 7.

Barnett [1] has described how jump lists function and has investigated the behavior of the jump list of a browser when files are uploaded and downloaded using the browser. Lyness [5] has explored jump lists further and has identified the structure and types of information recorded in a DestList stream contained in an AutoDest data file in a Windows 7 desktop operating system. Lyness executed anti-forensic actions on data files such as removing entries from a jump list and discovered that the attempts can be detected in the DestList stream data. Lallie and Bains [3] have presented an overview of the AutoDest data file structure and have documented numerous artifacts related to file accesses and program execution; they suggest that research should focus on timeline development based on the information extracted from jump list files.

Smith [13] has used jump lists to detect fraudulent documents created on a Windows system. In particular, Smith showed that the information maintained in jump list files is useful forensic evidence in financial fraud cases because the files record all file creation and opening activities. More recently, Singh and Singh [10] have conducted the first investigation of jump lists in the Windows 10 operating system and have discovered that modifications of and/or additions to certain portions of jump list data files prevent existing forensic tools from working properly. Singh and Singh also examined the new DestList structure and compared it against the DestList structures in older Windows versions. They developed the JumpListExt tool for extracting information stored in jump list data files, individually as well as collectively. This information is very useful for constructing user activity timelines.

3. Locations and Structures of Jump Lists

The data files created by the jump list feature are hidden by default, but users can view them by browsing the complete path. Two types of data files are associated with the feature: (i) AutoDest (automatic destinations); and (ii) CustDest (custom destinations). Users may also locate the data files by entering *Shell:Recent\automaticDestinations* in the Run command as shown in Figure 1. The files are located at the following paths:

- **AutoDest:** *C:\Users\UserName\AppData\Roaming\Microsoft\Windows\Recent\AutomaticDestinations*

- **CustDest:** *C:\Users\UserName\appData\Roaming\Microsoft\Windows\Recent\CustomDestinations*

Larson [4] was the first to study jump lists as a resource for user activity analysis and presented the anatomy of jump lists in Windows 7

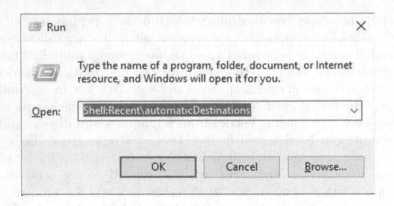

Figure 1.   Locating jump list data files in Windows.

platforms. Each jump list file has a 16-digit hexadecimal number called
the AppID (application identifier) followed by an extension. The AppID
is computed by the Windows operating system using a CRC-64 checksum
based on the file path of the application. An application that is executed
from two different locations has two different AppIDs associated with the
application. A script is available for computing AppIDs based on the
file paths [2]. A list of known AppIDs is available at [6, 9].

The structure of an AutoDest data file conforms to the Microsoft OLE
(object linking and embedding) file format [7]. The AutoDest file has
two types of streams: (i) SHLLINK; and (ii) DestList. A data file may
have multiple SHLLINK streams, all of which have a structure similar
to a shortcut (LNK) file. On the other hand, the DestList stream, which
has a special structure, records the order of file accesses and access count
of each file, which could serve as the MRU and MFU lists, respectively.
The header length of 32 bytes in a DestList stream is fixed in all Windows
distributions. However, the semantics of the fields in the DestList stream
header differ in Windows distributions.

Table 1 presents the DestList stream header fields and their semantics
in four Windows operating system distributions. The DestList stream
header records useful information such as the version number, total current entries, last issue entry ID number, pinned entries and the numbers
of added/deleted entries in the jump list.

Figure 2 shows the binary data in a DestList stream header in Windows 10 Pro v1511. Comparison of the DestList header in Windows 10
against the header in Windows 7/8 reveals that most of the fields are
same, but the semantics of two fields are different. For example, the
value of the first four bytes in Windows 10 is 3 or 4 (version number)
whereas it is 1 (first issued entry ID number) in Windows 7/8. Also,

Table 1. DestList headers and entry lengths in four Windows distributions.

Operating System	Header Length (Bytes)	Header Version (Offset 0)	Entry Length (Bytes)
Windows 7 Profesional	32	0x00000001 (1)	114
Windows 8/8.1 Pro x64	32	0x00000001 (1)	114
Windows 10 Pro v1511	32	0x00000003 (3)	130
Windows 10 Pro v1607	32	0x00000004 (4)	130

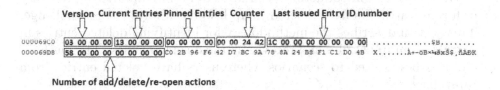

Figure 2. DestList stream header structure in Windows 10 Pro v1511.

the value of the last eight bytes of the DestList header appears to be double that of the total current entries in the list. When an entry is added, deleted or pinned, or an existing entry is re-opened, the value is incremented by one. Singh and Singh [10] have described the process for computing the access counts of removed entries. Table 1 presents the DestList headers for various Windows distributions.

CustDest files are created by applications with their AppIDs followed by the extension `customDestinations-ms`. These jump lists are specified by the applications using the ICustomDestinationList API [4]. Compared with AutoDest files, CustDest files have a different structure of sequential MS-SHLLINK binary format segments. CustDest files record the artifacts related to user web history on the system. For example, the file `969252ce11249fdd.customDestinations-ms`, which is created by Mozilla Firefox, records the web history and timestamps. Windows Media Player creates the file `74d7f43c1561fc1e.customDestinations-ms`, which records the file paths of music files that have been played.

4.   Experiments and Results

This section discusses the experimental objectives, methodology and results related to the recovery of forensic artifacts from AutoDest jump lists in a Windows 10 Pro v1511 system.

4.1   Experimental Objectives

The principal objectives of the experiments were to: (i) retrieve deleted entries from jump list data files; (ii) identify the names of applications based on their AppIDs; (iii) determine the connected removable media properties using jump list information; (iv) list the most recently used and most frequently used files on a per application basis; and (v) identify the files accessed during a particular boot session.

4.2   Experimental Methodology

Ever since the introduction of jump lists in Windows 7, the recovery of forensic artifacts from deleted jump lists has always been a challenge. This section describes the methodology for identifying deleted entries in AutoDest jump list files and recovering the deleted entries. The methodology is best suited to scenarios where users have deleted entries from jump lists.

The first step in the methodology is to locate the AutoDest data files by entering *Shell:Recent\automaticDestinations* in the Run command. If the data files are available at the specified location, then it is possible to obtain the AppIDs and, thus, the names of the applications. The data files are then parsed individually or as a whole using the JumpListExt tool. The procedure outlined in Figure 3 is used to detect entries removed from an AutoDest data file. The jump list file must be parsed manually in order to carve the deleted entries. Manual analysis of the DestList header provides information about the number of deleted entries and their access counts. In the experiments, FTK Imager 3.4.2.6 was used to acquire the jump list files.

4.3   Experimental Set-Up

Two Windows systems were set-up for the experiments, one as the suspect system and the other as the forensic server. Several applications were installed on the suspect system, including host-based user applications (default Windows installation), user applications, portable applications (without installation and writing any configuration settings to the disk) and Windows Store apps, were used to create the jump lists. Various hypothetical activity scenarios were simulated by opening test

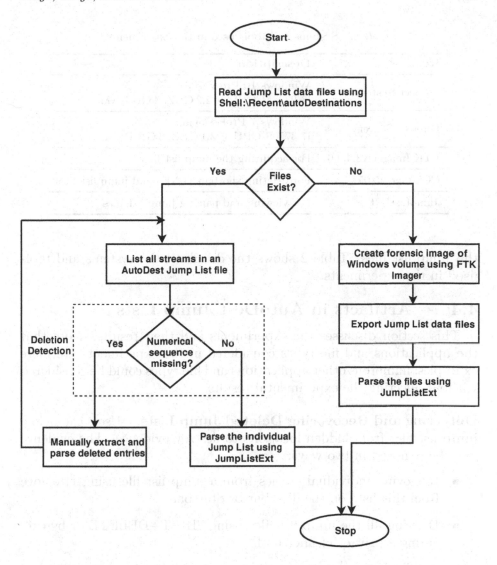

Figure 3. Identifying and recovering deleted entries in AutoDest jump lists.

files with the applications; the test files were opened from the internal hard disk. Also, in some cases, the applications and files were installed and opened from removable storage devices. The CCleaner application was used to delete jump lists and recent items. The forensic server was loaded with FTK Imager, which was used to recover and examine the deleted jump lists. The JumpListExt tool was used to parse and view

Table 2.   Systems and tools used in the experiments.

Item	Description
Suspect System	Windows 10 Pro v1709 i3-2328M CPU @ 2.2 GHZ, 4 GB RAM
Forensic Server	Windows 7 Professional i7-3770S CPU @ 3.1 GHZ, 4 GB RAM
FTK Imager v3.4.2.6	For acquiring the jump list files
CCleaner v5.05	For deleting shortcut (LNK) and jump list files
JumpListExt	For viewing and parsing jump list files

the jump list files. Table 2 shows the details of the systems and tools used in the experiments.

4.4   Artifacts in AutoDest Jump Lists

This section discusses the experiments and their results. Note that the applications and file types considered in the experiments are mere examples; numerous other applications and file types could be considered without affecting the experimental results.

Detecting and Recovering Deleted Jump Lists.   Users can delete jump list files from hidden locations to destroy evidence. The evidence may be removed in two ways:

- Removing individual entries from a jump list file using "Remove from this list" on the Taskbar or Startbar.

- Deleting all the jump list files using SHIFT+DELETE or by executing a privacy cleaner tool.

It is difficult for a normal user to detect the removal of individual entries from a jump list file. However, a forensic analyst can detect the removal by parsing the header of the DestList stream of the AutoDest jump list file. If a few entries have been removed from the list, then the values of the total number of current entries and the last issued entry ID number would be different. The difference gives the number of entries removed from the list. Note that (partial) data belonging to a removed entry may still reside in the corresponding jump list file. An automated tool is not available for carving the individual entries that have been removed. However, a forensic analyst can carve the entries via manual analysis of binary data in the jump list file.

Table 3. Effective size of an AutoDest file before and after entry removal.

Before Entry Removal				After Entry Removal		
	Entry	Size			Entry	Size
	1	995			1	995
SHLLINK	2	941		**SHLLINK**	2	941
Streams	3	952		**Streams**	3	952
	4	997				
DestList Stream		902		**DestList Stream**		668
Effective Size		4,787		**Effective Size**		3,576

The Adobe Reader application was used to open four PDF files, which created the file `de48a32edcbe79e4.automaticDestinations-ms`. The individual SHLLINK streams and the DestList stream were extracted and their sizes (in bytes) were recorded (Table 3). The sizes of the two types of streams were determined using the following Python script:

```
import olefile as J
ole = J.OleFileIO("AppID.automaticDestinations-ms", "rb")

# lists all streams in the AutoDest file
print(ole.listdir(streams = True, storages = False))

# lists size of all streams in the AutoDest file
for item in ole.listdir():
        print(ole.get_size(item))
```

The total size of the two types of streams, SHLLINK and DestList, was $(995 + 941 + 952 + 997) + 902 = 4,787$ bytes. Next, entry number 4 was removed from the jump list associated with Adobe Reader by selecting the option "Remove from this list" on the Startbar. The two types of streams were extracted once again and their total size was computed to be 3,576 bytes. If all the data related to entry number 4 (997 bytes) had been removed, then the number of remaining data bytes can be computed as follows:

$$Remaining\ Bytes = E_B - (E_A + Entry\ Size) \tag{1}$$

where E_B and E_A are the effective sizes before and after removal, respectively.

Upon applying Equation (1), a total of $4,787 - (3,576 + 997) = 214$ bytes of the removed entry persisted in the AutoDest jump list file of

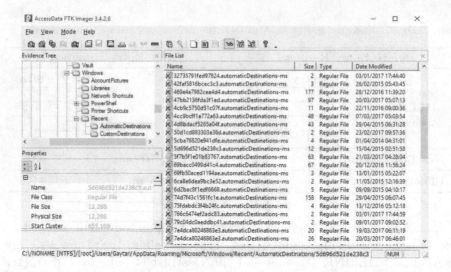

Figure 4.   Deleted jump lists shown in FTK Imager.

the application. However, these bytes could only be carved by analyzing the binary data of the jump list file.

The following observations were made when conducting the experiments:

- Removing individual entries reduces the DestList stream size by 130 bytes plus the size (in bytes) of the file name in Unicode.

- Partial data pertaining to the deleted entries may reside in the SHLLINK streams.

- The overall size of the jump list may or may not be reduced.

- The size of the residual data may be computed using Equation (1).

Another set of experiments was performed to reproduce a situation where a user deliberately deletes a few or all the jump list files to hide activities performed on fixed or removable media. A user may also destroy evidence in the files by browsing the locations and manually deleting them using SHIFT+DELETE. In the experiments, jump lists and recent documents were deleted by running a privacy protection tool (CCleaner).

FTK Imager was used to create an image of the Windows volume (comprising the Windows 10 operating system) to recover the deleted jump list files (Figure 4). The deleted jump list data files were then exported to a different volume. Following this, the exported files were parsed and analyzed using the JumpListExt tool. Useful information

Table 4. AppIDs and application names.

AppID	Application Name
1bc392b8e104a00e	Remote Desktop
*5f7b5f1e01b83767	Quick Access
*4cb9c5750d51c07f	Movies and TV (Windows Store App)
4cc9bcff1a772a63	Microsoft Office PowerPoint 2013 x64
9b9cdc69c1c24e2b	Notepad (64-bit)
9ce6555426f54b46	HxD Hex Editor
12dc1ea8e34b5a6	Microsoft Paint
47bb2136fda3f1ed	Microsoft Office Word 2013 x64
69bacc0499d41c4	Microsoft Office Excel 2013 x64
*a52b0784bd667468	Photos (Windows Store App)
*ae6df75df512bd06	Groove Music (Windows Store App)
f01b4d95cf55d32a	Windows Explorer Windows 8.1/10
faef7def55a1d4b	VLC Media Player 2.1.5 x64
ff103e2cc310d0d	Adobe Reader 11.0.0 x64

related to file accesses was obtained. This included the most MRU and MFU lists corresponding to each user and application, file names, full file paths, file MAC timestamps, volume names and serial numbers from where the files were accessed, unique file volumes and object IDs.

Identifying the Names of Installed Applications. AppIDs of individual applications are computed by the Windows operating system based on the application file paths. AppIDs can be used to name the individual applications. Thus, if an AppID is known, it is possible to identify the name of the associated application. Table 4 lists the AppIDs of common applications. The AppIDs marked with asterisks correspond to default applications introduced in Windows 10.

During the experiments, it was observed that the AppID of an application gives the correct name only when the application is installed at its default location. Different AppIDs are produced when an application is installed at its default location and subsequently installed at another location. Also, the data files associated with applications remain on the hard disk even after the applications have been uninstalled.

Determining Connected Removable Media Properties. When applications are installed and files are opened from a removable media drive, drive properties such as drive type, removable media label, drive serial number and full paths to the accessed files can be determined from

E.No.	Modified	Accessed	Created	Drive Type	Volume Name	Serial No.	File Size	LocalBasePath
29	11/12/2016 18:03	11/16/2016 6:12	11/16/2016 6:12	Fixed	softwares	4196679291	260355	D:\PhD\PhD@1st semPapers_1998.pdf
30	03/10/2017 7:53	08/11/2017 5:24	08/11/2017 5:24	Fixed	Seagate Drive	537079081	71954	H:\forensics\ts_1.pdf
31	5/25/2017 4:05	08/11/2017 5:24	08/11/2017 5:24	Fixed	Seagate Drive	537079081	119758	H:\forensics\ts_2.pdf
2	5/20/2017 5:23	5/20/2017 5:34	5/20/2017 5:23	Fixed	IMP	213827794	143021	E:\EAadhaar_14168300941496.pdf
32	04/11/2017 10:57	08/11/2017 5:24	08/11/2017 5:24	Fixed	Seagate Drive	537079081	60544	H:\forensics\ts_3.pdf
33	4/23/2017 7:49	08/10/2017 18:30	08/06/2017 10:43	Removable	HP-USB	3259304349	769774	G:\confidential_2.pdf
34	4/23/2017 7:52	08/10/2017 18:30	08/06/2017 10:43	Removable	HP-USB	3259304349	1644489	G:\confidential_3.pdf
35	7/18/2017 15:24	08/10/2017 18:30	08/11/2017 5:32	Removable	HP-USB	3259304349	85924	G:\confidential_1.pdf
3	05/11/2017 12:31	5/16/2017 8:32	5/16/2017 8:32	Fixed	IMP	213827794	1024010	E:\REMA_MiniProject11-05-15_Ashish.pdf

Figure 5. Determining connected removable media properties.

the jump lists. These properties can be extracted from the individual SHLLINK streams in the AutoDest files.

To validate these hypotheses, experiments were conducted with two removable drives, an external hard drive labeled Seagate and a removable USB drive labeled HP-USB. Both the drives were seeded with applications and files. Adobe Reader XI application was installed from the HP-USB drive. Six test PDF files were opened with the application. Three files (`confidential_1.pdf`, `confidential_2.pdf` and `confidential_-3.pdf`) were from the HP-USB drive and the other three files (`ts_1.pdf`, `ts_2.pdf` and `ts_3.pdf`) were from the Seagate drive. Adobe Reader XI was then uninstalled, all the test files were deleted and both the drives were removed safely.

In order to determine the drive properties, the jump list for the AppID `ff103e2cc310d0d` corresponding to Adobe Reader XI was parsed and exported to a CSV file using the JumpListExt tool. Figure 5 presents the identified drive properties: (i) drive type; (ii) volume name/drive label; (iii) drive serial number; and (iv) complete paths to the test files.

E.No.	NetBIOS Name	Access Count	New(Timestamp)	New (MAC)	Data
19	john	2	8/13/2017 4:01	a4:17:31:1b:94:12	C:\Users\bhupi\Desktop\AppIDs.docx
10	john	88	08/07/2017 8:57	a4:17:31:1b:94:12	C:\Users\bhupi\Desktop\Forensics Value of Jump List in Windows 10.docx
18	john	9	08/11/2017 4:22	a4:17:31:1b:94:12	C:\Users\bhupi\Desktop\final1_jumplist_w10.docx
14	john	49	08/10/2017 4:05	a4:17:31:1b:94:12	C:\Users\bhupi\Desktop\final_jumplist_w10.docx
17	john	2	08/11/2017 4:22	a4:17:31:1b:94:12	C:\Users\bhupi\AppData\Roaming\Microsoft\Templates\Normal.dotm
11	john	41	08/07/2017 8:57	a4:17:31:1b:94:12	C:\Users\bhupi\Desktop\Jump List experiments.docx
16	john	18	08/10/2017 16:32	a4:17:31:1b:94:12	C:\Users\bhupi\Downloads\DIARA_Proposal.docx
12	john	2	06/09/2017 17:26	c8:cb:b8:5a:95:d0	D:\PhD@DIAT\DFL lab mannual\Digital Forensics Blogs\Digital Forensic Blogs.docx
15	john	1	06/09/2017 17:26	c8:cb:b8:5a:95:d0	D:\PhD@DIAT\DFL lab mannual\NTUSER.docx
13	john	1	05/10/2017 6:38	c8:cb:b8:5a:95:d0	D:\PhD@DIAT\PhD@1st sem\OS Security\Lecture Notes_Lec 01Sem 01_OSS.docx
9	john	3	08/07/2017 8:57	a4:17:31:1b:94:12	C:\Users\bhupi\Desktop\Forensics Value of Jump List in Windows 8.docx

Figure 6. MRU list for Microsoft Word 2013.

Determining MRU and MFU Lists. The DestList stream in an AutoDest file contains the entry ID numbers of the file entries. This information can be used to verify the order of the entries added to the list and, thus, the order of file accesses. Indeed, the DestList stream serves as the MRU list for the files accessed by an application. Figure 6

E.No.	NetBIOS Name	Access Count	New(Timestamp)	New (MAC)	Data
10	john	88	08/07/2017 8:57	a4:17:31:1b:94:12	C:\Users\bhupi\Desktop\Forensics Value of Jump List in Windows 10.docx
14	john	49	08/10/2017 4:05	a4:17:31:1b:94:12	C:\Users\bhupi\Desktop\final_jumplist_w10.docx
11	john	41	08/07/2017 8:57	a4:17:31:1b:94:12	C:\Users\bhupi\Desktop\Jump List experiments.docx
16	john	18	08/10/2017 16:32	a4:17:31:1b:94:12	C:\Users\bhupi\Downloads\DIARA_Proposal.docx
18	john	9	08/11/2017 4:22	a4:17:31:1b:94:12	C:\Users\bhupi\Desktop\final1_jumplist_w10.docx
8	john	5	08/03/2017 5:50	a4:17:31:1b:94:12	E:\jumplist paper\Forensics Value of Jump List in Windows 8.docx
9	john	3	08/07/2017 8:57	a4:17:31:1b:94:12	C:\Users\bhupi\Desktop\Forensics Value of Jump List in Windows 8.docx
19	john	2	8/13/2015 4:01	a4:17:31:1b:94:12	C:\Users\bhupi\Desktop\AppIDs.docx
17	john	2	08/11/2017 4:22	a4:17:31:1b:94:12	C:\Users\bhupi\AppData\Roaming\Microsoft\Templates\Normal.dotm
12	john	2	06/09/2017 17:26	c8:cb:b8:5a:95:d0	D:\PhD@DIAT\DFL lab mannual\Digital Forensics Blogs\Digital Forensic Blogs.docx
2	john	2	08/01/2017 8:06	a4:17:31:1b:94:12	D:\CDAC\CDAC Cyber Forensics worksop on 16 April 2015\cdac\NOTE).doc

Figure 7. MFU list for Microsoft Word 2013.

shows the MRU list for the files accessed by Microsoft Office Word 2013. The MRU list enables a forensic analyst to identify recently used files on a per application basis.

The newly-added four-byte field in the DestList entry structure from offset 116 to 119 is a counter that consistently increases as files are accessed. The field records the access counts of the individual entries. Sorting the entries based on decreasing order of access counts gives the list of MFU entries. Figure 7 shows the MFU list for the files accessed by Microsoft Office Word 2013. The MFU list enables a forensic analyst to identify the frequently used files on a per application basis.

E.No.	NetBIOS	Access Count	New(Timestamp)	New (MAC)	Seq. No.	Data
32	john	2	6/27/2017 7:13	c8:cb:b8:5a:95:d0	33395	C:\Users\bhupi\Downloads\py2exe-0.9.2.2.zip
341	john	16	08/10/2017 16:32	a4:17:31:1b:94:12	33412	C:\Users\bhupi\Downloads\Modified_DIARA_Proposal.docx
470	john	1	4/16/2017 8:30	c8:cb:b8:5a:95:d0	33372	C:\Users\bhupi\Downloads\lec8.pdf
352	john	2	08/11/2017 4:22	a4:17:31:1b:94:12	33413	C:\Python34\5f7b5f1e01b83767\LinkFiles.csv
351	john	4	08/11/2017 4:22	a4:17:31:1b:94:12	33413	C:\Python34\5f7b5f1e01b83767\DestList.csv
107	john	19	08/03/2017 5:50	a4:17:31:1b:94:12	33400	C:\Python34\JumpListParser.py
458	john	4	8/13/2017 4:01	a4:17:31:1b:94:12	33418	C:\Users\bhupi\Desktop\JumpListParser1.0\5f7b5f1e01b83767\DestList.csv
459	john	2	8/13/2017 4:01	a4:17:31:1b:94:12	33418	C:\Users\bhupi\Desktop\JumpListParser1.0\5f7b5f1e01b83767\LinkFiles.csv
469	john	1	4/28/2017 13:20	c8:cb:b8:5a:95:d0	33377	E:\Facebook app sqilte databse backup\DB\Stories.sqlite
468	john	1	4/28/2017 13:20	c8:cb:b8:5a:95:d0	33377	E:\Facebook app sqilte databse backup\DB\Friends.sqlite
465	john	2	4/28/2017 13:20	c8:cb:b8:5a:95:d0	33377	E:\Facebook app sqilte databse backup\DB\FriendRequests.sqlite

Figure 8. Files accessed in a boot session.

Identifying Files Accessed in a Boot Session. An AutoDest jump list with AppID 5f7b5f1e01b83767 (Quick Access) keeps track of all the files opened with an application. The JumpListExt tool was used to parse and export the jump list data to a CSV file. Two fields were found to be important for identifying all the files accessed during a particular boot session: (i) Sequence Number; (ii) Birth Timestamp. Entries corresponding to the files accessed during the same boot session have the same Sequence Number; the Birth Timestamp value represents the session boot time of the system (Figure 8). This information enables a forensic analyst to construct a timeline of user activities on a system under investigation.

5.   Conclusions

The Microsoft Windows 10 operating system introduced dozens of new features and modified the formats of older features such as jump lists. Jump lists are created by software applications to provide quick and easy access to recently-opened files associated with the applications. Jump lists are a rich source of evidence related to file accesses and applications that have been used. This chapter has proposed a new methodology for identifying and recovering deleted entries in the AutoDest type of jump list files. The methodology is best suited to scenarios where users have intentionally deleted entries from jump lists to hide evidence related to their activities.

The experimental research demonstrates that valuable information can be recovered about the files that were accessed and their timelines, applications used to access the files, MRU and MFU file lists, volume names and serial numbers of the devices from which the files were accessed, and the files accessed during a particular boot session. The experiments also empirically verify that user activity history can be retrieved from jump lists even after the associated software applications have been uninstalled and the files have been deleted. Additionally, jump list analysis reveal anti-forensic activities intended to thwart investigations. Indeed, jump list data files are a treasure trove of evidentiary artifacts that can be leveraged in forensic investigations.

Although major portions of DestList streams are well understood, the specific uses of certain fields are still unknown. Future research will investigate the unknown components of DestList streams. Also, research will focus on automating the carving of deleted entries from jump lists.

References

[1] A. Barnett, The forensic value of the Windows 7 jump list, in *Digital Forensics and Cyber Crime*, P. Gladyshev and M. Rogers (Eds.), Springer, Berlin-Heidelberg, Germany, pp. 197–210, 2011.

[2] Hexacorn, Jump list file names and AppID calculator, Hong Kong, China (`www.hexacorn.com/blog/2013/04/30/jumplists-file-names-and-appid-calculator`), 2013.

[3] H. Lallie and P. Bains, An overview of the jump list configuration file in Windows 7, *Journal of Digital Forensics, Security and Law*, vol. 7(1), pp. 15–28, 2012.

[4] T. Larson, Forensic Examination of Windows 7 Jump Lists, *LinkedIn SlideShare* (`www.slideshare.net/ctin/windows-7-forensics-jump-listsrv3public`), June 6, 2011.

[5] R. Lyness, Forensic Analysis of Windows 7 Jump Lists, *Forensic Focus* (articles.forensicfocus.com/2012/10/30/forensic-anal ysis-of-windows-7-jump-lists), October 30, 2012.

[6] M. McKinnon, List of Jump List IDs, *ForensicsWiki* (www. forensicswiki.org/wiki/List_of_Jump_List_IDs), December 19, 2017.

[7] Microsoft Developer Network, [MS-CFB]: Compound File Binary File Format, Microsoft, Redmond, Washington (msdn.microsoft. com/en-us/library/dd942138.aspx), 2018.

[8] NetMarketshare, Operating system market share (www.netmar ketshare.com/operating-system-market-share.aspx?qprid=1 0&qpcustomd=0), 2018.

[9] D. Pullega, Jump List Forensics: AppIDs, Part 1, *4n6k* (www.4n 6k.com/2011/09/jump-list-forensics-appids-part-1.html), September 7, 2011.

[10] B. Singh and U. Singh, A forensic insight into Windows 10 jump lists, *Digital Investigation*, vol. 17, pp. 1–13, 2016.

[11] B. Singh and U. Singh, A forensic insight into Windows 10 Cortana search, *Computers and Security*, vol. 66, pp. 142–154, 2017.

[12] B. Singh and U. Singh, Program execution analysis in Windows: A study of data sources, their format and comparison of forensic capability, *Computers and Security*, vol. 74, pp. 94–114, 2018.

[13] G. Smith, Using jump lists to identify fraudulent documents, *Digital Investigation*, vol. 9(3-4), pp. 193–199, 2013.

Chapter 5

OBTAINING PRECISION-RECALL TRADE-OFFS IN FUZZY SEARCHES OF LARGE EMAIL CORPORA

Kyle Porter and Slobodan Petrovic

Abstract   Fuzzy search is often used in digital forensic investigations to find words that are stringologically similar to a chosen keyword. However, a common complaint is the high rate of false positives in big data environments. This chapter describes the design and implementation of `cedas`, a novel constrained edit distance approximate string matching algorithm that provides complete control over the types and numbers of elementary edit operations considered in approximate matches. The unique flexibility of `cedas` facilitates fine-tuned control of precision-recall trade-offs. Specifically, searches can be constrained to the union of matches resulting from any exact edit combination of insertion, deletion and substitution operations performed on the search term. The flexibility is leveraged in experiments involving fuzzy searches of an inverted index of the Enron corpus, a large English email dataset, which reveal the specific edit operation constraints that should be applied to achieve valuable precision-recall trade-offs. The constraints that produce relatively high combinations of precision and recall are identified, along with the combinations of edit operations that cause precision to drop sharply and the combination of edit operation constraints that maximize recall without sacrificing precision substantially. These edit operation constraints are potentially valuable during the middle stages of a digital forensic investigation because precision has greater value in the early stages of an investigation while recall becomes more valuable in the later stages.

Keywords: Email forensics, approximate string matching, finite automata

1.   Introduction

Keyword search has been a staple in digital forensics since its beginnings, and a number of forensic tools incorporate fuzzy search (or

Published by Springer Nature Switzerland AG 2018. All Rights Reserved
G. Peterson and S. Shenoi (Eds.): Advances in Digital Forensics XIV, IFIP AICT 532, pp. 67–85, 2018.
https://doi.org/10.1007/978-3-319-99277-8_5

approximate string matching) algorithms that match text against keywords with typographical errors or keywords that are stringologically similar. These algorithms may be used to search inverted indexes, where every approximate match is linked to a list of documents that contain the match.

Great discretion must be used when employing these forensic tools to search large datasets because many strings that match (approximately) may be similar in a stringological sense, but are completely unrelated in terms of their semantics. Even exact keyword matching produces an undesirable number of false positive documents to sift through, where as much as 80% to 90% of the returned document hits could be irrelevant [2]. Nevertheless, the ability to detect slight textual aberrations is highly desirable in digital forensic investigations. For example, in the 2008 Casey Anthony case, in which Ms. Anthony was convicted and ultimately acquitted of murdering her daughter, investigators missed a Google search for a misspelling of the word "suffocation," which was written as "suffication" [1].

Digital forensic tools such as dtSearch [8] and Intella [24] incorporate methods for controlling the "fuzziness" of searches. While the tools use proprietary techniques, it appears that they utilize the edit distance [16] in their fuzzy searches. The edit distance – or Levenshtein distance – is defined as the minimum number of elementary edit operations that can transform a string X to a string Y, where the elementary edit operations are defined as the insertion of a character, deletion of a character and substitution of a character in string X. However, precise control of the fuzziness of searches is often limited. In fact, it may not be clear what modifying the fuzziness of a search actually does other than the results "looking" more fuzzy. For example, some tools allow fuzziness to be expressed using a value between 0 to 10, without clarifying exactly what the values represent.

The research described in this chapter has two contributions. The first is the design and implementation of a novel constrained edit distance approximate search `cedas` algorithm, which provides complete control over the types and numbers of elementary edit operations considered in approximate matches. The flexibility of search, which is unique to `cedas`, allows for fine-tuned control of precision-recall trade-offs. Specifically, searches can be constrained to the union of matches resulting from any exact edit operation combination of insertions, deletions and substitutions performed on the search term.

The second contribution, which is a consequence of the first, is an experimental demonstration of which edit operation constraints should be applied to achieve valuable precision-recall trade-offs in fuzzy searches of an inverted index of the Enron Corpus [4], a large English email dataset. Precision-recall trade-offs with relatively high precision are valuable because fuzzy searches typically have high rates of false positives and increasing recall is simply obtained by conducting fuzzy searches with higher edit distance thresholds. The experiments that were performed identified the constraints that produce relatively high combinations of precision and recall, the combinations of edit operations that cause precision to drop sharply and the combination of edit operation constraints that maximize recall without sacrificing precision substantially. These edit operation constraints appear to be valuable during the middle stages of an investigation because precision has greater value in the early stages of an investigation whereas recall becomes more valuable later in an investigation [17].

2.   Background

This section discusses the underlying theory and algorithms.

2.1   Approximate String Matching Automata

A common method for performing approximate string matching, as implemented by the popular `agrep` suite [25], is to use a nondeterministic finite automaton (NFA) for approximate matching. Since `cedas` implements an extension of this automaton, it is useful to discuss some key components of automata theory.

A finite automaton is a machine that takes a string of characters X as input and determines whether or not the input contains a match for some desired string Y. An automaton comprises a set of states Q that can be connected to each other via arrows called transitions, where each transition is associated with a character or a set of characters from some alphabet Σ. The set of initial states $I \subseteq Q$ comprise the states that are active before reading the first character. States that are active check the transitions originating from themselves when a new character is being read; if a transition includes the character being read, then the state pointed to by the arrow becomes active. The set of states $F \subseteq Q$ correspond to the terminal states; if any of these states become active, then a match has occurred. The set of strings that result in a match are considered to be accepted by the automaton; this set is the language L recognized by the automaton.

Figure 1 shows the nondeterministic finite automaton for approximate matching A_L, where the nondeterminism implies that any number of states may be active simultaneously. The initial state of A_L is the node with a bold arrow pointing to it; it is always active as indicated

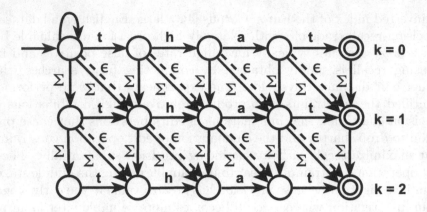

Figure 1. NFA matching the pattern "that" (allowing two edit operations).

by the self-loop. The terminal states are the double-circled nodes. Horizontal arrows denote exact character matches. Diagonal arrows denote character substitutions and vertical arrows denote character insertions, where both transitions consume a character in Σ. Since A_L is a nondeterministic finite automaton, it permits ϵ-transitions, where transitions are made without consuming a character. Dashed diagonal arrows express ϵ-transitions that correspond to character deletions. For approximate search with an edit distance threshold of k, the automaton has $k+1$ rows.

The automaton A_L is very effective at pattern matching because it checks for potential errors in a search pattern simultaneously. For every character consumed by the automaton, each row checks for potential matches, insertions, deletions and substitutions against every position in the pattern.

For common English text, it is suggested that the edit distance threshold for approximate string matching algorithms should be limited to one, and in most cases should never exceed two [9]. This suggestion is well founded because about 80% of the misspellings in English text are due to a single edit operation [5].

Let $L_{k=1}$ and $L_{k=2}$ be the languages accepted by automaton A_L with thresholds $k=1$ and $k=2$, respectively. The nondeterministic finite automaton A_T described in this section allows for different degrees of fuzziness that enable the exploration of the entire space between $L_{k=1}$ and $L_{k=2}$ in terms of the exact combinations of elementary edit operations applied to the search keyword. This automaton accepts the languages L_T, where $L_{k=1} \subseteq L_T \subseteq L_{k=2}$.

The automaton A_T is constructed in the following manner. The automaton that accepts $L_{k=2}$ can be viewed as the union of the languages accepted by each of its rows. For example, for an edit distance threshold of $k = 2$, the first row accepts the language comprising matches that have no edit operations performed on the keyword, the second row accepts the language of matches with one edit operation performed on the keyword and the third row accepts the language of matches with two edit operations performed on the keyword. The union of these subsets is a cover of $L_{k=2}$. An alternative cover of $L_{k=2}$ is the union of all the languages accepted by the automata for a specific number of insertions i, deletions e and substitutions s performed in a match such that $i + e + s \leq k$.

The following lemma proves the equivalence of the covers.

Lemma. Let L_k be the language accepted by an automaton such that k elementary edit operations are performed on a specified pattern. Let $L_{k=n}$ be the language accepted by the nondeterministic finite automaton for approximate matching with edit distance threshold n be equivalent to its cover $C_\alpha = \cup_{k=0}^{k=n} L_k$. Furthermore, let $L_{(i,e,s)}$ be equivalent to the language accepted by an automaton such that exactly i insertions, e deletions and s substitutions have been performed on a specified pattern. Let $C_\beta = \cup_{i,e,s:0 \leq i+e+s \leq n} L_{(i,e,s)}$. Then, $C_\alpha = C_\beta$.

Proof. For all $x \in L_k$, there exists $L_{(i,e,s)}$ such that $x \in L_{(i,e,s)}$, where $i + e + s = k$. Therefore, $C_\alpha \subset C_\beta$. For all $x \in L_{(i,e,s)}$ such that $i + e + s = k$, $x \in L_k$. Thus $C_\beta \subset C_\alpha$. □

By constraining the possible edit operations between the rows of the automaton A_T, each row of the automaton can correspond to a specific combination of i insertions, e deletions and s substitutions such that $i + e + s \leq k$ for edit distance threshold k instead of each row corresponding to some number of edit operations. This construction enables the accepted language L_T to be controlled by allowing terminal states $f \in F$ to remain in F or removing them from F. Specifically, some $L_{(i,e,s)}$ can be chosen to be not included in $C_\beta = \cup_{i,e,s:0 \leq i+e+s \leq n} L_{(i,e,s)}$.

2.2 NFA Definition

The constrained edit distance between two strings X and Y is the minimum number of edit operations required to transform X to Y given that the transformation obeys some pre-specified constraints T [19]. In general, constraints may be defined arbitrarily as long as they consider the numbers and types of edit operations. Let (i, e, s) be an element of T, the set of edit operations that constrain a transformation from string X to string Y, where (i, e, s) is an exact combination of edit operations. A_T may perform approximate searches where matches are constrained to the

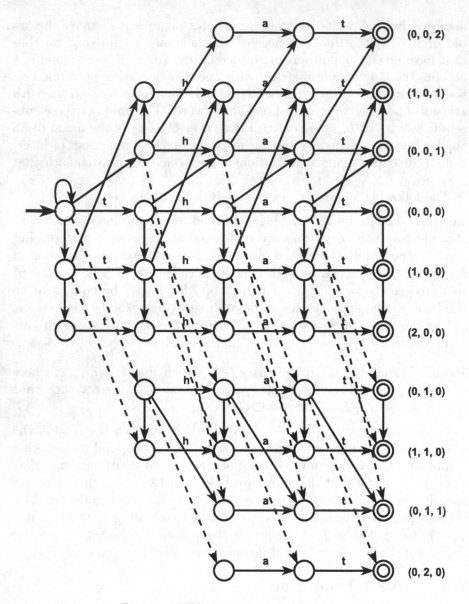

Figure 2. NFA matching the pattern "that."

allowed edit operation combinations in T. For example, the search may be constrained to approximate matches derived from the edit operation combinations $(0,0,0)$, $(1,0,1)$ and $(0,2,0)$. The corresponding accepted language is $L_{(0,0,0)} \cup L_{(1,0,1)} \cup L_{(0,2,0)}$.

Figure 2 shows the constrained edit distance nondeterministic finite automaton A_T. It uses the same symbol conventions as the nondeter-

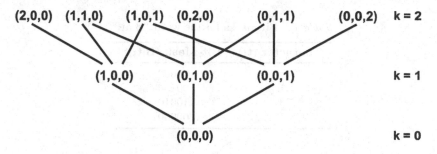

Figure 3. Partially ordered multisets (i, e, s).

ministic finite automaton in Figure 1, except that substitutions and insertions are expressed by diagonal and vertical transitions, respectively, where the transitions may go up or down. In order to ensure that each row $R_{(i,e,s)}$ of the automaton A_T corresponds to the accepted language $L_{(i,e,s)}$, it is necessary to engage the notion of a partially ordered set of multisets, which describes the edit operation transpositions that connect each row. The following definitions [12] are required:

Definition. Let X be a set of elements. Then, a multiset M drawn from set X is expressed by a function count M or C_M defined as $C_M : X \to N$, where N is the set of non-negative integers. For each $x \in X$, $C_M(x)$ is the characteristic value of x in M, which indicates the number of occurrences of elements x in M. A multiset M is a set if $C_M(x) = 0$ or 1 for all $x \in X$.

Definition. Let M_1 and M_2 be multisets selected from a set X. Then, M_1 is a submultiset of M_2 ($M_1 \subseteq M_2$) if $C_{M_1}(x) \le C_{M_2}(x)$ for all $x \in X$. M_1 is a proper submultiset of M_2 ($M_1 \subset M_2$) if $C_{M_1}(x) \le C_{M_2}(x)$ for all $x \in X$ and there exists at least one $x \in X$ such that $C_{M_1}(x) < C_{M_2}(x)$.

The set of multisets considered here comprises the elements (i, e, s), which implies that the multiset contains i insertions, e deletions and s substitutions. The cardinality of the multisets is no greater than the edit distance threshold k. The partial ordering of this set of multisets is the binary relation $\sim$, where for multisets M_1 and M_2, $M_1 \sim M_2$ means that M_1 is related to M_2 via $M_1 \subset M_2$.

Figure 3 presents the partially ordered multiset diagram D. Diagram D models the edit operation transitions between the rows of automaton A_T, where each multiset element (i, e, s) corresponds to row $R_{(i,e,s)}$ and each row of D corresponds to a sum of edit operations. As seen in D, every $R_{(i,e,s)}$ has a specific edit operation transition sent to it from a specific row. In this way, each row $R_{(i,e,s)}$ can determine which (and how

Table 1. Bit-masks for the word "that."

Character (t_j)	Bit-Mask ($B[t_j]$)
a	01000
h	00100
t	10010
*	00000

many) elementary edit operations are being considered in a match due to the partial ordering. For example, $R_{(1,0,0)}$ only has insertion transitions going to it from $R_{(0,0,0)}$, and $R_{(1,1,0)}$ only has deletion transitions going to it from $R_{(1,0,0)}$ (where one insertion has already taken place) and it only has insertion transitions going to it from $R_{(0,1,0)}$ (where one deletion has already taken place).

Finally, since the automaton is nondeterministic, it cannot be implemented directly using a von Neumann architecture.

2.3 Bit-Parallel Implementation

Bit-parallelism allows for an efficient simulation of a nondeterministic finite automaton. The method uses bit-vectors to represent each row of the automaton, where the vectors are updated via basic logical bitwise operations that correspond to transition relations of the automaton. Because bitwise operations update every bit in the bit-vector simultaneously, it updates the states in the row of the automaton simultaneously. If the lengths of the bit-vectors are not greater than the number of bits w in a computer word, then the parallelism reduces the maximum number of operations performed by a search algorithm by w [10].

In the bit-parallel nondeterministic finite automaton simulation, each row of the automaton for the search pattern X is expressed as a binary vector of length $|X| + 1$; this also requires the input characters to be expressed as vectors of the same size. Input characters t_j are handled by bit-masks. Thus, a table of bit-masks $B[t_j]$ is created, where each bit-mask represents the positions of the character t_j in pattern X. Table 1 shows the bit-masks when $X =$ "that." Characters that are not present in the pattern are expressed using the "*" symbol.

Algorithm 1 presents the bit-parallel simulation of automaton A_T. The algorithm is an extension of the simulation of the nondeterministic finite automaton for approximate string matching using the unconstrained edit distance; this was first implemented by Wu and Manber [26]. Therefore, the components of the A_T simulation are similar, the primary modifications being the transition relationships between rows

---

Algorithm 1: NFA update algorithm.

Initialize all rows R' to 0 except $R'(0,0,0) \leftarrow$ 0x00000001,
   $R'(0,1,0) \leftarrow$ 0x00000002, $R'(0,2,0) \leftarrow$ 0x00000004;

for *each input character t* **do**

   $R_{(0,0,0)} \leftarrow R'_{(0,0,0)}$;
   $R'_{(0,0,0)} \leftarrow ((R'_{(0,0,0)} << 1) \ \& \ B[t]) \ | \ $ 0x00000001;
   $R_{(1,0,0)} \leftarrow R'_{(1,0,0)}$;
   $R'_{(1,0,0)} \leftarrow ((R'_{(1,0,0)} << 1) \ \& \ B[t]]) \ | \ R_{(0,0,0)}$;
   $R_{(0,1,0)} \leftarrow R'_{(0,1,0)}$;
   $R'_{(0,1,0)} \leftarrow ((R'_{(0,1,0)} << 1) \ \& \ B[t]]) \ | \ (R'_{(0,0,0)} << 1)$;
   $R_{(0,0,1)} \leftarrow R'_{(0,0,1)}$;
   $R'_{(0,0,1)} \leftarrow ((R'_{(0,0,1)} << 1) \ \& \ B[t]]) \ | \ (R_{(0,0,0)} << 1)$;
   $R_{(0,1,1)} \leftarrow R'_{(0,1,1)}$;
   $R'_{(0,1,1)} \leftarrow ((R'_{(0,1,1)} << 1) \ \& \ B[t]) \ | \ (R_{(0,1,0)} << 1) \ | \ (R'_{(0,0,1)} << 1)$;
   $R_{(1,0,1)} \leftarrow R'_{(1,0,1)}$;
   $R'_{(1,0,1)} \leftarrow ((R'_{(1,0,1)} << 1) \ \& \ B[t]) \ | \ (R_{(1,0,0)} << 1) \ | \ R_{(0,0,1)}$;
   $R_{(1,1,0)} \leftarrow R'_{(1,1,0)}$;
   $R'_{(1,1,0)} \leftarrow ((R'_{(1,1,0)} << 1) \ \& \ B[t]) \ | \ R_{(0,1,0)} \ | \ (R'_{(1,0,0)} << 1)$;
   $R_{(2,0,0)} \leftarrow R'_{(2,0,0)}$;
   $R'_{(2,0,0)} \leftarrow ((R'_{(2,0,0)} << 1) \ \& \ B[t]) \ | \ R_{(1,0,0)}$;
   $R_{(0,2,0)} \leftarrow R'_{(0,2,0)}$;
   $R'_{(0,2,0)} \leftarrow ((R'_{(0,2,0)} << 1) \ \& \ B[t]) \ | \ (R'_{(0,1,0)} << 1)$;
   $R_{(0,0,2)} \leftarrow R'_{(0,0,2)}$;
   $R'_{(0,0,2)} \leftarrow ((R'_{(0,0,2)} << 1) \ \& \ B[t]) \ | \ (R_{(0,0,1)} << 1)$;
   if $(((R'_{(0,0,0)} \ \& \ R^B_{(0,0,0)}) \ | \ (R'_{(0,0,1)} \ \& \ R^B_{(0,0,1)}) \ | \ (R'_{(0,1,0)} \ \& \ R^B_{(0,1,0)}) \ |$
      $(R'_{(1,0,0)} \ \& \ R^B_{(1,0,0)}) \ | \ (R'_{(0,1,1)} \ \& \ R^B_{(0,1,1)}) \ | \ (R'_{(1,0,1)} \ \& \ R^B_{(1,0,1)}) \ |$
      $(R'_{(1,1,0)} \ \& \ R^B_{(1,1,0)}) \ | \ (R'_{(2,0,0)} \ \& \ R^B_{(2,0,0)}) \ | \ (R'_{(0,2,0)} \ \& \ R^B_{(0,2,0)}) \ |$
      $(R'_{(0,0,2)} \ \& \ R^B_{(0,0,2)})) \ \& \ ($0x00000001 $<< n - 1))$ **then**
         Match is found;
   end
end

---

and the number of rows. The rows of the automaton are denoted by bit-vectors $R_{(i,e,s)}$ and their updated values are denoted by $R'_{(i,e,s)}$. $R^B_{(i,e,s)}$ represents the Boolean values for whether or not row $R_{(i,e,s)}$ reports a match, which occurs when $R_{(i,e,s)}$ has a terminal state. For some i, e and s, the value $R^B_{(i,e,s)}$ is true when $(i, e, s) \in T$.

Each row is updated by first checking if the input character is an exact match for the row by computing $((R'_{(i,e,s)} << 1) \ \& \ B[t])$. This value is then bitwise ORed with potential transition relationships. $R_{(i,e,s)}$ checks for insertions, $(R'_{(i,e,s)} << 1)$ checks for deletions and $(R_{(i,e,s)} << 1)$ checks for substitutions from a row $R_{(i,e,s)}$. As mentioned above, incoming transitions for a row $R_{(i,e,s)}$ may be determined by checking against the incoming relations to the multiset (i, e, s) in diagram D in

Figure 3. After updating all the rows, matches are checked by bitwise ANDing each of the allowed rows and determining if any bit representing the terminal states is set to one.

2.4   Evaluation

The additional flexibility in specifying fuzziness comes at the cost of time and space. The time and space complexities of cedas can be specified in terms of the number of multisets in diagram D for an edit distance threshold k. This number is equal to the number of rows in Algorithm 1, which is $f(k) = \frac{1}{6}(k+1)(k+2)(k+3)$. Therefore, for keyword searches shorter than 64 characters on an x64 architecture, the worst-case space complexity is cubic in k and the worst-case time complexity is $O(k^3 n)$, where n is the length of the text searched. Obviously, this implies that the algorithm should not be applied to time sensitive tasks with massive throughput such as intrusion detection, or applied to a live search of massive forensic data with high edit distance thresholds k. However, this is sufficient for specifying the fuzziness of approximate searches over an index of emails, because the values of k should be low and the index acts as a data reduction mechanism. The experimentation described in the next section demonstrates that the algorithm runs approximately six times slower than agrep with an edit distance threshold of $k = 2$.

3.   Experimental Methodology

The flexibility of cedas was evaluated by specifying fuzziness in the context of an investigation of the Enron email dataset [4] and assessing the effectiveness of the constraints. The email messages were converted to the mbox format to simplify processing. Only the contents of the email bodies were examined.

In order to search the data, an inverted index of the emails was created using the mkid program [11], which yielded a database of index tokens. After deduplicating the tokens in the index, all the tokens were output to a single text file that was searched using cedas. Note that the choice of indexing algorithm affects the list of tokens because different algorithms may interpret delimiters differently and, therefore, would affect any search. The list of tokens used in the experiments totaled 460,800 unique words.

Twenty-eight different keywords related to the 2001 Enron scandal were used. This list of keywords was not compiled by a digital forensic investigator, so the choice of keywords could be improved. Keywords were chosen that were relevant to the case, but would not obviously

Table 2. Keyword list.

Word Length	Keywords
6	Cuiaba
7	BlueDog, BobWest, corrupt, illegal, launder, Sarzyna, scandal
8	bankrupt, Backbone, Fishtail, Margaux1, Shutdown, subpoena, Velocity, unlawful
9	collusion, Whitewing, Yosemite
10	Catalytica, conspiracy, KennethLay, litigation, reputation, suspicious
>10	ArthurAndersen, illegitimate, talkingpoints

produce an overwhelming number of false positives. Furthermore, no keyword that contained less than six characters was chosen.

Unconstrained fuzzy searching with an edit distance threshold of $k = 2$ for small keywords produces massive lists of words (often exceeding 10,000 words) that have to be analyzed manually. This can be viewed as a limitation of the proposed approach. Table 2 shows the list of search keywords. Many of the words were taken from Rodger Lepinsky's webpage on data science and the Enron corpus [15].

A case-insensitive fuzzy search for each keyword was conducted on the list of index tokens, and each search was done under 64 different constraints. A match occurred if a keyword was found as a substring of an index token with the allowed tolerance of edit operations as specified by the constraints in terms of $(i, e, s) \in T$. All the approximate matches found in the index were returned in a list. The elements (i, e, s) that were possibly not included in T were those in which the sum $i + e + s$ was equal to the edit distance threshold $k = 2$. Specifically, the automaton accepted $L_{(0,0,0)}, L_{(1,0,0)}, L_{(0,1,0)}, L_{(0,0,1)}$, but the inclusion of all possible combinations of languages $L_{(i,e,s)}$ such that $i + e + s = 2$ was allowed.

The effectiveness of a search for each constraint on each keyword was measured in terms of the precision and recall derived from the list of returned approximate matches. To understand the overall effectiveness of each constraint, the average precision and recall results for all the keywords under each constraint were computed as harmonic means. The harmonic mean was chosen because the arithmetic mean produced overly optimistic results for fuzzy searches under the chosen constraints.

3.1   Interpreting Match Results

Precision and recall have been used by researchers to gauge the effectiveness of approximate string matching algorithms [3, 20]. Precision is the proportion of retrieved items that are relevant whereas recall is the proportion of total relevant items retrieved [13]. As recall increases, precision tends to decrease. Precision and recall are expressed as:

$$\text{Precision} = \frac{|(\text{retrieved items}) \cap (\text{relevant items})|}{|(\text{retrieved items})|} \tag{1}$$

$$\text{Recall} = \frac{|(\text{retrieved items}) \cap (\text{relevant items})|}{|(\text{relevant items})|} \tag{2}$$

The precision and recall metrics are useful, but they are not perfect because the notion of relevance is subjective. Relevant terms are defined as being variations of the original term (e.g., obtaining "litigating" when searching for "litigation"), closely related to the original term in a semantic sense (e.g., obtaining "legalese" when searching for "illegal"), or misspellings of the original term. However, if a keyword is a substring of the examined index token and is clearly unrelated, then it is not considered relevant. For example, if the search term is "audit" and a hit is obtained for "AudiTalk," then the hit is not relevant. For this reason, the classification of relevant versus non-relevant hits for approximate hits is always a manual process.

Another shortcoming of the metrics is that it is not possible to compute the true precision and recall for every keyword; this is because the number of relevant words for each keyword in the Enron dataset is unknown. Therefore, a compromise was employed: the number of total relevant items was set to be equal to the items identified for each keyword for unconstrained approximate matching at the edit distance threshold $k = 2$. This implies that unconstrained approximate matching with $k = 2$ yields 100% recall, which is not necessarily true.

Finally, it is important to note that approximate string matching results are highly dependent on the specific data being matched and the keywords being used [6]. Therefore, utilizing `cedas` on an inverted index that was not derived from an English email corpus may produce different results.

4.   Experimental Results

This section describes the experimental results.

4.1   Precision and Recall

The results in this section reflect the effectiveness of each set of constraints T in terms of precision and recall, and identify the constraints that produce valuable results for investigating an English email corpus.

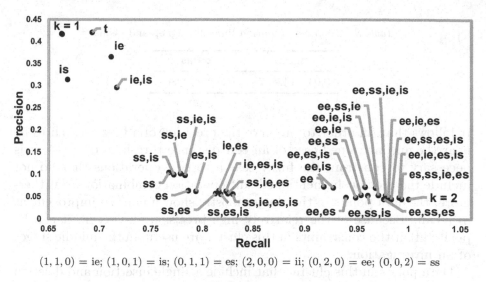

$(1, 1, 0) = $ ie; $(1, 0, 1) = $ is; $(0, 1, 1) = $ es; $(2, 0, 0) = $ ii; $(0, 2, 0) = $ ee; $(0, 0, 2) = $ ss

Figure 4. Precision-recall trade-off curve for various constraints.

Figure 4 shows the precision-recall trade-off curve for various constraints. Data points labeled $k = 1$ and $k = 2$ represent the results for unconstrained fuzzy searches with edit distance thresholds set to one and two, respectively.

As expected, the application of constraints to fuzzy searches of the Enron inverted index resulted in higher recall than an unconstrained fuzzy search with an edit distance threshold of $k = 1$, and better precision than an unconstrained fuzzy search with an edit distance threshold of $k = 2$. However, the primary interest is in the precision-recall trade-offs that are useful in an investigation. As mentioned in the introduction, a common complaint is the number of false positives produced by a fuzzy search, and the fact that precision is valued more than recall early in an investigation [17]. This implies that the constraints that produce results with relatively high precision are most useful in an investigation, because increased recall is easily obtained by increasing the edit distance threshold.

What is immediately apparent from the data is that there are several distinct clusters of data points, where each cluster is associated with different edit operation combinations. The cluster with the highest precision comprises all the data points near data point $k = 1$, where $(0, 1, 1), (0, 0, 2), (0, 2, 0) \notin T$. This means that matches under these constraints did not include edit operations with exactly two substitutions, a substitution and deletion, or two deletions performed on the keyword.

Table 3.   Average execution times for `agrep` and `cedas`.

agrep	cedas
0.0477142857 s	0.2795714286 s

It follows that, in order to preserve the precision of a fuzzy search to be near the unconstrained case of an edit distance threshold of $k = 1$, it is necessary to constrain the fuzzy search to edit operations that do not include the previously mentioned edit operation combinations. Furthermore, the data points in the cluster mostly show a marked improvement in recall. Because of the relatively high precision and recall, it can be posited that the constraints in this cluster are useful in the middle stages of an investigation.

Data points in this cluster that include a single insertion and deletion (*ie*) have very good precision-recall tradeoffs. To ensure that the results of a fuzzy search with these constraints are simply not due to the transposition edit operations for which adjacent characters may be swapped, the same tests were conducted using the `nrgrep` [18] algorithm to perform an unconstrained fuzzy search allowing transpositions with an edit distance threshold of $k = 1$. These results are represented by data point *t* and it can be seen that *ie* and *t* do not yield the same results.

4.2   Execution Time

The speed of `cedas` was evaluated by timing the unconstrained fuzzy search with an edit distance threshold of $k = 2$ for every keyword in the Enron inverted index. The average of these results was computed and compared with the average of the results obtained using `agrep`.

The results in Table 3 demonstrate that `cedas` executed nearly six times slower than `agrep` for an edit distance threshold $k = 2$. However, it should be noted that the `cedas` implementation was not optimized; therefore, it has the potential to run faster than measured.

4.3   Analysis and Suggestions

The gap in precision between the higher and lower data clusters is potentially shaped by the statistics of the English language. Additional experimentation is necessary to confirm this observation, but it is clearly easy to transform words to other words using many substitutions or deletions. By limiting the application of deletion and substitution edit operations, the structure of the original word is preserved. For this reason, if somewhat high precision is needed, it is appropriate to use a fuzzy search that does not include edit operations involving two deletions, two substitutions, or a single deletion and a single substitution.

To maximize the recall in the fuzzy search results without sacrificing precision as seen when applying many of the edit operation combinations, it is suggested that the set of constraints T should contain $(0,0,0)$, $(1,0,0)$, $(0,1,0)$, $(0,0,1)$, $(1,1,0)$, $(1,0,1)$, $(2,0,0)$; for the sake of brevity, the language accepted by this automaton is denoted by $L_{-(ee,ss,es)}$. The precision and recall of this language correspond to the data point ie, is. If more precision is needed with nearly as much recall, then the set of constraints T should contain $(0,0,0)$, $(0,0,0)$, $(1,0,0)$, $(0,1,0)$, $(0,0,1)$, $(1,1,0)$, $(2,0,0)$ (whose precision and recall correspond to data point ie). Ultimately, cedas users should choose constraints based on the precision-recall trade-offs they are willing to tolerate.

5.   Related Work

Fuzzy search algorithms are implemented in digital forensic tools such as dtSearch [8] and Intella [24]. However, the variables for setting the tolerated fuzziness in these tools do not always correlate directly with the edit distance thresholds. Whether or not these tools employ constrained edit distance algorithms is unknown because their techniques are proprietary. Nevertheless, they appear to be combining the edit distance measure with other types of distance measures, natural language processing and/or information retrieval techniques.

The agrep [25] and nrgrep [18] open-source tools may be used for fuzzy searches in digital forensic investigations. The tools incorporate various approximate matching algorithms, including edit-distance-based approximate matching, prefix matching, regular expression matching and other options. They can be considered to represent the cutting edge of bit-parallel nondeterministic finite automaton implementations for approximate matching in terms of speed and utility. However, the primary advantage of cedas compared with the edit distance matching algorithms used by the tools is its flexibility in constraining edit operations. The agrep tool does not implement constraints; as a result, specifying fuzziness in terms of edit distance operations is limited to setting the edit distance threshold. The nrgrep tool is more flexible in that it allows a user to set an edit distance threshold, use transpositions and define a subset of the edit operations used in a search. The last feature essentially constrains edit operations, thereby producing a subset of possible edit operation constraints as in the case of cedas. However, this type of matching cannot return results equivalent to $L_{-(ee,ss,es)}$.

Other researchers have also proposed constrained edit distance search algorithms. For example, Chitrakar and Petrovic [21, 22] have specified constrained edit distance search algorithms that employ row-based bit-parallelism. One algorithm specifies edit operation constraints in terms of the maximum number of allowed indels [21] (sum of insertions and deletions). A second algorithm expresses edit operation constraints in terms of the maximum allowed number of insertions, deletions and substitutions permitted in a match [22]. These algorithms also engage subsets of possible constraints permitted by cedas, but they cannot specify constraints that yield the language $L_{-(ee,ss,es)}$. Experiments by Chitrakar and Petrovic reveal that their algorithms are nearly as fast as agrep.

6.   Conclusions

This chapter has presented cedas, a novel constrained edit distance fuzzy search algorithm that performs approximate searches where the possible transformations on the search terms are constrained to any set of edit operation combinations with exactly i insertions, e deletions and s substitutions. The algorithm is a bit-parallel simulation of a nondeterministic finite automaton, in which the rows of the automaton are defined not by the number of elementary edit operations considered, but by the numbers and types of edit operations. This flexibility in defining edit operation constraints for approximate search is unique to cedas.

Experiments employed the cedas algorithm to perform constrained edit distance fuzzy searches for a list of keywords in an inverted index of the Enron email corpus. The average precision and recall results of searches applying various edit operation combination constraints identified the constraints that were the most valuable for fuzzy searches of an English email dataset. Because a common complaint against fuzzy search is its large number of false positives, edit operation constraints that yield high precision would be valuable in digital forensic investigations.

The experiments revealed that, in order to avoid the precision drop commonly seen in unconstrained fuzzy search at an edit distance threshold of $k = 2$, it is necessary to constrain fuzzy search to not include any matches involving two deletions, two substitutions, or a substitution and deletion. Fuzzy searches with an edit distance threshold of two and whose constraints did not include the previously mentioned edit operation combinations produced relatively high combinations of precision and recall, where the precision is somewhat reduced with an unconstrained edit distance threshold of $k = 1$ while also improving recall. To maximize the recall of a fuzzy search without significant precision reduction, the combination of edit operations (i, e, s) should be constrained to $(0,0,0)$, $(1,0,0)$, $(0,1,0)$, $(0,0,1)$, $(1,1,0)$, $(1,0,1)$ and $(2,0,0)$. These findings should be useful in the middle stages of an investigation because precision has greater value in the early stages and recall becomes more valuable later in an investigation [17].

The flexibility of cedas comes at a cost. The worst-case space complexity of the algorithm is cubic in k and the worst-case time complexity is $O(k^3 n)$ for searching keywords of length less than 64 characters on an x64 architecture, where k is the edit distance threshold and n is the length of the searched text. During the experiments, it was discovered that the average time taken to perform an unconstrained approximate search with edit distance threshold $k = 2$ on the inverted index of the Enron dataset and return the list of approximate matches increased from about 0.0477 seconds with agrep to about 0.2796 seconds with cedas. It is important to note that the cedas implementation has not been optimized. In fact, the space and time requirements can be reduced by dynamically generating the rows of the automaton that are necessary instead of simply removing terminal states from specific rows.

The implementation of cedas in a hardware architecture targeted for nondeterministic finite automata (e.g., Automata Processor [7]) could potentially run in linear time. Tracy et al. [23] have shown that the nondeterministic finite automaton for approximate matching (Figure 1) runs in worst-case linear time on the Automata Processor, where the hardware could maximally handle a nondeterministic finite automaton with a search pattern length of 2,730 characters with an edit distance threshold $k = 4$. The fastest bit-parallel nondeterministic finite automaton simulations of the same type of automaton require that search patterns do not exceed about 30 characters to preserve optimal results with a worst-case time complexity of $O(\lceil (m-k)(k+1)/w \rceil n)$ [14], where m is the length of the search pattern, k is the edit distance threshold and n is the length of the input. Finally, other improvements, such as those employed by other search tools, can also be made to cedas; these include prefix matching and character-specific fuzziness.

Acknowledgement

This research was supported by the Research Council of Norway Program IKTPLUSS under the R&D Project: "Ars Forensica – Computational Forensics for Large-Scale Fraud Detection, Crime Investigation and Prevention" (Grant Agreement 248094/O70).

References

[1] Associated Press, Casey Anthony detectives missed 'suffocation' search, *USA Today*, November 25, 2012.

[2] N. Beebe and J. Clark, Digital forensic text string searching: Improving information retrieval effectiveness by thematically clustering search results, *Digital Investigation*, vol. 4(S), pp. S49–S54, 2007.

[3] M. Bilenko, R. Mooney, W. Cohen, P. Ravikumar and S. Fienberg, Adaptive name matching in information integration, *IEEE Intelligent Systems*, vol. 18(5), pp. 16–23, 2003.

[4] W. Cohen, Enron Email Dataset, Machine Learning Department, Carnegie Mellon University, Pittsburgh, Pennsylvania (`www.cs.cmu.edu/~./enron`), 2015.

[5] F. Damerau, A technique for computer detection and correction of spelling errors, *Communications of the ACM*, vol. 7(3), pp. 171–176, 1964.

[6] R. da Silva, R. Stasiu, V. Moreira Orengo and C. Heuser, Measuring quality of similarity functions in approximate data matching, *Journal of Informetrics*, vol. 1(1), pp. 35–46, 2007.

[7] P. Dlugosch, D. Brown, P. Glendenning, M. Leventhal and H. Noyes, An efficient and scalable semiconductor architecture for parallel automata processing, *IEEE Transactions on Parallel and Distributed Systems*, vol. 25(12), pp. 3088–3098, 2014.

[8] dtSearch, Over 25 Federated and Concurrent Search Options, Bethesda, Maryland (`www.dtsearch.com/PLF_Features_2.html`), 2018.

[9] Elasticsearch, Fuzzy Query, Mountain View, California (`www.elastic.co/guide/en/elasticsearch/reference/current/query-dsl-fuzzy-query.html`), 2017.

[10] S. Faro and T. Lecroq, Twenty years of bit-parallelism in string matching, in *Festschrift for Borivoj Melichar*, J. Holub, B. Watson and J. Zdarek (Eds.), Prague Stringology Club, Prague, Czech Republic, pp. 72–101, 2012.

[11] Free Software Foundation, ID Database Utilities, GNU Operating System, Boston, Massachusetts (`www.gnu.org/software/idutils/manual/idutils.html`), 2012.

[12] K. Girish and J. Sunil, General relations between partially ordered multisets and their chains and antichains, *Mathematical Communications*, vol. 14(2), pp. 193–205, 2009.

[13] P. Hall and G. Dowling, Approximate string matching, *ACM Computing Surveys*, vol. 12(4), pp. 381–402, 1980.

[14] H. Hyyro, Improving the bit-parallel NFA of Baeza-Yates and Navarro for approximate string matching, *Information Processing Letters*, vol. 108(5), pp. 313–319, 2008.

[15] R. Lepinsky, Analyzing Keywords in Enron's Email, *Rodger's Notes* (www.rodgersnotes.wordpress.com/2013/11/24/analyz ing-keywords-in-enrons-email), 2013.

[16] V. Levenshtein, Binary codes capable of correcting deletions, insertions and reversals, *Soviet Physics Doklady*, vol. 10(8), pp. 707–710, 1966.

[17] D. Lillis and M. Scanlon, On the benefits of information retrieval and information extraction techniques applied to digital forensics, in *Advanced Multimedia and Ubiquitous Engineering*, J. Park, H. Jin, Y. Jeong and M. Khan (Eds.), Springer, Singapore, pp. 641–647, 2016.

[18] G. Navarro, NR-grep: A fast and flexible pattern-matching tool, *Software – Practice and Experience*, vol. 31(13), pp. 1265–1312, 2001.

[19] B. Oommen, Constrained string editing, *Information Sciences*, vol. 40(3), pp. 267–284, 1986.

[20] T. Rees, Taxamatch, an algorithm for near ('fuzzy') matching of scientific names in taxonomic databases, *PLoS ONE*, vol. 9(9), 2014.

[21] A. Shrestha Chitrakar and S. Petrovic, Approximate search with constraints on indels with application in spam filtering, *Proceedings of the Norwegian Information Security Conference*, pp. 22–33, 2015.

[22] A. Shrestha Chitrakar and S. Petrovic, Constrained row-based bit-parallel search in intrusion detection, *Proceedings of the Norwegian Information Security Conference*, pp. 68–79, 2016.

[23] T. Tracy, M. Stan, N. Brunelle, J. Wadden, K. Wang, K. Skadron and G. Robins, Nondeterministic finite automata in hardware – The case of the Levenshtein automaton, presented at the *Fifth Workshop on Architectures and Systems for Big Data*, 2015.

[24] Vound, Individual Solutions, Evergreen, Colorado (www.vound-software.com/individual-solutions), 2017.

[25] S. Wu and U. Manber, agrep – A fast approximate pattern-matching tool, *Proceedings of the USENIX Winter Technical Conference*, pp. 153–162, 1992.

[26] S. Wu and U. Manber, Fast text searching: Allowing errors, *Communications of the ACM*, vol. 35(10), pp. 83–91, 1992.

Chapter 6

ANTI-FORENSIC CAPACITY AND DETECTION RATING OF HIDDEN DATA IN THE Ext4 FILESYSTEM

Thomas Göbel and Harald Baier

Abstract   The rise of cyber crime and the growing number of anti-forensic tools demand more research on combating anti-forensics. A prominent anti-forensic paradigm is the hiding of data at different abstraction layers, including the filesystem layer. This chapter evaluates various techniques for hiding data in the ext4 filesystem, which is commonly used by Android devices. The evaluation uses the capacity and detection rating metrics. Capacity reflects the quantity of data that can be concealed using a hiding technique. Detection rating is the difficulty of finding the concealed artifacts; specifically, the amount of effort required to discover the artifacts. Well-known data hiding techniques as well as new techniques proposed in this chapter are evaluated.

Keywords: Anti-forensics, data hiding, ext4, filesystem forensics

1.   Introduction

The rise of cyber crime and the proliferation of anti-forensic software and tools that interfere with forensic investigations demand more research in the area of anti-forensics [15]. In 2007, Garfinkel [7] cautioned about the number of tools that were available to frustrate forensic investigations. More recently, Conlan et al. [4] have released a huge data set that includes 308 anti-forensic tools. While investigators generally take strong measures to keep digital evidence intact, malicious entities attempt to hide, remove, destroy or alter evidence, rendering forensic investigations difficult, time-consuming and expensive. Anti-forensics also deals with data hiding techniques [13]; a variety of artifact wiping tools and trail obfuscation methods are used to deliberately disorient forensic investigations.

© IFIP International Federation for Information Processing 2018
Published by Springer Nature Switzerland AG 2018. All Rights Reserved
G. Peterson and S. Shenoi (Eds.): Advances in Digital Forensics XIV, IFIP AICT 532, pp. 87–110, 2018.
https://doi.org/10.1007/978-3-319-99277-8_6

The popular ext4 filesystem is used as the default by Android and many Linux operating system distributions since kernel 2.6.28 [18]. It was created as the successor to the ext3 filesystem to keep up with increasing disk capacities and advanced features [10]. In the context of forensic investigations, it is important to know about the potential hiding places in ext4 volumes, especially due to the extensive use of ext4 in Android smartphones since version 2.3 Gingerbread [16].

Anderson et al. [1] conducted a study of data hiding in filesystem metadata and developed a steganographic filesystem. This resulted in the creation of StegFS [11], a steganographic filesystem based on ext2 that secured hidden data.

Various data hiding techniques for the ext2 and ext3 filesystems, as well as suitable countermeasures, are discussed in [3, 5, 12]. A security analyst named The Grugq [14] has developed several anti-forensic tools that hide data within ext2, but these tools have not been updated for newer versions of the ext filesystem. The most recent contribution is a low-level study and comprehensive forensic analysis of the most important ext4 filesystem data structures by Fairbanks [6]. This research also identified potential hiding places in ext4, such as HTree nodes, group descriptor growth blocks (GDGBs) and data structures in uninitialized block groups, but it did not study these hiding places any further.

Mathur et al. [10] have published extensive research related to the new ext4 filesystem. Wong [19] has created the *Ext4 Wiki*, an important reference for filesystem analysis. Both these references have been used in this research to locate possible hiding places in the ext4 filesystem. Essential information about the ext4 filesystem layout can be found in the source code of the Linux kernel (see, e.g., [17]).

Some academic research has focused on data hiding in previous versions of the ext filesystem. However, public research related to ext4 anti-forensics is practically non-existent.

This research focuses on the key question – How can data be hidden in an ext4 volume? In particular, the research differentiates between new methods and known techniques discussed in research related to previous ext filesystem versions, and studies their functionality in the context of ext4. New features and data structures of ext4 are analyzed and their efficacy in hiding data is evaluated; this helps identify specific filesystem structures that can be used to hide data. The data hiding methods are evaluated using two metrics: (i) capacity; and (ii) detection rating. Capacity expresses the amount of data that can be hidden whereas the detection rating expresses the difficulty of finding concealed artifacts (e.g., effort required on the part of forensic investigators). For this reason, ext4 volumes are examined using common, open-source forensic

Table 1. Overview of ext4 hiding techniques.

Data Hiding Techniques	Filesystems
Previous Techniques	
File and Directory Slack Space [3, 5]	ext2/ext3
Null Directory Entries [14]	ext2
Partition Boot Sector [12]	ext2/ext3
Superblock: Slack Space [3]	ext2/ext3
Superblock: Reserved Space [14]	ext2
Superblock: Backup Copies [12]	ext2/ext3
Group Descriptor Table: Slack Space [3]	ext2/ext3
Block Group Descriptor: Reserved Space [14]	ext2
Inode Table: Reserved Inodes [5, 12]	ext2/ext3
Inode: Reserved Space [14]	ext2
New Techniques	
Block Bitmap: Slack Space [*]	ext4
Inode Bitmap: Slack Space [*]	ext4
Inode: Slack Space/Extended Attributes [*]	ext4
Inode: Nanosecond Timestamps [*]	ext4
Group Descriptor Table: Backup Copies [*]	ext4
Group Descriptor Table: Growth Blocks [6]	ext4
Extent: Persistent Preallocation [*]	ext4
Data Structures in Uninitialized Block Groups [6]	ext4

tools such as FTK Imager, Autopsy and Sleuthkit. Finally, the research evaluates the forensic implications of the various data hiding methods.

Table 1 lists all the ext4 data hiding techniques evaluated in this research. The table is organized into two sections, one containing techniques applied to earlier versions of the ext filesystem and the other containing new or untested techniques for the ext4 filesystem. The new techniques, which are marked as [*], are the primary contributions of this research.

2. Background

This section discusses anti-forensics and the technical aspects of the ext4 filesystem.

2.1 Anti-Forensics

Baggili et al. [2] have observed that research papers combating anti-forensic techniques are vastly outnumbered by the number of websites that discuss how to exploit the digital forensic process [8]. Combating anti-forensics requires a consensus view and a standardized definition and categories of anti-forensic methods in order to develop mitigation strategies [8]. Definitions of anti-forensics were proposed in 2005 by Rogers [13] and in 2006 by Harris [8]. The most recent definition was formulated in 2016 by Conlan et al. [4], who summarized the previous definitions and defined anti-forensics as "attempts to alter, disrupt, negate, or in any way interfere with scientifically valid forensic investigations."

Anti-forensic techniques fall into several categories. Rogers [13] has proposed four categories: (i) data hiding; (ii) artifact wiping; (iii) trail obfuscation; and (iv) attacks against the digital forensic process and tools. A more recent taxonomy was specified by Conlan et al. [4]. This taxonomy adds a new category to Rogers' classification: (v) possible indications of anti-digital-forensic activity. It also specifies several subcategories in order to create a more comprehensive and up-to-date taxonomy. The methods considered in this research can be classified as data hiding techniques that are mapped to the filesystem manipulation subcategory in the extended taxonomy of Conlan et al. [4].

In general, there are three ways to hide data in an ext filesystem. First, data can be hidden in slack space. This is because ext has a fixed block size and a write operation that (in most cases) does not need an exact multiple of the block size, making slack space available in several places. Of course, it is important to distinguish between different types of slack space, for example, classical file/directory slack space and metadata slack space associated with several filesystem data structures.

The second way is to hide data in reserved space. Multiple locations distributed across the filesystem are reserved for future use, for example, reserved group descriptor growth blocks for future filesystem expansion. Reserved areas can also be leftovers from earlier versions that are no longer used.

The third way is to misuse filesystem structures to hide data. This approach is effective because it is difficult to distinguish hidden data from normal content. An analysis tool will not report an inconsistency if the hidden data matches the normal internal structures (i.e., there is no anomaly). An example is data hidden in inode timestamps, which the `e2fsck` tool would interpret as ordinary timestamps.

2.2   Ext4 Filesystem Layout

Figure 1 shows the ext4 filesystem layout. The filesystem allocates disk space in units of blocks comprising multiple sectors; the typical block size is 4 KiB. Blocks are, in turn, grouped into larger units called block groups.

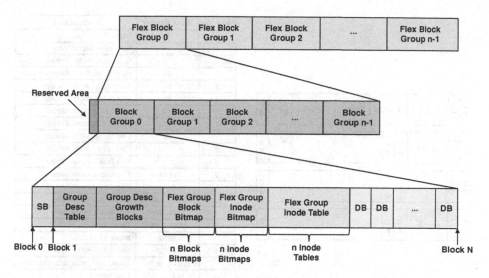

Figure 1. General ext4 filesystem layout.

The entire partition is divided into a series of block groups. The ext4 filesystem offers a new feature called a flexible block group (INCOMPAT_- FLEX_BG). This feature provides better performance by allowing the combination of several block groups into a single logical block group. The block metadata of multiple block groups (i.e., block bitmaps, inode bitmaps and inode tables) are placed close together as one long run in the first block group of the flexible block group.

Figure 2 shows an example ext4 filesystem layout with one flexible block group that includes four block groups (left-hand side of the figure), and the sparse feature.

A block group contains a number of data structures [19]. The first 1,024 bytes are reserved for the boot sector. Following this is the superblock, which generally starts after the reserved area at byte offset 1,024; the superblock is essential to smooth filesystem operation. It records various information about the layout, size and enabled features of the filesystem.

The superblock is followed by the group descriptor table (GDT). Each block group of the filesystem has a table entry, the so-called block group descriptor. It contains metadata about the block group, for example, the locations of the associated block bitmap, inode bitmap and inode table.

To support future expansion of the filesystem, mke2fs allocates several group descriptor growth blocks after the group descriptor table. If the sparse feature flag (RO_COMPAT_SPARSE_SUPER) is set, then redundant

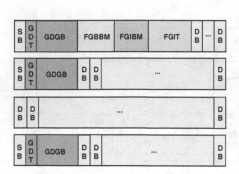

Block Grp.	Block Number	Data Structure
0	0	Super Block Copy
0	1	Group Descriptor Table
0	2 - 62	Group Descriptor Growth Blocks
0	63	Flex Group Block Bitmap
1	63	Flex Group Block Bitmap
2	63	Flex Group Block Bitmap
3	63	Flex Group Block Bitmap
0	67	Flex Group Inode Bitmap
1	68	Flex Group Inode Bitmap
2	69	Flex Group Inode Bitmap
3	70	Flex Group Inode Bitmap
0	71 - 1047	Flex Group Inode Table
1	1048 - 2024	Flex Group Inode Table
2	2025 - 3001	Flex Group Inode Table
3	3002 - 3978	Flex Group Inode Table
0	3979 - 32767	Data Blocks
1	32768	Super Block Copy
1	32769	Group Descriptor Table
1	32770 - 32830	Group Descriptor Growth Blocks
1	32831 - 65535	Data Blocks
2	65536 - 98303	Data Blocks
3	98304	Super Block Copy
3	98305	Group Descriptor Table
3	98306 - 98366	Group Descriptor Growth Blocks
3	98367 - 124999	Data Blocks

Figure 2. Example ext4 filesystem layout.

copies of the superblock, group descriptor table and group descriptor growth blocks are placed in groups whose group number is 0 or a power of 3, 5 or 7. Otherwise, each block group contains a backup copy.

Following this are the block bitmap, inode bitmap and inode table. The block bitmap tracks the usage of each data block in the block group. The inode bitmap records the entries in the inode table that are in use. The inode table contains the metadata of a file or directory (e.g., file owner, permissions and timestamps). While the bitmaps usually use one block each, the inode table uses multiple contiguous blocks. Leftover space is used by the data blocks that store actual user data.

3.　　Evaluation Methodology

An anti-forensic hiding approach seeks to conceal data. A user who employs such a technique is mainly interested in two aspects. The first aspect is the amount of data that can be hidden by the technique – the more, the merrier. The second is the ease with which hidden data can be discovered by a digital forensic expert – the harder, the better.

Table 2. Relevant metadata information in the ext4 test volumes.

Metadata Information	64 GiB Volume	500 GiB Volume
Block Size	4,096	4,096
Inode Size	256	256
Inode Range	1 – 4,194,305	1 – 32,768,001
Free Blocks	16,369,541	128,734,265
Free Inodes	4,194,293	32,767,989
GDT Size (in Blocks)	8	63
Number of Block Groups	512	4,000
Blocks per Block Group	32,768	32,768
Inodes per Block Group	8,192	8,192
Superblocks (with Sparse Feature)	13	18
Superblocks (without Sparse Feature)	512	4,000

Therefore, a hiding approach is evaluated based on: (i) capacity; and (ii) detection rating. Comparable evaluation metrics have not been proposed in the digital forensics literature.

- **Capacity:** The maximum hideable amount of data in bytes over the entire filesystem is specified for each technique. If there is insufficient space for an entire file to be hidden in one location, it can be divided into several pieces and hidden in multiple locations across the filesystem. Furthermore, the maximum hiding capacities of a 64 GiB volume (e.g., Android internal flash memory) and a 500 GiB volume (e.g., laptop SSD) are specified. Reasonable estimates of the hiding capacity were made based on information extracted from sample test images using Sleuthkit (Table 2).

- **Detection Rating:** The following detection rating scheme is employed:

  - The "easy" rating implies that a digital forensic investigator will typically find the hidden data.

  - The "advanced" rating implies that the hidden data would not ordinarily be found, but a digital forensic expert would find it if there is an anomaly.

  - The "difficult" rating implies that the hidden data would hardly ever be found.

The Sleuthkit, FTK Imager and Autopsy tools were used to obtain ratings of the data hiding techniques. Modern volumes are getting larger and forensic investigators often do not have the expertise or resources to perform manual examinations using hex editors. Forensic tools are used to examine volumes and alert investigators to anomalies. If an alert does not point an investigator to the hidden data, it can remain undetected.

The e2fsck and debugfs filesystem checking utilities in the e2fsprogs suite may be used to find filesystem inconsistencies and provide hints about hidden data. The e2fsck utility can be forced to check a filesystem using the -f argument. Beyond this, file carving can be used to obtain hidden data, but this is outside the scope of this research, which focuses on data hiding and detection using filesystem structures instead of treating the entire volume as an image without metadata.

It is important to note that detecting hidden data does not solve the problem of interpreting the hidden data. Therefore, after an anomaly indicates the presence of hidden data, reverse engineering and decryption techniques may have to be applied to determine the meaning of the hidden content. Obfuscated and encrypted data significantly complicate hidden data detection using carving techniques.

This research focuses on the capabilities of forensic tools to find hidden data in unexpected locations. When assessing the hiding techniques in this research, it was assumed that a forensic investigator would know the tools well, but not the details about the ext4 filesystem. Furthermore, it was assumed that the investigator would not examine the entire volume manually if nothing unexpected was encountered.

Experiments were performed on several images created using the dd command and formatted with certain ext4 settings using mke2fs. The data, which included JPG, TXT and ZIP files, and single ASCII characters, was subsequently hidden in the created images using dd.

4.   Hiding Methods Based on Previous Research

This section evaluates whether or not the hiding techniques proposed for ext2/ext3 or other filesystems work on the ext4 filesystem.

The experiments demonstrate that nine of the ten tested techniques still work. Table 3 lists each of the tested methods along with its hiding capacity and detection rating.

4.1   File and Directory Slack Space

Data can be hidden in file slack space [5] as well as in directory slack space [3]. Slack space hiding methods developed for previous ext versions also work on the ext4 filesystem.

The available slack space depends on the block size, amount of data stored in the corresponding block and number of allocated files. This makes it possible to conceal $\frac{BlockSize}{2} \cdot UsedInodes$ bytes on average. Just like any other file, ext4 directories are allocated in blocks. They contain

Table 3. Summary of adapted ext4 hiding techniques with hiding capacity and detection rating metrics.

Data Hiding Technique	Capacity (Bytes) (Usable Space)	Capacity 64 GiB Volume	Capacity 500 GiB Volume	Detection Rating
File/Directory Slack Space	$\frac{BlockSize \cdot UsedInodes}{2}$	8 GiB	62.5 GiB	Easy
Null Directory Entries	$(BlockSize - (3 \cdot 12) - 8) \cdot UsedDataBlocks$	61.77 GiB	485.8 GiB	Advanced
Partition Boot Sector	1,024	1,024 B	1,024 B	Easy
Superblock: Slack Space	$BlockSize - 1,024$	1.5 MiB	11.71 MiB	Easy
Superblock: Reserved Space	394	–	–	Easy
Superblock: Backup Copies	$BlockSize \cdot (BlockGroups - 1)$	2 MiB	15.62 MiB	Advanced
Group Descriptor Table: Slack Space	$GDTSize - (GroupDescSize \cdot BlockGroups)$	–	7.81 MiB	Easy
Block Group Descriptor: Reserved Space	$4 \cdot BlockGroups$	2 KiB	15.62 KiB	Advanced
Inode Table: Reserved Inodes	$2 \cdot (InodeSize - 20)$	472 B	472 B	Advanced
Inode: Reserved Space	$2 \cdot (Inodes - 8)$	8 MiB	62.5 MiB	Advanced

```
e2fsck 1.43.7 (16-Oct-2017)
Pass 1: Checking inodes, blocks and sizes.
Pass 2: Checking directory structure.
Directory inode 12, block #0: directory passes checks but fails
    the checksum.  Fix<y>? yes.
```

Figure 3. Repair of an directory inode checksum using e2fsck.

several directory entries, including at least one entry each for the current directory and parent directory. The available space depends on the number of directory entries. Data can be hidden in the space between the last directory entry and before the ext4_dir_entry_tail structure because the last existing entry points to this structure at the end of the block [19], leaving the remaining space unused. The downside of using slack space is that modifying the original file or directory often overwrites the hidden data; consequently, this method should be restricted to static files and directories.

Hidden data in file slack space does not cause an e2fsck or kernel warning. However, hidden data in directory slack space causes checksum errors. These can be fixed by e2fsck without losing the hidden data as shown in Figure 3. According to the information in Table 2, the 64 GiB volume provides about 8 GiB of available slack space on average whereas the 500 GiB volume provides about 62.5 GiB.

It is common knowledge that data can be hidden in file slack space; therefore, it is classified as easy to find. Common forensic tools check the file slack space by default. However, Autopsy does not show the file slack space automatically; directory slack space is visible using the built-in hex viewer. FTK Imager shows the file slack space in the file browser, but the directory slack space is not visible in the same way. The Sleuthkit command icat -s can help extract a file, including its slack space. Directory slack space should not be ignored during an investigation. Many seemingly useless small files or empty directories in a volume could indicate hidden data in file slack space and directory slack space. File carving can help distinguish hidden data from normal binary data in file slack space.

4.2   Null Directory Entries

The anti-forensic tool KY FS [14] shows how data can be hidden in an ext2 directory entry. In the ext4 filesystem, this can still be done by setting the values of the inode and name_len attribute of a directory entry to zero. After this is done, the directory entry appears as unused and is not visible in a normal file explorer. The length rec_len is set to the length of the entire block and data is then hidden in the name field of the entry. Note that 12 bytes each for the current directory, parent directory and structure ext4_dir_entry_tail at the end of the block including the checksum, as well as 8 bytes for the null directory entry itself, cannot be used to conceal data. With the exception of the above-mentioned entries $(BlockSize - (3 \cdot 12) - 8) \cdot UsedDataBlocks$ bytes remain to hide data.

In the experiments, 61.77 GiB of data could be hidden in the 64 GiB image and 485.8 GiB in the 500 GiB image. Invalid directory inode checksums can also be fixed by e2fsck as shown in Figure 3.

This is an advanced data hiding technique because null directory entries can be difficult to recognize among the variety of directory entries; in fact, their content would appear almost invisible at first sight. Hidden data can be viewed manually using the FTK Imager and Autopsy hex viewers, but no user notifications are provided. Forensic investigators should pay attention to the presence of numerous empty directories.

4.3 Partition Boot Sector

Piper et al. [12] have shown that the first 1,024 bytes (boot sector) of an ext2 volume can be used to hide data. This method is applicable to ext4. No errors are detected during a forced filesystem check.

The ability to hide data in the boot sector is well known and a forensic investigator should find it easy to find the hidden data. FTK Imager provides the option to examine the boot sector using its hex viewer. However, Autopsy has no option to show this data structure.

4.4 Superblock: Slack Space

Berghel et al. [3] mention that unused space exists behind the superblock up to the end of the block in the ext3 filesystem. In the ext4 filesystem, the superblock also has a total size of 1,024 bytes. In general, this provides $BlockSize - 2,048$ bytes of usable space in block group 0 and $BlockSize - 1,024$ bytes in each remaining block group, including a superblock backup copy, since the first superblock has an offset of 1,024 bytes to make room for the additional boot sector.

Hidden data does not affect e2fsck. The available space depends on whether the sparse_super feature flag is set. In the experiments, the 64 GiB volume provided 38 KiB of usable space with the sparse feature and 1,535 KiB without the feature. The 500 GiB volume provided 53 KiB of usable space with the sparse feature and 11.71 MiB without it.

Hidden data in the slack space of a superblock is easy to find because this area is normally empty. In fact, a forensic investigator should be

```
e2fsck 1.43.7 (16-Oct-2017)
ext2fs_open2: Superblock checksum does not match superblock.
e2fsck: Superblock invalid, trying backup blocks...
```

Figure 4. Automated repair of an invalid superblock.

suspicious if it is not empty. FTK Imager provides the option to examine a superblock with its hex viewer. However, Autopsy has no special option to show this data structure and does not provide any warnings.

4.5   Superblock: Reserved Space

The anti-forensic tool Data Mule FS has been shown to use 759 bytes in a superblock to hide data [14]. According to the Linux kernel source code [17], the reserved space in the ext4 superblock is 394 bytes (2 bytes in s_reserved_pad and 392 bytes in array s_reserved[98]). However, this hiding technique is useless. In the experiments, all the attempts at concealing data in the reserved space of the primary superblock failed because e2fsck generated invalid checksum errors. Subsequent recovery using the backups of the superblock overwrote the hidden content (Figure 4). However, as discussed in the next section, this behavior does not apply to the backup copies. Due to the warnings, data hidden in the reserved space of a superblock is easily spotted.

4.6   Superblock: Backup Copies

Piper et al. [12] have shown that it is possible to hide data in ext3 superblock backups. This data hiding method is still applicable to ext4. In fact, redundant superblocks can be fully used to hide data as long as the first superblock is undamaged. No warnings are issued when the volume is mounted or checked with e2fsck. If the sparse feature flag is not set, then $BlockSize \cdot (BlockGroups - 1)$ bytes are available to conceal data; otherwise, the space available is reduced to the number of block groups including the backups.

In the experiments, the 64 GiB volume provided about 48 KiB of space for data hiding with the sparse feature and 2 MiB without it. The 500 GiB volume provided about 68 KiB with the sparse feature and 15.62 MiB without it. However, data loss could occur if the first superblock is corrupted; this is because e2fsck attempts to restore the original data structure in all backups and overwrites the hidden content. Also, if no valid backup is found, a successful filesystem recovery is impossible.

This method is classified as advanced in terms of its difficulty. This is because real data is actually expected in the superblock backups, unlike slack space, which is normally empty. The superblocks can be viewed manually using FTK Imager with its hex viewer, but Autopsy has no such option. The e2fsck utility does not point to the manipulated backups, so hidden data may remain undetected. A forensic investigator should check for a missing sparse feature flag, which is set by default. The flag could have been deliberately removed by an attacker to obtain additional space for data hiding.

4.7　Group Descriptor Table: Slack Space

Berghel et al. [3] have identified the presence of group descriptor slack space in previous ext versions. The ext4 filesystem still has some slack space behind the group descriptor table when its last block is not completely filled with table entries. Hiding data in this slack space assumes that the filesystem will not grow in size because any added group descriptors would overwrite the hidden data.

The ext4 filesystem extends the group descriptor size from 32 to 64 bytes when the 64-bit feature is enabled. This provides $GDTSize - (GroupDescSize \cdot BlockGroups)$ bytes per table for hiding data. The number of group descriptor table backups depends on the sparse_super feature flag. Hidden data does not affect e2fsck.

In the experiments, data could not be concealed in the 64 GiB image because all the group descriptor table blocks were completely filled with group descriptors. However, the 500 GiB volume provided 2,048 bytes per table, corresponding to 36 KiB with the sparse feature and 7.81 MiB without the feature for the entire filesystem.

Just like any other method that hides data in slack space, this technique is rated as easy to detect. FTK Imager enables the group descriptor table to be examined using its hex viewer; Autopsy does not provide this option.

4.8　Block Group Descriptor: Reserved Space

Data Mule FS has utilized 14 bytes of reserved space to hide data in each ext2 group descriptor [14]. The Linux kernel source code [17] shows that ext4 group descriptors still have a 4-byte bg_reserved structure for padding when the 64-bit feature is enabled. The available storage per group descriptor table, which depends on the number of block groups, amounts to $4 \cdot BlockGroups$ bytes. Therefore, each group descriptor table in the 64 GiB volume provides 2 KiB of usable space while each group descriptor table in the 500 GiB volume provides 15.62 KiB of usable space.

```
e2fsck 1.43.7 (16-Oct-2017)
One or more block group descriptor checksums are invalid.
   Fix<y>? yes.
Group descriptor 0 checksum is 0x5009, should be 0x7d85.
   FIXED.
```

Figure 5.   Repair of an invalid group descriptor checksum.

After manipulating the group descriptors, e2fsck can be used to fix invalid checksums (Figure 5). No more errors occur in further filesystem checks.

FTK Imager provides the option to examine the group descriptor table with its hex viewer, but does not give any warnings; Autopsy has no such option. However, due to the fact that only four bytes per group descriptor are available, hidden data would almost certainly be spread over many group descriptors. If a forensic tool does not explicitly report a non-empty reserved field, the fragmented data can render the forensic investigation more difficult. Therefore, this data hiding technique is classified as advanced.

4.9   Inode Table: Reserved Inodes

Data hiding using reserved inodes has been discussed for ext2 and ext3 [5, 12]. In ext4, inodes 1 to 10 are reserved for internal filesystem use. Inode 0 is not used. Inode 11 is the first available inode and is typically used for the lost+found directory. However, the kernel source code [17] does not explicitly mention the use of inodes 9 and 10. According to Holen [9], inode 9 is used for snapshots by Next3fs and inode 10 is used for ext4 metadata replication. Both are non-standard options and are not used without a patched kernel.

```
e2fsck 1.43.7 (16-Oct-2017)
Pass 1: Checking inodes, blocks and sizes.
Inode 12 passes checks, but checksum does not match inode.
   Fix<y>? yes.
```

Figure 6.   Repair of an invalid inode checksum.

Tests have shown that the fields i_mode, i_blocks_lo, l_i_blocks_-hi, i_flags, i_size_high, l_i_checksum_lo and i_checksum_hi should not be manipulated because they cause errors in e2fsck. Therefore, $2 \cdot (InodeSize - 20)$ bytes remain, which provides 472 bytes in each test volume. The e2fsck utility corrects the inode checksums after manipulation (Figure 6).

It should be mentioned that data can be hidden in blocks that are marked bad using the reserved inode 1. The filesystem prevents bad blocks from being allocated to a file or directory. Any block can be added to the list of bad blocks (using e2fsck [-l bad_blocks_file] device), which provides almost unlimited space.

FTK Imager supports the examination of the inode table with its hex viewer; Autopsy has no such option. This data hiding technique is classified as advanced because reserved inodes are usually not assumed to be empty. Therefore, all inodes, including reserved inodes and slack space, should be analyzed by default using forensic software.

4.10   Inode: Reserved Space

Data Mule FS has utilized 10 bytes per ext2 inode to hide data [14]. However, the ext4 inode structure only has two bytes available in l_i_-reserved [17]. With the exception of the reserved inodes 1 to 8, this field can be abused, providing $2 \cdot (Inodes - 8)$ bytes for hiding data. Therefore, the 64 GiB volume offers approximately 8 MiB of space for hiding data and the 500 GiB volume offers 62.5 MiB. Invalid inode checksums can be fixed using e2fsck after data has been hidden (Figure 6).

FTK Imager provides the option to investigate the inode table manually; Autopsy has no special option.

The inode reserved space is mentioned in the ext4 documentation [19]. Nevertheless, this data hiding method is rated as advanced because the same situation applies as in the case of the group descriptor reserved space. Hidden data is hard to find when it is distributed in multiple entries across the inode table. An investigator should, therefore, keep an eye on the various reserved areas.

5.   New Hiding Methods

This section discusses locations for hiding data that have been identified during this research project. Some techniques have not been described in the literature because they are only applicable to ext4. Furthermore, this section verifies whether or not any of the potential ext4 hiding places proposed in the literature, but that have not been tested, actually work.

The experiments demonstrate that all eight tested techniques work. Table 4 summarizes the results of the eight techniques.

5.1   Block Bitmap: Slack Space

The block bitmap is one block in size because the number of blocks per block group corresponds to the number of bits of one block (e.g.,

Table 4. Summary of new ext4 hiding techniques with hiding capacity and detection rating metrics.

Data Hiding Technique	Capacity (Bytes) (Usable Space)	Capacity 64 GiB Volume	Capacity 500 GiB Volume	Detection Rating
Block Bitmap: Slack Space	$(BlockSize - (\frac{BlocksPerGroup}{8})) \cdot BlockGroups$	Variable	Variable	Easy
Inode Bitmap: Slack Space	$(BlockSize - (\frac{InodesPerGroup}{8})) \cdot BlockGroups$	1.5 MiB	11.71 MiB	Easy
Inode: Slack Space/ Extended Attributes	$(InodeSize - (128 + i\_extra\_isize)) \cdot Inodes$	384 MiB	3,000 MiB	Advanced
Inode: Nanosecond Timestamps	$15 \cdot UsedInodes$	60 MiB	469 MiB	Difficult
Group Descriptor Table: Backup Copies	$GDTSize \cdot (BlockGroups - 1)$ $GDTSize = BlockSize \cdot \lceil \frac{BlockGroups \cdot s\_desc\_size}{BlockSize} \rceil$	16 MiB	984 MiB	Advanced
Group Descriptor Table: Growth Blocks	$s\_reserved\_gdt\_blocks \cdot BlockSize \cdot (BlockGroups - 1)$	2 GiB	15.6 GiB	Advanced
Extent: Persistent Preallocation	16 TiB	Variable	Variable	Advanced
Data Structures in Uninitialized Block Groups	$DataStructureSize \cdot UninitBlockGroups$	Variable	Variable	Advanced

there are 32,768 blocks per block group with a default block size of 4,096 bytes). Default settings leave no room between the block bitmap and the end of the block. However, slack space can still exist because the number of blocks per group does not necessarily have to match the number of bits in a block, and it is adjustable during formatting. The command `mkfs.ext4 -g [image]` deliberately creates a filesystem with fewer blocks per group.

Several regions of block bitmap slack space exist, one in each block group. The amount of data that can be hidden depends on the number of block groups and amounts to $(BlockSize - (\frac{BlocksPerGroup}{8}))$. $BlockGroups$ bytes. The amount of usable slack space varies, but corresponds to the inode bitmap. Hidden data survives a forced check by `e2fsck`.

FTK Imager presents the block bitmaps in its hex viewer; Autopsy has no such option. Hidden data should be easy to find because, with the default filesystem settings, no slack space is available behind the block bitmap; if there is space, it should contain only zeros.

5.2   Inode Bitmap: Slack Space

There are fewer inodes than blocks per block group. Therefore, unlike the block bitmap, several bytes remain unused at the end of each inode bitmap with the default settings. The amount of usable space is repeated per block group and this provides $(BlockSize - (\frac{InodesPerGroup}{8}))$. $BlockGroups$ bytes. The 64 GiB volume can store 1.5 MiB of hidden data and the 500 GiB volume can store 11.71 MiB. The hidden data survives a forced check by `e2fsck`.

FTK Imager provides the option to view the inode bitmaps manually whereas Autopsy does not provide this option. The slack area behind the inode bitmap up to the end of the block normally contains zeros. Any other data would be easily found by a forensic investigator.

5.3   Inode: Slack Space/Extended Attributes

The ext2 and ext3 filesystems have an inode size of 128 bytes and leave no space for data hiding. The default size of an inode record in ext4 is 256 bytes [10]. It can even be set to the filesystem block size using the `mkfs.ext4 [-I inode size]` option at format time. The extra 128 bytes are divided into a range of fixed fields and a range of extended attributes as shown in Figure 7. Each inode contains the field `i_extra_isize`, which records the additional number of bytes for the fixed fields beyond the original 128 bytes. The extra space between the end of the inode structure and the end of the inode record is meant to store extended

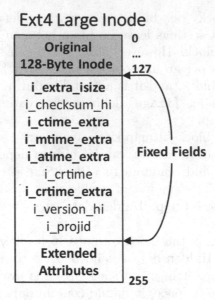

Figure 7.   Ext4 inode structure layout (adapted from [10]).

attributes, but it can also be used to hide data. The maximum concealable amount of data is $(InodeSize - (128 + i\_extra\_isize)) \cdot Inodes$. Thus, 384 MiB of space is available in the 64 GiB volume and 3,000 MiB in the 500 GiB volume (when i_extra_isize is set to 32). After an inode is manipulated, its checksum can be fixed by e2fsck (Figure 6). No warnings occur during additional checks.

If no extended attributes are used, the area behind the actual inode structure is normally empty and any hidden data would be suspicious. Since this is not generally the case and none of the tools give any indications of hidden data, the detection rating is advanced. Any inodes that do not have the default size of 256 bytes should raise further suspicion. In extreme cases, each inode can have the size of an entire block, thereby providing additional space.

5.4   Inode: Nanosecond Timestamps

With larger inodes (256 bytes), there is room to support nanosecond timestamps, so additional 32-bit i_[c|m|a|cr]time_extra fields were added to the original inode structure as shown in Figure 7. Since 30 bits are sufficient to enable nanosecond precision, the remaining two bits are used to extend the Unix epoch (new overflow date is 2446-05-10) [19]. If the additional precision for the timestamps is not required, then the four fields can conceal 16 bytes in each inode. However, the use of the lower two epoch bits leads to dates beyond the year 2038, which looks suspicious and could help reveal the hidden data. Therefore, it makes more sense to hide data only in the upper 30 bits of the nanosecond timestamps. This provides $15 \cdot UsedInodes$ bytes if all four timestamps are used. Thus, the 64 GiB volume offers almost 60 MiB of usable space while the 500GiB volume offers as much as 469 MiB of space. After the checksums of the manipulated inode entries are repaired (Figure 6), hidden data survives another forced e2fsck check and no warnings are given when the filesystem is mounted.

Data hidden in this manner is difficult to find. Common file explorers, as well as ls -la, do not support nanosecond accuracy. FTK Imager and Autopsy also do not show the nanosecond timestamps in their file explorers. Commands such as stat [file] or debugfs -R 'stat <inode>' [image] can parse the timestamps, but this does not provide concrete information about the hidden data. Furthermore, tests have shown that the istat command of Sleuthkit does not take the extra epoch bits into account and, therefore, timestamps beyond 2038 are not decoded properly. A forensic investigator should keep an eye on access or modification timestamps that occur before the creation time.

5.5 Group Descriptor Table: Backup Copies

During this research it was discovered that, in addition to the superblock backup copies, backups of the group descriptor table can be used to hide data. The amount of space depends on the size of the group descriptor table and corresponds to $GDTSize \cdot (BlockGroups - 1)$ if the sparse feature is disabled; otherwise, the space is reduced to the number of block groups including the backups. The 64 GiB volume provides 16 MiB and 384 KiB of usable space without and with the feature, respectively; the corresponding values for the 500 GiB volume are 984 MiB and 4 MiB, respectively. The e2fsck utility does not give any warnings. However, when the first group descriptor table is damaged, any hidden data is overwritten during the filesystem check.

As in the case of the superblock backups, this method is rated as advanced because real data is typically already present in this location. FTK Imager provides the option to examine the group descriptor table manually, but Autopsy does not. None of the tools give any warnings.

5.6 Group Descriptor Table: Growth Blocks

Reserved group descriptor table growth blocks enable the expansion of the group descriptor table and filesystem. Fairbanks [6] points out

```
e2fsck 1.43.7 (16-Oct-2017)
Pass 1: Checking inodes, blocks and sizes.
Inode 7 has illegal block(s). Clear<y>? no.
Too many illegal blocks in inode 7.
```

Figure 8.   e2fsck error after group descriptor table growth block manipulation.

that these additional blocks may be used to hide data. The number of reserved group descriptor table blocks for future filesystem expansion is stored in the superblock if the feature flag COMPAT_RESIZE_INODE is set. All attempts to hide data in reserved group descriptor table blocks of block group 0 failed because e2fsck generated errors (Figure 8).

However, there are several backups in other block groups where data can be hidden without raising any warnings (as in the case of the superblock/group descriptor table backups). The amount of space corresponds to $s\_reserved\_gdt\_blocks \cdot BlockSize \cdot (BlockGroups - 1)$. The 64 GiB volume provides about 2 GiB of space whereas the 500 GiB volume provides nearly 15.6 GiB of usable space.

Because of the e2fsck warning, hidden data in block group 0 is discovered easily. In this case, the error message relates to inode 7 (reserved group descriptor inode), which is an indication of errors in the group descriptor table blocks. However, this does not apply to other block groups. The data hiding technique is rated as advanced because the growth blocks are not a well-known ext4 data structure. FTK Imager and Autopsy do not provide any options to examine this data structure.

5.7   Extent: Persistent Preallocation

In the ext4 filesystem, the old indirect block mapping scheme is replaced with an extent tree. An extent no longer provides a one-to-one mapping from logical blocks to disk blocks; instead, it efficiently maps a large part of a file to a range of contiguous physical blocks [10]. Instead of saving many individual block numbers, an extent only has to save the first block number that it covers, the number of blocks it covers and the physical block number to which it points (Figure 9). The persistent preallocation feature permits the preallocation of blocks for a file, which typically extends its size (e.g., database) without having to initialize the blocks with valid data or zeros [10]. The most significant bit of the ee_len field in the ext4_extent structure indicates whether an extent contains uninitialized data. If the bit is set to one, the filesystem only returns zeros during a read of the uninitialized extent. For this reason, data can be hidden using persistent preallocation. Hidden data does not induce e2fsck errors or kernel warnings when a volume is mounted. The

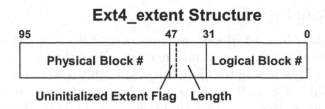

Figure 9. Ext4 extent structure (from [10]).

amount of space is limited to the maximum file size, which is 16 TiB in the case of 4 KiB blocks [6].

This is rated as an advanced data hiding technique because the uninitialized extent flag can be overlooked. However, few forensic investigators are knowledgeable about the new features introduced in ext4. Data that returns only zeros should be deemed suspicious. Additionally, Fairbanks [6] points out that uninitialized extents may contain remnants of previous data, making it even more important to examine them. Forensic tools should have the ability to show the real content of preallocated blocks instead of zero-filled blocks.

5.8 Uninitialized Block Groups

Data could be stored in several data structures in uninitialized block groups. This technique can be applied as long as the `uninit_bg` flag (`RO_COMPAT_GDT_CSUM`) is set on the volume. Three block group descriptor flags enable `mke2fs` to skip the initialization of parts of the block group metadata. The `INODE_UNINIT` and `BLOCK_UNINIT` flags enable the inode table/bitmap and block bitmap for the block group to be calculated and, therefore, the on-disk bitmap and table blocks are not initialized immediately during formatting. This is generally the case for an empty block group that only contains fixed-location metadata.

This technique provides considerable storage for hidden data. In fact, the entire space of the uninitialized inode/block bitmaps or inode tables can be used to hide data, instead of just the slack space. It is better to use block groups with high group numbers because they are initialized later. This offers $DataStructureSize \cdot UninitBlockGroups$ bytes for concealing data.

Hidden data does not affect a forced check by `e2fsck`. FTK Imager enables inode bitmaps to be viewed manually using its hex viewer; Autopsy has no such option. This technique has an advanced detection rating because many forensic investigators are not aware of this new ext4 data structure.

6.   Conclusions

Hidden data in ext4 filesystems may constitute valuable evidence in forensic investigations and should not be underestimated. Seventeen of the eighteen data hiding techniques tested in this research were found to be successful. New hiding places were discovered, previously-proposed techniques were proven to work and even very old methods were verified as still applicable. Most of the data hiding techniques exploit unallocated block space or specific reserved metadata fields of the ext4 filesystem.

The usable data hiding capacity strongly depends on the data structure and the filesystem settings and its size. Ext4 volumes are easily set up to provide enough space to hide data; for example, the sparse feature can be disabled, inode size can be set to the size of an entire block and larger numbers of inodes than usual can be created. The use of non-standard filesystem settings should be cause for alarm in a digital forensic investigation. However, even with default settings, adequate space – ranging from a few bytes to several gigabytes – is available to conceal data in the filesystem data structures. For example, malware could be hidden in various locations (e.g., on an Android smartphone) to remain partially undetectable. Also, data can be hidden in several data structures and distributed across the filesystem, making a forensic investigation much more difficult.

This research has shown that existing forensic tools, as well as filesystem checking utilities, do not recognize hidden data in locations that are not normally used. Ten of the techniques tested are rated as advanced and, therefore, require substantial forensic expertise. Data hidden in nanosecond timestamps is difficult to detect because it would be spread over several timestamps and would be very similar to normal data. The detection rates of forensic tools could be improved if official filesystem specifications were published, including standards of how reserved fields and unused space should be treated. This would help forensic tools keep up with changes to the specifications, enabling them to interpret all the data structures correctly and provide automatic warnings when hidden data is discovered.

Future research should focus on unresearched locations such as hash tree directories and non-essential fields such as the unused field in the extent tree. The use of the ext4 journal for data hiding should also investigated. Another important topic is the measurement of entropy of data in potential hiding places, which would enhance the detection of hidden data because anomalies are easily discovered in locations that normally contain null bytes. Finally, the implementation of an anti-forensic data hiding toolkit and detection utility would be invaluable to the digital forensic community.

Acknowledgement

This research was supported by the German Federal Ministry of Education and Research (BMBF) under the funding program Forschung an Fachhochschulen (Contract No. 13FH019IB6) and by the Hessen State (Germany) Ministry for Higher Education, Research and the Arts (HMWK) under CRISP (www.crisp-da.de).

References

[1] R. Anderson, R. Needham and A. Shamir, The steganographic file system, *Proceedings of the Second International Workshop on Information Hiding*, pp. 73–82, 1998.

[2] I. Baggili, A. BaAbdallah, D. Al-Safi and A. Marrington, Research trends in digital forensic science: An empirical analysis of published research, *Proceedings of the Fourth International Conference on Digital Forensics and Cyber Crime*, pp. 144–157, 2012.

[3] H. Berghel, D. Hoelzer and M. Sthultz, Data hiding tactics for Windows and Unix file systems, *Advances in Computers*, vol. 74, pp. 1–17, 2008.

[4] K. Conlan, I. Baggili and F. Breitinger, Anti-forensics: Furthering digital forensic science through a new extended granular taxonomy, *Digital Investigation*, vol. 18(S), pp. S66–S75, 2016.

[5] K. Eckstein and M. Jahnke, Data hiding in journaling file systems, *Proceedings of the Fifth Digital Forensic Research Workshop*, 2005.

[6] K. Fairbanks, An analysis of Ext4 for digital forensics, *Digital Investigation*, vol. 9(S), pp. S118–S130, 2012.

[7] S. Garfinkel, Anti-forensics: Techniques, detection and countermeasures, *Proceedings of the Second International Conference on Information Warfare and Security*, pp. 77–84, 2007.

[8] R. Harris, Arriving at an anti-forensics consensus: Examining how to define and control the anti-forensics problem, *Digital Investigation*, vol. 3(S), pp. S44–S49, 2006.

[9] V. Holen, Reserved ext2/ext3/ext4 inodes (www.vidarholen.net/contents/junk/inodes.html), 2012.

[10] A. Mathur, M. Cao, S. Bhattacharya, A. Dilger, A. Tomas and L. Vivier, The new Ext4 filesystem: Current status and future plans, *Proceedings of the Linux Symposium*, vol. 2, pp. 21–33, 2007.

[11] A. McDonald and M. Kuhn, StegFS: A steganographic file system for Linux, *Proceedings of the Third International Workshop on Information Hiding*, pp. 463–477, 1999.

[12] S. Piper, M. Davis, G. Manes and S. Shenoi, Detecting hidden data in Ext2/Ext3 file systems, in *Advances in Digital Forensics*, M. Pollitt and S. Shenoi (Eds.), Springer, Boston, Massachusetts, pp. 245–256, 2005.

[13] M. Rogers, Anti-forensics, presented at Lockheed Martin, San Diego, California, September 15, 2005.

[14] The Grugq, The art of defiling: Defeating forensic analysis, presented at *Black Hat USA*, 2005.

[15] C. Thuen, Understanding Counter-Forensics to Ensure a Successful Investigation, Department of Computer Science, University of Idaho, Moscow, Idaho (`pdfs.semanticscholar.org/d5b6/b658d9178dbcdf33e095a53c45b4f7a43fc8.pdf`), 2007.

[16] T. Ts'o, Android will be using ext4 starting with Gingerbread, Blog Entry (`thunk.org/tytso/blog/2010/12/12/android-will-be-using-ext4-starting-with-gingerbread`), December 12, 2010.

[17] T. Ts'o, Ext4 filesystem tree, Kernel.org git repositories (`git.kernel.org/pub/scm/linux/kernel/git/tytso/ext4.git`), 2018.

[18] D. Wong, Ext4 Howto, *Ext4 Wiki* (`ext4.wiki.kernel.org/index.php/Ext4_Howto`), 2015.

[19] D. Wong, Ext4 Disk Layout, *Ext4 Wiki* (`ext4.wiki.kernel.org/index.php/Ext4_Disk_Layout`), 2016.

Chapter 7

DETECTING DATA LEAKAGE
FROM HARD COPY DOCUMENTS

Jijnasa Nayak, Shweta Singh, Saheb Chhabra, Gaurav Gupta, Monika Gupta and Garima Gupta

Abstract   Document fraud has evolved to become a significant threat to individuals and organizations. Data leakage from hard copy documents is a common type of fraud. This chapter proposes a methodology for analyzing printed and photocopied versions of confidential documents to identify the source of a leak. The methodology incorporates a novel font pixel manipulation algorithm that embeds data in the pixels of certain characters of confidential documents in a manner that is imperceptible to the human eye. The embedded data is extracted from a leaked printed or photocopied document to identify the specific document that served as the source. The embedded data is robust in that it can withstand errors introduced by printing, scanning and photocopying documents. Experimental results demonstrate the efficiency, robustness and security of the methodology.

Keywords: Document fraud, data leakage detection, font pixel manipulation

1.   Introduction

People and organizations depend on documents for their day-to-day activities. The importance of documents has driven criminals to perpetrate a number of digitized document frauds. Document frauds involve manufacturing, counterfeiting, altering, selling and/or misusing documents for criminal purposes [4, 5]. Indeed, document frauds have become a global problem that requires serious attention on the part of digital forensic researchers and investigators.

Data leakage is a common but most serious threat. Incidents involving data breaches are reported almost daily. Large tranches of sensitive documents are lost or stolen; in many cases, they are posted on Internet sites such as Wikileaks. According to a 2016 report by In-

© IFIP International Federation for Information Processing 2018
Published by Springer Nature Switzerland AG 2018. All Rights Reserved
G. Peterson and S. Shenoi (Eds.): Advances in Digital Forensics XIV, IFIP AICT 532, pp. 111–124, 2018.
https://doi.org/10.1007/978-3-319-99277-8_7

foWatch [8], the United States ranked first with 451 leakage incidents, 54% of the total number of incidents; Russia was second with 110 leaks and the United Kingdom third with 39 leaks. Depending on the leaked documents, the incidents could impact national security, cause business losses, tarnish reputations and result in staggering financial penalties due to non-compliance of regulations or lawsuits.

To address the data leakage problem, researchers have proposed digital watermarking and data hiding techniques for a variety of digital media applications, including ownership protection, copy control, annotation and authentication. Data hiding has attracted the interest of the signal processing research community as a means for detecting and preventing data leakage. It is the art and science of inserting payloads (external information) in host content. Some techniques employ cryptographic algorithms [9]. Others leverage steganography to hide secret messages in host data while concealing the very existence of the secret messages [13].

While numerous algorithms and techniques have been proposed for hiding data in images, audios and videos, very little work has focused on data hiding in documents. The principal reason is that the continuous tone property inherent to images and videos does not hold for digital text documents. Furthermore, data hiding in binary images is challenging due to the lack of redundancy in the image carrier and the arbitrary flipping of pixel values that produces noticeable noise.

This chapter describes a novel methodology for detecting leakage from hard copy documents. The methodology embeds a quick response (QR) code in an original "cover" document in a manner that is imperceptible to the human eye. The embedded data is extracted later to identify if a leaked document is a printed version or photocopy of the original cover document. The methodology, which can withstand errors introduced by printing, scanning and photocopying the original document, does not require access to the original document to identify the source of the leak.

2.   Related Work

Zou and Shi [16] have proposed a data hiding technique involving inter-word space modulation that embeds exactly one bit of information in one line of text; the technique has been shown to be robust to printing, photocopying and scanning. He et al. [6] have developed a novel data hiding algorithm that combines block partitioning, discrete cosine transforms and pixel flipping. Block partitioning is performed, the matrix of characteristic values of each block is converted into the discrete cosine transform space and a coefficient matrix is generated; high frequency coefficients are modified based on a threshold. The detection process, which checks if the characteristic values change after applying the inverse discrete cosine transform, is robust to printing and scanning.

Wu and Liu [15] have developed a data hiding method that manipulates flippable pixels based on specific block-based relationships, enabling a significant amount of data to be embedded without creating noticeable artifacts. Shuffling is applied before embedding to equalize uneven embedding capacities from region to region. The hidden data can be extracted without using the original image. Moreover, the data can be extracted after high quality printing and scanning with the help of few registration marks.

Odeh et al. [11] have investigated steganographic algorithms that employ text files as carriers. Secret data is hidden in a text file by manipulating the fonts or inserting special symbols in the text file; the algorithms can be applied to Unicode and ASCII code regardless of the text file format. Villan et al. [14] have applied color quantization, which has a high information embedding rate, to digital and printed text documents. The color or luminance intensity of each character is quantized such that the human visual system is unable to distinguish between the original and quantized characters; however, the embedding can be detected by a specialized reader.

Por et al. [12] have developed a data hiding method that inserts external information into a Microsoft Word document in a manner that addresses the low embedding efficiency of text-based data hiding. The data hiding is reversible in that the embedded information can be extracted to completely reconstruct the original Word document. Dasare and Dhore [3] leverage the Microsoft Compound Document File Format (MCDFF) to hide data in unused areas of a Word document while ensuring that the changes made to the document are not visible. Culnane et al. [1] have enhanced the method of Zou and Shi [16] by applying multi-set modulation techniques to increase the data hiding capacities of binary document images; their approach employs automatic threshold computation, threshold buffering, shifted space distribution and letter space compensation techniques. In other work, Culnane et al. [2] have proposed a watermarking method for formatted text documents that is robust to printing and scanning. This method, which builds on their earlier work [1], treats a cover document as one long line of text and uses all the word spaces. Culnane et al. compute the threshold between letter and word spaces based on frequency distributions, and employ a new approach for threshold buffering.

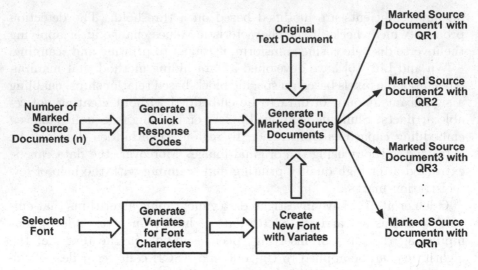

Figure 1. Document generation.

3. Methodology Overview

Identifying the specific document that leaked secret information is a challenging problem. During the past decade, researchers have developed several techniques for identifying the sources of leaks of digital documents. However, the problem is more challenging in the case of physical documents. In a typical use case, confidential documents with the same information are disseminated. Later, it is discovered that someone has leaked the information by taking a photographic image or making a photocopy of one of the disseminated documents. The determination of the source document that leaked the confidential information involves two processes: (i) document generation; and (ii) source identification.

3.1 Document Generation

Figure 1 shows the document generation process. The original text document, the number of marked source documents (copies) required and the selected font are provided as inputs. The user then identifies the specific font characters (letters and/or symbols) that should be modified to create variates whose changes are imperceptible to the naked eye. A new font is then created that contains the variate characters and the characters from the original font.

Let n be the number of marked source document copies that the user wishes to produce for dissemination. Then, n quick response codes are created, each with unique encoded data. Note that the user may

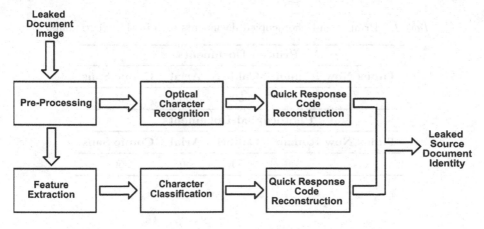

Figure 2. Source identification.

provide input for generating the quick response codes. Following this, the original text document, new font with variates and n quick response codes are used to produce the n marked source document copies, each embedded with a unique quick response code.

3.2 Source Identification

Figure 2 shows the source identification process. The image of the leaked document (camera capture or scanned image) is provided as input. The image is pre-processed, which involves document alignment, noise removal, binary conversion and text segmentation. The segmented character images are input to an optical character recognition (OCR) engine and to a feature extraction module that operate in parallel.

The optical character recognition engine produces the document text and reconstructs the quick response code embedded in the leaked document based on the occurrences and positions of the variate characters.

The feature extraction module extracts the features of each segmented character and passes them to a trained machine-learning-based classifier. The quick response code is then reconstructed based on the classified output characters and their occurrences and positions.

In the final step, the quick response codes generated by the optical character recognition engine and the machine-learning-based classifier are combined to produce a single quick response code; this serves to reduce the error rate. The quick response code is then decoded to extract the encoded information, which identifies the specific marked source document that was responsible for the leak.

Table 1.   Printed and photocopied documents used in the experiments.

Printed Documents			
Times New Roman	Calibri	Arial	Comic Sans
50	50	50	50
Photocopied Documents			
Times New Roman	Calibri	Arial	Comic Sans
50	50	50	50

4.   Experimental Setup

The proposed methodology identifies the specific source document responsible for a data leakage. This is accomplished by embedding secret information in the form of a unique quick response code in each source (cover) document. Certain font characters in the source documents are altered in a unique and imperceptible manner without affecting the document content. The source documents marked with the embedded quick response codes are then printed and distributed.

A marked document could be leaked in several ways. The original marked document could be released, or the marked original document could be photographed and the camera image could be disseminated, or the original marked document could be photocopied and the photocopy disseminated, or the original marked document could be scanned, emailed and subsequently printed. Additionally, a camera image of the document could be printed, photocopied and then disseminated, or a photocopy of the document could be photographed and the camera image disseminated, and so on.

The proposed solution requires a digitized version of the leaked physical document. It extracts the structure of the quick response code from the digitized version to determine which original marked source document was responsible for the leak.

In order to implement the proposed methodology, multiple commonly-used fonts were chosen in order to create confidential documents. Following this, various characters were selected from each font, a modified version or variate of each character was generated and a unique quick response code was embedded in each confidential document.

In the experiments, four fonts – Times New Roman, Calibri, Arial and Comic Sans – were chosen (Table 1). The A, E, a and g characters of the Times New Roman, Calibri, Arial and Comic Sans fonts were selected a genuine message

a ,enuine mess%ge

Figure 3. Selected font with variates.

for creating variates and embedding the quick response codes. For each font, 50 documents were created and printed using an HP Color LaserJet Pro MFP M177 printer. This yielded 200 (= 50 × 4) printed documents.

In order to verify the robustness of the proposed methodology, photocopies of the printed documents were considered in addition to the printed documents. Hence, the total number of documents used in the experiments was 400 (= 200 × 2). A Canon CanoScan Mark II scanner was used to produce digitized images of the 400 documents at 400 dpi.

5. Technical Details

This section provides additional technical details about the document generation and source identification processes.

5.1 Document Generation

The two principal steps involved in document generation are: (i) font pixel manipulation; and (ii) quick response code embedding.

Font Pixel Manipulation. The font pixel manipulation technique is used to manipulate certain characters of a font to create variates. The variates are minor modifications of the original characters. The variates are assigned new ASCII values associated with special characters that are rarely used. A new font is created that contains the original characters and the variates.

Figure 3 shows the original text "a genuine message" where the first instance of "g" and the second instance of "a" are shown in boldface for emphasis. The text on the second line replaces these two instances with their variates "," and "%," respectively. Note that the variates are denoted by different symbols ("," and "%") because they are essentially indistinguishable from the original characters ("g" and "a"). While the differences are imperceptible to the human eye in a low-resolution image, they can be detected in a high-resolution image.

Quick Response Code Embedding. The printing, scanning and photocopying processes add noise to a document, which makes it difficult to extract a watermark. Therefore, the proposed methodology incorporates a novel embedding technique in which data (i.e., quick re-

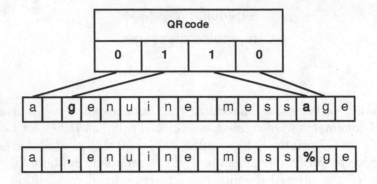

Figure 4. Mapping of a quick response code to text.

sponse code) is hidden in text using modified font characters. In the technique, the original two-dimensional quick response code, which consists of ones and zeros, is first converted to a single-dimensional array. The array is then mapped to the text in the document.

Again, assume that the text is "a genuine message" (Figure 4) and the chosen characters are "a" and "g." Furthermore, assume that the one-dimensional quick response code array that uniquely identifies the document is "0110." Only instances of "a" and "g" in the text may be replaced by their variates. A value of zero in the quick response code array indicates that the corresponding character is not replaced by its variate and a value of one indicates that the corresponding character is replaced by its variate. For example, since the array is "0110," the first instance of a chosen character ("a") is not replaced, the second instance of a chosen character ("g") is replaced with its variate, the third instance of a chosen character ("a") is replaced with its variate and the fourth instance of a chosen character ("g") is not replaced.

Figure 4 shows the mapping of the quick response code array to the text. Because the quick response code array is "0110," only the two characters ("g" and "a") highlighted in boldface are replaced by their variates (once again, denoted by the symbols "," and "%" because the variates are visually indistinguishable from the original characters). Thus, the marked document has miniscule differences from the original document that are imperceptible to humans.

5.2   Source Identification

Source identification involves the extraction of the quick response code from the leaked document image. Next, the quick response code is decoded to identify the original marked source document that was responsible for the leak. This section provides key technical details about the source identification process.

Pre-Processing In order to improve accuracy, the document image is pre-processed before submitting it to an optical character recognition engine. First, the orientation of the document is extracted using the Hough transform. Following this, the image is de-skewed.

Next, the image is converted to the CMYK subtractive color model; the K-channel is selected because it highlights only the black printed text and suppresses the other colors. The final pre-processing step involves the segmentation of each character in the image using vertical and horizontal profiling.

Feature Extraction. An optical character recognition engine and a machine-learning-based classifier are used to identify individual characters (including variates) in the segmented image. Of course, both the systems must be trained to accurately recognize characters using appropriate training sets.

In order to further improve the accuracy of character recognition, a feature extraction technique is applied to the pre-processed image. Because an image can be distorted by scaling, rotation and translation, the invariant moments feature extraction technique [10], which is independent of these operations, is employed. In this technique, the scaling, rotation and translation features corresponding to each character are extracted and fed to the classifier.

In the experiments, the extracted features comprised seven invariant moments that express the shape descriptors of characters. The invariant moments were computed using the following equations:

$$\phi_1 = \eta_{20} - \eta_{02}$$
$$\phi_2 = (\eta_{20} - \eta_{02})^2 + 4\eta_{11}^2$$
$$\phi_3 = (\eta_{30} - 3\eta_{12})^2 + (3\eta_{21} - \mu_{03})^2$$
$$\phi_4 = (\eta_{30} + \eta_{12})^2 + (\eta_{21}\mu_{03})^2$$
$$\phi_5 = (\eta_{30}3\eta_{12})(\eta_{30} + \eta_{12})[(\eta_{30} + \eta_{12})^2 \cdot 3(\eta_{21} + \eta_{03})^2] +$$
$$(3\eta_{21}\eta_{03})(\eta_{21} + \eta_{03})(3(\eta_{30} + \eta_{12})^2 \cdot (\eta_{21} + \eta_{03})^2)$$
$$\phi_6 = (\eta_{20} - \eta_{02})((\eta_{30} + \eta_{12})^2 - (\eta_{21} + \eta_{03})^2) - 4\eta_{11}(\eta_{30} +$$
$$\eta_{12})(\eta_{21} + \eta_{03})$$
$$\phi_7 = (3\eta_{21} - \eta_{03})(\eta_{30} + \eta_{12})[(\eta_{30} + \eta_{12})^2 - 3(\eta_{21} + \eta_{03})^2] +$$
$$(\eta_{30} - 3\eta_{12})(\eta_{21} + \eta_{03})[3(\eta_{30} + \eta_{12})^2 - (\eta_{21} + \eta_{03})^2)]$$

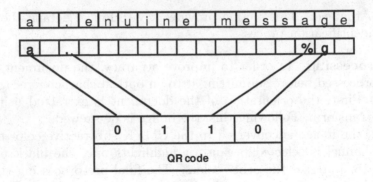

Figure 5.   Mapping of text to a quick response code.

where

$$\eta_{pq} \; = \; \mu_{pq}/\mu_{oo}^{\gamma} \quad \gamma = (p+q+2)/2, \; p+q = 2,3,...$$

$$\mu_{pq} \; = \; \int_{+\infty}^{-\infty} (x-\bar{x})^p (y-\bar{y})^q f(x,y) dx dy$$

Thus, the classifier is able to correctly identify the characters in a segmented document image.

Character Recognition and Code Reconstruction. In the final step, the segmented document image is passed to the trained optical character recognition engine and the machine-learning-based classifier, which output the document text. The output text includes all the variates of the chosen characters. When reconstructing the quick response code from the output text, only the chosen characters are retained because they may have been replaced with their variates based on the quick response code; the remaining characters in the text are ignored.

Figure 5 shows the mapping of the text "a ,enuine mess%ge" in the example document above, where (as before) the "," and "%" denote the variates of the characters "g" and "a," respectively. Since only the second and third instances of the chosen characters were replaced by their variates, the quick response code is determined to be "0110."

6.   Experimental Results

Experiments were performed on 400 documents, 200 printed documents and 200 photocopied documents. The images were input to a trained optical character recognition engine and two trained machine-learning-based classifiers in order to reconstruct the quick response codes.

Table 2. Accuracy of quick response code reconstruction.

	OCR-Based System		SVM-Based System		KNN-Based System	
	Times New Roman					
Characters	Printed	Photocopied	Printed	Photocopied	Printed	Photocopied
A,a	82.1	78.3	87.4	83.3	75.6	72.8
A,a,g	80.7	79.2	86.7	82.9	73.3	71.5
A,a,E,g	81.5	80.0	86.1	84.7	72.8	72.3
	Calibri					
Characters	Printed	Photocopied	Printed	Photocopied	Printed	Photocopied
A,a	81.2	81.0	86.1	82.7	73.2	72.1
A,a,g	80.8	79.1	85.3	81.1	74.9	73.7
A,a,E,g	80.6	78.2	84.2	83.1	73.3	71.6
	Arial					
Characters	Printed	Photocopied	Printed	Photocopied	Printed	Photocopied
A,a	83.4	83.3	85.9	84.3	73.5	72.2
A,a,g	82.3	81.7	86.2	85.6	76.6	74.3
A,a,E,g	82.8	81.8	83.4	84.9	74.1	73.8
	Comic Sans					
Characters	Printed	Photocopied	Printed	Photocopied	Printed	Photocopied
A,a	84.1	83.3	86.5	83.7	71.9	70.2
A,a,g	85.1	81.7	84.7	84.6	73.4	71.4
A,a,E,g	84.6	77.8	84.9	83.8	74.5	73.7

6.1 Optical Character Recognition

A trained Tesseract (version 3.02) optical character recognition engine was used to identify the characters and variates in the segmented document images. The Tesseract engine incorporates algorithms that learn features and classify characters. Before using the engine in the experiments, it was trained using 50 images of each character in each of the four fonts (including the variates).

Table 2 presents the quick response code reconstruction results (as percentages) for the printed and photocopied documents. The results clearly show that the trained optical character recognition engine performed better with the printed documents than with the photocopied documents; the errors were likely introduced while training the engine. All the reconstructed quick response codes were decoded successfully using the ZXing library. Additional experiments revealed that the quick response codes could be extracted and decoded successfully when the optical character recognition accuracy was greater than 90%.

6.2   Machine-Learning-Based Classification

Two machine-learning classifiers, a support vector machine (SVM) and a k-nearest neighbor (KNN) classifier, were trained using 184 samples of each character in the four fonts used in the experiments. For each font, 728, 754 and 13,780 samples were used, corresponding to alterations to two, three and four characters, respectively.

Table 2 shows the quick response code reconstruction accuracy rates (as percentages) for the machine-learning-based classifiers with printed and photocopied documents. The results demonstrate that the support vector machine performed better than the k-nearest neighbor classifier. Moreover, both the classifiers performed better with printed documents than with photocopied documents. All the quick response code were decoded successfully using the ZXing library.

7.   Conclusions

Data leakage from hard copy documents is a common type of document fraud. However, existing solutions for identifying the specific confidential document that was the source of a leak are not robust to printing, photocopying and scanning. The methodology described in this chapter incorporates a novel font pixel manipulation algorithm that embeds unique data in the pixels of certain characters of confidential documents in a manner that is imperceptible to humans. The embedded data is extracted from a leaked printed or photocopied version of an original confidential document to identify the specific document that was the source of the leak. Experimental results demonstrate that the methodology is robust in that it can withstand errors introduced by printing, scanning and photocopying documents.

Future research will focus on improving the identification accuracy using machine learning. Research will also extend the methodology to embed high-dimension color quick response codes in source documents.

References

[1] C. Culnane, H Treharne and A. Ho, A new multi-set modulation technique for increasing hiding capacity of binary watermarks for print and scan processes, *Proceedings of the International Workshop on Digital Watermarking*, pp. 96–110, 2006.

[2] C. Culnane, H. Treharne and A. Ho, Improving multi-set formatted binary text watermarking using continuous line embedding, *Proceedings of the Second International Conference on Innovative Computing, Information and Control*, 2007.

[3] A. Dasare and M. Dhore, Secure approach for hiding data in MS Word documents using MCDFF, *Proceedings of the International Conference on Computing, Communication, Control and Automation*, pp. 296–300, 2015.

[4] G. Gupta, C. Mazumdar, M. Rao and R. Bhosale, Paradigm shift in document related frauds: Characteristics identification for development of a non-destructive automated system for printed documents, *Digital Investigation*, vol. 3(1), pp. 43–55, 2006.

[5] G. Gupta, S. Saha, S. Chakraborty and C. Mazumdar, Document frauds: Identification and linking fake documents to scanners and printers, *Proceedings of the International Conference on Computing: Theory and Applications*, pp. 497–501, 2007.

[6] B. He, Y. Wu, K. Kang and W. Guo, A robust binary text digital watermarking algorithm for the print-scan process, *Proceedings of the WRI World Congress on Computer Science and Information Engineering*, pp. 290–294, 2009.

[7] Z. Huang and J. Leng, Analysis of Hu's moment invariants on image scaling and rotation, *Proceedings of the Second International Conference on Computer Engineering and Technology*, vol. 7, pp. 476–480, 2010.

[8] InfoWatch, Global Data Leakage Report 2016, Moscow, Russia (`info watch.com/report2016`), 2016.

[9] A. Menezes, P. van Oorschot and S. Vanstone, *Handbook of Applied Cryptography*, CRC Press, Boca Raton, Florida, 2001.

[10] J. Noh and K. Rhee, Palmprint identification algorithm using Hu invariant moments and Otsu binarization, *Proceedings of the Fourth Annual ACIS International Conference on Computer and Information Science*, pp. 94–99, 2005.

[11] A. Odeh, K. Elleithy, M. Faezipour and E. Abdelfattah, Highly efficient novel text steganography algorithms, *Proceedings of the Long Island Systems, Applications and Technology Conference*, 2015.

[12] L. Por, K. Wong and K. Chee, UniSpaCh: A text-based data hiding method using Unicode space characters, *Journal of Systems and Software*, vol. 85(5), pp. 1075–1082, 2012.

[13] V. Potdar and E. Chang, Visibly invisible: Ciphertext as a steganographic carrier, *Proceedings of the Fourth International Network Conference*, pp. 385–391, 2004.

[14] R. Villan, S. Voloshynovskiy, O. Koval, J. Vila, E. Topak, F. Deguillaume, Y. Rytsar and T. Pun, Text data-hiding for digital and printed documents: Theoretical and practical considerations, *Proceedings of SPIE–IS&T Electronic Imaging*, vol. 6072, pp. 607212-1–607212-11, 2006.

[15] M. Wu and B. Liu, Data hiding in binary images for authentication and annotation, *IEEE Transactions on Multimedia*, vol. 6(4), pp. 528–538, 2004.

[16] D. Zou and Y. Shi, Formatted text document data hiding robust to printing, copying and scanning, *Proceedings of the IEEE International Symposium on Circuits and Systems*, vol. 5, pp. 4971–4974, 2005.

III

NETWORK FORENSICS

Chapter 8

INFORMATION-ENTROPY-BASED DNS TUNNEL PREDICTION

Irvin Homem, Panagiotis Papapetrou and Spyridon Dosis

Abstract   DNS tunneling techniques are often used for malicious purposes. Network security mechanisms have struggled to detect DNS tunneling. Network forensic analysis has been proposed as a solution, but it is slow, invasive and tedious as network forensic analysis tools struggle to deal with undocumented and new network tunneling techniques.

This chapter presents a method for supporting forensic analysis by automating the inference of tunneled protocols. The internal packet structure of DNS tunneling techniques is analyzed and the information entropy of various network protocols and their DNS tunneled equivalents are characterized. This provides the basis for a protocol prediction method that uses entropy distribution averaging. Experiments demonstrate that the method has a prediction accuracy of 75%. The method also preserves privacy because it only computes the information entropy and does not parse the actual tunneled content.

Keywords: Network forensics, DNS tunneling, information entropy

1.   Introduction

Recent years have seen an increase in the use of DNS tunneling to stealthily perpetrate malicious activities such as exfiltrating sensitive data, hiding network attacks and orchestrating malware activities via botnet communications [23]. Several strains of malware such as the Morto worm [18] and Feederbot [9], and variants of point-of-sale malware such as BernhardPOS and FrameworkPOS [22] demonstrate the increased popularity of DNS tunneling to implement stealthy communications. The availability of DNS tunneling tools, such as NSTX, Iodine, dnscat, DeNiSe, OzymanDNS and Heyoka [19], have also enhanced the popularity and uptake of DNS tunneling.

© IFIP International Federation for Information Processing 2018
Published by Springer Nature Switzerland AG 2018. All Rights Reserved
G. Peterson and S. Shenoi (Eds.): Advances in Digital Forensics XIV, IFIP AICT 532, pp. 127–140, 2018.
https://doi.org/10.1007/978-3-319-99277-8_8

Preventive measures are unable to curtail these activities [22]. DNS tunneling detection mechanisms have been developed [6, 7], but they discover only 3% of attacks in sophisticated real-world cases [22]. Research has focused on improving the detection of tunneling [13, 14], but despite these efforts, network breaches that leverage tunneling are on the increase [18, 22].

Reactive security mechanisms such as network security monitoring and network forensic analysis techniques offer some promise. However, the techniques are often manual and labor intensive [8]. The techniques also require considerable expertise and are very time-consuming, taking up to seven months [17, 22]. Furthermore, available network forensic analysis tools only parse standardized network protocols; previously unseen or undocumented protocols commonly used in DNS tunneling require manual dissection [8]. New and innovative methods are sorely needed to alleviate these challenges and speed up the forensic analysis of tunneled network traffic.

The primary goals of network forensic analysis of tunneled networked traffic are to identify the carrier tunneling protocol, the internally tunneled protocol, the communicating parties, the content being tunneled and its significance. This work assumes that the identification of DNS tunneling has already been accomplished using, for example, the methods described in [6, 13]. Thus, the focus is on the next important task – the discovery of the network protocol being carried inside a DNS tunnel.

Little, if any, work has focused on the forensic analysis of DNS tunneling techniques. Also, no work has been done on identifying tunneled network protocols. To address this gap, this research has sought to develop a prediction mechanism that probabilistically identifies the network protocols carried in DNS tunnels. The hypothesis is that a network protocol exhibits a unique entropy distribution in its byte content during normal use. Furthermore, a network protocol carried in a tunneling mechanism maintains some similarity to its original byte entropy distribution. This enables the probabilistic matching of DNS tunneled traffic to a particular protocol with reasonable accuracy.

This research is limited to identifying the HTTP and FTP protocols when tunneled individually by a single DNS tunneling tool. The identification of the IP addresses of the communicating parties and the exact content transmitted in the messages of an internally-tunneled protocol are topics for future work. For simplicity, the focus is on the popular Iodine DNS tunneling tool, although the proposed approach could be applied to tools that use other DNS tunneling methods. Multilevel nesting of tunneled protocols is not considered, nor are encrypted protocols carried in tunneling protocols or tunneling protocols that use encryption, such as IPSec, SSH and SSL. The reason is that encryption makes information entropy uniform per block or per stream, rendering different portions of a message indistinguishable from each other. In any case, these are all interesting topics for future work.

The proposed method is implemented in a network protocol prediction tool. Experiments with the tool yield promising results with a prediction accuracy of 75%. Given the large volumes of network traffic captures encountered in digital investigations, the protocol prediction tool can help speed up the triage process as well as the analysis of network traffic. Specifically, a forensic analyst could identify network flows where a certain suspect protocol may be present in the network traffic, but is hidden by DNS tunneling. The tool also preserves privacy because it does not parse actual content; rather, it only computes the information entropy of a specific field in a packet.

2. Background and Related Work

Relatively few studies have sought to determine the protocols carried within a tunneling protocol. Bernaille and Teixeira [3] have classified the traffic of protocols tunneled over SSL using only the sizes of the first few packets of an SSL session. Their approach differentiates SSL traffic from normal traffic and uses a clustering mechanism based on Gaussian mixture models to distinguish between several protocols (HTTP, FTP, Bit-Torrent, edonkey, SMTP and POP3) tunneled over SSL. Dusi et al. [10] have employed statistical analysis of packet sizes and inter-arrival times to fingerprint normal SSH usage and when SSH is used for tunneling other protocols. Dusi et al. [11] subsequently extended their approach to distinguish HTTP tunneling traffic from normal HTTP traffic and to predict the presence of plaintext protocols such as POP3, SMTP, Chat and P2P in SSH and HTTP tunnels. Alshammari and Zincir-Heywood [2] have used Adaboost, C4.5 and genetic-programming-based classifiers to distinguish Skype and SSH traffic from other traffic, and to identify the type of application traffic (Shell, SFTP, SCP, local/remote forwarding or X11) in SSH tunnels.

Other researchers have focused on identifying proprietary protocols such as Skype and Spotify in other network traffic [1, 4, 15]. Song et al. [20] have extracted exact keystrokes from encrypted live SSH shell sessions, demonstrating the inference of content in tunnels.

Most studies on DNS tunneling have focused on detection. Born and Gustafson [6] have developed an n-gram character frequency analysis method for identifying domain names typical of DNS tunneling traffic. Xu et al. [23] have presented an anomaly detection method that contrasts the statistical and information-theoretic properties of payload content in normal DNS traffic from those of DNS tunneled traffic. Farnham [13] discusses several DNS tunneling tools and detection heuristics, including DNS request and response sizes, domain name entropy, use of uncommon resource records, volume of DNS requests per IP address or per domain, number of sub-domains per domain and presence of large numbers of orphaned DNS requests.

Davidoff and Ham [8] have developed initial methods for manually disassembling DNS tunneling traffic to recover the internally-carried protocols and data. However, no studies have focused on the automated prediction of network protocols carried in DNS tunneling traffic for the benefit of forensic analysis, which is the principal thrust of the research described in this chapter.

3.   DNS Tunnel Internals and Dataset Collection

The flexibility of the DNS protocol enables DNS tunneling tools to leverage a number of techniques [5]. Many tools append data as a sub-domain in the name field of queries, but they vary in their ease of use, throughput and invisibility to security mechanisms. For example, the dns2tcp tool uses TXT records, Iodine uses NULL records and DNScat uses CNAME records. Iodine and Heyoka use EDNS(0) extensions to increase throughput [5].

3.1   Tunneling with Iodine

The research described in this chapter employs the Iodine DNS (IP-over-DNS) tunneling tool due to its popularity, ease of use and availability of documentation [8]. Iodine encapsulates IPv4 packets in the payloads of DNS packets. By default, it uses NULL resource records, but it can also use other resource records such as PRIVATE, TXT, SRV, MX, CNAME and A. The query/answer name field in the resource record in use holds the encapsulated data.

Upstream data is compressed with GZIP and encoded. Encoding options include Base32, Base64 (or Base64u) and Base128. This is determined by checking for character set support at intermediate DNS servers. Downstream data is compressed with GZIP and encoded, as in the case of upstream data [12]. When encoding is applied, the downstream header is prepended with an ASCII character that signifies the encoding type that is used.

Tunneled data in the name field consists of a header and the fragment of the packet being tunneled, prepended as a sub-domain of the tunneling server. The header preceding the tunneled data contains metadata such as the user ID, codecs in use (Base32/64/128), fragment size, fragment number, sequence number, whether compression is used and a cache miss counter [12].

3.2 DNS Tunneling Setup and Dataset Capture

No well-known DNS tunneling network traffic captures are available and it is difficult to obtain network traffic captures involving malicious DNS activity [21]. As a result, a DNS tunnel was set up using the Iodine tool to create the experimental dataset.

The DNS tunneled traffic dataset was created by simulating the use of HTTP and FTP protocols, each in its own DNS tunnel. HTTP traffic over DNS was generated by performing simple web requests to eight websites, allowing for additional requests for extra content (images, CSS, JavaScript, Ads) to continue. The FTP protocol was simulated by downloading several files that were placed on an FTP server prior to the experiments. To ensure variation, the downloaded files were of different types, including image, PDF, text, audio, video and ZIP files. Twelve files were downloaded in all and stored at different paths on the FTP server.

The dataset comprised a total of 20 DNS tunneled traffic samples. Eight were HTTP communications, one for each of the eight websites. The other twelve were FTP communications involving logins, directory traversals and individual file downloads.

The control dataset for comparison of the tunneled network protocols against their plain versions was created by simulating normal HTTP web traffic and normal FTP traffic. The HTTP traffic was generated by visiting a randomly-chosen website with substantial content to be loaded. Normal FTP traffic was generated by logging into an FTP server and sequentially downloading three files. Multiple files were chosen due to the terse nature of FTP protocol commands.

4. Protocol Feature Trends and Analysis

The proposed method for network protocol prediction identifies patterns based on features found in plain protocol traffic that can be mapped to equivalent features in DNS tunneled traffic. Several features could be chosen to characterize the differences between protocols and the similarities across the plain and tunneled protocol versions; these include byte frequencies, information entropy and packet lengths. However, the proposed method employs information entropy analysis because it is inherently tied to the actual data bytes in packets. The idea is to observe normal HTTP and FTP traffic, and to compare the traffic against their

DNS tunneled equivalents that have been fragmented, encoded and compressed in the tunneling process.

4.1   Experimenting with Information Entropy

Measurements may be made at different levels of abstraction of a network packet to characterize its features: (i) IP packet level; (ii) transport level; and (iii) application level. Differences also can be identified between protocol client requests and server responses. HTTP and FTP have relatively small vocabularies of commands and content that go into requests, but their responses could include large amounts of data with considerable variation. Therefore, the focus is only on requests whose content and variation are more predictable and likely more significant for comparisons.

Information entropy is a measure of the variations of the components that make up a message. The proposed method computes the entropy of the bytes that make up a packet layer or field value as follows:

$$H(X) = -\sum_{i=1}^{n} p(x_i) \log p(x_i) \qquad (1)$$

where $p(x_i)$ is the probability of a particular byte occurrence and n is the number of byte occurrences.

The hypothesis underlying the use of entropy is that the request packets in a protocol flow have a specific entropy distribution. The hypothesis was tested by creating a simple Python program using the Scapy and Matplotlib libraries to measure information entropy and plot charts for visual analysis of the distribution trends.

4.2   Comparison of Plain and Tunneled Protocols

Figures 1(a) and 1(b) show the entropy distributions of application layer requests for plain HTTP and plain FTP network traffic, respectively. The traffic was filtered by taking only the packets containing application layer content and destined to port 80 and port 21 for HTTP and FTP, respectively. Thus, no transport layer features were present and no ACKs were observed because ACKs do not have any application layer content.

Figures 2(a) and 2(b) show the entropy distributions at the IP packet level for plain HTTP and FTP traffic, respectively. The traffic was filtered at a more granular level in that all the IP traffic from the client was captured. The packet entropy distributions contain packets with application data and packets with transport layer ACKs because HTTP

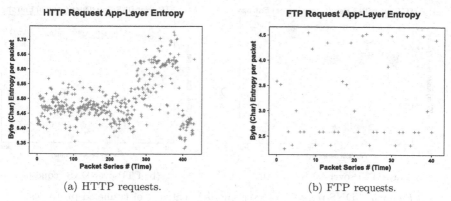

(a) HTTP requests. (b) FTP requests.

Figure 1. Application layer entropy of plain protocols.

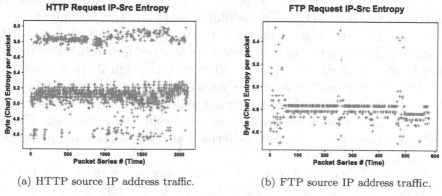

(a) HTTP source IP address traffic. (b) FTP source IP address traffic.

Figure 2. IP layer entropy of plain protocols.

and FTP both use TCP for the transport layer. The client ACKs acknowledge the receipt of prior server S-ACKs that originated from the delivery of requests to the server.

Figures 3(a) and 3(b) show the entropy distributions of HTTP-over-DNS traffic and FTP-over-DNS traffic, respectively. Specifically, the figures show the entropy of the query name field for DNS requests destined for DNS port 53. Because the filtering was based on the client side traffic destined for port 53, it includes tunneled application protocol request packets as well as those embodying transport layer properties (e.g., ACKs, sequencing and reliability information). Filtering was performed in this manner because no established methods exist for parsing and differentiating between application layer data and data from other layers of DNS tunneled traffic. Privacy was preserved because computa-

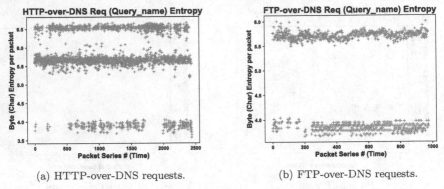

(a) HTTP-over-DNS requests.   (b) FTP-over-DNS requests.

Figure 3.   DNS request query name field entropy of tunneled protocols.

tions were performed over the packet content to generate metadata (i.e., entropy) without necessarily making sense of the actual content.

In the case of Base128 encoded traffic (default used by Iodine), the theoretical maximum entropy for completely random data tends towards eight bits. The distributions in Figures 1 through 3 show discernible variations between the protocols as well as between different layers of abstraction. The distributions are not uniformly distributed at the eight-bit value, demonstrating an absence of absolute randomness. The distributions also have different patterns that may indicate the presence of specific network protocols.

The HTTP application layer traffic entropy values in Figures 1(a) and 1(b) are significantly denser than those for FTP traffic. The FTP traffic has application layer packet entropy values around 4.5 and other values around 2.5 whereas the HTTP application layer traffic has most of its entropy values between 5.4 and 5.6.

In Figures 2(a) and 2(b), the density of packets appears to be less for FTP traffic than for HTTP traffic. There are three bands of clusters for HTTP traffic, with the densest band having entropy values between 4.9 and 5.3; the other two bands are around 4.6 and 5.8. FTP traffic has a single dense cluster of entropy values around the 4.8 mark. However, one could argue for the presence of two very sparse clusters around the 5.4 and 4.5 entropy values. These sparse clusters may be significant when one looks across the sequence of packets, where the hypothesized variations in entropy away from the 4.8 mark correspond to the FTP requests that initiated downloads of the three files.

Figures 3(a) and 3(b) reveal some clustering of the entropy values for HTTP-over-DNS traffic and FTP-over-DNS traffic, respectively. The HTTP-over-DNS traffic in Figure 3(a) appears to have three cluster bands – the densest band is around 5.6 and 5.8, the next less dense band is around 6.5 and the least dense band is in the 3.8 to 4.0 entropy range. The FTP-over-DNS traffic in Figure 3(b) has two main clusters of entropy values – one band is in the 5.6 to 5.8 range and the other is in the 3.8 to 4.0 range.

Shorter message sizes and smaller alphabets produce lower entropy values [3]. In the case of tunneled traffic with a fixed Base128 encoding, two types of traffic could have lower entropy values due to their shorter packet lengths. One is the ACKs from the transport layer and the other is the short query request messages (ping traffic) sent by a DNS tunneling tool to prevent DNS servers from timing out.

It can be postulated that the bands in Figures 3(a) and 3(b) around the 4.0 mark correspond to the entropy values of the pings because they are shorter (less than 30 bytes) than those of ACKs (at least 40 bytes) when seen in a manual DNS tunneling disassembly. This is reinforced by the fact that they are less dense in the HTTP traffic because an HTTP request can spawn several other HTTP requests to retrieve more content in order to load websites properly. These HTTP requests keep the connection between the DNS tunneling client and tunneling server open, resulting in fewer pings being generated for time-out prevention.

The bands in the 5.6 to 5.8 range for tunneled HTTP traffic and tunneled FTP traffic in Figures 3(a) and 3(b), respectively, likely correspond to ACKs in the transport layer. This inference is made primarily because the HTTP-over-DNS traffic has another band with higher entropy that likely corresponds to HTTP requests, which have higher entropy values because they are the longest messages. Also, the small repetitive pattern seen in the first 200 packets in Figure 3(b) appears to correspond to the downloading of the three files, implying that the band around the 4.0 mark contains FTP request packets hidden in the same cluster as the pings. This is reinforced by the fact that FTP commands in FTP requests are terse and have a fixed structure. This would contribute to a lower entropy than for the HTTP requests, which have a larger request header set and many more fields.

The clustering of different types of packets based on the effects that their content and lengths have on entropy implies that inherent distributions exist that can help distinguish between DNS tunneled traffic that contains different protocols. The different average values of the bands suggests that the average entropy of tunneled network traffic can help distinguish between internally-tunneled protocols. The next section discusses protocol prediction experiments that explore whether these trends and mean entropy values can identify internally-tunneled protocols.

5.   Protocol Prediction Experiments

The dataset containing 20 test traffic captures and two ground truth captures was used to determine the similarities between the entropy distributions (variables) of plain network traffic of a particular protocol and its equivalent DNS tunneled versions. A simple similarity metric based on the averages of the distributions (variables) was employed. This metric is referred to as "MeanDiff," which is the shortened form of "Mean Differences." It is computed as the absolute difference between the means of the two variables:

$$m(X, Y) = |\mu_X - \mu_Y| \qquad (2)$$

where the variable X corresponds to the entropy values of the ground truth protocol packet capture over time, and variable Y corresponds to the entropy values of a specific tunneled test capture.

5.1   Results

A classifier tool was written to evaluate the suitability of the Mean-Diff similarity metric for predicting the underlying protocol in a DNS tunneled network traffic capture. The classifier scripts are available at a GitHub repository [16].

The tool takes two ground truth traffic captures, one containing plain HTTP traffic and the other containing plain FTP traffic. It computes the entropy values of each packet in a capture stream at the IP packet level, generating two entropy distributions, one for HTTP traffic and the other for FTP traffic.

The tool then accepts a DNS tunneled traffic capture with an unknown internally-tunneled protocol. It performs random sampling by selecting a consecutive series of entropy values from the DNS tunneling capture. The random sample series length is set at 90% of the length of the ground truth capture used for comparison. One thousand samples are taken and the MeanDiff metric is calculated for each sample against the respective HTTP and FTP entropy distributions. An average of the 1,000 rounds is then taken as the MeanDiff score against the respective ground truth entropy distributions (HTTP and FTP) for a given DNS tunneled sample. This score is used as the basis for prediction, where MeanDiff is the distance metric. The ground truth protocol with the smallest MeanDiff score is deemed to be closest to the test DNS tunneled traffic sample. This ground truth protocol is the predicted internally-carried protocol.

Table 1. Sample run results.

No.	DNS Tunneled Sample	True Value	MeanDiff Prediction
1	[amazon]	HTTP	HTTP
2	[bbc]	HTTP	HTTP
3	[craigslist]	HTTP	FTP
4	[dsv.su.se]	HTTP	HTTP
5	[en.wikipedia]	HTTP	HTTP
6	[facebook]	HTTP	HTTP
7	[google]	HTTP	FTP
8	[youtube]	HTTP	FTP
9	[audio-wav]	FTP	HTTP
10	[audio-mp3]	FTP	HTTP
11	[img-jpg1]	FTP	FTP
12	[img-jpg2]	FTP	FTP
13	[img-png1]	FTP	FTP
14	[img-png2]	FTP	FTP
15	[pdf1]	FTP	FTP
16	[pdf2]	FTP	FTP
17	[txt1]	FTP	FTP
18	[txt2]	FTP	FTP
19	[video]	FTP	FTP
20	[zipfile]	FTP	FTP

5.2   Discussion

The classifier tool was applied to the dataset. Table 1 shows the actual and predicted protocols in a sample run. The MeanDiff metric yields a prediction accuracy of approximately 75%. Subsequent runs yielded 70% to 80% prediction accuracy, demonstrating the promise of the proposed approach for predicting DNS tunneled protocols. Note that five of the eight HTTP-over-DNS test samples were classified correctly, corresponding to a 62.5% recall (true positive) rate. Also, ten of the twelve FTP-over-DNS test samples were classified correctly, corresponding to an 83.3% recall.

The confusion matrix in Table 2 summarizes the classifier performance. The misclassification rate is 25%. The precision is 71.4% for HTTP and 76.9% for FTP. The false positive rate is 37.5% for the HTTP class and 16.7% for the FTP class. These results demonstrate the effectiveness of the method for predicting the underlying network protocols in DNS tunnels.

Table 2.   Classifier performance confusion matrix.

Predicted			
N = 20	HTTP	FTP	Total
HTTP	5	3	8
FTP	2	10	12
Total	7	13	20

Actual (HTTP, FTP rows)

6.   Conclusions

This research has taken on the challenging task of predicting the application protocols tunneled in DNS traffic. The exploration of the internal structure of DNS tunneling techniques contributed to the use of entropy distributions of packet bytes in a method for characterizing and predicting internally-tunneled protocols. Packet traces were visualized in order to identify patterns arising from various protocol packets due to their content and function. A classifier tool was developed and applied to a dataset of DNS tunneled traffic to evaluate the approach. Protocol classification based on entropy value averages yielded a prediction accuracy of 75%, indicating that the method holds promise.

DNS tunneling is increasingly leveraged in security breaches and other criminal activities. The proposed method assists forensic analysts in triaging and identifying DNS tunneling network traffic that may contain protocols of interest, enabling them to focus on specific DNS tunnel flows instead of having to analyze all the DNS tunneled traffic. The proposed method also preserves privacy because it only computes the information entropy and does not scrutinize the contents of packets. This is an important feature that enables the method to adhere to privacy laws that limit the invasive nature of forensic investigations.

This research is just the first foray into the relatively unexplored field of DNS tunneled traffic forensics. Although the 75% prediction accuracy obtained in the experiments is quite good, certain improvements can be made to improve the performance. One approach is to incorporate features in addition to information entropy in tunneled protocol classification; these features include packet lengths, inter-arrival times and character n-grams. A wider analysis of DNS tunneling techniques and candidate internally-tunneled protocols would help identify the best set of features for classification. Other statistical metrics that offer fine-grained differentiation of protocols should also be explored. Finally, machine learning and data mining techniques should be leveraged to improve protocol classification. For example, current research is employing dynamic time warping in time series analysis for robust matching of plain protocols against their DNS tunneled variants.

References

[1] R. Alshammari and A. Zincir-Heywood, Machine learning based encrypted traffic classification: Identifying SSH and Skype, *Proceedings of the IEEE Symposium on Computational Intelligence in Security and Defense Applications*, 2009.

[2] R. Alshammari and A. Zincir-Heywood, Can encrypted traffic be identified without port numbers, IP addresses and payload inspection? *Computer Networks*, vol. 55(6), pp. 1326–1350, 2011.

[3] L. Bernaille and R. Teixeira, Early recognition of encrypted applications, *Proceedings of the Eighth International Conference on Passive and Active Network Measurement*, pp. 165–175, 2007.

[4] D. Bonfiglio, M. Mellia, M. Meo, D. Rossi and P. Tofanelli, Revealing Skype traffic: When randomness plays with you, *ACM SIGCOMM Computer Communication Review*, vol. 37(4), pp. 37–48, 2007.

[5] K. Born, PSUDP: A passive approach to network-wide covert communications, presented at *Black Hat USA*, 2010.

[6] K. Born and D. Gustafson, Detecting DNS tunnels using character frequency analysis, *Proceedings of the Ninth Annual Security Conference*, 2010.

[7] M. Crotti, M. Dusi, F. Gringoli and L. Salgarelli, Detecting HTTP tunnels with statistical mechanisms, *Proceedings of the IEEE International Conference on Communications*, pp. 6162–6168, 2007.

[8] S. Davidoff and J. Ham, *Network Forensics: Tracking Hackers through Cyberspace*, Pearson Education, Upper Saddle River, New Jersey, 2012.

[9] C. Dietrich, C. Rossow, F. Freiling, H. Bos, M. van Steen and N. Pohlmann, On botnets that use DNS for command and control, *Proceedings of the Seventh European Conference on Computer Network Defense*, pp. 9–16, 2011.

[10] M. Dusi, M. Crotti, F. Gringoli and L. Salgarelli, Detection of encrypted tunnels across network boundaries, *Proceedings of the IEEE International Conference on Communications*, pp. 1738–1744, 2008.

[11] M. Dusi, M. Crotti, F. Gringoli and L. Salgarelli, Tunnel Hunter: Detecting application-layer tunnels with statistical fingerprinting, *Computer Networks*, vol. 53(1), pp. 81–97, 2009.

[12] E. Ekman and B. Andersson, Iodine Tunneling Protocol Documentation v502 (`github.com/yarrick/iodine`), 2014.

[13] G. Farnham, Detecting DNS Tunneling, InfoSec Reading Room, SANS Institute, Bethesda, Maryland, 2013.

[14] N. Hands, B. Yang and R. Hansen, A study on botnets utilizing DNS, *Proceedings of the Fourth Annual ACM Conference on Research in Information Technology*, pp. 23–28, 2015.

[15] E. Hjelmvik and W. John, Breaking and Improving Protocol Obfuscation, Technical Report No. 2010-05, Department of Computer Science and Engineering, Chalmers University of Technology, Goteborg, Sweden, 2010.

[16] I. Homem, TunnelStatsTests (`github.com/irvinhomem/Tunnel StatsTests`), 2016.

[17] Mandiant, M-Trends 2014 Annual Threat Report: Beyond the Breach, Alexandria, Virginia, 2014.

[18] OpenDNS, OpenDNS Security Talk: The Role of DNS in Botnet Command and Control, San Francisco, California, 2011.

[19] O. Santos, *Network Security with NetFlow and IPFIX: Big Data Analytics for Information Security*, Cisco Press, Indianapolis, Indiana, 2016.

[20] D. Song, D. Wagner and X. Tian, Timing analysis of keystrokes and timing attacks on SSH, *Proceedings of the Tenth USENIX Security Symposium*, article no. 25, 2001.

[21] M. Stevanovic, J. Pedersen, A. D'Alconzo, S. Ruehrup and A. Berger, On the ground truth problem of malicious DNS traffic analysis, *Computers and Security*, vol. 55, pp. 142–158, 2015.

[22] I. Valenzuela, Game Changer: Identifying and defending against data exfiltration attempts, presented at the *SANS Cyber Defense Summit*, 2015.

[23] K. Xu, P. Butler, S. Saha and D. Yao, DNS for massive-scale command and control, *IEEE Transactions on Dependable and Secure Computing*, vol. 10(3), pp. 143–153, 2013.

Chapter 9

COLLECTING NETWORK EVIDENCE USING CONSTRAINED APPROXIMATE SEARCH ALGORITHMS

Ambika Shrestha Chitrakar and Slobodan Petrovic

Abstract   Intrusion detection systems are defensive tools that identify malicious activities in networks and hosts. In network forensics, investigators often study logs that store alerts generated by intrusion detection systems. This research focuses on Snort, a widely-used, open-source, misuse-based intrusion detection system that detects network intrusions based on a pre-defined set of attack signatures. When a security breach occurs, a forensic investigator typically starts by examining network log files. However, Snort cannot detect unknown attacks (i.e., zero-day attacks) even when they are similar to known attacks; as a result, an investigator may lose evidence in a criminal case.

This chapter demonstrates the ease with which it is possible to defeat the detection of malicious activity by Snort and the possibility of using constrained approximate search algorithms instead of the default Snort search algorithm to collect evidence. Experimental results of the performance of constrained approximate search algorithms demonstrate that they are capable of detecting previously unknown attack attempts that are similar to known attacks. While the algorithms generate additional false positives, the number of false positives can be reduced by the careful choice of constraint values in the algorithms.

Keywords: Network forensics, constrained approximate search, Snort

1. Introduction

Alerts generated by network intrusion detection systems are one of the important sources of evidence in network forensic investigations. The alerts indicate illegal network connection attempts and provide information about the source IP address, time of event and type of illegal attempt, among other information. Indeed, it is very likely that most

© IFIP International Federation for Information Processing 2018
Published by Springer Nature Switzerland AG 2018. All Rights Reserved
G. Peterson and S. Shenoi (Eds.): Advances in Digital Forensics XIV, IFIP AICT 532, pp. 141–160, 2018.
https://doi.org/10.1007/978-3-319-99277-8_9

investigations begin by looking into this information. While alerts do not provide detailed information about malicious events, they can guide an investigator in the process of gathering evidence. Additionally, the log files that store intrusion detection system alerts can be presented as evidence in a court of law. Therefore, it is important to store as many alerts as possible and to reduce the number of false negatives (i.e., failures to raise alerts when suspicious activities take place).

Snort [7] is a widely-used, open-source, misuse-based system that detects intrusions based on a pre-defined set of attack signatures. The attack signatures are stored in its misuse database in the form of rule files, and exact searches are used to identify the signatures in real network traffic. Snort and many other intrusion detection systems engage Aho-Corasick search as their default algorithm [1]. This choice is motivated by the fact that the Aho-Corasick algorithm is fast enough for intrusion detection in networks with up to moderate bandwidth. In addition, it is easy to implement and is resistant to algorithmic attacks, where an attacker produces traffic that is difficult for search algorithms to detect efficiently.

Snort generates an alert when one of the known attack signatures is matched in incoming network traffic. Due to its use of exact search, Snort cannot detect unknown (i.e., zero-day) attacks even when they are similar to known attacks. Indeed, it could be enough for an attacker to change just a single bit in known attack traffic to evade Snort. In such an instance, a network forensic investigator could lose valuable evidence.

In order to detect attacks that are mutually similar and preserve the corresponding alerts in a log file, an attempt could be made to list all the variations of the known attack patterns and produce the corresponding signatures. However, this is impractical; in fact, it is impossible in the case of a zero-day attack. Another solution is to use regular expressions that enable input strings to be varied efficiently in an exact search algorithm. However, complex regular expressions are difficult to understand by human signature creators, which often results in erroneous signatures that produce large numbers of false positives and false negatives. Additionally, the interpretation of regular expressions by a machine is often very resource intensive. Moreover, it is impossible to create a regular expression that could be used to detect a zero-day attack.

A solution to these problems is to apply constrained approximate string matching instead of exact search. Approximate search [2, 13] allows some level of error tolerance in string comparisons. The errors are presented in the form of elementary edit operations such as insertions, deletions and substitutions. Constrained approximate search is based on *a priori* knowledge about possible edit operations that can be used in approximate matching. This knowledge can be obtained by reconnaissance and/or attacker profiling. A recent study [11] has demonstrated that constrained and unconstrained approximate search algorithms can detect zero-day suspicious activities. However, constrained approximate search algorithms produce fewer false positives and false negatives compared with unconstrained search algorithms.

This chapter demonstrates Snort evasion by an attacker, which results in the loss of evidence. Next, constrained approximate search algorithms, such as CRBP-OpType [12], CRBP-OpCount [11], modified CRBP-OpCount and CRBP-Indels (insertions and deletions taken together) [10], are employed to detect SQL injection attack signatures. These algorithms are implemented in a bit-parallel manner. The results obtained with the constrained approximate search algorithms are compared with those obtained with an unconstrained approximate search algorithm implemented using row-based bit-parallelism (RBP), which underlies the constrained RBP (CRBP) algorithms mentioned above. The experimental results demonstrate that the constrained and unconstrained approximate search algorithms can detect new attacks that are similar to known attacks up to a level of tolerance specified in advance. This facilitates the gathering of evidence related to network intrusions. However, trade-offs must be struck between the desired (small) numbers of false positives and the speed of the constrained approximate search algorithms to obtain quality results in reasonable time.

2. Evidence Detection Using Snort

Joshi and Pilli [4] have presented a generic process model for network forensics, which covers the preparation, detection, incident response, collection, preservation, examination, analysis, investigation and presentation processes. All these processes are connected and tools such as network intrusion detection systems play an important role in detecting attacks and collecting evidence. This section discusses the use of Snort as a tool for generating alerts associated with detected attacks.

Snort [7] is an open-source, network intrusion detection system that is supported by commercially-funded research and development efforts. Because of this, Snort is actively updated and its rules are freely available. Moreover, the rules may be customized or augmented as desired.

Snort compares known attack patterns against network traffic using the Aho-Corasick algorithm [1], a well-known, exact multi-pattern search algorithm. The known attack patterns are stored in the Snort misuse database in the form of rules. The rules define the type of traffic that is considered to be illegal in a monitored network. Snort generates alerts when it finds traffic that triggers one of its rules. The following example demonstrates how rules are triggered when Snort examines network packets or sessions.

Consider the following Snort rule:

```
alert tcp $EXTERNAL_NET any -> $HOME_NET $HTTP_PORTS (
    msg:"SQL 1 = 1 - possible sql injection attempt";
    flow:to_server,established; content:"1%3D1";
    fast_pattern:only; http_client_body;
    pcre:"/or\++1%3D1/Pi"; metadata:policy balanced-ips drop,
    policy security-ips drop, service http; reference:url,
    ferruh.mavituna.com/sql-injection-cheatsheet-oku/;
    classtype:web-application-attack; sid:30040; rev:2;)
```

This rule triggers on an SQL injection attempt. In the rule, all the fields outside the parentheses belong to the rule header and the parameters within the parentheses belong to the rule option (see the Snort manual [8] for more details).

In this particular case, the rule header tells Snort to trigger an alert on any TCP traffic coming from an external network $EXTERNAL_NET through any port to the destination/home network $HOME_NET and port number $HTTP_PORTS. $EXTERNAL_NET, $HOME_NET and $HTTP_PORTS are variables that can be defined in the Snort configuration file (`snort.conf`).

The rule option provides the exact requirements for traffic to generate the alert. The `flow:to_server` rule option guides Snort to perform a match on a proper TCP segment sent from the client to the server as a part of connection establishment. If this condition is met, the Snort examines the string 1%3D1 (or 1=1 because %3D is "=" in Unicode) in the payload of incoming traffic. The `fast_pattern` keyword tells Snort to further evaluate the rule only if the content is found in the payload. The `http_client_body` keyword restricts the search to the body of an HTTP client request. After meeting this condition, Snort examines the regular expression inside the `pcre` keyword (or followed by one or more whitespaces (\+ is an HTTP-encoded whitespace) that terminates with 1%3D1). The text inside the regular expression is not case sensitive.

This rule is assigned a class type of priority 1 and it is a second revision with a unique Snort identification (SID) number of 30040. More information about the attack is available in the URL provided by the `reference` keyword.

The Snort rule triggers the following alert for an OR 1=1 string in an HTTP request body:

```
[**] [1:30040:2] SQL 1 = 1 - possible sql injection attempt [**]
[Classification:  Web Application Attack] [Priority:  1]
{TCP} 10.0.2.15:40020 -> 10.0.2.25:80
```

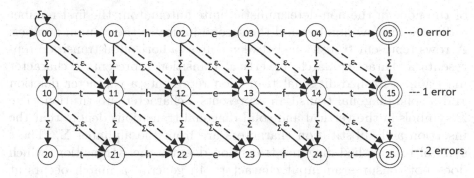

Figure 1. NFA for the search pattern "threat" permitting up to two errors [12].

The string [1:30040:2] in the first line of the alert has the structure [GID:SID:Revision] where GID is the generator ID that created the alert and SID and Revision are the same as in the rule above; this portion is followed by an alert message, which is provided by the message option of the rule. The second line provides information about the classification type and its priority. The third line shows TCP as the embedded protocol, which is followed by the source IP address:port number (10.0.2.15:40020) and the destination IP address:port number (10.0.2.25:80).

The alert text provides human readable information about the source, time of the event, type of attack attempt, etc., which could be used to gather additional evidence. Snort alerts can be presented as evidence in a court of law.

3.   Row-Based Bit-Parallelism

Row-based bit-parallelism (RBP) [13] has been exploited by many constrained approximate search algorithms such as CRBP-Indels [10], CRBP-OpType [12] and CRBP-OpCount [11]. In this technique, a non-deterministic finite automaton (NFA) for the search pattern is simulated in a row-wise fashion for each search symbol in order to find a match. Bit-parallelism is an important technique that speeds up a search algorithm. It reduces the number of multiple operations by a factor of the number of bits in a computer word [3].

Figure 1 shows a non-deterministic finite automaton for the search pattern "threat" that permits up to two errors [12]. Each row in the non-deterministic finite automaton represents a match with number of errors equal to the row number (row number starts with zero). The node with the self-loop is the initial state and the double-circled nodes in each row are the final states. The numbers inside a node indicate the position of the node in the non-deterministic finite automaton: the first number indicates the row number and the second indicates the column number. Arrows represent transitions between states: a horizontal transition represents a character match, a vertical transition represents a character insertion, a dashed-diagonal transition represents a character deletion and a solid-diagonal transition represents a character substitution. The Σ symbols in the vertical and solid-diagonal transitions denote that the insertion and substitution characters are from the alphabet Σ. The ϵ symbol in a dashed-diagonal transition denotes the ϵ-transition, which does not consume an input character. In general, a match occurs at a certain search symbol of the search string when a final state in the non-deterministic finite automaton is reached.

In order to simulate the non-deterministic finite automaton using row-based bit-parallelism, a search algorithm engages three processes: (i) bit-mask generation; (ii) non-deterministic finite automaton initialization; and (iii) search.

A bit-mask is created for all the unique characters of a search pattern. In this process, the length of the bit sequence for each character is equal to the length of the search pattern and the bit positions where the character exists in the search pattern are set to one; the other bits are set to zero.

In the non-deterministic finite automaton initialization process, each state of the non-deterministic finite automaton is assigned an activity bit, where one indicates an active bit that can be reached with a successful transition and zero indicates an inactive bit. The process of assigning bits in the non-deterministic finite automaton differs for various search algorithms [11–13].

The third process, performing the search, computes an update formula to search for a given search symbol. The following update formula [13] determines a sequence of bits for each row of the non-deterministic finite automaton for the given search symbol:

$$R'_0 \leftarrow ((R_0 << 1)|0^{m-1}1)\&B[t_j] \tag{1}$$

$$R'_i \leftarrow ((R_i << 1)\&B[t_j])|R_{i-1}|(R_{i-1} << 1)|(R'_{i-1} << 1)|1 \tag{2}$$

The first part of the update formula (Equation (1)) computes the horizontal transition for row zero while the second part of the update formula (Equation (2)) computes the horizontal, vertical, solid-diagonal, and dashed-diagonal transitions, respectively, for all the rows greater than zero. In the update formula, m is the length of the search pattern, $B[t_j]$ is the bit-mask of the character at position j of search string t, i is the row number, R is a sequence of bits of the row for a search symbol at position $j - 1$ and R' is a sequence of bits of the row for the search string at position j. A match is said to occur at position j of the search string when the last bit of any row is active.

4.   Constrained Approximate Search

Constrained approximate search applies *a priori* knowledge about edit operations and sets constraints on them while performing approximate matching. Example constraints include the maximum number of allowed indels, allowed types of edit operations and maximum number of allowed individual edit operations [12].

Sankoff and Kruskal [9] have specified a constrained edit distance calculation algorithm with constraints on the number of indels. In the algorithm, the indel distance value indicates the number of insertions, deletions or their combinations. The Sankoff-Indels algorithm [10] is a modified version of the constrained edit distance algorithm, which converts it to a constrained approximate search algorithm. The CRBP-Indels algorithm [10] is also a constrained approximate search algorithm that allows constraints on indels. This algorithm, which employs row-based bit-parallelism [13], uses counters in each state to control the use of indel operations. For example, if the number of indels is two, then the algorithm attempts to find matches by allowing maximum two insertions $(I = 2)$, maximum two deletions $(E = 2)$ or one insertion and one deletion $(I = 1$ and $E = 2)$. The Sankoff-Indels and CRBP-Indels algorithms have been applied in spam filtering to detect spam words that were modified but are still intelligible to humans [10].

The constraints on the types of edit operations enable users to specify the edit operations to be used in an approximate search algorithm. Examples include allowing only substitutions (if possible) or only deletions and substitutions. The CRBP-OpType algorithm [12] is a constrained approximate search algorithm that allows a subset of insertions, deletions and substitutions to be applied as constraints during approximate search. The algorithm exploits bit-parallelism and is, in fact, based on the RBP unconstrained search algorithm [13].

An experiment was performed to detect similar attack patterns. The results demonstrate that the CRBP-OpType algorithm exhibits better performance in terms of speed compared with the RBP unconstrained search algorithm. The simulated NR-grep tool [5] also enables a subset of edit operations (including transpositions) to be used as constraints in approximate matching. NR-grep is based on the BNDM algorithm [6], which exploits bit-parallelism to simulate a suffix automaton.

The constraint on the number of individual edit operations is another type of constraint used in approximate search. The constraint enables a user to set the maximum number of allowed individual edit operations. An example is allowing two insertions, one substitution and one deletion to find the occurrences of a search pattern in a search string.

The CRBP-OpCount algorithm [11] is a constrained approximate search algorithm that allows such constraints. The algorithm, which is also based on the RBP unconstrained search algorithm [13], uses counters for all the active bits of the non-deterministic finite automaton to control the allowed number of individual edit operations. Before applying the algorithm, the attack signatures in the content field of the alerts in the Snort `backdoor.rules` file are extracted and converted to hexadecimal values. The hexadecimal values are considered to be search patterns and search strings are created by introducing some errors.

An experiment was performed to find approximate matches using the CRBP-OpCount and RBP unconstrained search algorithms. The experimental results indicate that the CRBP-OpCount algorithm can reduce the number of false positives compared with the RBP unconstrained search algorithm. However, due to the space complexity introduced by the counters and computations, the CRBP-OpCount algorithm is slower than the RBP unconstrained search algorithm [11].

5.   Modified CRBP-OpCount Algorithm

This section provides details about the modified CRBP-OpCount algorithm, which improves on the CRBP-OpCount constrained approximate search algorithm [11].

The original CRBP-OpCount algorithm incorporates the same three processes as the RBP unconstrained search algorithm [13]: (i) bit-mask generation; (ii) non-deterministic finite automaton initialization; and (iii) search.

The bit-mask generation process is the same as in the RBP unconstrained search algorithm, but the initialization and search processes incorporate counters for all the active bits to control the allowed numbers of edit operations.

In the non-deterministic finite automaton initialization process, i consecutive bits from right to left are set to active for each row of the automaton, where $i = 0, 1, \ldots, k$. The active bits in each row are then assigned for all the possible counters by reducing each counter for row $i - 1$ by one on each edit operation.

The search process uses the same update formula as the RBP unconstrained search algorithm, but the transitions (for insertions, deletions

---

Algorithm 1: NFA initialization (modified CRBP-OpCount).

$R_0 \leftarrow 0^m$; $R_0.D_0 \leftarrow con$
for $i = 1$ *to* k **do**
    if $i \leq con[E]$ **then**
        $R_i \leftarrow 0^{m-1}1^i$
    end
    else
        $R_i \leftarrow 0^m$
    end
    for *all* j *such that* $R_i.D_j = 1$ **do**
        $R_i.C_j \leftarrow R_{i-1}.C_{j-1}[I, E-1, S]$
    end
    for *all* $R_i.D_0$ **do**
        $R_i.C_0 \leftarrow R_{i-1}.C_0[I-1, E, S]$, $R_{i-1}.C_0[I, E, S-1]$
        /* counter values should not be negative */
    end
end

---

and substitutions) are controlled by checking the corresponding counter values for the transitions from where the transitions must be initiated. A transition is successful and the bit to which the transition has to be directed is set to active when the counter value is greater than zero; otherwise, the bit is set to inactive. A match is found if the last bit of any row in the non-deterministic finite automaton can be reached by following the search process.

The modified CRBP-OpCount algorithm only differs from the original CRBP-OpCount algorithm in the initialization process of the non-deterministic finite automaton. The modified algorithm reduces the number of counters used during initialization compared with the original CRBP-OpCount algorithm. The original CRBP-OpCount algorithm uses all the possible counters for the active bits, although all of them are not needed in the search. By removing the unnecessary counters in the non-deterministic finite automaton initialization process, the modified CRBP-OpCount algorithm further reduces the unnecessary computations involving the counters during the search. As a consequence, the modified CRBP-OpCount algorithm saves storage while increasing the speed compared with the original CRBP-OpCount algorithm. In particular, the theoretical time complexity of the modified CRBP-OpCount algorithm is $O(knb)$ where k is the maximum number of allowed errors in the approximate search, n is the length of the search string and b is the counter computation for active bits in a row.

Algorithm 1 presents the pseudocode for non-deterministic finite automaton initialization in the modified CRBP-OpCount algorithm. Note

Table 1.   Non-deterministic finite automaton initialization.

Row	CRBP-OpCount	Modified CRBP-OpCount
0	$R_0 = 0000000$ $R_0.C_0 = [0, 2, 1]$	$R_0 = 0000000$ $R_0.C_0 = [0, 2, 1]$
1	$R_1 = 0000001$ $R_1.C_0 = [0, 1, 1], [0, 2, 0]$	$R_1 = 0000001$ $R_1.C_0 = [0, 1, 1]$
2	$R_2 = 0000011$ $R_2.C_0 = [0, 0, 1], [0, 1, 0]$ $R_2.C_1 = [0, 0, 1], [0, 1, 0]$	$R_2 = 0000011$ $R_2.C_0 = [0, 0, 1]$ $R_2.C_1 = [0, 0, 1]$
3	$R_3 = 0000111$ $R_3.C_0 = [0, 0, 0]$ $R_3.C_1 = [0, 0, 0]$ $R_3.C_2 = [0, 0, 0]$	$R_3 = 0000000$ $R_3.C_0 = [0, 0, 0]$

that *con* denotes the constraints on edit operations, k is the maximum number of allowed errors (i.e. tolerance), m is the length of the search pattern, R is a row, D is a status bit (0 or 1), j is a bit position and C is a counter for the active bits.

During the non-deterministic finite automaton initialization process of the modified CRBP-OpCount algorithm, i consecutive bits are set to one only for the rows starting from zero to the number of allowed deletions; otherwise, all the bits in all the rows are set to zero. The process of assigning counters for the active bits is also different compared with the original CRBP-OpCount algorithm. In the case of the modified CRBP-OpCount algorithm, *con* is assigned in position zero of row zero ($i = 0$). For rows greater than zero and for every active bit j, the deletion counter is decremented by one from the counter value of bit $j - 1$ of row $i - 1$. Counters for the insertions and substitutions are computed only for the zero positions of the rows. A check is made whether or not a counter value is greater than zero in bit zero of row $i - 1$. If it is greater than zero, then the value is decremented by one and stored in the counter of position zero of row i. Moreover, substitution is not applied when a deletion has already been applied for an active bit.

Table 1 shows all the bits and their counters for each row of the non-deterministic finite automaton. Note that the goal is to find distorted occurrences of the search pattern "threats" in the search string "treet" by allowing the constraint $con[I, E, S] = [0, 2, 1]$. The results in Table 1 reveal that the number of counters used by the modified CRBP-OpCount algorithm is less than the number required by the original CRBP-OpCount algorithm to solve the same problem. Other processes in the modified CRBP-OpCount algorithm (i.e., bit-mask and search) are not presented because they are the same as in the original CRBP-OpCount algorithm [11].

6.   Experimental Results

The experimental setup incorporated two virtual machines: (i) attacker machine; and (ii) victim machine. The host computer had a 2.7 GHz processor and 8 GB RAM. The attacker machine ran the Kali Linux operating system while the victim machine ran the Windows 7 operating system.

6.1   Evading Snort with a Buffer Overflow

In order to perform a buffer overflow attack, a vulnerable echo server was created on the victim machine. When executed, the echo server listened for incoming client connections and transmitted the same text received from the clients back to the clients. The echo server was made vulnerable by using function `vulnerable`, which was invoked before sending back the message transmitted by a client.

The `vulnerable` function is defined as follows:

```
int vulnerable_func(char *input){
    char buffer[16];
    strcpy(buffer, input);
    return 1;
}
```

The function copies the content of the `input` parameter into the `buffer` variable. The size of the `buffer` variable is fixed, but the `strcpy` function allows an input message of any size to be copied into the `buffer`. If the echo server receives input text longer than the defined size of the `buffer`, the program crashes.

The experiment sought to perform a buffer overflow attack and execute the `calc.exe` application on the victim machine. In order to accomplish this, it was necessary to find the EBP and EIP register contents so that the EIP return address could be replaced with a new address that starts the malicious code that invokes `calc.exe`. After some trials and debugging, it was discovered that the EBP register contained the GGGG value when the text AAAABBBBCCCCDDDDEEEEFFFFGGGGHHHH... was sent. A new ESP address was then added manually and the text AAAABBBBCCCCDDDDEEEEFFFFGGGG was combined with the address in reverse order. When the client message AAAABBBBCCCCDDDDEEEEFFFFGGGG [new ESP address][code to execute calc.exe] was sent to the victim machine, the application crashed and `calc.exe` was executed.

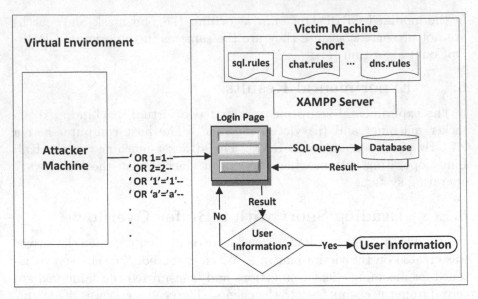

Figure 2.   Using Snort to detect selected SQL injection patterns.

The following is the hexadecimal representation of the shellcode that executed `calc.exe`:

```
6681e4fcff31d2526863616c6389e65256648b72308b760c8b76
0cad8b308b7e188b5f3c8b5c1f788b741f2001fe8b4c1f2401f9
0fb72c5142ad813c0757696e4575f18b741f1c01fe033caeffd7cc
```

Snort did not have a rule corresponding to this buffer overflow attack. Therefore, it was unable to detect the attack and log it for subsequent analysis.

6.2   Evading Snort with SQL Injection

Figure 2 shows the experimental setup for performing SQL injection attacks from the attacker machine and using Snort on the victim machine to detect the injection attacks.

A vulnerable website was hosted on the victim machine using the XAMPP web server. The vulnerable website contained a login form for a user to enter login credentials. In the case of a valid login, the user was redirected to access his/her user information page; otherwise, the user was redirected to the login page with an error message. The login form on the vulnerable website allowed any characters in the username and password fields. However, the username field accepted a maximum of 16 characters. The PHP programming language was used to create the vulnerable website and MySQL to create the database.

The validation of user credentials on the login page of the vulnerable website was performed using the following SQL statement:

```
SELECT * FROM users WHERE uname='$uname' and pass='$pass'
```

This SQL statement fetches all the details from the user table in the database when the username (uname) and password (pass) field values match the username ($uname) and password ($pass) values provided in the user login form.

In the experiment, Snort had the default set of rules, which were downloaded from the website snort.org. Snort was always started when the victim machine started. The SQL statement used in the experiment to authenticate users could be modified by the attacker to inject a malicious SQL statement, this is referred to as a SQL injection attack.

Two SQL injection attack patterns were employed: (i) OR 1=1; and (ii) '1'='1. The Snort rule corresponding to the second pattern is:

```
alert tcp $EXTERNAL_NET any -> $HOME_NET $HTTP_PORTS (
    msg:"SQL 1 = 1 - possible sql injection attempt";
    flow:to_server,established; content:"%271%27%3D%271";
    fast_pattern:only; http_client_body; metadata:policy
    balanced-ips drop, policy security-ips drop, service http;
    reference:url, ferruh.mavituna.com/sql-injection-cheatsheet
    -oku/; classtype:web-application-attack; sid:30041; rev:2;)
```

The rule triggers an alert for a possible SQL injection attempt when the '1'='1 attack pattern is found in the payload content of the network traffic.

In the experiment, the attacker entered the inputs ' OR 1=1-- and ' OR '1'='1'-- in the username field. These inputs modified the SQL statements as follows:

```
SELECT * FROM users WHERE uname='' OR 1=1-- and pass=''
SELECT * FROM users WHERE uname='' OR '1'='1'-- and pass=''
```

Since the username and password fields in the login page were not validated, the malicious SQL statements enabled the attacker to successfully log into the system. Specifically, the attacker was logged in with the user credentials that were located at the top of the user list in the database. In the two malicious SQL statements, the blank username was ORed with the valid arithmetic operations (1=1 and '1'='1', respectively) and everything that followed was commented with --. This demonstrates that the SQL statements were valid regardless of what the attacker entered in the password field.

Snort detected both the SQL injection attacks because the rules for detecting the ' OR 1=1-- and ' OR '1'='1'-- attack patterns were

included in the Snort rule set. However, there are unlimited variations of these attack patterns. For example, ` OR 2=2--` and ` OR
9=9--` corresponding to the ` OR 1=1--` attack pattern; and ` OR
'2'='2'--`, ` OR 'a'='a'--` and ` OR 'a1'='a1'--` corresponding to
the ` OR '1'='1'--` attack pattern. Since Snort does not incorporate
rules for these attack pattern variations, by default it was unable to
detect SQL injection attempts corresponding to these attack patterns.

6.3   Detecting Similar Attack Patterns

The next set of experiments applied four constrained approximate
search algorithms (CRBP-OpType, CRBP-Indels, CRBP-OpCount and
modified CRBP-OpCount) and one unconstrained approximate search
algorithm based on row-based bit-parallelism to find randomly-created
similar attack patterns such as 1=1 and '1'='1'.

In order to perform the experiments, 200 similar variations of the attack pattern 1=1 and 11,280 variations of the attack pattern '1'='1'
were generated. Only ten strings among the 200 similar variations of
the 1=1 search pattern could cause harm and only 80 strings of the
11,280 variations of the '1'='1' search pattern could cause harm. In
both cases, more strings were created that did not cause any harm but
could be indications of attack attempts; the detection of such a string
corresponds to a false positive. There could be fewer false positives in a
real-world scenario, but the numbers were deliberately increased to evaluate the performance of the constrained approximate search algorithms.

Figure 3 shows two simulations in which approximate search algorithms were applied to find the occurrences of the attack patterns 1=1
and '1'='1' in the list of their randomly-generated similar variations
(search strings). In both cases, all the approximate search algorithms
were executed 30 times and the average time required by each algorithm
was taken as its final execution time. The output also includes the
performance of the algorithms based on the false positive results they
generated.

Table 2 shows the false positive results generated by the algorithms
for the two attack patterns. The true positive error (TP) corresponds
to the number of attack patterns detected as harmful that were actually
harmful. The false positive error (FP) is the number of attack patterns
detected as harmful that were not actually harmful. The true negative
error (TN) is the number of attack patterns that were not detected and
that were not harmful.

The results in Table 2 show that, for the search pattern 1=1, all the
constrained approximate search algorithms produced the same num-

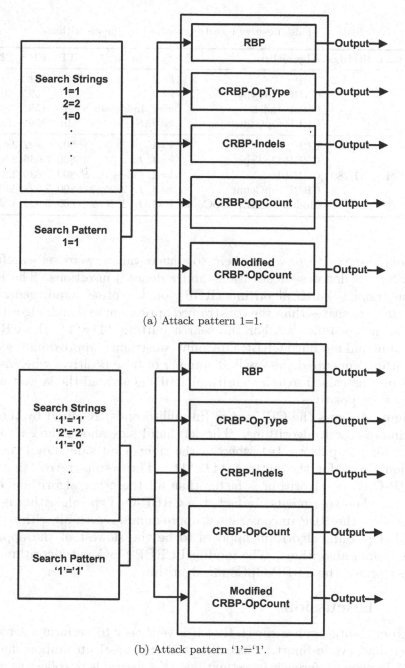

(a) Attack pattern 1=1.

(b) Attack pattern '1'='1'.

Figure 3. Applying approximate search algorithms with two SQL injection patterns.

Table 2.   False positive results generated by the algorithms

Pattern Strings		Algorithm	Tolerance	TP	FP	TN
1=1	200	RBP	$k=2$	10	181	9
		CRBP-OpType	$k=2, S$	10	159	31
		CRBP-Indels	$k=2$, indels$=0, S$	10	159	31
		CRBP-OpCount	$k=2, S$	10	159	31
'1'='1'	11,280	RBP	$k=4$	800	7,802	2,678
		CRBP-OpType	$k=4, IS$	800	7,636	2,844
		CRBP-Indels	$k=4$, indels$=2, S$	800	7,636	2,844
		CRBP-OpCount	$k=4, I=2, S=2$	800	5,928	4,552
		Modified CRBP-OpCount	$k=4, I=2, S=2$	800	5,928	4,552

ber of false positives when their tolerance values were set carefully. Note that S denotes substitutions and I denotes insertions. The RBP unconstrained search algorithm (RBP), on the other hand, generated more false positives than the constrained approximate search algorithms with same tolerance k. For the search pattern '1'='1', the CRBP-OpCount and modified CRBP-OpCount constrained approximate search algorithms generated the smallest number of false positives whereas the RBP unconstrained search algorithm (RBP) generated the largest number of false positives.

Figure 4 shows the CPU times (in milliseconds) required by the approximate search algorithms. The left-hand side shows the execution speed for the pattern 1=1 whereas the right-hand side shows the execution speed for the pattern '1'='1'. The results reveal that the CRBP-OpType algorithm is faster than all the other algorithms evaluated in the experiments. In fact, the CRBP-OpType algorithm is also faster than the RBP unconstrained approximate search algorithm. The CRBP-OpCount algorithm appears to be the slowest of the approximate search algorithms. The modified CRBP-OpCount algorithm also outperformed the CRBP-OpCount algorithm.

7.   Discussion

Experimentation has shown that it is very easy to perform a zero-day attack and evade Snort. Since Snort alerts constitute important evidence in network forensic investigations, it is desirable to collect as many relevant Snort alerts as possible. The experimental results reveal that approximate search algorithms (constrained and unconstrained) can be applied by Snort to collect more network forensic evidence by detecting attack signatures that are similar to those of known attacks. However,

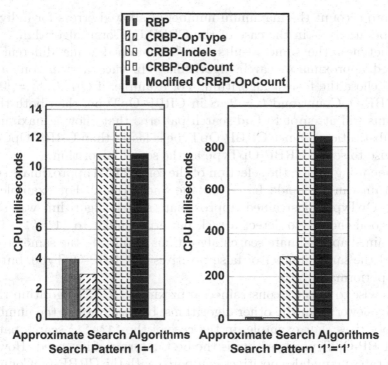

Figure 4. Speed comparison of the approximate search algorithms.

the results indicate that many false positives can be generated and the search speed can suffer if the wrong type of algorithm is selected with improper constraint parameters.

Comparisons of the speeds of the approximate search algorithms considered in this research (RBP unconstrained search, CRBP-OpType, CRBP-Indels, CRBP-OpCount and modified CRBP-OpCount) reveal that the CRBP-OpType algorithm exhibits the best performance while the CRBP-OpCount algorithm yields the worst performance. However, the overall performance of each algorithm also depends on the number of false positives it generates.

It is easy to use the RBP unconstrained search algorithm because all that a user needs to consider is the maximum number of allowed errors k. In the case of the constrained approximate search algorithms, it is recommended to acquire and engage *a priori* knowledge about the search problem. Constrained approximate search algorithms vary according to the types of constraints they can handle and their speeds also depend on the constraints. For example, the CRBP-OpType algorithm can consider the subset of edit operations to be used, but is unable to take into account the maximum number of allowed errors for individual edit operations as in the case of the CRBP-OpCount algorithm.

Sometimes, the same results can be obtained using different constrained approximate search algorithms. In such a situation, a user should chose the fastest algorithm. For example, if $C[I, E, S] = [0, 0, 2]$ in CRBP-OpCount and $k = 2$, S in CRBP-OpType, then both the algorithms will attempt to find search patterns that allow a maximum of two substitutions. Since CRBP-OpType is faster than CRBP-OpCount, it is wise to select CRBP-OpType as the search algorithm.

When using Snort, the selection of the constrained approximate search algorithm can be made based on the Snort rules. For example, the CRBP-OpType constrained approximate search algorithm was shown to be good enough to detect attack patterns similar to '1'='1'. Other constrained approximate search algorithms applied to the same problem yielded the same number of false positives as CRBP-OpType, but with lower performance.

It is wise to select a constrained approximate search algorithm that is slightly slower than the other algorithms, but will reduce the number of false positives. For example, in the case of the '1'='1' search pattern, the CRBP-OpType algorithm is the best in terms of its speed. However, it generates many false positives compared with the CRBP-OpCount and modified CRBP-OpCount algorithms. Since the CRBP-OpCount and modified CRBP-OpCount constrained approximate search algorithms differ only in their speed, it is better to select the modified CRBP-OpCount algorithm over CRBP-OpCount for search problems for which both the algorithms are suitable.

8.   Conclusions

Evidence from a network intrusion detection system such as Snort is very valuable in a network forensic investigation. However, Snort cannot detect zero-day attacks even when they are similar to known attacks; as a result, Snort does not record evidence pertaining to these attacks. This research has demonstrated that the problem can be addressed by incorporating a constrained approximate search algorithm in Snort. Constrained approximate search algorithms, which are more powerful than exact search, enable users to set constraints on edit operations and control searches based on their requirements. The experimental results reveal that all the approximate search algorithms (constrained and unconstrained) can detect zero-day attacks that are similar to known attacks. However, they differ in their speed and in the number of false positives they generate.

References

[1] A. Aho and M. Corasick, Efficient string matching: An aid to bibliographic search, *Communications of the ACM*, vol. 18(6), pp. 333–340, 1975.

[2] R. Baeza-Yates and G. Navarro, Faster approximate string matching, *Algorithmica*, vol. 23(2), pp. 127–158, 1999.

[3] S. Faro and T. Lecroq, Twenty years of bit-parallelism in string matching, in *Festschrift for Borivoj Melichar*, J. Holub, B. Watson and J. Zdarek (Eds.), Prague Stringology Club, Prague, Czech Republic, pp. 72–101, 2012.

[4] R. Joshi and E. Pilli, *Fundamentals of Network Forensics: A Research Perspective*, Springer-Verlag, London, United Kingdom, 2016.

[5] G. Navarro, NR-grep: A fast and flexible pattern-matching tool, *Software – Practice and Experience*, vol. 31(13), pp. 1265–1312, 2001.

[6] G. Navarro and M. Raffinot, A bit-parallel approach to suffix automata: Fast extended string matching, *Proceedings of the Annual Symposium on Combinatorial Pattern Matching*, pp. 14–33, 1998.

[7] M. Roesch, Snort – Lightweight intrusion detection for networks, *Proceedings of the Thirteenth USENIX Conference on System Administration*, pp. 229–238, 1999.

[8] M. Roesch and C. Green, Snort Users Manual 2.9.9, The Snort Project (`manual-snort-org.s3-website-us-east-1.amazonaws.com`), 2017.

[9] D. Sankoff and J. Kruskal, *Time Warps, String Edits and Macromolecules: The Theory and Practice of Sequence Comparison*, Addison Wesley, Reading, Massachusetts, 1983.

[10] A. Shrestha Chitrakar and S. Petrovic, Approximate search with constraints on indels with application in spam filtering, *Proceedings of the Norwegian Information Security Conference*, pp. 22–33, 2015.

[11] A. Shrestha Chitrakar and S. Petrovic, Constrained row-based bit-parallel search in intrusion detection, *Proceedings of the Norwegian Information Security Conference*, pp. 68–79, 2016.

[12] A. Shrestha Chitrakar and S. Petrovic, CRBP-OpType: A constrained approximate search algorithm for detecting similar attack patterns, in *Computer Security*, S. Katsikas, F. Cuppens, N. Cuppens, C. Lambrinoudakis, C. Kalloniatis, J. Mylopoulos, A. Anton and S. Gritzalis (Eds.), Springer, Cham, Switzerland, pp. 163–176, 2018.

[13] S. Wu and U. Manber, Fast text searching: Allowing errors, *Communications of the ACM*, vol. 35(10), pp. 83–91, 1992.

Chapter 10

TRAFFIC CLASSIFICATION AND APPLICATION IDENTIFICATION IN NETWORK FORENSICS

Jan Pluskal, Ondrej Lichtner and Ondrej Rysavy

Abstract   Network traffic classification is an absolute necessity for network monitoring, security analyses and digital forensics. Without accurate traffic classification, the computational demands imposed by analyzing all the IP traffic flows are enormous. Classification can also reduce the number of flows that need to be examined and prioritized for analysis in forensic investigations.

This chapter presents an automated feature elimination method based on a feature correlation matrix. Additionally, it proposes an enhanced statistical protocol identification method, which is compared against Bayesian network and random forests classification methods that offer high accuracy and acceptable performance. Each classification method is used with a subset of features that best suit the method. The methods are evaluated based on their ability to identify the application layer protocols and the applications themselves. Experiments demonstrate that the random forests classifier yields the most promising results whereas the proposed enhanced statistical protocol identification method provides an interesting trade-off between higher performance and slightly lower accuracy.

Keywords: Protocol identification, application identification, machine learning

1. Introduction

Network traffic classification is an important technique used in network monitoring, security analyses and digital forensics. In digital forensics, file types can be identified by file extensions or by searching for magic numbers at the beginning of files; known files can be identified using databases of hash values. The identification of file types and filtering of known files reduce the amount of data that needs to be analyzed. Do-

© IFIP International Federation for Information Processing 2018
Published by Springer Nature Switzerland AG 2018. All Rights Reserved
G. Peterson and S. Shenoi (Eds.): Advances in Digital Forensics XIV, IFIP AICT 532, pp. 161–181, 2018.
https://doi.org/10.1007/978-3-319-99277-8_10

ing the same with network traffic is much more complicated because each data transfer contains specific and temporary characteristics that depend on the network state, network utilization and locations of communications endpoints. The correct classification of network traffic enables an automated analyzer to determine which application protocol parser to use to extract information carried by an IP flow (a packet sequence identified by the same source and destination IP addresses, transport protocol ports and transport protocol type). This, in turn, helps speed up a forensic investigation by reducing the number of unclassified IP flows.

Traditional traffic classification methods identify applications based on the TCP or UDP ports that are used. This provides only limited accuracy (60–80%) because many applications use random or non-standard ports [3, 24], for example, peer-to-peer applications, multimedia streaming applications, computer games and tunneled traffic. Advanced traffic classification utilizes supervised machine learning methods based on payload analysis, statistical methods and hybrid approaches [17, 19, 26, 27, 29]. Each technique has its advantages and disadvantages. For example, payload analysis of encrypted communications is unacceptably inaccurate. Statistical and hybrid approaches demonstrate that it is not necessary to rely exclusively on packet content [5, 12, 21], but that it is possible to combine structural and behavioral features to increase detection accuracy [16].

Unsupervised machine learning methods can classify unknown network traffic [9] into unlabeled clusters based on their similarity. An expert investigator, upon inspection of a few samples of a cluster, can label the entire cluster.

Several researchers have investigated machine learning approaches for traffic classification. Most of the research has focused on classifying network traffic to identify the application layer protocol in order to support intelligent network filtering and security monitoring. While traffic classification for network forensics stems from the same ideas, there are some notable differences. Network forensics analysis can be performed off-line on captured data. In this case, accuracy is more important than speed. Thus, a combination of several methods or applications that are slower, but more accurate, can be considered.

In network forensics, an investigator can compensate for incorrect results by performing additional manual inspections of results. For example, some methods return a probability vector that can be inspected to consider different results.

Additionally, in network forensics, classification must be deterministic because forensic principles require that all results be verifiable.

Also, classification methods can be tuned by an investigator and can be repeated with different parameter sets to increase sensitivity while decreasing specificity.

Machine learning algorithms for network traffic classification have been studied since the 1990s. The most common algorithms include support vector machines [12], decision tree algorithms [21] and probabilistic [5] and statistical methods [16, 19], all of which involve supervised learning. The unsupervised k-means clustering algorithm [9] groups traffic based on its significant features. If the feature set is selected properly, a machine learning method can exceed 90% accuracy [26].

Surveys of classification methods by Nguyen and Armitage [27] and Namdev et al. [26] discuss protocol identification. Classification methods for encrypted traffic are reviewed in [29]. Al Khater and Overill [2] have proposed the use of machine learning algorithms to improve traffic classification methods for digital forensic applications. Foroushani and Zincir-Heywood [10] have demonstrated the possibility of identifying high-level application behaviors from encrypted network service communications. Dai et al. [6] and Miskovic et al. [23] have described methods for fingerprinting mobile applications based on their communications. Erman et al. [8] have explored flow-based classification and have proposed a semi-supervised classification method that can accommodate known and unknown applications.

While traffic classification has been applied extensively to network monitoring and security analysis, significantly less research has focused on traffic discrimination for network forensics. This research makes some key contributions to the field of network forensics. The first is the creation of a dataset that provides a means to reliably acquire ground truth for experiments. Typical datasets use information inferred from `17-filter` [28] or `nmap` [1] and, therefore, offer only approximations of the real information. Shang and Huang [28] have shown that the precision of these techniques is always one (no false positives), but the recall varies between 0.67 and 0.87. This means that 13–33% of the samples are not labeled and the researchers would have excluded them from the datasets because they lacked labels [1, 12]. Therefore, the remaining dataset is already classifiable via deep packet inspection and is less relevant to finding better classification methods. In other cases, researchers do not include information about the data used in their experiments, or the descriptions are vague and not reproducible [28], or they do not describe how to annotate data with labels without errors [5].

For these reasons, this research captured one week's worth of packet data in an environment with eight hosts, which translates to roughly

20 GB. The data was automatically tagged with complete information about the origin application.

This research has also developed an enhanced statistical protocol identification (ESPI) method that leverages a machine-learning-based classifier. Upon evaluating the results of related studies, two additional classifiers, a Bayesian network classifier and a random forests classifier, were selected for comparison. This chapter describes all three methods and shows that they can be used to identify application layer protocols and even the applications that used the protocols. This is important because application identification provides more information about network traffic compared with what can be gleaned from the identified application layer protocols. Consider a situation where HTTPS is used to create an encrypted tunnel. A tool capable of recognizing applications (e.g., Google Drive, iTunes and OneDrive) in network traffic instead of merely the application layer protocol (e.g., HTTPS) is useful in several domains. Notably, in forensic analysis, application identification could significantly reduce the amount of data to be analyzed compared with conventional approaches.

2.   Data Collection and Preprocessing

Network traffic classification takes a network traffic capture file as input, typically in the PCAP format. The captured traffic is then split into a collection of layer 4 conversations represented by one or two IP flows for one-way or two-way communications, respectively. The experiments described in this chapter employed an annotated dataset captured by Microsoft Network Monitor, which provides application labels for almost all conversations. The dataset contains regular network traffic generated by eight user workstations running the Windows operating system. The final capture file has the following characteristics:

- **PCAP File Size:** 19.5 GB.
- **PCAP Format:** Microsoft NetMon 2.x.
- **Capture Duration:** 119 hours.
- **Number of Packets:** 27,616,138.
- **Number of Layer 7 Conversations:** 269,459.
- **Number of Application Protocols:** 58.
- **Number of Communicating Applications:** 93.

Information about the dataset is available at `pluskal.github.io/AppIdent` and the dataset itself can be downloaded from `nes.fit.vutbr.cz/AppIdent`.

Before the capture file could be used, additional post-processing steps from previous work [22] were applied to enhance data extraction. The final post-processing step used a round of experiments with the enhanced statistical protocol identification method. Based on these initial results, a second instance of the dataset was created that contained ground truth about the application protocols. The ground truth supported manual hierarchical clustering analysis of the results.

The post-processing steps improved the traffic classification accuracy by reducing the noise in the extracted features caused by the following items:

- Important TCP session control information, such as synchronization segments and finalization segments, may be missing.

- Sequence numbers may overflow in long-running TCP conversations. This can result in incorrect interpretation, causing single conversations to be split or two unrelated IP flows to be joined into a single conversation.

- The joining of capture files from multiple probes must address issues related to possible packet duplication and the proper ordering of packets belonging to the same conversation.

- Some IP packets may be missing or be duplicated (e.g., in the case of TCP retransmission).

- Finally, associated IP flows in bidirectional conversations must be paired correctly.

Matousek et al. [22] have shown that other network forensic solutions do not effectively address these issues. This implies that adopting the proposed additional steps would also be beneficial in the context of network traffic classification. To address these issues, Netfox Detective (`github.com/nesfit/NetfoxDetective`), a custom tool created for these use cases, was used to process the captured PCAP files.

2.1 Application Conversations and Messages

In addition to addressing the basic issues related to processing layer 4 conversations, Netfox Detective also enabled the dataset to be processed to track layer 7 conversations and to approximate individual application messages. This increased the classification accuracy by identifying application communications patterns. It also eliminated remnants of network packet fragmentation in the Internet layer and TCP retransmission in the transport layer. Packet fragmentation and TCP retransmission are independent of application communications patterns and, thus, can negatively impact classification.

An application message was identified in the reassembled stream based on the transport protocol. The following rules were used for identification:

- If a stream uses the UDP transport protocol, then the entire payload of each UDP datagram is considered to be a single application message.

- In the case of the TCP transport protocol, segments are separated into application messages based on packets with PSH, RST or FIN flags, or based on timeouts.

These rules are simple to implement and yield accurate approximations of application messages in most cases.

3.   Classification Methods

Using machine learning algorithms to classify traffic is by no means a new concept in the field of network forensics. However, the typical use case is to identify the application protocol [27, 29]. In this research, the approach was expanded to also identify the application that created the traffic. This provides more information that can be used by a forensic investigator for easier and more precise analysis.

This section describes revisions to the commonly-used feature sets [16, 19, 25] to address the task at hand and presents a feature elimination method based on feature correlation to improve the accuracy of the created classifiers. Finally, the proposed enhanced statistical protocol identification method is described along with two other classification methods from the literature that have yielded promising traffic identification results.

3.1   Feature Set

The quality of a feature set directly influences classification accuracy [32]. Common features used for traffic classification are related to key aspects of packet communications and network architecture. These include port numbers, transport protocol type, starting sequence of payload bytes, pattern occurrence, message length and message timing. Researchers have identified a list of possible features comprising 92 items that are invariant to network line characteristics [16, 19, 25]. The list is available at `github.com/pluskal/AppIdent`.

Machine learning algorithms achieve the best performance when the selected features are orthogonal (i.e., no correlation exists between the features) [14]. Several approaches have been proposed for calculating feature correlations, including the Pearson, Spearman, Kendall correlation formulas [31] and covariance matrix [13]. This research opted for the covariance matrix method due to its ease of implementation.

The covariance matrix provides a correlation value for each pair of features. This matrix was used to design an automated two-step procedure for eliminating features. In the first step, a covariance matrix was calculated based on a chosen ratio of training data to verification data (t/v). In the second step, based on a maximum allowed correlation value, feature pairs with higher correlation values were identified and features that were, on average, more correlated with all the other features, were iteratively removed from the feature set. The resulting feature set was used by the selected classification method and could be evaluated to find the optimal set.

In the experiments, more than 80% of the feature pairs had correlation values of 0.5 or higher. Table 1 lists the features that remained after feature elimination was performed on sample data with training to verification ratios of 0.1 and 0.2, based on accepted correlation values up to 0.5. Note that the correlation column shows the maximal-allowed correlation values of features listed on the corresponding line and higher. These feature sets were used by the Bayesian network and random forests classifiers.

Most of the features describe flow characteristics instead of individual packet characteristics. This confirms the assumption that relying on a signature or some pattern in packet content gives better results for encrypted or less-structured traffic.

3.2 Enhanced Statistical Protocol Identification

Hjelmvik [16] developed the statistical protocol identification (SPID) method for use with the NetworkMiner tool. The learning phase of the method creates a database of protocol fingerprints for identifying application protocols. The features utilized by the statistical protocol identification method are called "protocol attribute meters," each conveying different information. Some items are scalar values representing payload data size, number of packets in a session or port number. Other items are composite values, such as a tuple comprising packet direction, packet ordering, packet size and byte value frequency.

The original implementation uses about 35 protocol attribute meters and extracts information from the first few packets of IP flows to achieve better speed compared with other classification methods that analyze entire IP flows. The distance between the analyzed data to a

Table 1. Features remaining after elimination based on t/v ratios of 0.1 and 0.2.

Correlation	Feature (t/v = 0.1)	Feature (t/v = 0.2)
	BytePairsReoccuringDownFlow	
	DirectionChanges	
	First3BytesEqualDownFlow	First3BytesEqualDownFlow
	FirstBitPositionUpFlow	FirstBitPositionUpFlow
	FirstPayloadSize	
	MinInterArrivalTimeDownFlow	
	MinInterArrivalTimePackets UpAndDownFlow	MinInterArrivalTimePackets UpAndDownFlow
	MinPacketLengthDownFlow	MinPacketLengthDownFlow
	NumberOfBytesDownFlow	
	NumberOfPacketsUpFlow	
	PacketLengthDistribution DownFlow	PacketLengthDistribution DownFlow
	PacketLengthDistribution UpFlow	
		ThirdQuartileInterArrival TimeUp
		ByteFrequencyUpFlow
		MaxSegmentSizeDown
		MaxSegmentSizeUp
		MinInterArrivalTimePackets UpFlow
		NumberOfBytesUpFlow
		ThirdQuartileInterArrival TimeDown
<0.25	PUSHPacketsDown	PUSHPacketsDown
	ThirdQuartileInterArrival TimeDown	
		NumberOfBytesUpFlow
<0.3		FirstPayloadSize
	ByteFrequencyUpFlow	
	MinPacketLengthUpFlow	MinPacketLengthUpFlow
	NumberOfPacketsPerTimeUp	
		DirectionChanges
		BytePairsReoccuringDownFlow
<0.4		MeanPacketLengthUpFlow
<0.5	MeanPacketLengthUpFlow	

known protocol fingerprint is computed using the Kullback-Leibler divergence and the best matching protocol fingerprint has the smallest sum of Kullback-Leibler divergences over all the attributes. Kohnen et al. [19] have developed a new version of the statistical protocol identification method by adding support for UDP and handling streaming protocols using a different set of protocol attribute meters.

The research described here has drawn on this work in creating the enhanced statistical protocol identification method. The research was motivated by the fact that a forensic investigator is more interested in the precision of identification than its speed (although quicker identification is important); therefore, completed conversations are analyzed instead of just the first few packets. Additionally, as mentioned above, the intent is to identify application protocols as well as the applications themselves; therefore, approximated application messages instead of individual packets are analyzed. The enhanced statistical protocol identification method also uses a different set of features (92 features selected as described in Section 3.1) and a different method for computing the distances between measured values and learned protocol fingerprints.

The following three functions are employed:

- Function f computes the divergence of a measured value to a fingerprint value.

- Function g returns a normalized feature value for an actual measured value.

- Function w returns the weight of a feature for a protocol fingerprint.

The divergence from a learned fingerprint is computed as the Euclidean distance [7] of the weighted divergences for individual features:

$$d_{x,c} = \sqrt{\sum_{i=0}^{n} \left(w_i(c) \cdot f_i(g_i(x_i), c_i)\right)^2} \qquad (1)$$

where $x_1, \ldots, x_n$ denote the current flow protocol feature values; $c_1, \ldots, c_n$ denote the normalized feature values in the protocol fingerprint; and $w_i(c)$ denotes the weight of the ith feature in protocol fingerprint c.

Equation (1) is used to compute the difference d_{x,c^j} for each protocol fingerprint c^j. The identified protocol or application k is the one such that $d_{x,c^k} = min(d_{x,c^1} \ldots d_{x,c^m})$.

Compared with other machine learning methods, the enhanced statistical protocol identification method does not suffer from overfitting due to the use of correlated features because it assigns weights on a per-feature basis. This property renders the enhanced statistical protocol identification method readily extensible to classifying new protocols and incorporating features unique to the new protocols, which could be correlated with features of other protocols.

3.3   Bayesian Network Classifier

The Bayesian network classifier [11] relies on Bayes' theorem, which defines the probability of an event based on prior knowledge about the conditions related to the occurrence of the event. The classifier incorporates Bayesian belief networks that are constructed during the learning phase. A Bayesian network is a directed acyclic graph and a set of conditional probability tables. Nodes in the network represent feature variables and edges represent conditional dependencies. The probability tables provide probability functions for the nodes.

A Bayesian network classifier identifies the application protocol by determining the node (or set of nodes) with the highest probability for the given input feature values. The advantage of the Bayesian network classifier is that it also computes the probability that the conversation belongs to the identified protocol. This information enables a forensic investigator to decide whether or not to analyze the conversation.

3.4   Random Forests Classifier

Random forests is an ensemble method that constructs multiple C4.5 decision trees during the training phase; the trees are used for classification in the verification phase, where the mode of the partial results is selected as the resulting class [4]. This makes the random forests classifier prone to overfitting [15]. Random forests are parametrized by multiple variables such as the forest count, join, and training to verification ratio. Optimal values for the parameters are determined by cross-validation and computation of an out-of-bag error that estimates the performance of specific parameter combinations. Because the classifier computes the out-of-bag error, there is no need to employ a separate data verification phase. Therefore, the random forests classifier can be trained on the entire dataset, although this approach can be computationally expensive.

4.   Experimental Procedures and Results

This section presents the experimental procedures and the results obtained using the three classification methods. The experiments were designed with three goals in mind. The first goal was to compare results yielded by machine learning and statistical methods that share the same base feature set, but involve fundamentally-different approaches to classification. The second goal was to observe how the training set size and feature elimination ratio impact the accuracy of application protocol and application classification. The third goal was to prove (or disprove) that application classifiers can identify network traffic based on the applications that generated the traffic.

The Netfox Detective tool was employed as middleware for parsing and processing the captured traffic into application conversations and messages. The feature elimination algorithm and classification methods were implemented as modules in Netfox Detective for easy integration with input data. A standalone application was used to automate the experimental procedure with different parameters. The enhanced statistical protocol identification method was implemented from scratch. The Bayesian network and random forests classifiers were implemented using the Accord.NET library of machine learning algorithms.

4.1 Experimental Procedures

As mentioned above, Netfox Detective was used to parse and process the captured traffic and to extract the full set of feature values for the resulting conversations (feature vectors). Each feature vector was annotated with a label that identified the level of classification using the ground truth from the original capture file. The following labels were used:

- **Application Protocol:** Each application protocol was labeled using a tuple with the components: (i) transport protocol type; and (ii) destination transport layer port or manually assigned label (e.g., TCP_http).

- **Application:** Each application was labeled using a tuple with the components: (i) transport protocol type; (ii) destination transport layer port or manually assigned label; and (iii) application process information (e.g., tcp_http_skypeexe).

Because this task was time-intensive, but only had to be done once, the results were saved in a separate binary file. A custom application was developed to automatically execute the same experiment, but with different configuration parameter values (classification method, training to verification ratio and accepted correlation value for feature elimination). All the experiments involved the following five steps:

- **Step 1 (Dataset Generation):** The available data was split into two disjoint datasets based on the training to verification ratio. The first dataset was used for training and the second for verification.

- **Step 2: (Feature Elimination):** The experiments using the Bayesian network and random forests classifiers used the training dataset created in Step 1 with the feature elimination algorithm described in Section 3.1. The experiments using the enhanced statistical protocol identification method employed the accepted correlation value of one to include all the features; this is because, as explained in Section 3.2, the enhanced statistical protocol identification method does not require feature elimination.

- **Step 3: (Training):** The training dataset created in Step 1 was used to train the three classifiers:

  - **Bayesian Network Classifier:** A classifier was trained for each group of feature vectors with the same label.

  - **Random Forests:** The optimal parameters specified in Section 3.4 corresponded to the most accurate classifier.

  - **Enhanced Statistical Protocol Identification Classifier:** For each group of feature vectors with the same label, an application protocol fingerprint was computed using function g.

- **Step 4 (Verification):** A cross-validation phase was used to determine the best classifiers created in Step 3. Specifically, the classifiers were used to classify each conversation from the verification dataset. They returned either: (i) multiple labels; or (ii) single labels:

  - **Multiple Labels:** Multiple labels were returned as a set of probabilities or distances. The set was ordered and the label with the highest probability or shortest distance was selected. In the case of the Bayesian network classifier, each Bayesian classifier yielded a probability of the current conversation belonging to the class of interest (application protocol or application) represented by the classifier. In the case of the enhanced statistical protocol identification classifier, the Euclidean distance between the specific conversation to each application protocol or application fingerprint was returned.

  - **Single Label:** The random forests classifier returned a single label.

- **Step 5 (Label Comparison):** In each case, the label was compared against the annotation and the statistical properties of each classification method were computed.

Table 2. Configurations of the classification methods.

Classification Method	Experiment ID	Training to Verification Ratio	Highest Feature Correlation Used
Bayesian Network	B1	0.1	0.3
	B2	0.2	0.5
	B3	0.5	0.5
	B4	0.1	0.2
	B5	0.2	0.25
	B6	0.5	0.25
ESPI	ESPI1	0.7	1
	ESPI2	0.2	1
Random Forests	RF1	0.1	0.4
	RF2	0.2	0.4
	RF3	0.1	0.5
	RF4	0.2	0.5

4.2   Experimental Results

The automated application ran many experiments with various configurations of parameters with the goal of identifying the configurations that yielded the best results. The experiments were organized based on the classification methods. For better comparisons, the most successful experiments for each method with various training to verification ratios were employed.

Table 2 lists the configurations of the classification methods with the best results. The last column specifies the highest feature correlation values used for feature elimination. The experiments were split into two categories. Experiments B1, B2, B3, ESPI1, RF1 and RF2 used classifiers for application protocol identification, for which the complete dataset contained 58 application protocol tags. The remaining experiments B4, B5, B6, ESPI2, RF3 and RF4 used classifiers for application identification, for which the complete dataset contained 93 application tags. All the experimental results are available at **pluskal.github.io/AppIdent**. The figures and tables in this section show the truncated results of the experiments. The truncation was performed by selecting the best experiment in each category as a baseline. The 20 most accurately identified labels are shown for all the experiments in a category.

The labels returned by the classification methods were compared with the ground truth from the original captured data and separated into four categories defined by the confusion matrix in Table 3. Note that a classi-

Table 3. Confusion matrix for a single label (application protocol or application).

Classification Result Ground Truth	Positive	Negative	Total
Positive	True Positive (TP)	False Positive (FP)	P
Negative	False Negative (FN)	True Negative (TN)	N
Total	P'	N'	$P + N$

fication result is positive when the classifier returns that the conversation can be labeled with the label and negative when it cannot. The ground truth is positive when the conversation in the dataset is actually labeled with the label and negative when it is not.

The F-measure, also referred to as the balanced F-score [14], was used to compare the classification methods. This single score is computed as the harmonic mean of the precision and recall using the equation:

$$F = 2 \times \frac{precision \times recall}{precision + recall} \tag{2}$$

where the precision and recall are computed from the corresponding confusion matrix values using the equations:

$$precision = \frac{TP}{TP + FP} \tag{3}$$

$$recall = \frac{TP}{TP + FN} = \frac{TP}{P} \tag{4}$$

Figure 1 presents the visualization of the application protocol identification results. The two random forest classifiers (RF1 and RF2) were very accurate. The Bayesian network classifier (B3) also performed very well, but it required a larger training set, a training to verification ratio of 0.5 and more features (see Table 2).

Figure 2 presents the visualization of the application identification results. The two random forest classifiers again yielded the best results. However, in this case, the Bayesian network classifiers were outperformed by the enhanced statistical protocol identification classifier, which also provided the best trade-off between performance and accuracy.

Figure 3 provides the aggregate statistics for all the classes. The number in each cell corresponds to the number of labels that were classified with F-measures greater than or equal to the F-measure value. Note that the size of the shaded area in a cell is proportional to the number of labels classified in the cell.

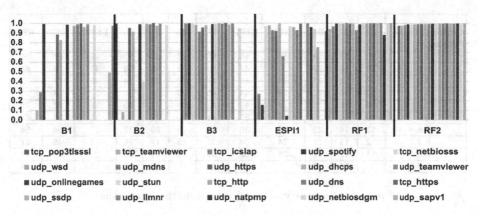

Figure 1. Performance of application protocol classifiers using the F-measure.

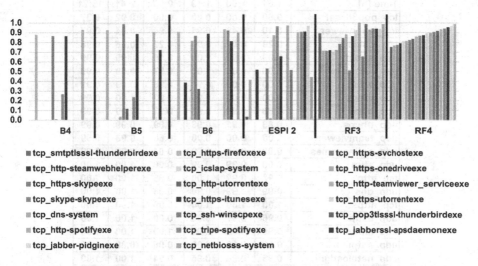

Figure 2. Performance of application classifiers using the F-measure.

Figure 4 presents the results of the performance comparison of application protocol classifiers. The first row shows the times required to complete all the steps involved in the experiments. The remaining rows show the F-measure scores of each evaluated method for the top 20 labels based on the most successful experiment in the category.

Figure 5 presents the results of the performance comparison of application classifiers. Once again, the first row shows the times required to complete all the steps involved in the experiments. The remaining rows show the F-measure scores of each evaluated method for the top 20 labels based on the most successful experiment in the category.

GreaterOrEqual F-Measure	B1	B2	B3	ESPI1	RF1	RF2	B4	B5	B6	ESPI2	RF3	RF4
0.0	58	58	58	58	58	58	93	93	93	93	93	93
0.1	21	19	23	33	47	51	22	25	36	43	83	83
0.2	16	18	23	31	45	47	22	23	34	40	77	77
0.3	14	18	22	29	41	45	20	22	34	37	74	75
0.4	14	16	22	29	40	43	19	22	30	36	68	70
0.5	14	14	22	28	37	41	19	22	29	31	63	63
0.6	13	14	22	26	36	39	16	20	27	27	54	58
0.7	12	13	21	24	34	37	15	17	26	22	45	47
0.8	11	12	19	21	32	36	13	13	26	20	38	41
0.9	8	12	18	17	26	31	7	12	15	17	25	28

Figure 3. Summary of classification method performance.

AppProtocol	B1	B2	B3	ESPI1	RF1	RF2
Time [h]	1:01	1:08	1:13	0:50	2:41	13:21
tcp_pop3tlsssl	0.00	0.00	0.00	0.00	0.92	0.97
tcp_teamviewer	0.10	0.49	0.94	0.94	0.94	0.97
tcp_icslap	0.29	0.97	0.99	0.27	0.96	0.98
udp_spotify	0.99	0.99	1.00	0.15	0.99	0.99
tcp_netbiosss	0.00	0.00	1.00	0.97	0.99	0.99
udp_wsd	0.00	0.08	0.98	0.98	0.99	0.99
udp_mdns	0.00	0.00	0.91	0.92	1.00	0.99
udp_https	0.88	0.95	0.95	0.92	0.99	0.99
udp_dhcps	0.83	0.91	0.98	0.99	0.99	0.99
udp_teamviewer	0.00	0.00	0.00	0.66	0.93	0.99
udp_onlinegames	0.98	0.98	0.99	0.04	0.99	0.99
udp_stun	0.00	0.39	0.99	0.96	1.00	1.00
tcp_http	0.97	0.99	1.00	0.96	1.00	1.00
udp_dns	0.99	0.99	0.99	0.93	1.00	1.00
tcp_https	1.00	1.00	1.00	0.99	1.00	1.00
udp_ssdp	0.96	0.97	0.98	0.00	1.00	1.00
udp_llmnr	0.99	0.99	0.99	1.00	1.00	1.00
udp_natpmp	0.00	0.00	0.00	0.96	0.88	1.00
udp_netbiosdgm	0.98	0.98	0.95	0.94	1.00	1.00
udp_sapv1	0.00	0.00	0.00	0.75	1.00	1.00

Figure 4. Performance comparison of application protocol classifiers.

5.   Conclusions

This research has focused on the important network forensics problem of identifying network applications in addition to just application protocols in network traffic flows. It has studied various aspects of applying machine learning methods and the selection of features that characterize application behavior, such as message timing, content length and TCP flags instead of features related to network line characteristics. An automated feature elimination method based on the feature correlation

AppProtocol	B4	B5	B6	ESPI 2	RF3	RF4
Time [h]	0:53	1:03	2:00	1:11	20:13	23:20
tcp_smtptlsssl-thunderbirdexe	0.00	0.00	0.00	0.03	0.89	0.75
tcp_https-firefoxexe	0.88	0.93	0.91	0.41	0.71	0.77
tcp_https-svchostexe	0.00	0.00	0.00	0.00	0.71	0.77
tcp_http-steamwebhelperexe	0.00	0.00	0.38	0.52	0.72	0.79
tcp_icslap-system	0.00	0.00	0.00	0.00	0.70	0.81
tcp_https-onedriveexe	0.00	0.03	0.82	0.00	0.72	0.81
tcp_https-skypeexe	0.86	0.99	0.87	0.53	0.78	0.82
tcp_http-utorrentexe	0.01	0.11	0.32	0.01	0.84	0.83
tcp_http-teamviewer_serviceexe	0.00	0.00	0.00	0.87	0.88	0.86
tcp_skype-skypeexe	0.27	0.24	0.00	0.96	0.51	0.87
tcp_https-itunesexe	0.86	0.89	0.89	0.65	0.86	0.87
tcp_https-utorrentexe	0.00	0.00	0.00	0.00	0.92	0.89
tcp_dns-system	0.00	0.00	0.00	0.97	1.00	0.89
tcp_ssh-winscpexe	0.00	0.00	0.00	0.51	0.65	0.91
tcp_pop3tlsssl-thunderbirdexe	0.00	0.00	0.00	0.00	0.98	0.92
tcp_http-spotifyexe	0.93	0.91	0.93	0.90	0.93	0.93
tcp_tripe-spotifyexe	0.00	0.00	0.92	0.91	0.94	0.94
tcp_jabberssl-apsdaemonexe	0.00	0.72	0.81	0.91	0.94	0.95
tcp_jabber-pidginexe	0.00	0.00	0.00	0.97	0.94	0.97
tcp_netbiosss-system	0.00	0.00	0.90	0.44	0.98	0.99

Figure 5. Performance comparison of application classifiers.

matrix was employed to improve the classification results. Additionally, this research has developed the enhanced statistical protocol identification method, which was compared against the Bayesian network and random forests classification methods from the literature that offer high accuracy and acceptable performance.

The experimental results confirm that application protocols as well as the applications that generate network traffic can be classified with high confidence. For example, NetBIOS service and DNS were identified accurately and several common applications that use the HTTP(S) application protocol were identified with high accuracy. Similarly, it was possible to distinguish between communications traces of OneDrive, Skype, iTunes, Spotify, Steam and μTorrent clients, although all of them use the same application protocol (HTTPS).

The random forests classifier achieved the best results, confirming the results obtained by other researchers [20, 30] who experimented with machine learning approaches for traffic classification. The enhanced statistical protocol identification classifier yielded better results than the Bayesian network classifier and was much faster than the Bayesian network and random forests classifiers.

Classification accuracy is mainly determined by the quality of the selected features. This research has employed features based on previous observations and intuition. Future research should focus on the systematic analysis and selection of feature sets that could improve classification accuracy and robustness.

To improve the identification of applications that employ the same application protocol (e.g., removing errors when `tcp_http_skypeexe` is classified as `tcp_http_firefoxexe`, or vice-versa), future research should focus on hierarchical classification methods. An example is hierarchical clustering based on enhanced statistical protocol identification fingerprints. A forensic investigator could then infer the actual application classes by visual cluster analysis. This approach could also be extended to other levels such as application message level.

Future research should also consider combining multiple classifiers [18] to increase the confidence in the results. Research should also focus on semi-supervised classification methods [8] that enable the creation of models from partially-labeled data.

Finally, experiments should be conducted to extend the classification models and evaluate the properties of other datasets. The classification methods considered in this work require accurate models. Creating such models requires the analysis of large numbers of traffic samples. Experimenting with different datasets could provide more accurate classification models and valuable insights into the properties of individual classification methods.

A reference implementation is available under an MIT license from GitHub at `pluskal.github.io/AppIdent`. This includes the framework for parsing captured data, extracting features and eliminating features, along with the three classifiers described in this chapter and the standalone application that automated the experiments. The dataset is available at `nes.fit.vutbr.cz/AppIdent` to facilitate the reproducibility of the experiments and to serve as a benchmarking platform for testing other machine-learning-based application identification methods.

References

[1] S. Alcock and R. Nelson, Libprotoident: Traffic Classification Using Lightweight Packet Inspection, Technical Report, WAND Network Research Group, Computer Science Department, University of Waikato, Hamilton, New Zealand, 2012.

[2] N. Al Khater and R. Overill, Forensic network traffic analysis, *Proceedings of the Second International Conference on Digital Security and Forensics*, 2015.

[3] T. Auld, A. Moore and S. Gull, Bayesian neural networks for Internet traffic classification, *IEEE Transactions on Neural Networks*, vol. 18(1), pp. 223–239, 2007.

[4] L. Breiman, Random forests, *Machine Learning*, vol. 45(1), pp. 5–32, 2001.

[5] E. Bursztein, Probabilistic identification of hard to classify protocols, *Proceedings of the Second IFIP WG 11.2 International Conference on Information Security Theory and Practices: Smart Devices, Convergence and Next Generation Networks*, pp. 49–63, 2008.

[6] S. Dai, A. Tongaonkar, X. Wang, A. Nucci and D. Song, NetworkProfiler: Towards automatic fingerprinting of Android apps, *Proceedings of the IEEE International Conference on Computer Communications*, pp. 809–817, 2013.

[7] M. Deza and E. Deza, *Encyclopedia of Distances*, Springer-Verlag, Berlin Heidelberg, Germany, 2009.

[8] J. Erman, A. Mahanti, M. Arlitt, I. Cohen and C. Williamson, Offline/real-time traffic classification using semi-supervised learning, *Performance Evaluation*, vol. 64(9-12), pp. 1194–1213, 2007.

[9] A. Finamore, M. Mellia and M. Meo, Mining unclassified traffic using automatic clustering techniques, *Proceedings of the Third International Conference on Traffic Monitoring and Analysis*, pp. 150–163, 2011.

[10] V. Foroushani and A. Zincir-Heywood, Investigating application behavior in network traffic traces, *Proceedings of the IEEE Symposium on Computational Intelligence for Security and Defense Applications*, pp. 72–79, 2013.

[11] N. Friedman, D. Geiger and M. Goldszmidt, Bayesian network classifiers, *Machine Learning*, vol. 29(2-3), pp. 131–163, 1997.

[12] G. Gomez Sena and P. Belzarena, Early traffic classification using support vector machines, *Proceedings of the Fifth International Latin American Networking Conference*, pp. 60–66, 2009.

[13] I. Guyon and A. Elisseeff, An introduction to variable and feature selection, *Journal of Machine Learning Research*, vol. 3(March), pp. 1157–1182, 2003.

[14] J. Han, M. Kamber, and J. Pei, *Data Mining: Concepts and Techniques*, Morgan Kaufmann Publishers, Waltham, Massachusetts, 2012.

[15] T. Hastie, R. Tibshirani and J. Friedman, *The Elements of Statistical Learning – Data Mining, Inference and Prediction*, Springer, New York, 2009.

[16] E. Hjelmvik, The SPID Algorithm – Statistical Protocol Identification, Gavle, Sweden (`www.iis.se/docs/The_SPID_Algorithm_-_Statistical_Protocol_IDentification.pdf`), 2008.

[17] J. Khalife, A. Hajjar and J. Diaz-Verdejo, A multilevel taxonomy and requirements for an optimal traffic-classification model, *International Journal of Network Management*, vol. 24(2), pp. 101–120, 2014.

[18] J. Kittler, Combining classifiers: A theoretical framework, *Pattern Analysis and Applications*, vol. 1(1), pp. 18–27, 1998.

[19] C. Kohnen, C. Uberall, F. Adamsky, V. Rakocevic, M. Rajarajan and R. Jager, Enhancements to statistical protocol identification (SPID) for self-organized QoS in LANs, *Proceedings of the Nineteenth International Conference on Computer Communications and Networks*, 2010.

[20] J. Li, S. Zhang, Y. Xuan and Y. Sun, Identifying Skype traffic by random forests, *Proceedings of the International Conference on Wireless Communications, Networking and Mobile Computing*, pp. 2841–2844, 2007.

[21] Y. Luo, K. Xiang and S. Li, Acceleration of decision tree searching for IP traffic classification, *Proceedings of the Fourth ACM/IEEE Symposium on Architectures for Networking and Communications Systems*, pp. 40–49, 2008.

[22] P. Matousek, J. Pluskal, O. Rysavy, V. Vesely, M. Kmet, F. Karpisek and M. Vymlatil, Advanced techniques for reconstruction of incomplete network data, *Proceedings of the Seventh International Conference on Digital Forensics and Cyber Crime*, pp. 69–84, 2015.

[23] S. Miskovic, G. Lee, Y. Liao and M. Baldi, AppPrint: Automatic fingerprinting of mobile applications in network traffic, *Proceedings of the Sixteenth International Conference on Passive and Active Measurement*, pp. 57–69, 2015.

[24] A. Moore and K. Papagiannaki, Toward the accurate identification of network applications, *Proceedings of the Sixth International Workshop on Passive and Active Network Measurement*, pp. 41–54, 2005.

[25] A. Moore, D. Zuev and M. Crogan, Discriminators for Use in Flow-Based Classification, Technical Report RR-05-13, Department of Computer Science, Queen Mary, University of London, London, United Kingdom, 2013.

[26] N. Namdev, S. Agrawal and S. Silkari, Recent advancements in machine learning based Internet traffic classification, *Procedia Computer Science*, vol. 60, pp. 784–791, 2015.

[27] T. Nguyen and G. Armitage, A survey of techniques for Internet traffic classification using machine learning, *IEEE Communications Surveys and Tutorials*, vol. 10(4), pp. 56–76, 2008.

[28] C. Shen and L. Huang, On the detection accuracy of the l7-filter and OpenDPI, *Proceedings of the Third International Conference on Networking and Distributed Computing*, pp. 119–123, 2012.

[29] P. Velan, M. Cermak, P. Celeda and M. Drasar, A survey of methods for encrypted traffic classification and analysis, *International Journal of Network Management*, vol. 25(5), pp. 355–374, 2015.

[30] Y. Wang and S. Yu, Machine learned real-time traffic classifiers, *Proceedings of the Second International Symposium on Intelligent Information Technology Applications*, vol. 3, pp. 449–454, 2008.

[31] I. Zezula, On multivariate Gaussian copulas, *Journal of Statistical Planning and Inference*, vol. 139(11), pp. 3942–3946, 2009.

[32] L. Zhen and L. Qiong, A new feature selection method for Internet traffic classification using ML, *Physics Procedia*, vol. 33, pp. 1338–1345, 2012.

Chapter 11

ENABLING NON-EXPERT ANALYSIS OF LARGE VOLUMES OF INTERCEPTED NETWORK TRAFFIC

Erwin van de Wiel, Mark Scanlon and Nhien-An Le-Khac

Abstract   Telecommunications wiretaps are commonly used by law enforcement in criminal investigations. While phone-based wiretapping has seen considerable success, the same cannot be said for Internet taps. Large portions of intercepted Internet traffic are often encrypted, making it difficult to obtain useful information. The advent of the Internet of Things further complicates network wiretapping. In fact, the current level of complexity of intercepted network traffic is almost at the point where data cannot be analyzed without the active involvement of experts. Additionally, investigations typically focus on analyzing traffic in chronological order and predominately examine the data content of the intercepted traffic. This approach is overly arduous when the amount of data to be analyzed is very large.

This chapter describes a novel approach for analyzing large amounts of intercepted network traffic based on traffic metadata. The approach significantly reduces the analysis time and provides useful insights and information to non-technical investigators. The approach is evaluated using a large sample of network traffic data.

Keywords: Internet taps, network forensics, traffic metadata analysis

1.   Introduction

Lawful interception is used by law enforcement in many middle and high level criminal investigations. Investigations of intercepted traffic cover voice and network data [19]. This work focuses on intercepted network data that is a valuable source of evidence in crimes such as child abuse material distribution [23], cloud hosted services [19], industrial espionage [10], dead drops [10, 17], malicious software distribution [17], instant messaging [22], piracy [18] and illegal content distribution [17].

© IFIP International Federation for Information Processing 2018
Published by Springer Nature Switzerland AG 2018. All Rights Reserved
G. Peterson and S. Shenoi (Eds.): Advances in Digital Forensics XIV, IFIP AICT 532, pp. 183–197, 2018.
https://doi.org/10.1007/978-3-319-99277-8_11

However, investigating these crimes is challenging for non-technical personnel because of the difficulty in interpreting network data.

Analysis of the data can also be very labor-intensive. Placing a telephone or IP tap requires special investigatory powers. In The Netherlands, the legal power is provided by the Special Investigative Powers Act (Bijzondere Opsporings Bevoegdheid in Dutch). Dutch telecommunications law requires every provider to make data interception equipment available to law enforcement. Law enforcement is also permitted to intercept data at locations without service provider involvement, such as when intercepting data from wireless access points.

Ideally, all digital forensic evidence should be analyzed by expert investigators. However, the reality is that there are simply too many cases that require expert analysis and the case backlog is often too large [15]. As a result, evidence processing by non-experts has become a necessity in law enforcement agencies around the world [16].

Analysis of intercepted data from an IP tap is often conducted by non-technical investigators who analyze the data in chronological order. In a typical scenario, an investigator analyzes data collected over a period of four weeks. The investigator works with the first day of the IP tap data and the analysis software presents all the data for the day starting from 0:00 to 23:59. If the focus is on HTTP-based web traffic, each web visit is displayed in a list view by the software. The investigator then selects a row and the contents of the website are displayed. The only option in such a scenario is for the investigator to examine every web visit sequentially. As a result, it would take a considerable amount of time to analyze the IP tap traffic over the entire four-week period. The analysis software may provide options to filter on text strings and protocols such as HTTP or FTP, but the investigator must know in advance the search terms to be used in the filtering.

A solution is to analyze all the traffic and create text filters based on knowledge about the case. However, this task is challenging because even ordinary Internet users produce vast amounts of traffic, and the traffic will increase significantly as the use of the cloud increases [5, 9].

This chapter proposes a novel approach for analyzing large streams of intercepted data from IP taps. Instead of analyzing the data chronologically, the approach identifies what lies behind an intercepted Internet connection and produces an overview of the extracted information that can be interpreted by non-technical investigators. This chapter also describes the Network Intell system, which instead of focusing on data content, analyzes metadata related to the protocols seen in the data. This reduces the time required to analyze the intercepted traffic. It also provides a quick way to retrieve intelligence information – essentially a clear view of what is seen behind an IP tap. For example, if an investigator knows that a mobile phone is present, then he can focus on data related to mobile phone protocols. The performance of the system is evaluated using a large sample of network traffic data.

2. Background

Several tools have been developed for analyzing intercepted network traffic. However, the majority of the tools require highly-specialized knowledge for their effective use.

The available tools can be divided in two groups. The first group comprises tools created for professionals with high levels of networking knowledge such as network administrators and digital investigators with advanced network protocol expertise. These tools analyze network traffic at the packet level and extract data for deeper analysis.

The second group comprises specialized network forensic tools that analyze captured traffic. While these tools are not as complex as those in the first group, they still require specialized networking knowledge. Most of the tools are available as freeware or as professional versions that cost between $500 and $1,000. The tools employ the well-known PCAP packet capture format.

2.1 Network Forensic Analysis Tools

The NetworkMiner tool was created by Hjelmvik [7] in 2007. The tool splits network traffic and extracts data from within the traffic. The latest version of NetworkMiner can distinguish between hosts, but this feature cannot be used when a network connection in a lawful interception scenario is analyzed; in such a scenario, the captured traffic appears to come from a single IP address (tapped IP address). Additionally, NetworkMiner does not scale well with increasing data size. For example, the analysis of a 1.25 GB capture takes more than 21 minutes. NetworkMiner parses all the information and the results may be analyzed by scrolling the list view. However, the tool is too advanced to be used effectively by non-technical investigators.

The Xplico tool extracts application data from a network capture [3]. Network traffic is broken down to the protocol level and metadata is extracted for each protocol. Xplico can be used to analyze relatively large network capture datasets. It parses all the information and the results can be viewed and analyzed via a web interface. Although the tool is easy to operate, an investigator still needs to review and analyze the data. Moreover, the tool cannot identify the devices behind the captured network point because it does not incorporate the knowledge required to interpret the data.

The popular Wireshark network analyzer breaks traffic down to the packet level, and can even analyze broken and half packets. Wireshark also supports the reconstruction of network flows, data analysis using advanced filtering and deep packet inspection. However, Wireshark can be difficult to use by non-technical investigators. Additionally, it is relatively slow when performing filtering and running modules. This is because each filter and module must be executed on the entire dataset. Filter creation is also very slow because each filter has to be tested on the entire database. Wireshark only supports single capture files, although it is possible to connect multiple captures using third-party tools. Moreover, Wireshark requires significant amounts of time to analyze the large volumes of intercepted network traffic encountered in a forensic investigations involving residential or corporate users.

2.2   Traffic Metadata Analysis Tools

Several tools are available for examining and/or extracting metadata from capture files. An example is the p0f tool [24]. This tool employs passive traffic fingerprinting to identify the entities involved in TCP/IP communications. However, in order to obtain the best results, the tool must be executed on the target network (i.e., network on which the interception is conducted). This is almost never possible in the case of lawful interception because the actual capture takes place at the Internet provider. The p0f tool can only identify or fingerprint traffic coming from the tapped IP address, which is typically a single router or gateway.

Justniffer is another tool that focuses on metadata in network capture files [12]. The tool targets request and response information from various protocols. Justniffer exports information in a log format and provides Python scripts that support network forensic functionality.

3.   Network Intell System

This section specifies the requirements of a system for analyzing large amounts of intercepted network traffic. The requirements are realized by the proof-of-concept Network Intell system, which is also described in this section.

3.1   System Requirements

The Network Intell system is not intended to be a one-size-fits-all solution. Instead, it should greatly facilitate the analysis of large amounts of network traffic to discover evidence relevant to digital forensic investigations. Another key requirement is speed of analysis. Casey [1] has specified a number of requirements for network traffic processing tools [1]. The Network Intell system should satisfy the following requirements:

- **Tcpdump Format:** This format is desired because the WinPcap library is used to parse network traffic. Thus, the proposed system should be designed to handle PCAP traffic.

- **Reliable Protocol Identification:** Deep packet inspection must be used where possible to identify different protocols.

- **Data Reduction:** The actual contents of rebuilt packet streams need not be stored. Instead, the system should focus on metadata and only store packet information. This increases the speed of automated analysis and reduces the storage requirements.

- **Keyword Search:** The system should identify devices and their usage behind an Internet connection based on custom queries. It particular, it should search for metadata items using keywords. Since data content is not stored, it is not possible to search the contents.

- **Read-Only Feature:** The parsed traffic is stored in an SQLite database. The stored data should be accessed as needed, but no modifications should be made to the database.

A key requirement is that Network Intell should be operable by digital investigators and/or non-technical investigators. A digital investigator would be able to input and change the rules that identify the devices and objects behind an intercepted network point. A non-technical investigator would simply operate the system and report the results in an investigative report or pass the results for further analysis by a digital investigator. Any user should be allowed to edit the rules.

3.2   System Design

Figure 1 shows the Network Intell architecture. The system has three main components: (i) network parser; (ii) fragmented traffic reassembler; and (iii) protocol analyzer/parser.

Network Parser. The system splits protocol data to produce usable metadata. This metadata is stored in a SQLite database that may be queried later for devices and objects behind the intercepted network address. The technical requirements define the traffic that is used as a

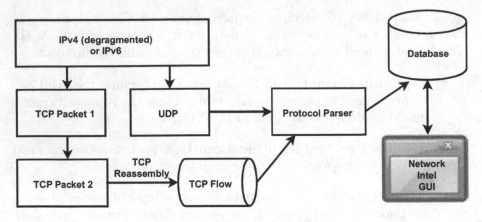

Figure 1.   Network Intell architecture.

parsing object. The most useful protocols in the traffic are selected for parsing. Each parsed protocol is stored in its own database table.

WinPcap provides options for intercepting live network traffic and opening stored packet captures (PCAP files). However, the Network Intell system is designed to only operate on stored packet captures. As stated above, the interception of network packets is done at a service provider. The function pcap_open_offline in WinPcap is used to open offline stored packet captures. By opening a packet capture in this manner, it is possible to loop through all the stored packets.

The first requirement is to only include Ethernet packets from the network access layer. The next requirement is to only parse Ethernet packets with IPv4 or IPv6 headers from the Internet layer. This is motivated by the fact that, as of June 2016, 10.88% of the computing systems that accessed Google used IPv6 [11] and the percentage has grown to 18.09% as of January 2018 [6]. The parser selects Ethernet packets with IPv4 or IPv6 headers associated with the TCP, UDP or ICMP protocols. At this stage, ICMP packets are also logged.

The final requirement is the application layer. This layer is the most important because the final results stored in the database are associated with the application layer protocols that are selected.

Fragmented Traffic Reassembler.   The most complex part of network analysis is packet reassembly. Packet reassembly occurs at two layers: (i) IP layer; and (ii) TCP layer.

IP fragmentation can be caused by IPv4 routers that fragment IPv4 packets when they are transferred to other networks [13]. Reassembly of the fragmented packets is done by the receiving endpoint. Since IPv4 packets do not necessarily arrive in order, it is difficult to reassemble the packets in the correct order without errors. Fragmented packet reassembly is performed using the IP datagram reassembly algorithms described in RFC 815 [2].

Network Intell uses code implemented in the IPTraf tool [8]. Several attack vectors target the manner in which IP fragmentation is handled. However, protection from IP fragmentation attacks is beyond the scope of this work. In any case, IPv4 fragmentation is not seen very often and IPv6 routers do not support fragmented IPv6 packets.

TCP reassembly is the next step in rebuilding network streams and data. Analysis tools rely on proper TCP reassembly to rebuild traffic.

Rebuilding TCP packets produces streams (also called flows). Considerable research has focused on TCP reassembly (see, e.g., Wagener et al. [21]). Problems that occur during IPv4 reassembly also occur in TCP reassembly. Exploits can be used to bypass the reassembly process and can even crash the software. Protection against TCP reassembly attacks is not in the scope of this research, although it could be considered in future tests of the system.

Network Intell uses a portion of the code in the `tcpick` TCP reassembly tool [4]. The modified code also incorporates a requirement that every TCP connection must have a complete three-way handshake. The three-way TCP handshake involves an exchange of packets before a TCP connection is established.

In a three-way TCP handshake, three packets are exchanged between a client and server with the first SYN packet being the most important packet. ACK and SEQ numbers are used in the reassembly process. The sender of the SYN packet is the initiator of the connection and is identified as the "TCP flow from" entity. Without a SYN packet it would be very complex to identify the entity that started the connection because packets may not arrive in the same order as they were sent. Therefore, a complete three-way handshake is needed before a connection can be parsed for a higher-level protocol.

Network Intell relies on a four-tuple mechanism for packet reassembly: (i) source IP address; (ii) destination IP address; (iii) source port; and (iv) destination port. Each reassembled connection must start with a SYN; this is needed to identify the entity that started the connection and, thus, determine the client side and the server side. It is possible to create flows that do not have starting SYNs, but this introduces packet reassembly errors. Specifically, the sending and receiving endpoints can get switched and incorrect assumptions are made during traffic analysis. An example is when an HTTP request from an external entity is directed to the intercepted network point. Without a SYN packet, the request could be identified as traffic originating from inside the intercepted network point and headed outside the network.

Network Intell rebuilds each flow in memory and stores the metadata associated with the flow in the database. The stored metadata includes the client and server IP addresses, the duration of the flow and the amount of traffic that was intercepted. Flows remain active until a RST or FIN packet is received in the TCP flow. After the flow information metadata is exported to the database, the flow is removed from memory.

Network Intell also provides the option to export a complete flow. This is useful for analyzing specific connections and data transfers. However, the option is currently disabled because disk I/O slows down the analysis. When a flow does not receive the RST or FIN terminating packets, then the flow needs to be shut down after a period of time. This feature is built into Network Intell, but more testing is required to determine the correct timing for flow termination. In any case, since Network Intell works on captured traffic, real-time analysis of live traffic is not an issue.

Protocol Analyzer/Parser.   After IP packets are defragmented and TCP packets are reassembled to create a stream or flow, they are parsed by the protocol analyzer. The first step is to identify the contents of the network stream. Casey [1] recommends that traffic should not be filtered based on protocol because of the risk that other traffic can be tunneled through a protocol such as HTTP. For the same reason, it is not advisable to filter traffic based on port number. Although port numbers are exported to a log file, the actual contents of the reassembled packets are used to identify the protocols employed in the application layer. The only exception is the DNS protocol, which is analyzed based its port number (port 53).

Filtering the contents of TCP streams is referred to as deep packet inspection. This technique is useful for detecting protocols hidden inside network traffic. However, it is a complex process because it can cause false hits based on the keywords used to identify protocols. Therefore, it has to be continually evaluated and adjusted where needed, a task that can only be done by a skilled network forensic investigator.

The key functions of Network Intell are to analyze different application layer protocols and store important metadata in a SQLite database. Network Intell conducts deep packet inspection by searching for specific keywords in packet headers. First, it looks for protocol-specific details such as an HTTP header that ends with "\r\n\r\n." Next, it searches for specific keywords such as "GET" and "POST" that are bound to the protocol. Based on the results, the reconstructed packets are identified by their protocol. This method is based on the approach used by Xplico

Figure 2. Network Intell main menu.

to identify protocols. Currently, Network Intell employs deep packet inspection to identify HTTP, FTP, SMTP and POP3 protocol packets. Because deep packet inspection is used, these protocols are detected even when they run on ports other than their default ports.

4. System Implementation

As described above, Network Intell analyzes intercepted network traffic. Win32 C was chosen as the programming language to ensure adequate speed of analysis. The Pelles C Microsoft Windows development environment was used to create 32/64-bit C language code [14].

Network Intell maintains several logs. The results of each analysis and the network packets can be exported to a separate log file. The system also can export each TCP stream/flow to a binary file. This enables research to be conducted on unknown network traffic and the content to be verified for consistency. Figure 2 shows the Network Intell main menu functionality, which includes analysis, search, detection rule editing, report creation, settings and help.

The main – and initial – function is analysis. A non-technical investigator can execute this function if he/she knows which capture files need to be investigated. The system asks for the names of the network capture files in the PCAP format. After the files are input, the MD5 and SHA1 hashes of the files are computed. Also, the numbers of packets in the files are counted. The PCAP format does not save packet counts in the header. The only safe way to count packets is to open a capture file and loop through all the packets with a counter running. The result of the analysis is a tree view with an overview of the analyzed items. Since all the metadata is stored in a SQLite database, a user is allowed to include new items as shown in Figure 3.

Detection rule editing is another important Network Intell function. The detection rule editor facilitates the input and modification of rules. A detection rule type must be selected, the result name entered, the parent selected and, of course, the search query entered with partial or exact match options (Figure 4).

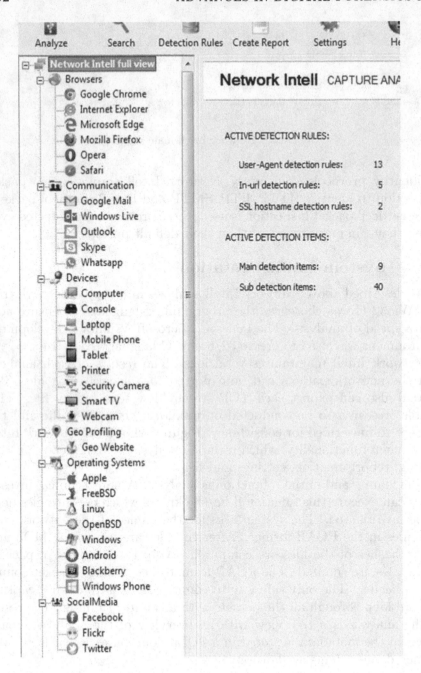

Figure 3.   Network Intell analysis options.

5.   System Evaluation

This section describes the results of evaluating the Network Intell system. The evaluation used intercepted network traffic in open source captures and home network captures.

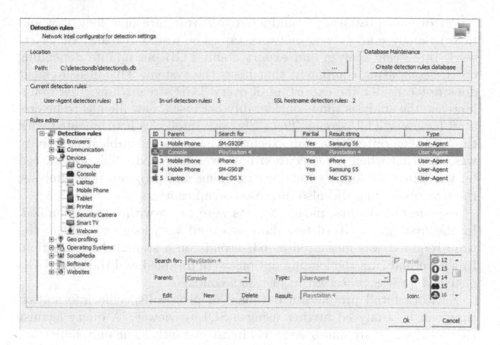

Figure 4. Network Intell detection rules.

The following evaluation scheme was employed:

- Each protocol was tested using a protocol-specific PCAP file.

- The results obtained using Network Intell were compared against those obtained using other network forensic tools such as Wireshark. The only differences were seen at TCP stream/flow level. Wireshark also identifies streams without a starting SYN packet; however, Network Intell cannot handle such streams and needs a SYN packet to identify a TCP stream/flow.

- Personal network traffic was captured at the router level to mimic intercepted network traffic. Most errors were detected during this test because personal network traffic has a lot of content that is not handled by Network Intell. An example is secure DNS traffic, which causes an error in the parsing code.

- Network Intell has not as yet been tested on a real-world investigation. The system is designed to be used by experts as well as non-experts. However, it will be extended to enhance usability; complex configurations will not be required to use the final system.

Performance tests were conducted to investigate how long it would take to analyze an average network tap. The results revealed that Network Intell can analyze and export about 1 GB per minute depending on the computing equipment that hosts the system. This measurement does not consider the exporting of every TCP stream/flow; this would increase the analysis time considerably because a new file has to be created for every TCP stream/flow. Network Intell was instrumented with timers to compute the overall execution time. Considerable disk activity was observed when the execution data was analyzed. This was caused by the extensive logging for error checking and program flow analysis; the execution time was also increased significantly.

As a result, the first measurements were taken with logging enabled. In the first run, 1 GB of test data was used with logging enabled; the time required was measured as 63 seconds on a standard workstation. In the second run, the logging options were disabled and the same 1 GB of test data was processed in just 35 seconds.

Network Intell produces a database of protocol-specific information that can be analyzed further using a SQLite viewer. A query against the SQLite capture database runs almost instantly. The only limitation is when the amount of data approaches the maximum size of a SQLite database (more than 140 TB). No performance testing was performed on the analysis time because it takes less than a second to produce the tree view. The information presented after the analysis of a PCAP file is completed can be used by a digital forensic investigator to check the number of streams that were analyzed and for any errors that may have occurred.

The research goal has been to develop a system that produces useful results from large volumes of data intercepted via a network tap. Instead of analyzing the data in a chronological manner, the Network Intell system identifies what lies behind the intercepted connection and produces an overview of the discovered information. The system is easy to use by experts as well as non-experts; in fact, it can be operated almost via single button actions. Network Intell is fast – it analyzes approximately 1 GB of data per minute with logging enabled and requires just 34 seconds to analyze 1 GB of data without logging enabled. This analysis speed is comparable to or exceeds the performance of other available tools. Finally, Network Intell appears to be able to handle "big data" scenarios. Specifically, good performance was achieved with 1 GB capture files; in contrast, other network analysis tools either cannot handle files of this size or become very slow after loading files of this size.

6. Conclusions

The chapter has presented a new approach for analyzing large amounts of intercepted network traffic and Network Intell, its proof-of-concept implementation. Network Intell exhibits good performance – it can analyze intercepted network traffic in the PCAP format at speeds of around 20 seconds per 200 MB. The analyzed information is stored in a SQLite database that can be queried to identify the devices used behind a network tap and obtain useful statistics about the captured traffic. Network Intell can be used by digital forensic investigators with technical expertise as well as by non-expert investigators.

Network Intell offers a good mix of functionality and performance, but is a proof-of-concept system and several enhancements are possible. For example, the current version engages detection rules input by users. Future research will attempt to employ the Fingerbank database [20] accessible at `www.fingerbank.org`, a device database containing MAC addresses and user-agent device detection information. Additionally, it is ineffective to employ complete user agent strings in lawful interception scenarios because browser software is updated very frequently. Consequently, future work will use detection rules based on browser names instead of complete user agent strings with version numbers.

References

[1] E. Casey, Network traffic as a source of evidence: Tool strengths, weaknesses and future needs, *Digital Investigation*, vol. 1(1), pp. 28–43, 2004.

[2] D. Clark, IP Datagram Reassembly Algorithms, RFC 815 (`tools.ietf.org/html/rfc815`), 1982.

[3] G. Costa and A. De Franceschi, Xplico: Open Source Network Forensic Analysis Tool (NFAT) (`www.xplico.org`), 2018.

[4] duskdriud, `tcpick` version 0.2.1 (`tcpick.sourceforge.net`), 2005.

[5] J. Farina, M. Scanlon, N. Le-Khac and M. Kechadi, Overview of the forensic investigation of cloud services, *Proceedings of the Tenth International Conference on Availability, Reliability and Security*, pp. 556–565, 2015.

[6] Google, IPv6 Adoption Statistics, Mountain View, California (`www.google.com/intl/en/ipv6/statistics.html`), 2018.

[7] E. Hjelmvik, Passive network security analysis with NetworkMiner, *(IN)SECURE Magazine*, issue 18, pp. 18–21, October 2008.

[8] G. Java, IPTraf: IP Network Monitoring Software (`iptraf.seul.org`), 2005.

[9] T. Lillard, *Digital Forensics for Network, Internet and Cloud Computing: A Forensic Evidence Guide for Moving Targets and Data*, Syngress, Burlington, Massachusetts, 2010.

[10] B. Nelson, A. Phillips and C. Steuart, *Guide to Computer Forensics and Investigations*, Cengage Learning, Boston, Massachusetts, 2016.

[11] V. Nicolls, N. Le-Khac, L. Chen and M. Scanlon, IPv6 security and forensics, *Proceedings of the Sixth International Conference on Innovative Computing Technology*, pp. 743–748, 2016.

[12] O. Notelli, Justniffer, Plecno, Milan, Italy (`justniffer.source forge.net`), 2014.

[13] N. Olifer and V. Olifer, *Computer Networks: Principles, Technologies and Protocols for Network Design*, John Wiley and Sons, Chichester, United Kingdom, 2006.

[14] P. Orinius, Pelles C (`www.smorgasbordet.com/pellesc`), 2017.

[15] D. Quick and K. Choo, Impacts of increasing volume of digital forensic data: A survey and future research challenges, *Digital Investigation*, vol. 11(4), pp. 273–294, 2014.

[16] M. Scanlon, Battling the digital forensic backlog through data deduplication, *Proceedings of the Sixth International Conference on Innovative Computing Technology*, pp. 10–14, 2016.

[17] M. Scanlon, J. Farina and M. Kechadi, Network investigation methodology for BitTorrent Sync: A peer-to-peer based file synchronization service, *Computers and Security*, vol. 54, pp. 27–43, 2015.

[18] M. Scanlon, A. Hannaway and M. Kechadi, A week in the life of the most popular BitTorrent swarms, *Proceedings of the Fifth Annual Symposium on Information Assurance*, pp. 32–36, 2010.

[19] H. Schut, M. Scanlon, J. Farina and N. Le-Khac, Towards the forensic identification and investigation of cloud hosted servers through non-invasive wiretaps, *Proceedings of the Tenth International Conference on Availability, Reliability and Security*, pp. 249–257, 2015.

[20] J. Spooren, D. Preuveneers and W. Joosen, Mobile device fingerprinting considered harmful for risk-based authentication, *Proceedings of the Eighth European Workshop on System Security*, article no. 6, 2015.

[21] G. Wagener, A. Dulaunoy and T. Engel, Towards an estimation of the accuracy of TCP reassembly in network forensics, *Proceedings of the Second International Conference on Future Generation Communications and Networking*, vol. 2, pp. 273–278, 2008.

[22] D. Walnycky, I. Baggili, A. Marrington, J. Moore and F. Breitinger, Network and device forensic analysis of Android social-messaging applications, *Digital Investigation*, vol. 14(S1), pp. S77–S84, 2015.

[23] A. Yasinsac and Y. Manzano, Policies to enhance computer and network forensics, *Proceedings of the IEEE Workshop on Information Assurance and Security*, pp. 289–295, 2001.

[24] M. Zalewski, p0f (`lcamtuf.coredump.cx/p0f3`), 2014.

Chapter 12

HASHING INCOMPLETE AND UNORDERED NETWORK STREAMS

Chao Zheng, Xiang Li, Qingyun Liu, Yong Sun and Binxing Fang

Abstract   Deep packet inspection typically uses MD5 whitelists/blacklists or regular expressions to identify viruses, malware and certain internal files in network traffic. Fuzzy hashing, also referred to as context-triggered piecewise hashing, can be used to compare two files and determine their level of similarity. This chapter presents the stream fuzzy hash algorithm that can hash files on the fly regardless of whether the input is unordered, incomplete or has an initially-undetermined length. The algorithm, which can generate a signature of appropriate length using a one-way process, reduces the computational complexity from $O\left(n\log n\right)$ to $O(n)$. In a typical deep packet inspection scenario, the algorithm hashes files at the rate of 68 MB/s per CPU core and consumes no more than 5 KB of memory per file. The effectiveness of the stream fuzzy hash algorithm is evaluated using a publicly-available dataset. The results demonstrate that, unlike other fuzzy hash algorithms, the precision and recall of the stream fuzzy hash algorithm are not compromised when processing unordered and incomplete inputs.

Keywords: Fuzzy hashing, network traffic, approximate matching, file tracking

1.   Introduction

Identifying content in network traffic is important in deep packet inspection applications such as malware detection, data leakage prevention and digital forensics. In these applications, a search is made for predefined signatures in packet payloads, which could be string patterns, cryptographic hash values, etc. For example, Snort inspects file content using regular expressions and Suricata (`suricata-ids.org`) computes the MD5 checksums of files.

In order to deal with new security threats, several researchers have focused on identifying similar files and file fragments in network traffic

© IFIP International Federation for Information Processing 2018
Published by Springer Nature Switzerland AG 2018. All Rights Reserved
G. Peterson and S. Shenoi (Eds.): Advances in Digital Forensics XIV, IFIP AICT 532, pp. 199–224, 2018.
https://doi.org/10.1007/978-3-319-99277-8_12

using techniques such as Bloom filters [1], machine learning [8] and fuzzy fingerprints [21]. However, increased network throughput and network transmission optimization technologies have rendered these approaches infeasible. Scarce computational resources prevent the execution of complex algorithms on high throughput traffic in deep packet inspection applications. Additionally, emerging technologies such as multi-thread downloading, P2P file sharing and cyberlocker file uploading make it impractical to acquire ordered file streams during or even after transmission.

Fuzzy hashing, also referred to as context-triggered piecewise hashing (CTPH), essentially slices an input file into pieces using a context-triggered algorithm and hashes each piece. Compared with cryptographic hash algorithms such as MD5 and SHA1, fuzzy hashing can recognize files that are changed in a subtle manner (e.g., by inserting just a single character in a document). This feature makes fuzzy hashing very appealing in deep packet inspection applications. However, current fuzzy hash algorithms only work on intact and stored files. Indeed, when applying fuzzy hashing to files in transmission, a number of challenges are encountered that are quite different from conventional scenarios. The challenges include incomplete capture, unordered fragments and very high buffering requirements.

This chapter proposes an improved fuzzy hash algorithm that can detect similar files in network traffic under real-time, incomplete input and limited memory constraints. This so-called stream fuzzy hash (SFH) algorithm can be applied to streamed and unordered data. The algorithm employs a compact structure to record the computed contexts and hashes unordered fragments individually with almost no buffering, generating a proper-length signature via a one-way process. Experiments demonstrate that the stream fuzzy hash algorithm can hash data at 68 MB/core/s in a typical multi-thread transfer scenario while consuming no more than 5 KB memory per file regardless of the file size. The ability of the stream fuzzy hash algorithm to track files transmitted in network traffic is very useful in network measurement, malicious software detection and data leakage protection applications.

2.   Preliminaries

This section discusses the fuzzy hash algorithm, which is the primitive version of the stream fuzzy hash algorithm presented in this chapter. Next, it presents the Tillich-Zémor (TZ) hash that is used as a strong hash by the stream fuzzy hash algorithm due to its concatenation property, which saves memory.

2.1   Fuzzy Hashing

Cryptographic hash algorithms such as MD5 and SHA1 have good avalanche effects, which means that flipping a single bit of a file causes drastic changes to its hash value. While this is a highly desirable security property of cryptographic hash algorithms, digital forensic investigators are interested in a hash algorithm that can be used to compare two distinctly different items and determine their fundamental level of similarity. Context-triggered piecewise hashing, also referred to as fuzzy hashing, is one of many such options. Unlike a cryptographic hash, a fuzzy hash is not designed to be difficult to reverse by an adversary, making it unsuitable for cryptographic purposes. The concept of fuzzy hashing was pioneered in **spamsum** [23] and Nilsimsa [25]. Kornblum [14] formalized the concept and developed **ssdeep** for use in digital forensics.

Non-propagation is a property unique to fuzzy hashing. In a fuzzy hash, only the part of the signature that corresponds linearly to the changed part of the binary is changed. This means that a small change to any part of the plaintext will leave most of the signature intact.

Alignment robustness is another important property. Most hash algorithms are very alignment sensitive. Deleting or inserting a single byte in the plaintext generates a completely different hash value. The core of the fuzzy hash algorithm is a rolling hash that produces a series of reset points in the binary. Each reset point depends only on the immediate context.

Fuzzy hashing uses a block size variable b to trigger a reset point. The block size is computed using the following equation:

$$b_{init} = b_{min}2^{\left\lfloor log_2\left(\frac{n}{Sb_{min}}\right)\right\rfloor} \tag{1}$$

where b_{min} is the (constant) minimum block size, S is the (constant) expected fuzzy hash length and n is the input file size. The equation helps ensure that the fuzzy hash result of a given file is neither too long for efficient comparisons nor too short to avoid collisions. Note that the file size is not always available in network traffic; this issue, which poses some challenges, is discussed later.

In the case of a rolling hash function with window k, if an input sequence of k bytes $c_1c_2\ldots c_k$ satisfies the condition:

$$\text{rolling hash}\,(c_1c_2\ldots c_k)\,\bmod\,b = b - 1 \tag{2}$$

then a reset point is positioned at c_k. Statistically, the smaller the value of b, the greater the number of reset points that are triggered.

The strong hash based on the Fowler-Noll-Vo (FNV) algorithm is used to produce hash values of the regions between two reset points. The resulting signature comes from the concatenation of a single character from the Fowler-Noll-Vo hash per reset point. A signature is produced if the length is not more than $S/2$ characters. Specifically, the fuzzy hash algorithm reduces the block size from b to $b/2$ and the algorithm is executed iteratively until a signature of at least $S/2$ characters is produced. Some researchers [2, 6] have proposed improvements to reduce the computations, but the iterative processing has not been eliminated. The string edit distance algorithm is used to measure the similarity percentage of fuzzy hash values computed for different files.

2.2 Tillich-Zémor Hash

The Tillich-Zémor [22] hash function maps a binary string to a matrix over a finite field of matrices with determinant one. Each element in the alphabet is first mapped to a matrix from a generator set. Next, the corresponding matrices are multiplied according to their order in the binary string. The security of the Tillich-Zémor hash to certain attacks has been proven to be equivalent to associating a Cayley graph with the hash function.

The Tillich-Zémor hash has: (i) a defining parameter; and (ii) a hash algorithm:

- **Defining Parameter:** This parameter is an irreducible polynomial $P_n(X)$ of degree n in the range 130 to 170.

- **Tillich-Zémor Hash Algorithm:** Let A and B be the matrices:

$$A = \begin{pmatrix} X & 1 \\ 1 & 0 \end{pmatrix} \quad B = \begin{pmatrix} X & X+1 \\ 1 & 1 \end{pmatrix}$$

and let $\pi = \{0,1\} \rightarrow \{A, B\}$ be a mapping where $0 \rightarrow A$ and $1 \rightarrow B$. Then, the hash code of a binary message $x_1 x_2 \ldots x_k$ is the matrix product:

$$\pi(x_1)\pi(x_2)\ldots\pi(x_k)$$

where the computations are performed in the quotient field $F_{2^n} = F_2[X]/P_n(X)$ of 2^n elements.

Since the Tillich-Zémor hash uses the group $SL_2(G)$ to present a bit of input data and multiply matrices to produce the hash result, it has the concatenation property. This feature is of interest to the stream fuzzy hash algorithm presented in this chapter.

Note that this presentation only provides an overview of Tillich-Zémor hashing, so mathematical details and proofs are omitted. However, it should be noted that several attacks have targeted the collision resistance and pre-image resistance properties of the Tillich-Zémor hash function [10, 17]. Fortunately, the vulnerabilities have been addressed in recent research [12, 13]. As a result, the Tillich-Zémor hash is still strong enough for non-cryptographic purposes.

3. Challenges

As mentioned above, fuzzy hashing has been applied in many domains to determine the fundamental level of similarity between a pair of files. However, several challenges are encountered when applying fuzzy hashing to network traffic in order to identify similar files in transmission.

One challenge is that the file size is not known initially; typically, it cannot be determined until the end of a transmission. For example, if an HTTP session is non-keep-alive or chunked, the content-length region is optional [9]. This is not a problem for hash algorithms such as MD5 and SHA-1 that do not require the file size. However, the file size is a crucial parameter in a fuzzy hash implementation. This is because it is used as the input to produce a trigger value (or block size) for generating pieces for hashing.

Another challenge is one-way processing. In order to generate a signature of the proper length, fuzzy hashing must adjust the rolling hash trigger value and calculate it iteratively. Because network traffic often has high throughput (e.g., 10 Gb Ethernet), it is impractical to store the file content, so there is no opportunity for recomputation.

Unordered input also poses a challenge. State-of-the-art networking technologies split a file into fragments for transmission efficiency and agility, such as multi-thread downloading, P2P file sharing and cyber-locker services. Figure 1 shows a typical multi-thread transfer scenario, where the grey block represents a file fragment. At time t_3, any file offset in the range 0–3 M may appear. The fuzzy hash algorithm can only perform its computations from the file header or a reset point, meaning that unordered fragments must be buffered until all the preceding data has been received. In the worst case, almost the entire file has to be buffered, which makes the memory consumption unacceptable.

Finally, incomplete capture is a challenge. Files captured from network traffic are often incomplete due to packet loss and processing errors. Packet loss is a common problem in intrusion detection and data leakage protection systems because they cannot deal with bursts of network traffic or attacks. A human user may also compromise the integrity of a captured file, for example, by dragging the progress bar on an on-line video or manually terminating a transfer session.

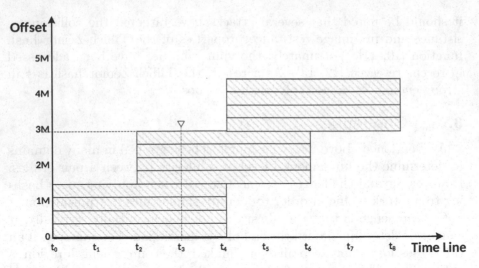

Figure 1. Example of an out-of-sequence transfer.

4.   Stream Fuzzy Hashing Algorithm

This section describes the design and implementation of the stream fuzzy hash algorithm.

4.1   Overview

As mentioned above, a fuzzy hash algorithm uses a rolling hash to generate reset points and a strong hash technique to produce hash values for each piece between two reset points. The stream fuzzy hash algorithm uses a context to record the computational result of each discrete data segment. Since unordered data segments are common and each segment generates a segment context, an interval tree [7] is used to efficiently organize the file segment contexts. The stream fuzzy hash algorithm uses the Tillich-Zémor hash instead of the Fowler-Noll-Vo hash, enabling each discrete segment to be buffered using no more than six bytes. A fine-grained adaptive mechanism is employed to generate a fuzzy hash signature via a one-way process. If a file is confirmed to be incomplete after transmission, the missing parts of a file do not affect other intervals because each signature is generated individually.

Figure 2 illustrates the three basic operations in the stream fuzzy hash algorithm:

- **Updating:** This operation updates the segment context with an incoming data segment. There are no limitations on the data size and starting offset.

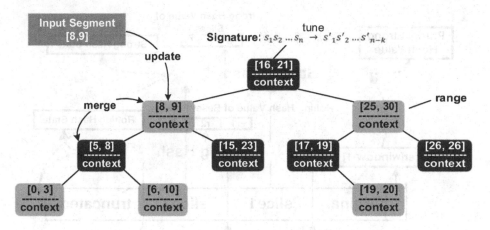

Figure 2. Stream fuzzy hash algorithm operations.

- **Merging:** This operation merges adjacent segment contexts when an input data fills the gap of the interval tree.

- **Tuning:** This operation tunes the block size during hashing if the current signature length exceeds the upper limit. This enables the generation of a signature with the proper length via a one-way process.

4.2 Segment Contexts

The stream fuzzy hash algorithm uses a context to represent the fuzzy hash computation of a data segment while it is being processed. The data segment, which may belong to any part of the original file, has no minimum length limit. As shown in Figure 3, a rolling hash is computed for each byte of a data segment with marginal data, sliced data or truncated data:

- Marginal data comprises data in the range before the first reset point to which a strong hash cannot be applied.

- Sliced data comprises data in the range between two reset points to which a strong hash can be applied.

- Truncated data comprises data in the range from the last reset point to the end to which a strong hash can be applied, but the result is an incomplete hash.

A hash algorithm must hash data from the beginning of a file. Since a strong hash cannot be applied to the marginal data portion before a reset

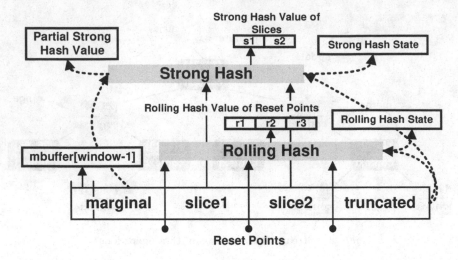

Figure 3. Data segment context.

point, the data is buffered in the context. However, buffering marginal data can cause a severe memory overload; in the worst case, the entire file has to be buffered. This is infeasible when hashing multi-gigabit files.

The Tillich-Zémor hash used in the stream fuzzy hash algorithm has two attractive features:

- **Concatenation Property:** Partial Tillich-Zémor hashing satisfies the concatenation property. This is because the Tillich-Zémor hash uses the group $SL_2(G)$ to present a bit of input data and multiplies matrices to produce the hash result. For example, the Tillich-Zémor hash of $d_1 d_2 d_3$ can be computed individually as follows:

$$hash_{TZ}(d_1 d_2 d_3) = hash_{TZ}(d_1 d_2) \, hash_{TZ}(d_3) \qquad (3)$$

This design is conducive to parallel computing. In the stream fuzzy hash algorithm, the marginal part is separated into a partial Tillich-Zémor hash value and a buffer of size $rolling window - 1$ (six bytes for each discrete data segment in the algorithm implementation).

- **Computational Efficiency:** Tillich-Zémor hashing is computationally efficient. Matrix multiplications are performed in the quotient field F_{2^n}, which are easily computed using a few shifts and XORs of 150-bit quantities per message bit. Because the stream fuzzy hash is a non-cryptographic hash function, the strong hash

Table 1. Context components.

Symbol	Description
mbuff	Marginal data buffer of context, may have a reset point
msize	Size of *mbuff* buffer, up to six bytes
ps	Partial strong hash value of unbuffered marginal data
$state_r$	Rolling hash state of truncated data
$state_s$	Strong hash state of truncated data, a matrix in group $SL_2(G)$
$array_r$	Array storing rolling hash values of reset points
$array_s$	Array storing strong hash matrices between reset points
$backup_s$	Backup of $array_s$ before the last tuning operation

result is reduced by recording only a Base64 encoding of the six least significant bits (LS6B [23]) of each hash value; $n = 8$ is used instead of the range 130–170 to define the quotient field F_{2^n}. The following irreducible polynomial is employed:

$$F_{2^n} = x^8 + x^4 + x^3 + x^2 + 1 \tag{4}$$

Table 1 presents the context components produced after Tillich-Zémor hashing.

4.3   Context Updating

An interval tree is employed for context updating. It is a tree data structure that holds intervals such that all the intervals that overlap with any given interval or point can be determined efficiently. In this work, the interval tree implementation is based on a red-black tree. This dynamic data structure enables the efficient insertion and deletion of an interval in $O(\log n)$. Because intervals in the tree cannot overlap, the query time is also $O(\log n)$.

When a new data segment is received, the stream fuzzy hash algorithm finds the segment context by querying the interval tree with the starting offset and ending offset of the data segment. If the new data segment overlaps with a previous data segment (e.g., due to retransmission), for convenience of computing, the duplicate portion of the new segment is discarded. The remaining input data is used to update the context as in the original fuzzy hash algorithm, except that the stream fuzzy hash algorithm replaces the Fowler-Noll-Vo hash with the Tillich-Zémor hash.

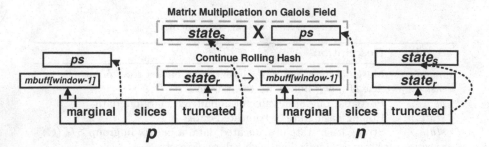

Figure 4.   Merging two adjacent contexts.

4.4   Context Merging

Discrete segment contexts in the interval tree could become adjacent
if an incoming segment fills the gap; this situation triggers the merging
operation. Merging adjacent segment contexts decreases the number of
nodes in the interval tree, thereby reducing the search time.

Figure 4 illustrates the process of merging two adjacent contexts p
and q. It is based on the associative property of the Tillich-Zémor hash,
where strong hash values of discrete fragments can be computed individually and concatenated when they are consecutive. Also, the rolling
hash is continued with the six bytes in *mbuff*.

4.5   Block Size Tuning

The number of reset points generated by the rolling hash function
is determined by three parameters: (i) file length; (ii) randomness (entropy) of file content; and (iii) block size. For ease of comparison, a
fuzzy hash should limit its signature length to a specific range. The
original fuzzy hash algorithm achieves this goal by iteratively adjusting
the initial block size and recomputing the hash value until the desirable
signature length is obtained. However, this method is infeasible for files
in transmission. On one hand, the file length may not be known before
the computation, which means that Equation (1) cannot be used to compute the initial block size. On the other hand, using a fixed block size
renders the signature length unpredictable and there is no opportunity
for recalculation in a one-way process.

The stream fuzzy hash algorithm employs an adaptive mechanism to
tune the block size during hashing. In the tuning process, the rolling
hash value of each reset point (stored in $array_r$) is tested by a new block
size, which is the current block size multiplied by a tuning factor k that

```
3072:Xk/maCm4yLYtRIFDFnVfHHqx1Jl+[0:432501]
7wr6Es3+TaKxONfbN[6130147:1160163]#12288:XCht
bFS6pHp9GZ[0:432501]1Z1hze2[6130147:1160163]
```

Figure 5. Example signature.

satisfies the following equation:

$$r \bmod (k \times b) = k \times b - 1 \Rightarrow r \bmod b = b - 1 \qquad (5)$$

Obviously, if an appropriate reset point exists for a new block size, then it must be one of the surviving reset points. This guarantees that the final signature is independent of the timing of the tuning operation. After a new reset point is selected, the temporary hash result is refined by multiplying each strong hash value between the reset points.

The tuning factor k also determines whether or not a partial file can be compared. As discussed later in this chapter, a larger tuning factor k generates a longer signature.

A tuning operation is chosen carefully. Let S be the expected signature length. Then, a tuning operation is deemed to be necessary when the current reset point number is larger than $k \times S$. In certain cases, the file entropy may be extremely low (e.g., a string of repeated characters); this yields rolling hash values with less diversity. Tuning the block size based on these hash values causes a dramatic reduction in the number of reset points. To avoid this, every rolling hash value is tested with a new block size before tuning is performed. The tuning operation is aborted when the number of eligible reset points is less than the expected signature length S.

4.6 Signature Generation

After all the transferred data is input, the stream fuzzy hash algorithm initiates an inorder traversal of the interval tree to visit every context. Each strong hash value is mapped to a Base64 space with LS6B and the data range is in the format [*left offset* − *right offset*] to mark gaps. To enhance partial file matching, the stream fuzzy hash signature for block size b is $k \times b$, where k is the tuning factor. Repeated computations are not necessary because the signature of a block of size b is a precedent result of $k \times b$, which is stored in $backup_s$ by the tuning operation. The format of the stream fuzzy hash signature is $blocksize{:}hash_b{:}\ hash_{\frac{b}{k}}[range_{start} - range_{end}]$. Figure 5 shows an example stream fuzzy hash signature with an expected length of 64, block size of 3,072 and tuning factor of 4.

Since the stream fuzzy hash algorithm uses the same rolling hash function as ssdeep, the two signatures should have the same length for the same input. Some files may not yield an appropriate number of pieces for any block size. The ssdeep algorithm addresses this problem by combining the last few pieces of a message into a single piece. In contrast, the stream fuzzy hash algorithm keeps all the pieces separate and generates a longer signature to preserve more details of the input.

5. Signature Comparison

The stream fuzzy hash signature length depends on the block size and entropy of the input. Since the file is determinate, it can be assumed that a missing number of signature characters is linearly correlated with the missing length. Since s_1 is generated by the transferred file, n_i spaces are used for each gap in s_1, where n_i is given by:

$$n_i = \left\lfloor \frac{GapBytes|s_1|}{ComputeBytes} \right\rfloor \tag{6}$$

Let s_1' be the filled signature and s_2 be the signature of the intact target file. The Levenshtein distance (LE) of s_1 and s_2 is refined using the following equation:

$$e(s_1, s_2) = LE(s_1', s_2) - \frac{|s_1|(|s_1'| - |s_1|)}{|s_1'|} \tag{7}$$

As in [14], the final match score in the range 0 to 100 is computed using the equation:

$$M = 100 - \frac{100\, e(s_1, s_2)}{|s_1'| + |s_2|} \tag{8}$$

A higher match score indicates a greater probability that the source files have blocks of values in common and in the same order.

5.1 Partial File Matching

Two stream fuzzy hash signatures are comparable if and only if they have been generated using the same block size. As described above, block size tuning is driven by the input data and missing data postpones the tuning operation. A partial file may have a different block size from its original file. In fact, although the stream fuzzy hash signature with block size b has length b/k, it is still possible that a partial file has a different block size.

Assume that the reset points are evenly distributed over the entire file and consider a partial file with integrity rate m and tuning factor

k. Then, the probability that the partial file can be compared with the original file is given by:

$$p = \frac{k^2 m - 1}{k^2 m - km} \quad m \in (0, 1], \ k \in \mathbf{N} \tag{9}$$

Note that the even distribution is used just to simplify the problem; in practice, the distribution of reset points is strongly correlated with the dataset. For the desired stream fuzzy hash signature length S, a complete file with final block size b has two reset point numbers, one is L_b and the other is $L_{\frac{b}{k}}$, which is the precedent result of final tuning. L_b satisfies the following inequality:

$$S \leq L_b \leq kS \tag{10}$$

The partial file signature is generated with block size b' and its reset point number $L_{b'}$ satisfy the following inequality:

$$S \leq L_{b'} \leq kS \tag{11}$$

The partial file is comparable when:

$$b' = b \text{ or } b' = \frac{b}{k}$$

Based on Equation (11), $b' = b$ is satisfied if and only if:

$$S \leq mL_b \leq kS \Leftrightarrow \frac{S}{m} \leq L_S \leq \frac{kS}{m} \tag{12}$$

Similarly, $b' = \frac{b}{k}$ is satisfied if and only if:

$$S \leq mL_{\frac{b}{k}} \leq kS \Leftrightarrow S \leq mkL_b \leq kS \Leftrightarrow \frac{S}{mk} \leq L_b \leq \frac{S}{m} \tag{13}$$

The concatenation of Equations (12) and (13) yields:

$$\frac{S}{mk} \leq L_b \leq \frac{kS}{m} \tag{14}$$

Since $kS \leq \frac{kS}{m}$, $m \in (0, 1]$, this inequility can be written as:

$$\frac{S}{mk} \leq L_b \leq kS \tag{15}$$

Since the reset points are evenly distributed, if L_b satisfies Equation (10), then the probability p that L_b also satisfies Equation (15) is given by:

$$p = \frac{kS - \frac{S}{mk}}{kS - S} = \frac{k^2 m - 1}{k^2 m - km} \tag{16}$$

A larger tuning factor k can be used to obtain a better comparison probability. However, this generates a longer signature that increases the storage requirements and comparison overhead. Therefore, it is necessary to trade-off comparison efficiency versus the ability to perform partial matching. For example, for a tuning factor $k = 3$ and integrity rate $m = 0.3$, the comparison probability is 0.94. Based on Equation (16), a partial file is always comparable when $m \geq \frac{1}{k}$. Equation (16) is also confirmed later in this chapter when the application of the stream fuzzy hash algorithm on a real dataset is evaluated.

It is important to note that the ability of the stream fuzzy hash algorithm to perform partial file matching not only enables a deep packet inspection application to identify incomplete captured files, but also allows hazardous transmissions to be stopped.

5.2   Comparing Massive Numbers of Files

Deep packet inspection and intrusion prevention systems maintain signature sets of valuable files and malicious software that run into millions of elements. For example, NIST's National Software Reference Library [15] maintains a large public database of known content that covers more than 50 million files. A naive solution for dealing with massive numbers of signatures is to compare all pairs by brute force, which is obviously impractical. Fortunately, the large-scale approximate matching problem has been well studied in connection with string similarity search [24]. The proposed approach adopts a classical method from the string similarity search domain to speed up comparisons.

The method involves indexing the stream fuzzy hash signatures using n-grams:

- **Index Creation:** An n-gram is a contiguous sequence of n characters from a sequence of text. The original design of the fuzzy hash algorithm requires that similar hashes must have a common 7-gram. Thus, each signature in the set is split into many 7-grams. Each 7-gram is treated as a key and the signature itself as a value. The key-value pair is then inserted into a hash table.

- **Signature Querying:** The signature to be queried is also split into several 7-grams. Every 7-gram in the hash table is examined to find candidate signatures. The 7-gram implementation was selected because the original fuzzy hash algorithm required similar hashes to have a common 7-gram. A threshold c is selected for querying based on a predefined similarity baseline. When a candidate signature shares more than c 7-grams with a query, then Equation (8) is applied to determine their similarity.

Table 2. Normalized TLSH distances versus ssdeep scores.

TLSH Distance	< 60	< 50	< 30	< 20	< 10	< 1
ssdeep Score	> 0	> 30	> 70	> 80	> 90	100

6. Evaluation

This section evaluates the correctness of the stream fuzzy hash algorithm and its hashing speed and signature length using the t5 corpus [19]. The t5 corpus contains 4,457 files and 1.8 GB of data. In particular, the stream fuzzy hash algorithm is compared against ssdeep v2.13 (sourceforge.net/projects/ssdeep), sdhash v3.4 (roussev. net/sdhash/sdhash.html) and TLSH v3.7 (github.com/trendmicro/ tlsh), which were the latest versions available when the experiments were conducted. ssdeep is the *de facto* standard for malware analysis domain; it is currently the only similarity digest supported by Virus-Total (www.virustotal.com). sdhash is a widely-applied fuzzy hash implementation. ssdeep and sdhash are both supported by NIST's National Software Reference Library [15]. TLSH [16] is an open-source fuzzy matching library developed by Trend Micro.

6.1 Correctness

The first set of experiments sought to evaluate the ability of the stream fuzzy hash algorithm to identify similarities between files compared with other fuzzy hash algorithms. Note that the results can contain false positives (non-similar pairs identified as similar) and false negatives (similar pairs not identified as similar).

The ssdeep, sdhash and stream fuzzy hash schemes score the similarity between two files in a range from 0 to 100, where 0 corresponds to a mismatch and 100 is a perfect match (or near-perfect match); a lower score means a lower confidence level. However, TLSH uses a different scheme to score the similarity between two digests – a distance score of zero means that the files are identical (or nearly identical) and increasing score values above zero represent greater distances between the files.

In order to compare the four schemes using a common basis, the TLSH distance was normalized to a range from 0 to 100 based on the results obtained by Oliver et al. [16]. Table 2 shows the TLSH distances and ssdeep scores with the proximate false positive and recall rates considered to be the same.

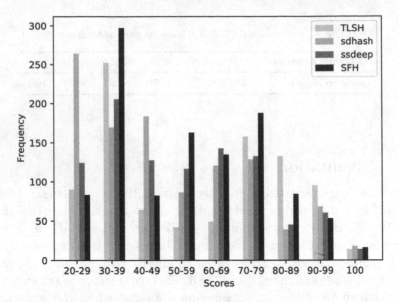

Figure 6. Distributions of the detected pairs in t5.

Figure 6 shows the distributions of the detected pairs obtained by the four hash algorithms.

Recall. Because there are $n(n-1)/2$ pairs in a set of n files, there are almost 10 million pairs in t5 and it is not possible to determine all the pairs by hand. Therefore, an assumption was made that only (true and false) positives would be detected by an algorithm and, if a correlation was not discovered by an algorithm, then it did not exist. This is appropriate because the intent was to compare the performance of the stream fuzzy hash algorithm relative to the other algorithms instead of in absolute terms based on the ground truth.

Drawing on previous research [16, 19], a strict threshold value was set for each algorithm. Below the threshold, all positive results were ignored as the false positive rate rose to 10%. The four algorithms detected 387 similar pairs in total using the threshold values listed in Table 3. Note that the TLSH threshold is not a score, but a distance.

Precision. The 387 unique file pairs were reviewed manually. A total of 256 pairs were identified as true positives. The following definition was employed to determine a correct similar pair (true positive):

- TXT and HML files that use the same boilerplate or share more than 10% common content.

Table 3. Comparison of the precision and recall rates for t5.

	Threshold	True Positives	False Positives	Precision	Recall
TLSH	20	146	95	60.6%	57.0%
sdhash	80	109	16	87.2%	42.6%
ssdeep	80	126	14	90.0%	49.2%
SFH	80	155	17	90.1%	60.5%
Total	–	256	131	–	–

- PDF, DOC, PPT and XLS files that are syntactically correlated beyond their formats.

- JPG and GIF files that have visual similarities.

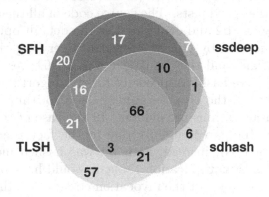

Figure 7. Intersections of the true positive sets for t5.

Note that the focus of the true positive definition is not on determining the percentage of similar pairs, but to compare the four algorithms on the same real-world dataset. Figure 7 shows the intersections of the true positive sets for the four algorithms. The overlaps vary because the thresholds are more rigorous than those in [19]. Note that, for readability, Figure 7 does not show all the intersections.

Table 3 compares the precision and recall rates of the four algorithms applied to t5. Note that the use of Tillich-Zémor hashing by the stream fuzzy algorithm does not decrease the precision and recall rates.

6.2   Hashing Speed for Sequential Inputs

This section evaluates the hashing speed of the stream fuzzy hash algorithm, which is a crucial property in deep packet inspection appli-

Table 4. Hashing speeds for sequential t5.

	MD5	TLSH	sdhash	ssdeep	SFH
Time (s)	2.62	149.53	60.70	31.03	27.01
Speed (MB/s)	703	12	30	59	68

cations. MD5 was added to the four evaluated algorithms to provide readers with an intuitive understanding of the relative speeds of the algorithms.

The computer used in the experiments had a multicore Intel Xeon E5-2698 v3 CPU with a frequency of 2.30 GHz. All the algorithms were executed on one logic core with hyper-threading enabled. The operating system used was Linux RedHat 7.2 (kernel 3.10). The t5 corpus was used as the input in the speed tests. The source code of all the algorithms was compiled with `gcc -O2` and configured as the default option. The MD5 results were generated by OpenSSL v1.0.0. Every algorithm processed the files sequentially and the chunk size was 4,096 bytes.

Table 4 shows the hashing speeds of the five algorithms. The performance gaps between the cryptographic hash algorithm (MD5) and the four fuzzy hash algorithms are evident. In the case of the stream fuzzy hash algorithm, the gap is mainly due to the fact that a block hash function was not used; instead, each bit was hashed individually. By querying the Galois multiplication table, it would have been possible to hash eight bits per call, but the invocation cost would still be more than a block hash. In the case of MD5 (and SHA1), an input message was broken up into 512-bit blocks, which `ssdeep` and the stream fuzzy hash algorithm processed byte-by-byte.

The `ssdeep` algorithm has to recalculate an n-byte input $O(\log n)$ times to find the proper block size and requires $O(n)$ time for each computation, making the total execution time $O(n \log n)$. For the stream fuzzy hash algorithm with block size tuning, no recalculation is needed after the block size is adjusted, so the total execution time is $O(n)$. However, the complexity of the Tillich-Zémor hash weakens this advantage.

6.3   Hashing Speed for Unordered Inputs

The stream fuzzy hash algorithm is designed to hash files in transmission. Therefore, the unordered input of a multi-thread download was simulated. The chunk size was 1,460 bytes in order to simulate a generic TCP payload. Sequential inputs are preconditions for all the other algo-

Table 5. Hashing speeds for t5 multi-thread downloading.

	4 Threads	8 Threads	16 Threads	Random Order
Speed (MB/s)	67.8	67.8	67.6	61.3
Space (KB)	2.39	3.40	4.90	310.20

rithms evaluated in this research; therefore, they could not be compared with the stream fuzzy hash algorithm in this set of experiments.

Table 5 shows the hashing speeds of the stream fuzzy hash algorithm for different numbers of concurrent fragments. No significant slowdown was observed even when the input order was completely random. The memory consumption in the case of sixteen concurrent fragments was 4.90 KB, which is practical for deep packet inspection applications.

6.4 Comparison of Incomplete Files

As discussed earlier, files captured from network traffic may be incomplete for a number of reasons. It has also been shown that, if the product of the integrity rate m and the tuning factor k is greater than one, then the partial file has a same block size as the original file. Experiments were conducted to validate this theoretical result on real data.

In the experiments, for each file in t5, only a portion of m (0 to 0.5) from the first byte of the file was provided as input to the stream fuzzy hash algorithm. If the block size of an incomplete file was the same as that of the complete file, then, by design, the two files were deemed to be comparable. The choice of the threshold score may be left to the user.

Figure 8 shows the incomplete file comparison probabilities obtained for various tuning factors k. Note that the results mostly fit with the predictions made by Equation (9).

6.5 Stream Fuzzy Hash Algorithm Deployment

This section discusses a case study involving the deployment of the stream fuzzy hash algorithm to provide an intuitive understanding of the practicalities involved in handling real network traffic. In the case study, the stream fuzzy hash algorithm was integrated as a plug-in in a carrier-grade deep packet inspection system to identify malicious Android app installation packages in network traffic. The stream fuzzy hash algorithm proved to be very flexible because it does not require buffering

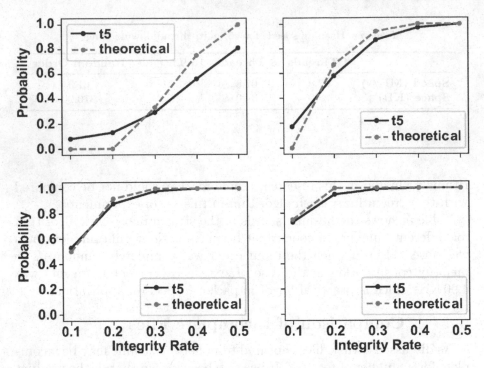

Figure 8. Incomplete file comparison probabilities for various tuning factors.

and segment rearrangement; as a result, it was readily integrated with the deep packet inspection system.

The following steps were involved in detecting malicious Android app installation packages:

- Malicious Android app samples were downloaded from VirusShare (`virusshare.com`). In all, 35,397 files with a total size of 52.82 GB were downloaded and a stream fuzzy hash algorithm signature was computed for each file.

- To enhance comparison efficiency, the 35,397 signatures were indexed as described in Section 5.2.

- The deep packet inspection system was deployed at an Internet service provider. It processed traffic at about 10 Gbps. The stream fuzzy hash algorithm plug-in identified app package transmissions based on their URLs. The plug-in provided the packets of the HTTP session as input to the stream fuzzy hash algorithm. Thus, a data structure containing the stream fuzzy hash algorithm signatures and URLs was created.

ALARM URL: res.cnappbox.com/libs/AdUnion50.apk
ALARM SFH: 6144:n6mrnX64nT0tgi8Wa5gQCY6xZyn+O5ClxXYDlnv+
 HA8VSNfbUTxx1AzeR3VKlxhO4DOaR[0:401688]
Sample SFH: 6144:n6mrnX64nT0tgi8Wa5gQCY6xZyn+O5ClxXYDlnv+
 HA8VSNfbUTxx1AzeR3VKlxhO4DOaR[0:401688]
File name: AdUnion50.apk
Detection ratio: 26 / 57
Analysis date: 2017-03-10 04:34:56 UTC (2 days, 22 hours ago)
Result: Android.Adware.Plankton.A

(a) Suck ads.

ALARM URL:ndl.mgccw.com/mu3/app/20140406/03/1396724471646/co
 m.tufan.soccerhighlights.apk?md5=5d37a2a6a6316ce464e
 0529e2b54d027
ALARM SFH:49152:bEDHVo6WMAfK9OWbUKyb8Ndibunp8zTyyV2Nk6/
 WrT4qYyvcj0bpfYlxcAOLVcJwESJuUymBMGiT1oxvK2yRP
 v6zuh8EFguWLQ29kSgrCWdvXawlKVXdWkNQVF6k34U4
 XC9KcF/jFlS4Hx0SB4S9+TNfm4Q+dG[0:6157658]
Sample SFH:49152:mV+SligSbZbGE3+5lmmFDVZMDBhtZgMDEhx2tSE
 DHVo6WMAfK9OWbUKyb8Ndibunp8zTyyV2Nk6/WrT4qYyv
 cj0bpfYlxcAOLVcJwESJuUymBMGiT1oxvK2yRPv6zuh8EFg
 uWLQ29kSgrCWdvXawl[0:6162751]
File name: com.tufan.soccerhighlights_21.apk
Detection ratio: 16 / 56
Analysis date: 2016-04-06 02:31:47 UTC (11 months, 1 week ago)
Result: Adware.AndroidOS.LeadBolt.a (v)

(b) Football Highlights app.

Figure 9. Malicious app packages detected by the stream fuzzy hash algorithm.

- The signature of the app in the previously-constructed index was queried to measure the similarity. An alarm was raised when the distance as computed by Equation (7) was less than a fixed threshold.

In the case study, the deep packet inspection system processed 184,688 Android APK downloads and raised fourteen alarms associated with ten apps. To verify the results, the suspected app packages were retrieved using the recorded URLs and uploaded to VirusTotal for further examination.

Four app packages were downloaded successfully and two of them were identified as malicious (true positives). Figure 9 shows the two malicious app packages. The Football Highlights app was detected based on similarity, a capability that is not provided by conventional detection methods. Visual checks of the two false positive app binaries revealed that their file contents were quite similar to malicious samples. They shared 95% mutual content and presumably used the same development components. Thus, the false positive results are due to the concepts underlying approximate matching as opposed to a flaw in the proposed stream fuzzy hash algorithm.

7.   Related Work

Fuzzy hash algorithms have evolved over the years. Kornblum [14] developed the ssdeep open-source fuzzy hash algorithm, which has been widely used to find similar files. Chen and Wang [6] and Breitinger and Baier [2] have proposed approaches for improving the performance of fuzzy hashing. However, these researchers and others have not considered the challenges involved in applying fuzzy hashing to network traffic.

The sdhash algorithm [18] has also been widely used for similar file detection. It attempts to find the features in each neighborhood that have the lowest empirical probability of being encountered by chance. Each of the selected features is hashed and placed in a Bloom filter. When a Bloom filter reaches its capacity, a new filter is created until all the features are accommodated. Thus, an sdhash similarity digest comprises a sequence of Bloom filters. The sdhash digest length is about 2 to 3% of the input length, which is different from the bounded digest of the fuzzy hash algorithm (64 to 128 bytes). Because it retains more details of the original file, sdhash is better at embedded object detection than ssdeep [19]. However, retaining these details increases the storage and comparson overhead. For example, sdhash generated digests totaling 101 GB for the 50 million files in the National Software Reference Library [15]; in contrast, ssdeep generated only 1.2 GB of digests for the same set of files.

MinHash [4] and SimHash [5] have been widely adopted in industry to identify potential duplicated text files. They belong to the family of locality-sensitive hash (LSH) algorithms. Shrivastava and Li [20] claim that MinHash outperforms SimHash on binary data, but it is curious that locality-sensitive hash algorithms are rarely employed in digital forensic applications. Harichandran et al. [11] note that a locality-sensitive hash algorithm attempts to map similar objects to the same bucket whereas approximate matching yields similarity digests that can be compared to a desired threshold. Several other open-source algorithms and tools, such as Nilsimsa [25], TLSH [16], MRSH-v2 [3], have also been developed to detect similar files.

8. Stream Fuzzy Hash Algorithm Limitations

Although the stream fuzzy hash algorithm has important security applications, it is by no means cryptographically secure. Additionally, the stream fuzzy hash algorithm cannot handle files that have been compressed or encrypted.

As a hash function, the stream fuzzy hash algorithm has two principal limitations:

- **Collisions:** Like the original fuzzy hash algorithm, the stream fuzzy hash algorithm maps a file chunk to a six-bit value. Therefore, the possibility always exists that two distinct chunks will map to the same hash. Moreover, two files that have identical stream fuzzy hash signatures could still be different files. Kornblum [14] has shown that the probability of a failure to detect a change is 2^{-12} to 2^{-6}. In the case of two completely-random files with signatures of length S, the probability of an exact match is $\left(2^{-6}\right)^S$. Of course, the expected signature length can be increased to reduce collisions, but this increases the time and space requirements.

- **Signature Comparison:** Meaningful signature comparisons can only be performed on files with the same block size. This is not a problem for different files that match approximately, but it is a useful feature because different block sizes means that two files are quite different in terms of size as well as content. In the case of partial file matching, as discussed in Section 5.1, the cut-off of $1/k$ of a file is always compared, where k is the tuning factor. Below this level, the block sizes are too different to make meaningful comparisons. Embedded file detection is similar because a small embedded object can be considered to be a portion of the larger object.

9. Conclusions

The stream fuzzy hash algorithm is specifically designed to hash files and file fragments captured from network traffic in real time. The algorithm leverages the context-triggered piecewise hashing concept, employs the Tillich-Zémor hash as a strong hash function and uses an interval tree to index the computed segment contexts, rendering it very effective at handling unordered and incomplete inputs. With block size tuning, the stream fuzzy hash algorithm can hash a data stream using one-way processing. Additionally, compared with the ssdeep algorithm, the stream fuzzy hash algorithm reduces the computational complexity from $O\left(n \log n\right)$ to $O\left(n\right)$.

Experimental results demonstrate that the stream fuzzy hash algorithm has a hashing speed of 68 MB/s per CPU core and consumes just 5 KB of memory per file. Moreover, compared with the other fuzzy hash algorithms, the precision and recall of the stream fuzzy hash algorithm are not compromised when processing unordered and incomplete inputs.

The integration of the stream fuzzy hash algorithm in a carrier-grade deep packet inspection system to identify malware in network traffic demonstrates the applications potential of the algorithm. A deep packet inspection system incorporating the stream fuzzy hash algorithm can identify valuable files (e.g., containing intellectual property) in egress traffic and malicious software in ingress traffic. Another significant benefit is the ability to perform partial file matching in the context of deep packet inspection – this makes it possible to identify files before transmission completes and to stop attacks before they can be realized.

Interested readers may access **github.com/mesasec/sfh** for the source code related to this project.

Acknowledgements

The authors wish to thank Vassil Roussev for his assistance with the evaluation conducted in this research. This research was supported in part by the National Key R&D Program of China under Grant No. 2016YFB0801304.

References

[1] F. Breitinger and I. Baggili, File detection on network traffic using approximate matching, *Journal of Digital Forensics, Security and Law*, vol. 9(2), pp. 23–35, 2014.

[2] F. Breitinger and H. Baier, Performance issues about context-triggered piecewise hashing, *Proceedings of the International Conference on Digital Forensics and Cyber Crime*, pp. 141–155, 2011.

[3] F. Breitinger and H. Baier, Similarity preserving hashing: Eligible properties and a new algorithm MRSH-v2, *Proceedings of the International Conference on Digital Forensics and Cyber Crime*, pp. 167–182, 2012.

[4] A. Broder, On the resemblance and containment of documents, *Proceedings of the Conference on Compression and Complexity of Sequences*, pp. 21–29, 1997.

[5] M. Charikar, Similarity estimation techniques from rounding algorithms, *Proceedings of the Thirty-Fourth Annual ACM Symposium on the Theory of Computing*, pp. 380–388, 2002.

[6] L. Chen and G. Wang, An efficient piecewise hashing method for computer forensics, *Proceedings of the First International Workshop on Knowledge Discovery and Data Mining*, pp. 635–638, 2008.

[7] T. Cormen, C. Leiserson, R. Rivest and C. Stein, *Introduction to Algorithms*, MIT Press, Cambridge, Massachusetts, 2009.

[8] Y. Elovici, A. Shabtai, R. Moskovitch, G. Tahan and C. Glezer, Applying machine learning techniques for detection of malicious code in network traffic, *Proceedings of the Annual Conference on Artificial Intelligence*, pp. 44–50, 2007.

[9] R. Fielding, J. Gettys, J. Mogul, H. Frystyk, L. Masinter, P. Leach and T. Berners-Lee, Hypertext Transfer Protocol – HTTP/1.1, RFC 2616, 1999.

[10] M. Grassl, I. Ilic, S. Magliveras and R. Steinwandt, Cryptanalysis of the Tillich-Zémor hash function, *Journal of Cryptology*, vol. 24(1), pp. 148–156, 2011.

[11] V. Harichandran, F. Breitinger and I. Baggili, Bytewise approximate matching: The good, the bad and the unknown, *Journal of Digital Forensics, Security and Law*, vol. 11(2), pp. 59–77, 2016.

[12] K. Joju and P. Lilly, Pre-image of Tillich-Zémor hash function with new generators, *Applied Mathematical Sciences*, vol. 7(85), pp. 4237–4248, 2013.

[13] K. Joju and P. Lilly, Improved form of Tillich-Zémor hash function, *International Journal of Theoretical Physics and Cryptography*, vol. 6, pp. 24–29, 2014.

[14] J. Kornblum, Identifying almost identical files using context-triggered piecewise hashing, *Digital Investigation*, vol. 3(S), pp. S91–S97, 2006.

[15] National Institute of Standards and Technology, National Software Reference Library (NSRL), Gaithersburg, Maryland (www.nist.gov/software-quality-group/national-software-reference-library-nsrl), 2018.

[16] J. Oliver, C. Cheng and Y. Chen, TLSH – A locality sensitive hash, *Proceedings of the Fourth Cybercrime and Trustworthy Computing Workshop*, pp. 7–13, 2013.

[17] C. Petit and J. Quisquater, Pre-images for the Tillich-Zémor hash function, *Proceedings of the International Workshop on Selected Areas in Cryptography*, pp. 282–301, 2010.

[18] V. Roussev, Data fingerprinting with similarity digests, in *Advances in Digital Forensics VI*, K. Chow and S. Shenoi (Eds.), Springer, Heidelberg, Germany, pp. 207–226, 2010.

[19] V. Roussev, An evaluation of forensic similarity hashes, *Digital Investigation*, vol. 8(S), pp. S34–S41, 2011.

[20] A. Shrivastava and P. Li, In defense of MinHash over SimHash, *Proceedings of the Seventeenth International Conference on Artificial Intelligence and Statistics*, pp. 886–894, 2014.

[21] X. Shu and D. Yao, Data leak detection as a service, *Proceedings of the International Conference on Security and Privacy in Communications Systems*, pp. 222–240, 2012.

[22] J. Tillich and G. Zémor, Hashing with SL_2, *Proceedings of the International Cryptology Conference*, pp. 40–49, 1994.

[23] A. Tridgell, `spamsum` (`github.com/tridge/junkcode/tree/master/spamsum`), 2002.

[24] S. Wandelt, J. Wang, S. Gerdjikov, S. Mishra, P. Mitankin, M. Patil, E. Siragusa, A. Tiskin, W. Wang, J. Wang and U. Lesser, State-of-the-art in string similarity search and join, *ACM SIGMOD Record*, vol. 43(1), pp. 64–76, 2014.

[25] Wikipedia, Nilsimsa Hash (`en.wikipedia.org/wiki/Nilsimsa_Hash`), 2018.

[26] C. Winter, M. Schneider and Y. Yannikos, F2S2: Fast forensic similarity search through indexing piecewise hash signatures, *Digital Investigation*, vol. 10(4), pp. 361–371, 2013.

Chapter 13

A NETWORK FORENSIC SCHEME USING CORRENTROPY-VARIATION FOR ATTACK DETECTION

Nour Moustafa and Jill Slay

Abstract   Network forensic techniques help track cyber attacks by monitoring and analyzing network traffic. However, due to the large volumes of data in modern networks and sophisticated attacks that mimic normal behavior and/or erase traces to avoid detection, network attack investigations demand intelligent and efficient network forensic techniques. This chapter proposes a network forensic scheme for monitoring and investigating network-based attacks. The scheme captures and stores network traffic data, selects important network traffic features using the chi-square statistic and detects anomalous events using a novel correntropy-variation technique. An evaluation of the network forensic scheme employing the UNSW-NB15 dataset demonstrates its utility and high performance compared with three state-of-the-art approaches.

Keywords: Network forensics, cyber attacks, correntropy-variation technique

1.   Introduction

Due to increases in the number and sophistication of network-based attacks, effective techniques and tools are required to conduct network forensic investigations. The WannaCry ransomware attack on Microsoft Windows systems in May 2017 infected more than 230,000 computers in about 150 countries [3]. Advanced techniques are required to analyze network traffic in order to identify potential security policy abuses and information assurance violations, along with their sources [4, 11, 27].

Although extracting network packets for forensic analysis is simple in theory, it requires accurate inspection due to large and diverse network flows [10, 11]. Accurate inspection requires an advanced feature

© IFIP International Federation for Information Processing 2018
Published by Springer Nature Switzerland AG 2018. All Rights Reserved
G. Peterson and S. Shenoi (Eds.): Advances in Digital Forensics XIV, IFIP AICT 532, pp. 225–239, 2018.
https://doi.org/10.1007/978-3-319-99277-8_13

selection method that selects only relevant information, including attack patterns. Identifying the key features supports the aggregation of network observations and investigations of the attack evidence [22].

Several commercial and open-source tools such as NetDetector Suite, PyFlag and Xplico have been developed to support network forensic investigations [6]. These tools collect and analyze flow information in network packets (e.g., IP addresses and port numbers) [9, 11]. However, this information is increasingly unreliable due to device mobility and dynamic IP address allocation [6]. Consequently, exploring dependencies of flow information without analyzing the transitions between flows is challenging.

This chapter presents a high-performance network forensic scheme that supports attack detection and attack source identification. The scheme relies on network traffic captures by the `tcpdump` sniffing tool and stores the captures in a MySQL database to support the analysis and aggregation of network traffic data. Important features related to anomalous activities are selected using the chi-square statistic [5, 15]. Following this, a correntropy-variation technique is applied to determine risk levels for normal and attack samples. The network forensic scheme is evaluated against three state-of-the-art approaches using the UNSW-NB15 dataset [18], which contains comprehensive data related to normal and abnormal network traffic.

2.   Related Work

Several network forensic schemes have been proposed in the literature [11, 13, 16]. A typical scheme captures and logs network traffic data in a database to support attack investigations. Important traffic attributes are stored, including flow identifiers such as source/destination IP addresses and ports, along with statistical information about packets such as packet size and packet interval. Sometimes, network packets are marked at routers as network flows move from senders to receivers [13]. A number of machine learning and heuristic approaches have been proposed for modeling and detecting network attacks [7, 11]. These approaches typically employ a training phase to distinguish between normal and suspicious samples, and a testing phase in which the training results are applied to normal and suspicious samples [18].

A number of network forensic frameworks have been proposed [4, 10–12, 27]. Khan et al. [12] have proposed a traceback-based framework for identifying the origins of network packets, especially in investigations of distributed denial-of-service (DDoS) and IP spoofing attacks. Wang et al. [27] have developed a topology-assisted deterministic packet marking technique based on IP traceback for tracking denial-of-service and distributed denial-of-service attacks. Cheng et al. [4] have employed a cloud-based traceback architecture to tackle access control challenges in cloud systems; their goal is to prevent users from requesting traceback information for malicious reasons.

Converged-network-based frameworks have been proposed for investigating attacks on VoIP communications networks [10, 11]. Attackers have been known to target voice communications by injecting attack packets or modifying legitimate voice packets. Ibrahim et al. [10] have designed an evidence model for investigating attacks on VoIP communications networks by framing hypotheses based on the collected information. He et al. [9] have modeled network vulnerabilities using evidence graphs; network vulnerability evidence and reasoning techniques are used to reconstruct malicious scenarios and backtrack to the network packets to obtain the original evidence. Attack-graph-based frameworks have been employed to discover and visualize possible attack paths in networks [11]. Liu et al. [14] have combined Bayesian inference and evidence graphs; their approach reduces false positive rates by computing the posterior probabilities in the evidence graphs.

Khan et al. [11] have proposed a framework that addresses the scalability problem by distributing network forensic servers and data agent systems [11]. Tafazzoli et al. [23] have proposed a network forensic architecture that comprises five components: (i) collection and indexing; (ii) database management; (iii) analysis; (iv) analysis results communication; and (v) database for collecting and analyzing anomalous patterns.

Finally, network intrusion detection and prevention frameworks are widely used to monitor traffic and mitigate attacks. Network forensic schemes based on intrusion detection typically employ static and dynamic inspection of network traffic to detect anomalies [16]. Wang et al. [26] have proposed hybrid attack detection and distributed forensic techniques for machine-to-machine networks; their techniques specifically combat distributed denial-of-service attacks.

Although existing network forensic frameworks support attack and other incident investigations, they are falling behind in their ability to cope with the large traffic volumes encountered in modern networks. Additionally, network forensic techniques require considerable time and space resources, especially when investigating large-scale distributed networks without aggregating relevant flows that include attack traffic. These challenges have motivated the development of the proposed network forensic scheme for monitoring and investigating network-based attacks. The scheme captures and stores network data, selects impor-

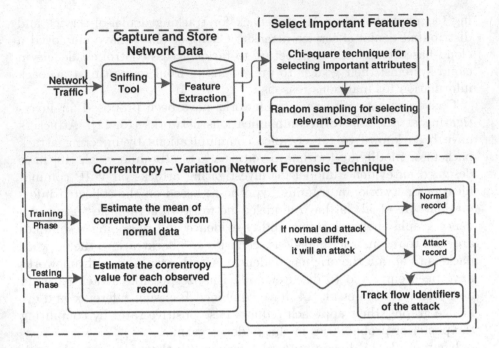

Figure 1. Proposed network forensic scheme.

tant network features using the chi-square statistic and helps investigate anomalous events using a novel correntropy-variation technique.

3.   Network Forensic Scheme

The key tasks in network forensics are to log attacker activities and apply forensic techniques to analyze the logged data. This provides valuable information about the attacker and the attack mechanism [8].

Figure 1 illustrates the proposed network forensic scheme. The first step captures network packets via sniffing and stores the captured network packets in a database to facilitate attack investigations. The second step selects important features and removes extraneous and redundant information that might negatively impact attack investigations. The third step investigates attacks and their origins using the novel correntropy-variation technique.

3.1   Capturing and Storing Network Data

The large numbers and volumes of flows in modern networks demand an aggregation method that starts from capturing packets to storing them in a database for supporting network forensic investigations. The tcpdump tool is used to capture raw packets from network interfaces.

Network traffic is sniffed at edge devices, in particular, ingress routers in order to collect relevant flows based on their source and destination IP addresses and ports, and protocols. Following this, several packet features are extracted from the captured traffic using the Bro and Argus tools (which were also used to create the UNSW-NB15 dataset).

Traffic data features for each network flow across the network are stored in a MySQL database. The flows are recorded using MySQL Cluster CGE, which can handle large-scale data and support real-time processing.

MySQL functions are used to aggregate data using multiple attributes of the traffic features. This addresses the drawbacks of tools such as Netflow and sFlow that can handle only one feature at a time. Attack path investigations are simplified when the flows between source and destination IP addresses are counted and tracked. For example, distributed denial-of-service attacks send large numbers of pings to disrupt a target; if these pings are monitored and counted, then the attack origins can be identified using the correntropy-variation technique discussed in Section 3.3.

The non-stationary properties of flows between IP addresses and ports are totaled by applying the `Count` function for all possible combinations of flows:

- `Select COUNT(*) as flows, srcip, dstip from network_data group by srcip, dstip;`

- `Select COUNT(*) as flows, srcip, srcport from network_data group by srcip, srcport;`

- `Select COUNT(*) as flows, dstip, dsport from network_data group by dstip, dsport, srcport;`

In the queries, `flows` is a network flow between two IP addresses, `srcip` is the source IP address, `dstip` is the destination IP address, `srcport` is the source port number and `dsport` is the destination port number. Each query retrieves the number of flows that match the specified features.

The collected flows should not include duplicated flows or missing flows. Consequently, uniform random sampling is employed to select arbitrary samples in which no flow is included more than once. All the samples have the same selection probability; moreover, a given pair of samples has the same probability of selection as the other pairs. Uniform random sampling reduces data bias and simplifies data analysis [25].

3.2   Feature Selection

In addition to selecting relevant network flows, it is necessary to identify the important features in the flows. The chi-square (χ^2) feature selection method [5, 15] is employed due to its simplicity and ease of implementation in real-time applications. The χ^2 statistic measures the occurrences of two independent variables associated with their class label, following which the highest ranked variable is selected as an important feature. The χ^2 statistic is computed using the following equation:

$$\chi^2 = \sum_i \frac{(O_i - E)^2}{E} \tag{1}$$

where O_i is the observed value of a sample flow and E is the expected value (mean) of the sample flows.

3.3   Correntropy-Variation Technique

The correntropy-variation technique combines the correntropy measure [2] to estimate the similarities between normal and attack samples, and a variation threshold for discovering attack samples. Correntropy is a nonlinear similarity function that reveals the relationships between normal and anomalous samples whereas variation estimates how different anomalous samples are from normal samples.

The correntropy V_σ of two random variables, f_1 and f_2, is estimated by:

$$V_\sigma(f_1, f_2) = E[\kappa_\sigma(f_1 - f_2)] \tag{2}$$

where σ is the kernel size, $E[.]$ is the expected value of the features and $K_\sigma(.)$ is the Gaussian kernel function computed using the equation:

$$K_\sigma(.) = \frac{1}{\sqrt{2\Pi} \cdot \sigma} \exp(-\frac{(.)^2}{2\sigma^2}) \tag{3}$$

The joint probability density function ($P_{F_1, F_2}(f_1, f_2)$) is not identified. However, a finite number of samples $\{f_i, f_j\}_{i,j=1}^M$ are known. Consequently, the correntropy is computed using the equation:

$$\hat{V}_{M,\sigma}(A, B) = \frac{1}{M} \sum_{i,j=1}^M K_\sigma(f_i - f_j) \tag{4}$$

In order to apply the correntropy measure to multivariate network data, the correntropy is computed for normal and malicious samples.

The mean of the correntropy values of normal samples $corpy^{normal}$ is computed during the training phase using the following equation:

$$\mu(corpy^{normal}) = \frac{1}{N} \cdot corpy^{normal} \tag{5}$$

where N is the number of normal samples.

During the testing phase, the correntropy value $corpy^{test}$ is estimated for each sample using Equations (4) and (5).

A baseline between $\mu(corpy^{normal})$ and each $corpy^{test}$ value is created using the standard deviation measure δ, which estimates the amount of variation between the mean of the normal correntropy values and the correntropy values of test samples. If the absolute value of the variation is greater than or equal 2δ (i.e., two standard deviations), then the test sample is considered to be an attack; otherwise, it is normal:

- **Attack:** if $|\mu(corpy^{normal}) - corpy^{test}| \geq 2\delta$.

- **Normal:** otherwise.

This is because, at a distance of two standard deviations or more, the test sample is so far from the dispersion of normal correntropy values that it does not fit within the distribution of normal samples.

The absolute variation $|\mu(corpy^{normal}) - corpy^{test}|$ is normalized to obtain a risk level for each sample in the range $[0, 1]$. The normalized risk level RL of a (normal or test) sample is given by:

$$RL = \frac{|corpy^{normal/test} - min(corpy^{normal})|}{max(corpy^{normal}) - min(corpy^{normal})} \tag{6}$$

where $min(corpy^{normal})$ and $max(corpy^{normal})$ are the minimum and maximum correntropy values over all the normal samples, respectively. The risk levels, which specify the extent to which anomalous samples deviate from normal samples, enable the identification of attack samples with low false alarm rates.

The flow identifiers of attack samples are associated with their estimated risk levels. If the risk level has a value of one, then the attack poses the greatest risk to an organization because it sends many flows to a specific destination (e.g., a distributed denial-of-service attack). An attack sample with a risk level of zero poses the least risk to the organization. Table 1 provides information about selected samples in the UNSW-NB15 dataset along with their risk levels. Note that anomalous samples (i.e., attacks) have higher risk levels of at least 0.5 compared with normal samples that have risk levels less than 0.5.

Table 1.   Selected samples with their risk levels.

Source IP Address	Source Port	Dest. IP Address	Dest. Port	Protocol	Label	Risk Level
149.171.126.14	179	175.45.176.3	33159	TCP	0	0.23
175.45.176.1	15982	149.171.126.14	5060	UDP	0	0.11
175.45.176.3	63888	149.171.126.14	179	TCP	0	0.25
175.45.176.2	7434	149.171.126.16	80	TCP	1	0.83
175.45.176.0	15558	149.171.126.13	179	TCP	1	0.72

4.   Results and Discussion

This section presents the results and discusses their significance.

4.1   Dataset and Evaluation Metrics

The performance of the proposed scheme was evaluated using the UNSW-NB15 dataset because it comprises a large collection of contemporary legitimate and anomalous activities. The dataset contains approximately 100 GB of network packets and about 2,540,044 feature vectors maintained in four CSV files. Each vector contains 47 features and the class label. The data is categorized into ten classes, one class corresponding to normal activities and nine classes corresponding to security events and malware activities: (i) analysis; (ii) denial-of-service; (iii) exploits; (iv) fuzzers; (v) generic; (vi) reconnaissance; (vii) backdoors; (viii) shellcode; and (ix) worms.

The performance of the proposed scheme for identifying and tracking attacks was evaluated using two metrics: (i) accuracy; and (ii) false alarm rate (FAR):

- **Accuracy:** The accuracy is the percentage of legitimate and suspicious samples that are correctly identified:

$$Accuracy = \frac{(TP + TN)}{TP + TN + FP + FN} \times 100 \qquad (7)$$

- **False Alarm Rate:** The false alarm rate is the percentage of normal and malicious samples that are incorrectly classified:

$$False\ Alarm\ Rate = \frac{FP + FN}{TP + TN + FP + FN} \times 100 \qquad (8)$$

Note that TP and TN are the numbers of true positives and true negatives, respectively; and FP and FN are the numbers of false positives and false negatives, respectively.

Table 2.   Features selected for investigating attacks.

Weight	Feature	Feature Description
0.592	sbytes	Source to destination bytes
0.558	swin	Source TCP window advertisement
0.552	dttl	Destination to source time to live
0.551	stcpb	Source TCP sequence number
0.550	dtcpb	Destination TCP sequence number
0.549	dwin	Destination TCP window advertisement
0.513	smean	Mean flow packet size transmitted by source
0.489	sload	Source bits per second

4.2   Pre-Processing and Feature Selection

The software used in the evaluation was developed using the R language and executed on a workstation with an i7 CPU and 16 GB RAM running the Windows 7 operating system. Three random samples, with 100,000, 200,000 and 300,000 items, were selected from the UNSW-NB15 dataset to extract important features using the chi-square statistic and investigate attack activities using the correntropy-variation technique. Table 2 lists the eight features that were selected based on their high chi-square values.

Feature vectors with five flow identifiers (i.e., source IP address, source port, destination IP address, destination port and protocol type) were selected using the uniform random sampling technique.

Table 1 shows five samples selected from the USNW-NB15 dataset, along with their computed risk levels. The risk levels were subsequently associated with their flow identifiers to analyze the evidence for attack activity. The chi-square statistic and uniform random sampling ensured the selection of features and samples that reflected legitimate and suspicious network activities.

4.3   Network Forensic Evaluation

Correntropy differentiates between legitimate and attack samples; this is because it estimates the nonlinear similarities between the samples. Figure 2 shows that the correntropy values of normal samples have fewer peaks than the correntropy values for attack samples. Thus, different attack types could be identified and investigated using the five flow identifiers associated with their risk levels.

Table 3 shows the results of evaluating the performance of the correntropy-variation technique. The evaluation metrics are the overall accu-

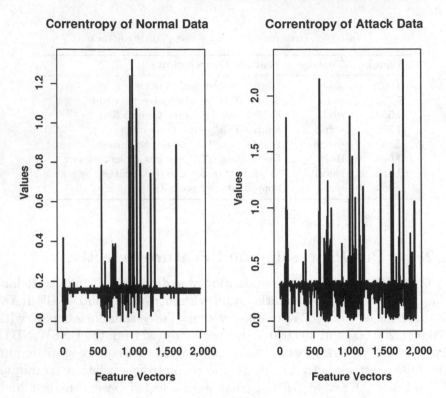

Figure 2.   Correntropy of normal and attack samples.

Table 3.   Performance of the correntropy-variation technique.

Sample Size	Accuracy	FAR
100,000	94.31%	5.69%
200,000	95.72%	4.28%
300,000	95.98%	4.02%

racy and false alarm rate for the features listed in Table 2. Note that
the overall accuracy improves from 94.31% to 95.98% while the overall
false alarm rate falls from 5.69% to 4.02% as the sample size increases
from 100,000 to 300,000.

Table 4 shows that the proposed scheme recognizes different attack
samples in the dataset. Specifically, the accuracy of detecting normal
samples increases from 92.12% to 93.29% as the sample size increases
from 100,000 to 300,000. Also, the accuracy of detecting malicious samples increases from a low of 45.82% for worms to a high of 97.55% for
denial-of-service attacks.

Table 4. Comparison of accuracy values for three sample sizes.

Sample Types	Sample Size 100,000	Sample Size 200,000	Sample Size 300,000
Normal	92.12%	93.16%	93.29%
Analysis	88.26%	89.45%	90.22%
Denial-of-Service	95.71%	95.13%	97.55%
Exploits	76.47%	77.82%	77.19%
Fuzzers	64.33%	65.23%	66.28%
Generic	83.56%	87.52%	88.87%
Reconnaissance	58.38%	59.24%	60.32%
Backdoors	54.42%	71.23%	72.42%
Shellcode	65.76%	66.48%	65.98%
Worms	45.82%	45.92%	48.87%

The results obtained with the proposed correntropy-variation network forensic (CV-NF) technique are compared against those obtained with three state-of-the art approaches, namely the filter-based support vector machine (FSVM) technique [1], multivariate correlation analysis (MCA) technique [24] and artificial immune system (AIS) technique [20] using the UNSW-NB15 dataset. The results in Figure 3 reveal that the proposed technique outperforms the other three techniques in terms of accuracy as well as the false alarm rate.

The correntropy-variation network forensic technique produces the best results because it estimates the correntropy values for normal and test samples, and subsequently identifies samples that are more than two standard deviations away from the mean of normal samples as attacks. The filter-based support vector machine and artificial immune system techniques undergo training and validation with large numbers of normal and malicious samples. In contrast, the multivariate correlation analysis technique relies on correlations between attributes using a Gaussian mixture model; however, it may not precisely identify the boundaries between normal and malicious mixture models [19].

5.   Conclusions

The network forensic scheme described in this chapter is designed for monitoring and investigating network-based attacks in real-time. The scheme involves three steps: capturing and storing network traffic data, selecting important traffic features and investigating anomalous traffic. The chi-square statistic and uniform random sampling are used to select sample features and samples, respectively; and the novel correntropy-variation technique is leveraged to identify samples with high risk levels

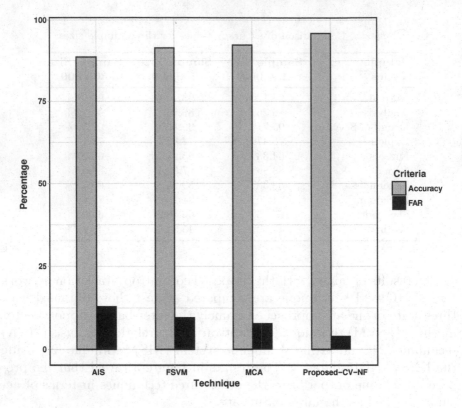

Figure 3. Comparison of the performance of the four techniques.

based on their flow identifiers (potential attacks). The case study employing the UNSW-NB15 dataset demonstrates the efficiency and efficacy of the network forensic scheme, especially its higher accuracy and lower false alarm rate compared with three state-of-the-art network attack detection approaches. Future research will attempt to re-target the proposed network forensic scheme for use in cloud and fog computing environments.

References

[1] M. Ambusaidi, X. He, P. Nanda and Z. Tan, Building an intrusion detection system using a filter-based feature selection algorithm, *IEEE Transactions on Computers*, vol. 65(10), pp. 2986–2998, 2016.

[2] R. Bao, H. Rong, P. Angelov, B. Chen and P. Wong, Correntropy-based evolving fuzzy neural system, to appear in *IEEE Transactions on Fuzzy Systems*.

[3] R. Brandom, A new ransomware attack is infecting airlines, banks and utilities across Europe, *The Verge*, June 27, 2017.

[4] L. Chen, D. Divakaran, A. Ang, W. Lim and V. Thing, FACT: A framework for authentication in cloud-based IP traceback, *IEEE Transactions on Information Forensics and Security*, vol. 12(3), pp. 604–616, 2017.

[5] Y. Chen and M. Chen, Using chi-square statistics to measure similarities for text categorization, *Expert Systems with Applications*, vol. 38(4), pp. 3085–3090, 2011.

[6] N. Clarke, F. Li and S. Furnell, A novel privacy preserving user identification approach for network traffic, *Computers and Security*, vol. 70, pp. 335–350, 2017.

[7] A. Diamah, M. Mohammadian and B. Balachandran, Network security evaluation method via attack graphs and fuzzy cognitive maps, *Proceedings of the Fourth International Conference on Intelligent Decision Technologies*, vol. 2, pp. 433–440, 2012.

[8] B. Hazarika and S. Medhi, Survey of real-time security mechanisms in network forensics, *International Journal of Computer Applications*, vol. 151(2), 2016.

[9] J. He, C. Chang, P. He and M. Pathan, Network forensic method based on evidence graph and vulnerability reasoning, *Future Internet*, vol. 8(4), article no. 9, 2016.

[10] M. Ibrahim, M. Abdullah and A. Dehghantanha, VoIP evidence model: A new forensic method for investigating VoIP malicious attacks, *Proceedings of the International Conference on Cyber Security, Cyber Warfare and Digital Forensics*, pp. 201–206, 2012.

[11] S. Khan, A. Ghani, A. Wahab, M. Shiraz and I. Ahmad, Network forensics: Review, taxonomy and open challenges, *Journal of Network and Computer Applications*, vol. 66, pp. 214–235, 2016.

[12] S. Khan, M. Shiraz, A. Wahab, A. Ghani, Q. Han and Z. Rahman, A comprehensive review of the adaptability of network forensic frameworks for mobile cloud computing, *The Scientific World Journal*, vol. 2014, article id. 547062, 2014.

[13] Y. Li, Y. Wang, F. Yang, S. Su and D. Yan, Deterministic packet marking based on the coordination of border gateways, *Proceedings of the Second International Conference on Education Technology and Computers*, vol. 2, pp. 154–161, 2010.

[14] C. Liu, A. Singhal and D. Wijesekera, A probabilistic network forensic model for evidence analysis, in *Advances in Digital Forensics XII*, G. Peterson and S. Shenoi (Eds.), Springer, Heidelberg, Germany, pp. 189–210, 2016.

[15] H. Liu and H. Motoda, *Computational Methods of Feature Selection*, Chapman and Hall/CRC, Boca Raton, Florida, 2008.

[16] J. Liu, G. Tian and S. Zhu, Design and implementation of a network forensic system based on intrusion detection analysis, *Proceedings of the International Conference on Control Engineering and Communications Technology*, pp. 689–692, 2012.

[17] W. Liu, P. Pokharel and J. Principe, Correntropy: Properties and applications in non-Gaussian signal processing, *IEEE Transactions on Signal Processing*, vol. 55(11), pp. 5286–5298, 2007.

[18] N. Moustafa and J. Slay, UNSW-NB15: A comprehensive data set for network intrusion detection systems (UNSW-NB15 Network Data Set), *Proceedings of the Military Communications and Information Systems Conference*, 2015.

[19] N. Moustafa, J. Slay and G. Creech, Novel geometric area analysis technique for anomaly detection using trapezoidal area estimation in large-scale networks, to appear in *IEEE Transactions on Big Data*.

[20] P. Saurabh and B. Verma, An efficient proactive artificial immune system based anomaly detection and prevention system, *Expert Systems with Applications*, vol. 60, pp. 311–320, 2016.

[21] A. Shalaginov and K. Franke, Big data analytics by automated generation of fuzzy rules for network forensic readiness, *Applied Soft Computing*, vol. 52, pp. 359–375, 2017.

[22] M. Srinivas and A. Sung, Identifying significant features for network forensic analysis using artificial intelligence techniques, *International Journal of Digital Evidence*, vol. 1(4), 2003.

[23] T. Tafazzoli, E. Salahi and H. Gharaee, A proposed architecture for network forensic systems in large-scale networks, *International Journal of Computer Networks and Communications*, vol. 7(4), pp. 43–56, 2015.

[24] Z. Tan, A. Jamdagni, X. He, P. Nanda and R. Liu, A system for denial-of-service attack detection based on multivariate correlation analysis, *IEEE Transactions on Parallel and Distributed Systems*, vol. 25(2), pp. 447–456, 2014.

[25] S. Thompson, *Sampling*, John Wiley and Sons, Hoboken, New Jersey, 2012.

[26] K. Wang, M. Du, Y. Sun, A. Vinel and Y. Zhang, Attack detection and distributed forensics in machine-to-machine networks, *IEEE Network*, vol. 30(6), pp. 49–55, 2016.

[27] X. Wang and X. Wang, Topology-assisted deterministic packet marking for IP traceback, *Journal of China Universities of Posts and Telecommunications*, vol. 17(2), pp. 116–121, 2010.

IV

CLOUD FORENSICS

Chapter 14

A TAXONOMY OF CLOUD ENDPOINT FORENSIC TOOLS

Anand Kumar Mishra, Emmanuel Pilli and Mahesh Govil

Abstract   Cloud computing services can be accessed via browsers or client applications on networked devices such as desktop computers, laptops, tablets and smartphones, which are generally referred to as endpoint devices. Data relevant to forensic investigations may be stored on endpoint devices and/or at cloud service providers. When cloud services are accessed from an endpoint device, several files and folders are created on the device; the data can be accessed by a digital forensic investigator using various tools. An investigator may also use an application programming interface made available by a cloud service provider to obtain forensic information from the cloud related to objects, events and file metadata associated with a cloud user. This chapter presents a taxonomy of the forensic tools used to extract data from endpoint devices and from cloud service providers. The tool taxonomy provides investigators with an easily searchable catalog of tools that can meet their technical requirements during cloud forensic investigations.

Keywords: Cloud computing, forensics, tool taxonomy

1.   Introduction

In 1999, the U.S. National Institute of Standards and Technology (NIST) [33] initiated the Computer Forensic Tool Testing (CFTT) Program to develop specifications and test methods for digital forensic tools. The tool specifications, test procedures, test criteria, test sets and test hardware require descriptions of tool functionality. NIST subsequently developed a tool catalog based on the specifications targeted for tool developers and users. However, to enhance the use of the catalog by the digital forensics community, a taxonomy of cloud forensic tools is required that describes the tool attributes desired by users. The taxonomy should provide a searchable catalog of forensic tools, enabling

© IFIP International Federation for Information Processing 2018
Published by Springer Nature Switzerland AG 2018. All Rights Reserved
G. Peterson and S. Shenoi (Eds.): Advances in Digital Forensics XIV, IFIP AICT 532, pp. 243–261, 2018.
https://doi.org/10.1007/978-3-319-99277-8_14

digital forensic investigators to find specific tools that can fulfill their technical requirements during cloud forensic investigations.

This chapter presents a taxonomy of cloud forensic tools. The taxonomy classifies tools into two broad categories. The first category comprises tools that are applied to local endpoint devices to collect artifacts that remain after cloud services have been used by web browsers or client applications. The second category comprises tools that leverage cloud application programming interfaces (APIs) and require user credentials to extract data and metadata from cloud user accounts. Several forensic tools claim to extract cloud-specific data from endpoint devices and cloud service providers. Therefore, this chapter also highlights the data that can be extracted from endpoint devices and via APIs from cloud service providers. Additionally, the chapter describes a case study involving data extraction from an endpoint device that used the OneDrive cloud service.

2.   Cloud Forensics

Computer and mobile device forensic tools can be applied to extract and analyze cloud data artifacts residing on endpoint devices. Cloud service providers provide APIs for accessing cloud data; these APIs can also be used to collect data during forensic investigations.

Cloud forensics is the application of digital forensic science in cloud computing environments, and involves hybrid forensic approaches such as virtual, network and live forensics [44]. Cloud forensics is not possible without the involvement of the various cloud actors – service providers, consumers, brokers, carriers and auditors. Zawoad and Hasan [47] state that computer forensic principles and procedures can be applied in cloud computing environments. According to NIST [35], "[c]loud computing forensic science is the application of scientific principles, technological practices and derived and proven methods to reconstruct past cloud computing events through the identification, collection, preservation, examination, interpretation and reporting of digital evidence." Cloud forensics also faces novel legal issues arising from the multi-jurisdiction and multi-tenancy features of the cloud.

3.   Taxonomy of Cloud Endpoint Forensic Tools

Cloud services are accessed via client software, a web browser or an app from a personal computer or mobile device. When cloud services are used, multiple files and folders (e.g., synchronized files and folders, prefetch files and cached files) may be created on the endpoint device. Digital forensic tools can be used to collect and analyze the artifacts from storage devices and physical memory. When a web browser or mobile device app is used to connect to cloud services and perform upload, download and data access operations, logs and other useful information are generated that can identify the user and provide details about user activities.

Cloud APIs made available by cloud service providers may be used to access evidence in the cloud upon presenting user credentials. The APIs provide valuable cloud user information such as file and folder contents, metadata (file ID, size, name, version, date and time and file type) and details about file and folder operations. Figure 1 presents a taxonomy of cloud endpoint forensic tools.

3.1 Evidence in Endpoint Devices

This section discusses the potential sources of cloud-related digital evidence in cloud endpoint devices.

- **Client Software:** Cloud client software is installed on local devices to interact with cloud service provider resources. An investigator may check and verify the software using hash values. A shortcut may also be created when client software is installed. The shortcut may contain a link to locally-stored data.

- **Synchronized File Folder:** This folder is created on a local device when client software is installed. The folder may automatically synchronize with a cloud server when the endpoint device is connected to the Internet.

- **Recycle Bin:** The recycle bin folder is an important place to check for deleted data in a forensic investigation. Cloud-related data may be recoverable even after synchronized data has been deleted. Two files, $I and $R, are created when data is deleted from the recycle bin folder. These files are very important from the forensic point of view. $I contains file metadata such file size, path, date and time whereas $R enables the deleted data to be restored [22].

- **Directory:** A directory maintains information about the files and folders it holds, including file/folder names, sizes and creation dates and times. The directory listing of a cloud client folder provides useful information in a forensic investigation.

- **Dynamic Link Library Files:** Dynamic link library files contain code, data and resources that enable the execution of programs in a Windows environment [30]. These files are important in a

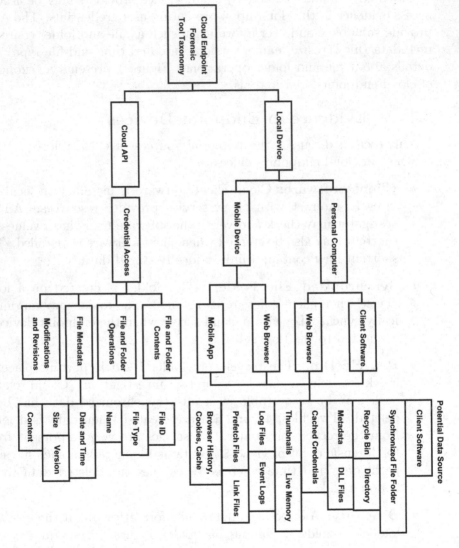

Figure 1.   Endpoint forensic tool taxonomy.

forensic investigation. For example, an experimental installation of OneDrive on a Windows 10 system resulted in the creation of more than 122 dynamic link library files.

- **Cached Credentials:** Credentials may be stored in the system credential manager, which records the user name, password, system type and network address. The credentials, which are stored on the hard drive, may be protected by the Data Protection Application Programming Interface (DPAPI) [34].

- **Thumbnails:** Thumbnails are stored in a database when images are uploaded or downloaded from the cloud. The thumbnail database can be very useful in a forensic investigation [34].

- **Live Memory:** Information about running processes can be found in live memory (RAM). Live memory analysis using the Volatility tool during the execution of OneDrive yielded its `*.exe` file, process ID, date and time. The names of dynamic link library files related to the OneDrive application were also found in live memory.

- **Log Files:** Multiple files and folders are created on an endpoint device during client software installation. Moreover, a log file is maintained when user data is synchronized with a cloud service provider. These log files keep records of communicated data such as file size, file creation time and file edit time.

- **Event Logs:** Windows systems maintain various event logs. A forensic investigator may find useful information about application events, security events, system events and hardware events in these logs.

- **Prefetch Files:** A prefetch file is created whenever an application is started [28]. The prefetch files may contain valuable information pertaining to applications.

- **Link Files:** A link file is a shortcut file that is used to open an application in a Windows system. The file stores information about the file path, size, MAC time and address [27]. When a cloud client application is installed, a shortcut file is created to open the folder and synchronize the data.

- **Browser History:** The browser history records the websites visited, visit times and user profile information. Cloud services are often accessed via web browsers such as Internet Explorer, Mozilla

Firefox, Google Chrome, Safari, Opera and Microsoft Edge. When a website is visited, the browser history records key information unless the URL is visited in the unidentified (i.e., incognito or private) mode. Analysis of the URLs in the browser history provides useful information about the cloud services accessed and user IDs, along with icon files.

- **Browser Cookies:** When a website is visited, cookie files created by the web browser are stored on the endpoint device; these files contain personally-identifiable information and user preferences. A forensic investigator can extract user names, addresses, email, user IDs, etc. from browser cookies.

- **Browser Cache:** The browser cache holds temporary Internet files, including downloaded HTML files, style sheets, scripts and images from web servers for faster loading of web pages. The cache information is useful for browser fingerprinting.

3.2 Evidence Recoverable via Cloud APIs

Cloud service providers supply cloud APIs that support data collection from cloud services. A forensic investigator can obtain data directly from a cloud service provider using the appropriate API and credentials (if needed).

Cloud APIs also enable computer programs to interact with cloud data. Several cloud service providers supply APIs that enable third parties to build applications that can be integrated with their cloud services. While these APIs were not created for forensic purposes, they provide very useful information in forensic investigations. For example, the Google Drive API v3 [14] manages Google Drive files using operations such as file uploading, downloading, searching, detecting changes and updating file sharing permissions. The extractable information includes the list of files, file metadata (file name, file ID, file type, date and time, size, version, etc.), thumbnails and revision history. File and folder metadata include file and folder names, special notifications, and editing and deletion information.

The following data extracted using cloud APIs is valuable in forensic investigations:

- **File Content:** Cloud APIs can provide the contents of specified files. Google Drive provides this functionality via the DriveFile and DriveFolder interfaces [15].

- **Metadata:** Metadata is data about a file or folder. Google Drive provides more than ten operations (e.g., copy, create, delete, get, list and update) that create file metadata. The metadata includes file name, size, ID, hash value, extension, edit times (creation, update and modification) and location. A forensic investigator would be very interested in knowing when files were viewed, modified and shared.

■ **Operations Log:** Cloud storage services enable users to perform operations such as uploading, downloading, editing, sharing, deleting and moving files and folders. These operations generate logs with information such as the name of the downloaded file, user name, file ID, hash value, file size and download details.

■ **Revision History:** Most of the time, when a user updates a file with a newer version, the file is directly modified in the cloud. The cloud service may maintain a revision history, which enables a user to revert to previous versions of a file. A cloud API may be used to obtain revision information for analyzing files and folders.

4.   Cloud Endpoint Forensic Approaches

Tables 1 through 3 summarize the principal cloud endpoint forensic approaches. Each table has five columns. The first column identifies the researchers who presented or developed the approaches. The remaining columns identify the endpoint devices used by the researchers to access cloud services, the specific cloud services accessed during their experiments, and the cloud service access methods (web browser and desktop/mobile app).

Roussev et al. [42, 43] have presented a method for collecting data using cloud APIs from services such as Dropbox, Box, Google Drive, Microsoft OneDrive and Google Docs. They employed a dispatcher written in Python (`kumodd.py`) on top of the cloud APIs to collect and filter data from cloud services that require user credentials for access. The extracted information included the file download date, application version, username, file name, file ID, file size, remote path, download path, revisions and hash values, and timestamps.

5.   Cloud Endpoint Device Forensic Tools

This section discusses the digital forensic tools that may be used to extract and analyze data residing in endpoint devices that have accessed cloud services via web browsers or client applications. The following information about forensic tools for cloud endpoint devices is based on vendor documentation:

Table 1. Cloud endpoint forensic approaches.

Researchers	Endpoint Devices	Cloud Services Accessed	Cloud Service Access Method	
			Web Browser	Desktop/Mobile App
Dykstra and Sherman [7]	Windows 2008 R2 Server	Amazon EC2	N/A	N/A
Chung et al. [4]	Windows PC, Mac, iPhone, Android	Amazon S3, Google Docs, Dropbox, Evernote	Internet Explorer, Mozilla Firefox	Dropbox Client, Evernote Client
Marturana et al. [26]	Windows PC	Google Docs, Flickr, PicasaWeb, Dropbox	Internet Explorer, Mozilla Firefox, Google Chrome	Dropbox Client
Hale [20]	Windows PC	Amazon Cloud Drive	Internet Explorer, Mozilla Firefox, Google Chrome	Amazon Cloud Drive Client
Koppen et al. [21]	Windows PC, iPad, Mobile Device	Google Docs, Dropbox, Windows Live Mesh	Internet Explorer	Dropbox Client, Windows Live Mesh
Epifani [11]	Windows 7 PC	Dropbox, Google Drive, SkyDrive, iCloud	Mozilla Firefox, Internet Explorer	Dropbox Client, Google Drive Client, SkyDrive Client
Martini and Choo [25]	Windows PC, Mobile Device	ownCloud	Internet Explorer, Mozilla Firefox, Google Chrome	ownCloud Sync Client, iOS ownCloud App

Table 2. Cloud endpoint forensic approaches (continued).

Researchers	Endpoint Devices	Cloud Services Accessed	Cloud Service Access Method	
			Web Browser	Desktop/Mobile App
Grispos et al. [16]	iOS Mobile Device, Android Mobile Device	Dropbox, Box, SugarSync	N/A	Cloud Service Mobile App
Quick and Choo [38]	Windows 7 PC, iPhone	SkyDrive	Mozilla Firefox, Internet Explorer, Google Chrome, Apple Safari	SkyDrive Client
Quick and Choo [39]	Windows 7 PC, iPhone	Dropbox	Mozilla Firefox, Internet Explorer, Google Chrome, Apple Safari	Dropbox Client
Quick et al. [40]	Windows 7 PC, iPhone	Google Drive	Mozilla Firefox, Internet Explorer, Google Chrome, Apple Safari	Google Drive Client
Federici [12]	Windows 7 PC	Dropbox, Google Drive, Microsoft Skydrive	Internet Explorer, Mozilla Firefox	Dropbox Client, Google Drive Client, SkyDrive Client
Oestreicher [36]	Mac OS System	iCloud	N/A	iCloud App
Grispos et al. [17]	iOS Mobile Device, Android Mobile Device	Dropbox, Box, SugarSync, Syncplicity	N/A	N/A

Table 3. Cloud endpoint forensic approaches (continued).

Researchers	Endpoint Devices	Cloud Services Accessed	Web Browser	Cloud Service Access Method Desktop/Mobile App
Blakeley et al. [2]	Windows 8.1 PC	hubiC	Internet Explorer, Google Chrome, Mozilla Firefox	hubiC Client
Mehreen and Aslam [29]	Windows 8 PC	Dropbox	N/A	Dropbox Metro UI
Daryabar et al. [5]	iOS Mobile Device, Android Mobile Device	Mega	N/A	Mega v1 App
Daryabar et al. [6]	iOS Mobile Device, Android Mobile Device	OneDrive, Box, Google Drive, Dropbox	N/A	N/A
Rahman et al. [41]	Android Mobile Device	Google Drive, Dropbox, OneDrive	N/A	N/A
Thamburasa et al. [46]	Windows 7 PC	IDrive, Mega	Internet Explorer, Google Chrome, Mozilla Firefox	IDrive Client, Mega Cloud Drive
Easwaramoorthy et al. [8]	Windows 7 PC	OneDrive, Amazon Cloud Drive	Internet Explorer, Google Chrome, Mozilla Firefox	Client Software

- **Internet Evidence Finder:** Internet Evidence Finder [28] extracts and analyzes cloud artifacts from computers, smartphones and tablets. The digital artifacts include synced files/folders, file names, file sizes, dates/times, user IDs, URLs, file sharing settings and privacy settings.

- **Dropbox Decryptor:** Dropbox Decryptor [24] decrypts SQLite database files such as `filecache.dbx` and `config.dbx` that are created when a user accesses Dropbox.

- **UFED Cloud Analyzer:** The UFED Cloud Analyzer [3] is a mobile device data extractor that requires user credentials to retrieve information. It can extract data from more than 25 cloud data sources, including Facebook, WhatsApp, Google Services, iCloud Services, OneDrive and Dropbox.

- **EnCase eDiscovery:** EnCase eDiscovery [18, 19] may be used to collect electronically-stored information and preserve data from an onsite device or computer as well as from cloud-based data services.

- **Oxygen Forensic Detective:** The Oxygen Forensic Detective tool [37] extracts data from more than 35 cloud sources, including iCloud applications, Google services, cloud-based storage services and email services.

- **XRY Cloud:** XRY Cloud [32] is a forensic tool for mobile devices. With the appropriate user credentials, XRY Cloud provides data access to cloud services such as iCloud, Twitter, Google and Facebook.

- **Elcomsoft Cloud eXplorer:** Elcomsoft Cloud eXplorer [9] is a mobile device forensic tool that extracts data from Google services; it needs user credentials for data retrieval.

- **Elcomsoft Phone Breaker:** Elcomsoft Phone Breaker [10] is a mobile device forensic tool that extracts data from the Apple iCloud; it needs user credentials for data retrieval.

- **Belkasoft Acquisition Tool:** The Belkasoft Acquisition tool [1] acquires images of digital data from hard drives, removable drives, mobile devices and computer RAM, as well as cloud data from iCloud, Google Drive and Google Plus.

- **F-Response Now Cloud Services:** F-Response Now Cloud Services [13] provides read-only access to remote systems, including cloud services.

- **MailXaminer:** MailXaminer [45] is an email forensic tool for investigations involving iCloud, Office365, Rackspace, Gmail, Hotmail and Live Exchange Server.

6.   OneDrive Forensics Case Study

This section describes a case study involving OneDrive forensics. In the case study, a OneDrive client application was installed on a computer running Windows 10. Files and folders were updated via the client application as well as using a web browser. The OneDrive application created multiple files and folders during the updates.

Data was extracted using WinPrefetchView v1.35, RAMMap v1.5, Volatility, RAM Capture and DumpIt. Due to space constraints, it is not possible to describe all the results. However, information is presented to enable readers to appreciate the amount of forensically-relevant data that can be found using a OneDrive Client API.

The following data was extracted and analyzed:

- **OneDrive Process Path:** The path (`C:\Users\UserName\App Data\Local\Microsoft\OneDrive\OneDrive.exe`) may be used to check if the client software was installed.

- **Application File:** The application file is located at `C:\Users\ UserName\AppData\Local\Microsoft\OneDrive\17.3.6517.08 09\OneDriveSetup`.

- **Synchronized File Folder:** OneDrive creates a local folder (`C: \Users\UserName\OneDrive`) in the client system to synchronize user data.

- **Hash Values:** MD5 hash values were checked before uploading the file `reference.txt` to OneDrive and after downloading the file from cloud storage. The MD5 hash value `C8E6450CBA8290B08C53A 6EE5138DC89` was not changed during this process.

    Next, file `reference.txt` was edited and saved and the file was downloaded once again. The MD5 hash value of the file was observed to have changed to `867C329748FAF41223351331945F84ED`. As expected, the hash value of the edited file was different from the hash value of the previous version of the file.

- **Account Information:** The following account information was obtained:
    - *User Email ID:* `userid@hotmail.com`.
    - *Cloud Storage Used:* 10 MB of 5 GB.
    - *Microsoft OneDrive:* Version 2016 (Build 17.3.6517.0809).

- **Cached Credentials:** The cached credentials were stored on the hard drive and protected by the Data Protection Application Programming Interface.

- **OneDrive Log Data:** The following files were found at `C:\Users \UserName\AppData\Local\Microsoft\OneDrive\logs\Person al`:
  – `SyncEngine.odl`: This file was created after syncing a file to OneDrive; the file name and file hash were synced in the logs.
  – `TraceArchive.ETL` and `TraceCurrent.ETL`: These files hold the folder attributes.
  – `SyncDiagnostics.log`: This file keeps track of the current operations (e.g., files remaining to be synced).

- *Prefetch Files:* The file `ONEDRIVE.EXE-CA61B35B.pf` was found; it contained the following information:
  – *ClientPolicy:* This was located at `C:\Users\UserName\AppData \Local\Microsoft\OneDrive\settings\Personal\CLIENTPOLI CY.INI`; the useful information included the share URL, file URL, etc.
  – *$MFT (Master File Table):* This table was located at `C:\Users\ UserName\AppData\Local\Microsoft\OneDrive\logs\Persona l\SyncEngine-2016-9-13.558.6736.7.aodl`.
  – *CollectOneDriveLogs (Windows Batch Files):* These files were found at `C:\Users\UserName\AppData\Local\Microsoft\OneDr ive\17.3.6517.0809\CollectOneDriveLogs`.
  – *ApplicationSettings XML File:* This file was located at `C:\Users \UserName\AppData\Local\Microsoft\OneDrive\settings\Pe rsonal\ApplicationSettings`; the UserCID was found to be 6205 14542fa58fa4.
  – `FileSync.LocalizedResources.dll`: This dynamic link library was found at `C:\Users\UserName\AppData\Local\Microsoft\On eDrive\17.3.6517.0809\FileSync.LocalizedResources.dll`.

- *Browser Password (Saved by User):* The following navigation was performed: Google Chrome → Settings → Show Advanced Settings → Passwords and Forms → Manage Passwords → Click on Saved Passwords → Show → (will ask for password) → (OneDrive password is displayed in a readable format).

- *Registry Files:* These files contained information about tuning parameters, device configuration and user preferences. Example registry files were:
  – `HKEY_CURRENT_USER\Software\Microsoft\OneDrive`.

- HKEY_CLASSES_ROOT\OneDrive.SyncFileInformationProvid
er.

- **Memory Inspection:** Memory was captured and stored in the
ANAND-20160917-062356.raw file. A total of 122 dynamic link
library files were found in raw memory. Example files were:
  - C:\Users\UserName\AppData\Local\Microsoft\OneDrive\17
.3.6517.0809\LoggingPlatform.dll.
  - C:\Users\UserName\AppData\Local\Microsoft\OneDrive\17
.3.6517.0809\qt5gui.dll.
  - C:\Users\UserName\AppData\Local\Microsoft\OneDrive\17
.3.6517.0809\filesync.resources.dll.

- **Browser Information:** The following browser information was
obtained:
  - *Local Storage:* The user ID was found at C:\Users\UserName\
AppData\Local\Google\Chrome\UserData\Default\LocalStor
age.
  - *Application Cache:* The cache was located at C:\Users\UserName
\AppData\Local\Google\Chrome\UserData\Default\Applicat
ionCache.
  - *History:* The history information, which included login data,
file uploaded, file downloaded, client ID, URL, date and time, was
located at C:\Users\UserName\AppData\Local\Google\Chrome\
UserData\Default\History.
  - *Cookies:* Cookies were located at C:\Users\UserName\AppData\
Local\Google\Chrome\UserData\Default\Cookies.

- **Metadata Extraction via Cloud API:** The Microsoft Graph
RESTful web API was used to access Microsoft cloud services [31].
The permissions were modified to access the OneDrive cloud service and the GET method was used to read data. The query
graph.microsoft.com/v1.0/me/drive/root/children was used
on "all the items on the drive."

The query yielded metadata for all the files that had been uploaded
to OneDrive. Table 4 shows the metadata obtained for one of the
files, IMG_5202.jpg.

7.   Conclusions

The taxonomy of cloud endpoint forensic tools presented in this chapter covers potential digital evidence sources in endpoint devices as well

Table 4.   Metadata extracted using the cloud API.

Source	Contents
Drive Information	Last Modified Date and Time; Drive ID; App Display Name and ID; User Display Name and ID; File and Folder Path
File and Folder Information	Name; Size (Bytes); Hash Value; MIME Type; Creation Time; Image; cTag (Item Content); eTag (Metadata and Content)
Photograph Information	Camera Make; Camera Model; Focal Length; fNumber; ISO; Capture Date and Time; Exposure Numerator; Exposure Denominator
URL Information	Web URL; Download URL

as evidence residing in cloud service provider resources that can be accessed using cloud APIs. Thus, it provides a valuable framework for understanding cloud forensic tools and comparing their functionality. The taxonomy, which supports tool selection as well as requests for increased tool functionality, will be submitted for incorporation in the NIST Computer Forensics Tool Testing Project Tool Catalog. It is hoped that the taxonomy will help advance tool specification and development efforts by vendors, and also enable digital forensic professionals to describe their needs and find tools that meet their needs.

Acknowledgement

The authors wish to thank Barbara Guttman, Software Quality Group Leader at the NIST Information Technology Laboratory for her valuable advice on various aspects of this research.

References

[1] Belkasoft, Belkasoft Acquisition Tool, Menlo Park, California (belkasoft.com/bat), 2018.

[2] B. Blakeley, C. Cooney, A. Dehghantanha and R. Aspin, Cloud storage forensics: hubiC as a case-study, *Proceedings of the Seventh IEEE International Conference on Cloud Computing Technology and Science*, pp. 536–541, 2015.

[3] Cellebrite, UFED Cloud Extractor, Petah Tikva, Israel (www.cellebrite.com/Mobile-Forensics/Products/ufed-cloud-analyzer), 2018.

[4] H. Chung, J. Park, S. Lee and C. Kang, Digital forensic investigation of cloud storage services, *Digital Investigation*, vol. 9(2), pp. 81–95, 2012.

[5] F. Daryabar, A. Dehghantanha and K. Choo, Cloud storage forensics: Mega as a case study, *Australian Journal of Forensic Sciences*, vol. 49(3), pp. 344–357, 2017.

[6] F. Daryabar, A. Dehghantanha, B. Eterovic-Soric and K. Choo, Forensic investigation of OneDrive, Box, GoogleDrive and Dropbox applications on Android and iOS devices, *Australian Journal of Forensic Sciences*, vol. 48(6), pp. 615–642, 2016.

[7] J. Dykstra and A. Sherman, Acquiring forensic evidence from infrastructure-as-a-service cloud computing: Exploring and evaluating tools, trust and techniques, *Digital Investigation*, vol. 9(S), pp. S90–S98, 2012.

[8] S. Easwaramoorthy, S. Thamburasa, G. Samy, S. Bhushan and K. Aravind, Digital forensic evidence collection of cloud storage data for investigation, *Proceedings of the International Conference on Recent Trends in Information Technology*, 2016.

[9] Elcomsoft Proactive Software, Elcomsoft Cloud eXplorer, Moscow, Russia (`www.elcomsoft.com/ecx.html`), 2018.

[10] Elcomsoft Proactive Software, Elcomsoft Phone Breaker, Moscow, Russia (`www.elcomsoft.com/eppb.html`), 2018.

[11] M. Epifani, Cloud storage forensics, presented at the *SANS European Digital Forensics Summit*, 2013.

[12] C. Federici, Cloud Data Imager: A unified answer to remote acquisition of cloud storage areas, *Digital Investigation*, vol. 11(1), pp. 30–42, 2014.

[13] F-Response, F-Response Universal, Tampa, Florida (`www.f-response.com`), 2018.

[14] Google, Google Drive API v3, Mountain View, California (`developers.google.com/apis-explorer`), 2018.

[15] Google, Google Drive APIs, Mountain View, California (`developers.google.com/drive`), 2018.

[16] G. Grispos, W. Glisson and T. Storer, Using smartphones as a proxy for forensic evidence contained in cloud storage services, *Proceedings of the Forty-Sixth Hawaii International Conference on System Sciences*, pp. 4910–4919, 2013.

[17] G. Grispos, W. Glisson and T. Storer, Recovering residual forensic data from smartphone interactions with cloud storage providers, in *The Cloud Security Ecosystem: Technical, Legal, Business and Management Issues*, R. Ko and K. Choo (Eds.), Syngress, Boston, Massachusetts, pp. 347–382, 2015.

[18] Guidance Software, EnCase eDiscovery, Pasadena, California (`www.guidancesoftware.com/encase-ediscovery?cmpid=nav_r`), 2018.

[19] Guidance Software, EnCase Forensic 8, Pasadena, California (`www.guidancesoftware.com/encase-forensic?cmpid=nav_r`), 2018.

[20] J. Hale, Amazon Cloud Drive forensic analysis, *Digital Investigation*, vol. 10(3), pp. 259–265, 2013.

[21] J. Koppen, G. Gent, K. Bryan, L. DiPippo, J. Kramer, M. Moreland and V. Fay-Wolfe, Identifying remnants of evidence in the cloud, in *Digital Forensics and Cyber Crime*, M. Rogers and K. Seigfried-Spellar (Eds.), Springer, Heidelberg, Germany, pp. 42–57, 2012.

[22] T. Leschke, Cyber dumpster-diving: $Recycle.Bin forensics for Windows 7 and Windows Vista, presented at the *Department of Defense Cyber Crime Conference*, 2010.

[23] Magnet Forensics, Artifacts, Herndon, Virginia (`www.magnetforensics.com/artifacts`), 2018.

[24] Magnet Forensics, Dropbox Decryptor Version 1.3, Herndon, Virginia (`www.magnetforensics.com/free-tool-dropbox-decryptor`), 2018.

[25] B. Martini and K. Choo, Cloud storage forensics: ownCloud as a case study, *Digital Investigation*, vol. 10(4), pp. 287–299, 2013.

[26] F. Marturana, G. Me and S. Tacconi, A case study on digital forensics in the cloud, *Proceedings of the International Conference on Cyber-Enabled Distributed Computing and Knowledge Discovery*, pp. 111–116, 2012.

[27] J. McQuaid, Forensic Analysis of LNK Files, Magnet Forensics, Herndon, Virginia (`www.magnetforensics.com/computer-forensics/forensic-analysis-of-lnk-files`), August 6, 2014.

[28] J. McQuaid, Forensic Analysis of Prefetch files in Windows, Magnet Forensics, Herndon, Virginia (www.magnetforensics.com/computer-forensics/forensic-analysis-of-prefetch-files-in-windows) August 6, 2014.

[29] S. Mehreen and B. Aslam, Windows 8 cloud storage analysis: Dropbox forensics, *Proceedings of the Twelfth International Bhurban Conference on Applied Sciences and Technology*, pp. 312–317, 2015.

[30] Microsoft, Dynamic-Link Libraries, Redmond, Washington (msdn.microsoft.com/en-us/library/windows/desktop/ms682589(v=vs.85).aspx), 2018.

[31] Microsoft, Use the Microsoft Graph API, Redmond, Washington (developer.microsoft.com/en-us/graph/docs/concepts/use_the_api), 2018.

[32] MSAB, XRY – Extract, Stockholm, Sweden (www.msab.com/products/xry/#cloud), 2018.

[33] National Institute of Standards and Technology, Computer Forensics Tool Testing (CFTT) Program, Gaithersburg, Maryland (www.cftt.nist.gov), 2018.

[34] Network Associates, Windows Data Protection, Microsoft, Redmond, Washington (msdn.microsoft.com/en-us/library/ms995355.aspx), 2001.

[35] NIST Cloud Computing Forensic Science Working Group, NIST Cloud Computing Forensic Science Challenges, Draft NISTIR 8006, Information Technology Laboratory, National Institute of Standards and Technology, Gaithersburg, Maryland, 2014.

[36] K. Oestreicher, A forensically-robust method for acquisition of iCloud data, *Digital Investigation*, vol. 11(S2), pp. S106–S113, 2014.

[37] Oxygen Forensics, Oxygen Forensic Detective, Alexandria, Virginia (www.oxygen-forensic.com/en/products/oxygen-forensic-detective), 2018.

[38] D. Quick and K. Choo, Digital droplets: Microsoft SkyDrive forensic data remnants, *Future Generation Computer Systems*, vol. 29(6), pp. 1378–1394, 2013.

[39] D. Quick and K. Choo, Dropbox analysis: Data remnants on user machines, *Digital Investigation*, vol. 10(1), pp. 3–18, 2013.

[40] D. Quick, B. Martini and K. Choo, *Cloud Storage Forensics*, Syngress, Boston, Massachusetts, 2014.

[41] N. Rahman, N. Cahyani and K. Choo, Cloud incident handling and forensics-by-design: Cloud storage as a case study, *Concurrency and Computation: Practice and Experience*, vol. 29(14), 2016.

[42] V. Roussev, I. Ahmed, A. Barreto, S. McCulley and V. Shanmughan, Cloud forensics – Tool development studies and future outlook, *Digital Investigation*, vol. 18, pp. 79–95, 2016.

[43] V. Roussev, A. Barreto and I. Ahmed, API-based forensic acquisition of cloud drives, in *Advances in Digital Forensics XII*, G. Peterson and S. Shenoi (Eds.), Springer, Heidelberg, Germany, pp. 213–235, 2016.

[44] K. Ruan, J. Carthy, T. Kechadi and I. Baggili, Cloud forensics definitions and critical criteria for cloud forensic capability: An overview of survey results, *Digital Investigation*, vol. 10(1), pp. 34–43, 2013.

[45] SysTools Software, MailXaminer, Pune, India (`www.mailxaminer.com/product`), 2018.

[46] S. Thamburasa, S. Easwaramoorthy, K. Aravind, S. Bhushan and U. Moorthy, Digital forensic analysis of cloud storage data in IDrive and Mega cloud drive, *Proceedings of the International Conference on Inventive Computation Technologies*, 2016.

[47] S. Zawoad and R. Hasan, Cloud Forensics: A Meta-Study of Challenges, Approaches and Open Problems, Technical Report, Department of Computer Science, University of Alabama at Birmingham, Birmingham, Alabama, 2013.

Chapter 15

A LAYERED GRAPHICAL MODEL FOR CLOUD FORENSIC MISSION ATTACK IMPACT ANALYSIS

Changwei Liu, Anoop Singhal and Duminda Wijesekera

Abstract   Cyber attacks on the systems that support an enterprise's mission can significantly impact its objectives. This chapter describes a layered graphical model designed to support forensic investigations by quantifying the mission impacts of cyber attacks. The model has three layers: (i) an upper layer that models operational tasks and their interdependencies that fulfill mission objectives; (ii) a middle layer that reconstructs attack scenarios based on the interrelationships of the available evidence; and (iii) a lower level that uses system calls executed in upper layer tasks in order to reconstruct missing attack steps when evidence is missing. The graphs constructed from the three layers are employed to compute the impacts of attacks on enterprise missions. The National Vulnerability Database – Common Vulnerability Scoring System scores and forensic investigator estimates are used to compute the mission impacts. A case study is presented to demonstrate the utility of the graphical model.

Keywords: Mission attack impact, cloud forensic analysis, layered graphical model

1.   Introduction

Organizational missions that abstract activities envisioned by organizations are usually defined at the high-level as a collection of business processes. Cyber attacks on enterprise infrastructures that support such missions can cause significant impacts. Meanwhile, a growing number of business processes and services are being hosted by cloud operator data centers. Given that most network infrastructures, including cloud infrastructures, rely on hardware and software assets, attacks that target these assets could significantly impact the missions they support.

G. Peterson and S. Shenoi (Eds.): Advances in Digital Forensics XIV, IFIP AICT 532, pp. 263–289, 2018.
https://doi.org/10.1007/978-3-319-99277-8_15

Therefore, analyzing and quantifying the mission impacts of cyber attacks are very important to infrastructure risk managers who seek to mitigate security threats and improve mission resilience.

NIST's National Vulnerability Database – Common Vulnerability Scoring System (NVD-CVSS) provides impact estimates of exploitable vulnerabilities in information technology systems [8]. Several approaches use the Common Vulnerability Scoring System to predict the impacts of multi-step attacks on assets by considering all possible attack paths [7, 9, 15]. However, evaluating all the attack paths is infeasible for a forensic investigator intending to assess the damage because of the large number of attack paths generated when all possible vulnerabilities are considered. Additionally, the scoring system only considers publicly-reported vulnerabilities, not zero-days.

Because post-attack artifacts obtained during forensic investigations provide information that can be used to analyze attacks, the proposed layered graphical model uses this information to quantify the impacts of attacks on organizational missions. The graphical model comprises three layers and two mapping algorithms. The upper layer models operational tasks and their interdependencies that constitute the final mission as a collection of choreographed tasks. The middle layer collects evidence from intrusion detection systems and event logs to reconstruct attack scenarios. The lower layer reconstructs potentially missing attack steps using system calls executed to fulfill the upper layer tasks; this is required when evidence needed to reconstruct the attack scenarios in the middle layer is not available. Finally, the two mapping algorithms integrate the information obtained from the three layers to ascertain how mission execution was impacted during the attacks.

The three layers of graph-like dependency information provide a means to compute attack impacts on organizational missions using the National Vulnerability Database – Common Vulnerability Scoring System or forensic investigator estimates. A case study is presented to demonstrate the utility of the graphical model, in particular, how it can be used to migrate attack risks in network infrastructures, including those supporting cloud services. The model is unique because it provides an integrated forensic analysis framework that quantifies the mission impacts of multi-step attacks in complex enterprise infrastructures.

2.   Background and Related Work

This section briefly discusses cloud forensics and related research.

2.1   Cloud Forensics

Digital forensic investigators seek evidence of attack activities on computers and networks. Evidence on a computer typically resides in physical memory or on the hard disk; the evidence may be recovered using imaging and data analysis tools [13]. Evidence from a network is typically obtained in the form of network traffic capture files. Some network forensic tools, such as Snort, are also used for intrusion detection.

In the case of cloud environments, NIST [6] has defined deployment models such as software-as-a-service (SaaS), platform-as-a-service (PaaS) and infrastructure-as-a-service. Software-as-a-service enables clients to use service provider applications running on a cloud infrastructure. Platform-as-a-service enables clients to deploy cloud client applications that use programming languages, libraries, services and tools supported by a cloud provider. Infrastructure-as-a-service provides clients with the ability to provision processing, storage, networks and other computing resources.

According to Ruan et al. [12], cloud forensics is a subset of network forensics because it follows the main phases of network forensics, albeit with techniques tailored to cloud computing environments. Evidence acquisition is different in a software-as-a-service deployment compared with an infrastructure-as-a-service deployment. In the case of a software-as-a-service deployment, a forensic investigator depends entirely on the cloud service provider. In contrast, in an infrastructure-as-a-service deployment, an investigator can acquire evidence from virtual machine images that execute on client computer systems.

2.2   Related Work

Attackers tend to use multi-step, multi-stage attacks to bypass security countermeasures and impact important business services. Several researchers have proposed models for estimating the mission impacts of such attacks by considering all known vulnerabilities. Sun et al. [16] have proposed a multi-layer impact evaluation model for estimating mission impacts. At the bottom is a vulnerability layer that maps to an asset layer, then to a service layer and finally to the top mission layer. This layered design enables mission impacts to be computed using the National Vulnerability Database – Common Vulnerability Scoring System scores and the relationships between missions and lower-level vulnerabilities. However, the model does not incorporate a methodology for constructing attack paths.

· Other researchers [15] have combined mission dependency graphs with attack paths generated by the MulVAL attack graph generation tool [11] to estimate the mission impacts of attacks on cloud infrastructures. Noel et al. [9] have designed a cyber mission impact assessment framework that analyzes all attack paths leading to attack goals to evaluate potential mission impacts; their framework leverages the Business Process Modeling Notation (BPMN) and a topological-vulnerability-analysis-based attack graph generation tool [2]. However, these approaches depend on attack paths constructed from vulnerability information provided by the bug report community (including NIST's National Vulnerability Database – Common Vulnerability Scoring System) to assess the impacts of attacks. As a result, the approaches do not scale to large infrastructures and cannot handle zero-day attacks.

Digital forensic researchers have employed post-attack evidence and correlation rules to reconstruct attack scenarios in investigations of criminal activities and enterprise incidents [4, 17]. For example, Liu et al. [3] have integrated the MulVAL Prolog logic-based tool with a vulnerability database and an anti-forensics database to ascertain the admissibility of evidence and explain missing evidence caused by anti-forensic activities [3]. Liu et al. [5] have also extended this work by using system calls to reconstruct attack scenarios in which certain attack steps cannot be determined due to missing evidence. However, no research in digital forensics has focused on assessing the mission impacts of attacks on enterprise infrastructures.

3.   Graphical Model

Figure 1 shows the layered graphical model for mission impact evaluation. The lower layers reconstruct attack paths, enabling attacks to be mapped to tasks and missions in the upper layer in order to compute the mission impact.

3.1   Upper Layer

The upper layer of the model represents tasks and missions in terms of business processes and connects them to business process diagrams (BPDs) using the Business Process Modeling Notation. Components such as tasks, events, sequencing, exclusive choices, parallel gateways, message flows and pools [1] are used to construct business process diagrams.

Definition 1. (Business Process Diagram): A business process diagram is a five-tuple $(Pool, T, E, C, OP)$ that satisfies the following conditions:

- T is a set of tasks and E is a set of events.

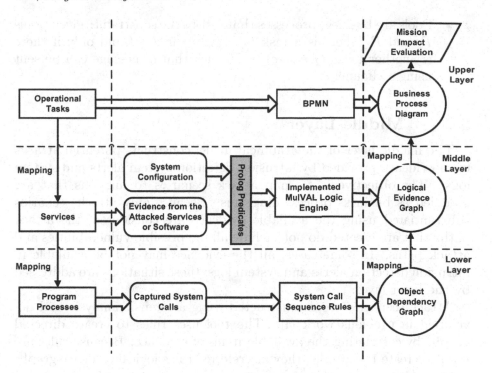

Figure 1. Layered graphical model for mission impact evaluation.

- Let E^{send}, E^{rec} be disjoint subsets of E and let $e_{start}, e_{end} \in E$ be the start and end events, respectively. Then, the set of events $E = \{e_{start}\} \cup \{e_{end}\} \cup E^{send} \cup E^{rec}$ comprises the start, end, message sending and message receiving events, respectively.

- The set of communicating tasks is $T^{com} = \{(t, e_{send}, c), (t, e_{rec}, c)\}$ where $t \in T$, $e_{send} \in E^{send}$, $e_{rec} \in E^{rec}$, $c \in C$.

- The set of operations $OP = \{F, M, XOR, ;\}$ comprises the parallel fork, parallel merge, exclusive choice and sequencing operations.

- C is a set of channels.

Business processlets and a business process are defined as follows:

- $t \in T \cup T^{com}$ is a processlet.

- If P and Q are processlets, then $P; Q$, $F(P, Q)M$ and $P(XOR)Q$ are processlets.

- If $P \in T \setminus T^{com}$ and e_{start}, e_{end} are the start and end events, then $e_{start}; P; e_{end}$ is a business process.

- Pools are business processes that satisfy the constraint: given pools P_1 and P_2, there is a task (t_1, e_{send}, c) in P_1 if and only if there is another task (t_2, e_{rec}, c) in P_2 such that a message can be sent using a channel c.

3.2   Middle Layer

The middle layer of the graphical model constructs potential attacks from evidence provided by intrusion detection system alerts and system logs. The objective is to map attack scenarios to missions that are modeled as business process diagrams. Because only attack scenarios substantiated using the available evidence are considered, the attack paths that are created do not include all the possible vulnerabilities and attack paths. In some cases, all the evidence may not be available in intrusion detection alerts and system logs; these situations are addressed by the lower layer.

Attack scenarios are reconstructed using a forensic analysis tool developed in previous work [4]. The tool uses rules to create directed graphs by correlating the available items of evidence. Because rules are used to create the graphs, they are referred to as logical evidence graphs (LEGs) [4].

Definition 2. (Logical Evidence Graph): A logical evidence graph is a six-tuple (N_r, N_f, N_c, E, L, G) where N_f, N_r and N_c are disjoint sets of nodes comprising fact, rule and consequence fact nodes, respectively. $E \subseteq ((N_f \cup N_c) \times N_r) \cup (N_r \times N_c)$ is the evidence, L is a mapping from nodes to labels and $G \subseteq N_c$ is a set of observed attack events. Every rule node has one or more fact nodes or consequence fact nodes from prior attack steps as its parents and a consequence fact node as its only child. Node labels consist of instantiations of rules or sets of predicates specified as follows:

1. A node in N_f is an instantiation of predicates that codifies system states, including access privileges, network topology and known vulnerabilities associated with host computers. The following predicates are used:

   - hasAccount(_principal,_host,_account), canAccessFile(_host, _user,_access,_path) and other predicates model access privileges.

   - attackerLocated(_host) and hacl(_src,_dst,_prot,_port) model network topology, including attacker location and network reachability information.

- vulExists(_host,_vulID,_program) and vulProperty(_vulID,_-range,_consequence) model node vulnerabilities.

2. A node in N_r describes a single rule of the form $p \leftarrow p_1 \wedge p_2 \cdots \wedge p_n$. The rule head p is an instantiation of a predicate from N_c, which is the child node of N_r in the logical evidence graph. The rule body comprises p_i ($i = 1..n$), which are predicate instantiations of N_f from the current attack step and N_c from one or more prior attack steps that comprise the parent nodes of N_r.

3. A node in N_c represents the predicate that codifies the post-attack state as the consequence of an attack step. The two predicates execCode(_host,_user) and netAccess(_machine,_protocol,_port) are used to model the attacker's capability after an attack step. Valid instantiations of these predicates after an attack update valid instantiations of the three predicates listed in item 1 above.

3.3   Lower Layer

The lower layer of the model uses instances of interactions between services and the execution environment to obtain evidence that is not provided by intrusion detection system alerts and system logs. In such situations, the interaction instances are obtained from system call logs. This is done because it is assumed that the missing evidence is due to the use of anti-forensic techniques, the limitations of forensic tools and/or the execution of zero-day attacks. Because there are many system calls, only the calls highlighted in [14] are considered; these calls are listed in the third column of Table 1. The first column of the table presents abstractions of the system calls. A process that makes system calls creates dependencies between itself and other processes, files or sockets for network connections. The dependencies are modeled as object dependency graphs (ODGs).

Definition 3. (Object Dependency Graph): The reflexive transitive closure of $\rightarrow$ defined in Table 1 is an object dependency graph. An object dependency graph is a three-tuple (V_O, V_E, D) where V_O is the set of vertices comprising objects (processes P, files F and sockets S), V_E is the set of textual descriptions of events (second column of Table 1) and D is the set of dependency edges listed in the first column of Table 1.

3.4   Mappings

The left-hand and right-hand portions of Figure 1 show the system resource mapping and graph mapping, respectively. The resource mapping

Table 1.   System call dependencies.

Dependency	Event Description	Unix System Calls
process → file	process modifies file	write, pwrite64, rename, mkdir, linkat, link, symlinkat, etc
file → process	process reads file	stat64, lstat6e, fsat64, open, read, pread64, execve, etc.
process ↔ file	process uses/ modifies file	open, rename, mount, mmap2, mprotect, etc.
process1 → process 2	process1 creates/ terminates process2	vfork, fork, kill, etc.
process → socket	process writes socket	write, pwrite64, etc.
socket → process	process checks/ reads socket	fstat64, read, pread64, etc.
process ↔ socket	process reads/writes/ checks socket	mount, connect, accept, bind, sendto, send, sendmsg, etc.
socket ↔ socket	process reads/ writes socket	connect, accept, sendto, sendmsg, recvfrom, recvmsg

obtained from the infrastructure configuration and software deployment is used to map graphs. This is accomplished by mapping the attacked services in the corresponding vertices of business process diagrams, logical evidence graphs and object dependency graphs so that the source graphs can be mapped to the destination graphs. A logical evidence graph is easily mapped to a business process diagram by matching the attacked services to the corresponding tasks supported by the services. An object dependency graph is mapped to a logical evidence graph using depth-first search as specified in Algorithm 1.

In Algorithm 1, all the object nodes in an object dependency graph are initially marked as not been checked by using the color WHITE as shown in the for-loop in Lines 1–3. Then, for each unchecked object node V_O (Lines 4–5), the algorithm repeatedly calls function Find(V_O,LEG). The function call is on Line 10 and the function itself is located at Lines 28–41.

The function finds the matching post-attack status node in the logical evidence graph by checking if the attacked service in the logical evidence graph is the same as the attacked service in the object dependency graph.

Algorithm 1: Mapping an OEG to a LEG.

Input: $ODG = (V, V_E, D)$ and $LEG = (N_r, N_f, N_c, E, L, G)$.

Output: LEG integrated with attack paths from the ODG.

```
1  for each node V_O in ODG do
2      color[V_O] ← WHITE
3  end
4  for each node V_O in ODG do
5      if V_O == WHITE then
6          for each node N_c in LEG do
7              color[N_c] ← WHITE
8          end
9          //Search for the corresponding N_c1 in LEG
10         N_c1 = Find(V_O, LEG)
11         //If there is a matching N_c1
12         if N_c1 ≠ ∅ then
13             color[V_O] ← BLACK
14             //Check if object parent matches the corresponding N_c1 parent
15             N_c2 = Find(parent(V_O), LEG)
16             //If there is no matching parent, add the missing attack step from
                  ODG to LEG
17             if N_c2 ≠ parent(N_C1) then
18                 LEG ← Flow(N_c1, V_E); LEG ← Flow(V_E, N_c2)
19             end
20         end
21         else
22             //If there is no matching parent, add the new object to LEG
23             LEG ← V_O; color[V_O] = GRAY
24         end
25         V_O = child(V_O)
26     end
27 end
28 Function Find(V_O, LEG)
29 for each post-attack status N_c from LEG do
30     //Check if there is a matching N_c for V_O
31     if (N_c.service == V_O.service AND
32     color[N_c] == WHITE then
33         color[N_c] ← BLACK
34         return N_c
35     end
36     else
37         color[N_c] ← GRAY
38         N_c ← child post-attack status node of N_c
39     end
40 end
41 return ∅
```

If such a post-attack status node (say N_{c1}) is found (Line 12), then the algorithm checks if the attack step between node V_O and its parent parent(V_O) in the object dependency graph has a mapping attack step between node N_{c1} and its parent parent(N_{c1}) in the logical evidence graph (Line 15). If no matching attack step exists, then one is added to the logical evidence graph (Line 18). If no mapping post-attack status node N_{c1} exists in the logical evidence graph for node V_O in the object dependency graph (Line 21), then one is added to the logical evidence graph (Line 23), and the search continues (Line 25) until all the nodes in the object dependency graph are checked (i.e., colored).

3.5 Computing Mission Impacts

The mission impact of an attack is quantified using the [0,1] interval. This section provides details about the mission impact computations.

Computing Attack Impact Scores. In a logical evidence graph, the term $P(a)$ is used to denote the impact of an attack a on services deployed on a host computer. NIST's National Vulnerability Database – Common Vulnerability Scoring System lists vulnerabilities and assigns impact scores. If attack a is found in the database, then the corresponding score is used as the value for $P(a)$. If attack a is not found in the database, then expert knowledge is used to assign the impact score $P(a)$.

As proposed in [3], the cumulative impact score of attacks on the same service is computed using the equation:

$$P(a) = P(a_1) \cup P(a_2) \tag{1}$$

where a_1 and a_2 are two different attacks on the same service and:

$$P(a_1) \cup P(a_2) = P(a_1) + P(a_2) - P(a_1) \times P(a_2) \tag{2}$$

Assigning Weights to Tasks and Missions. The weight of the mission impact of an attack on a task is also quantified using the [0,1] interval. The higher the weight, the greater the importance of the task to the mission of a business process.

Computing Mission Attack Impacts. In this step, a logical evidence graph is mapped to the corresponding business process diagram and the mission impact of attacks $I(T)$ on a task T is computed using the following equation:

$$I(T) = weight \times P(T) \tag{3}$$

where $P(T)$ is the impact of attacks on task T in the business process diagram.

Depending on the mapping relationship from the attacked service(s) (represented by a, a_1, a_2) in a logical evidence graph to a task (represented by T) in a business process diagram, $P(T)$ is computed using the following equations for a one-to-one mapping relationship and a many-to-one mapping relationship, respectively:

$$P(T) = P(a) \tag{4}$$
$$P(T) = P(a_1) \cup P(a_2) \tag{5}$$

Computing the Cumulative Mission Impact. In some cases, the cumulative impact of attacks on the final mission is required to estimate the overall damage. The cumulative impact of attacks on the final mission C is computed in the following ways depending on the relationships existing between the tasks comprising a business process:

$$C(M) = \text{Max}\{I(T_1), I(T_2), \ldots, I(T_n)\} \tag{6}$$
$$C(M) = \text{Max}\{I(T_1), I(T_2), I(T_4) \ldots, I(T_n)\} \tag{7}$$
$$C(M) = \text{Max}\{I(T_1), I(T_3), I(T_4) \ldots, I(T_n)\} \tag{8}$$
$$C(M) = \text{Max}\{C(M_{before}), I(T_2')\} \tag{9}$$

- $C(M)$ is computed using Equation (6) when the tasks $T_1, T_2, \ldots, T_n$ comprising the final mission M have sequential relationships with each other or only some tasks among all the sequential tasks (e.g., T_2 and T_3) have parallel fork relationships with the predecessor task (T_1) and parallel merge relationships with the successor task (T_4).

- $C(M)$ is computed using Equations (7) or (8) when the tasks $T_1, T_2, \ldots, T_n$ comprising the final mission M include tasks (e.g., T_2 and T_3) that have exclusive decision relationships with the predecessor task (T_1) and successor task (T_4), and all the other tasks ($T_4, \ldots, T_n$) have sequential relationships with each other. Specifically, depending on whether task T_2 or task T_3 is chosen by the business process, either Equation (7) or Equation (8) is used to compute $C(M)$.

- Suppose tasks $T_1, T_2, \ldots, T_n$ comprise the final mission M in a pool and let $C(M_{before})$ denote the cumulative mission attack impact of M without any message passing from other pools. Then, Equation (9) is used to compute $C(M)$ if there is message passing

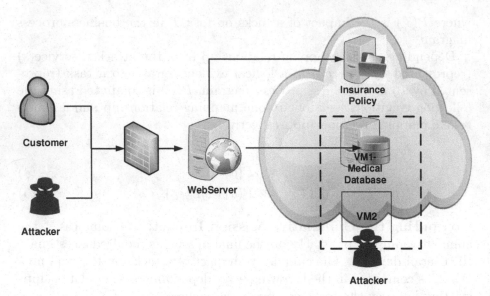

Figure 2. Experimental network.

between a task (T_2) in the pool and another task (T_2') in a different pool.

4. Case Study

This section uses a case study to demonstrate the utility of the proposed graphical model.

4.1 Experimental Network and Attacks

Figure 2 shows the experimental network used in the case study. The network was configured to manage customer medical records and health insurance policy files. The medical records and files were stored on two virtual machines (VM1 and VM2) in a private cloud deployed using OpenStack (Juno 2014.2.3) with a Xen hypervisor. OpenStack is a collection of Python-based software projects that manage access to pooled storage, computing and network resources that reside on one or more machines in a cloud system [10]. The projects include Neutron (networking), Nova (compute), Glance (image management), Swift (object storage), Cinder (block storage) and Keystone (authorization and authentication). OpenStack can be used to deploy a variety of cloud models, but is mostly deployed as an infrastructure-as-a-service.

In the experimental network, authenticated users were able to access the file server to retrieve policy files using `ssh` and to query the medical records stored on the database server using MySQL queries via a web application.

It was assumed that the attacker's objectives were to steal customer medical records, prevent medical record availability and modify health insurance policies. In the experiment, a simulated attacker probed the deployed web and cloud services, and launched four attacks: (i) SQL injection attack; (ii) denial-of-service (DoS) attack; (iii) cross-VM side-channel attack; and (iv) social engineering attack.

SQL Injection Attack. The web application did not sanitize user inputs. The attacker was able to exploit this vulnerability via a SQL injection attack (CWE-89) in order to access customer medical records. The following query was employed:

- `Select * from profile where name = 'Alice'`
  `and (password = 'alice' or '1' = '1')`

where `profile` is the database name and '1'= '1' is the payload that enables the query to bypass the password check. The SQL injection query retrieved all the customer medical records.

Denial-of-Service Attack. According to NIST's National Vulnerability Database, CVE-2015-3241 vulnerability in OpenStack Nova (compute) versions 2015.1 through 2015.1.1, 2014.2.3 and earlier enables authenticated users to cause denial-of-service by resizing and deleting virtual machine instances; the process of resizing and deleting an instance is called instance migration. Because of CVE-2015-3241, the migration process does not terminate when an instance is deleted, enabling an authenticated user to bypass user quota enforcement and deplete the available disk space by repeatedly performing instance migration.

In the experiment, the attacker played the role of a malicious privileged infrastructure-as-a-service user and launched a denial-of-service attack on the database server by repeatedly resizing and deleting VM2 that resided in the same physical machine as the database server (VM1).

Cross-VM Side-Channel Attack. Side-channel attacks can be used to extract fine-grained information across virtual machines that reside in the same hypervisor [19]. In the experimental network, the cache side-channel attack [18] shown in Figure 3 was launched against VM1 and VM2 that ran on the same multi-core processor (Intel quad-core i7). The cache side-channel attack leveraged the transparent page sharing feature implemented in hypervisors such as VMware ESXi and Xen.

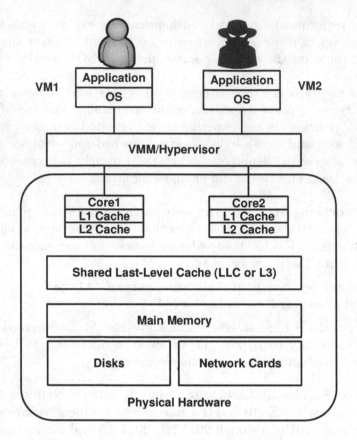

Figure 3.   Cross-VM side-channel attack using a shared last-level cache.

This feature automatically identifies identical pages of virtual memory and consolidates them in a single physical memory page. In the experiment, the attacker exploited transparent page sharing to evict a specific memory line (i.e., memory unit in cache containing a fixed number of bytes) from all levels of the processor cache hierarchy, waited for a period of time and measured the time taken to load the data from the corresponding memory line. Because retrieving data from memory takes more time than retrieving it from cache levels closer to the core, the attacker was able to use the timing information and the data in the corresponding memory lines to obtain confidential information about the victim.

Since the attack leverages the implementation weakness in GnuPG 1.x before version 1.4.16 to obtain the information used to extract the private encryption key, GnuPG 1.4.12 was installed on VM1 (medical database server) while its copy and the spy program simultaneously executed on VM2. The copy of the attacked program executable was required because the attacker used the transparent page sharing feature, which coalesced memory pages from the victim's virtual machine VM1 and the attacker's virtual machine VM2.

Social Engineering Attack. The attacker executed a social engineering attack on the file server to obtain the administrator's credentials (username and password). The attacker then logged into the file server as the administrator and modified insurance policy files on the file server.

Evidence Capture. In order to capture evidence of attacks, the experimental network employed Wireshark for monitoring network traffic and Snort for intrusion detection; moreover, all the servers were configured to log user access. Additionally, to obtain evidence of attacks missed by Snort and the service logs, system calls by user processes in the two virtual machines were recorded.

4.2 Three Levels of Graphs

The network configuration, service deployment information and captured evidence were used to construct the three levels of graphs, which included a business process diagram, two logical evidence graphs and two object dependency graphs.

Business Process Diagram. Figure 4 shows the business process diagram of the experimental network. The network incorporated three pools: (i) Pool 1 (web interface); (ii) Pool 2 (public cloud service); and (iii) Pool 3 (infrastructure-as-a-service).

The business process in Pool 1 is the web interface for the clients (medical customers); it comprises the start and end events, two consecutive tasks (Enter Username/Password and Send Request) and an exclusive gateway for tasks (Review Policy File and Review Medical Records) depending on the client's request.

The business process in Pool 2 comprises the start and end events, one task (Check User Request) followed by an exclusive gateway that directs to two tasks (Request Policy Files and Request Customer Databases) depending on the message passed from task Send Request in Pool 1. In each decision task branch, there is an exclusive decision gateway (File Available and Data Available) followed by tasks that either send the requested data (Send Policy File or Send Customer Medical Records) via message passing back to the clients or reject the client request.

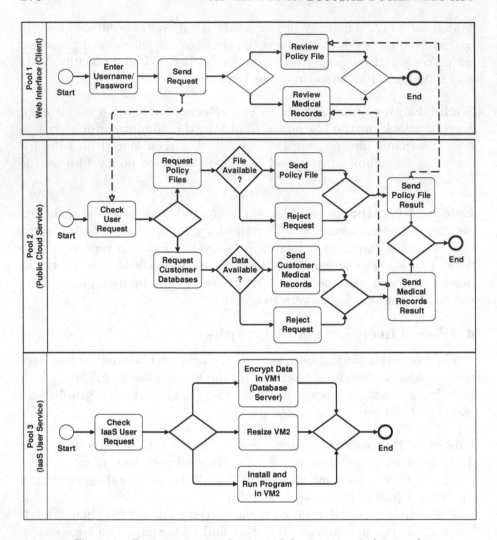

Figure 4. Business process diagram of the experimental network.

The business process in Pool 3 describes the user services; it comprises three tasks (Encrypt Data in VM1, Resize VM2 and Install and Run Program in VM2) that are the exclusive decisions of the Check IaaS User Request task. For each of the three business processes in the three pools, the last task(s) before the end event is taken to represent the entire business process mission(s).

Logical Evidence Graph. Table 2 shows evidence pertaining to the SQL injection attack, which includes the timestamps, machine IP addresses, Snort alerts and database access logs. Using the evidence, it

Table 2. SQL injection attack Snort alerts and database server log.

Timestamp	Machine	IP Address	Snort Alerts and Database Access Logs
	Attacker	129.174.124.122	
06/13/2017: 14:37:27	Web Server	129.174.124.184	SQL Injection Attack (CWE-89)
06/13/2017: 14:37:34	Database Server	129.174.124.35	Access from 129.174.124.184

```
2017-07-18 07:52:00.237 DEBUG oslo_concurrency.processutils
   [req-f79c7911-04ed-4a0c-adbe-0ae0a487c0f7 admin admin]
   Running cmd (subprocess): mv /opt/stack/data/nova/instances/
   bd1dac18-1ce2-44b5-93ee-967fec640ff3= /opt/stack/data/nova/
   instances/bd1dac18-1ce2-44b5-93ee-967fec640ff3_resize from
   (pid=41737)} execute /usr/local/lib/python2.7/dist-packages
   /oslo_concurrency/processutils.py:344
2017-07-18 07:52:00.253 DEBUG oslo_concurrency.processutils
   [req-f79c7911-04ed-4a0c-adbe-0ae0a487c0f7 admin admin] CMD
   "mv /opt/stack/data/nova/instances/bd1dac18-1ce2-44b5-93ee-
   967fec640ff3 /opt/stack/data/nova/instances/bd1dac18-1ce2-
   44b5-93ee-967fec640ff3_resize" returned: 0 in 0.016s from
   (pid=41737) execute /usr/local/lib/python2.7/dist-packages/
   oslo_concurrency/processutils.py:374
2017-07-18 07:52:00.254 DEBUG oslo_concurrency.processutils
   [req-f79c7911-04ed-4a0c-adbe-0ae0a487c0f7 admin admin]
   Running cmd (subprocess): mkdir p /opt/stack/data/nova/
   instances/bd1dac18-1ce2-44b5-93ee-967fec640ff3 from
   (pid=41737) execute /usr/local/lib/python2.7/dist-packages/
   oslo_concurrency/processutils.py:344
```

Figure 5. OpenStack Nova API call logs.

can be asserted that the attacker used a typical SQL injection with payload '1' = '1' to attack the customer database in the database server. Snort failed to capture evidence of the denial-of-service attack that exploited the vulnerability CVE-2015-3241 in OpenStack Nova services. The OpenStack application programing interface (API) logs provide information about user operations of running instances; some of the log entries are shown in the screenshot in Figure 5, where the second line in each entry is the user operation. This information leads to the conclusion that the user in VM2 (i.e., attacker in the experiment) kept resizing and deleting instances in VM2, which resided in the same physical ma-

```
/* initial attack location and final attack status */
attackerLocated(internet).
attackGoal(execCode(database,user)).
/* network access configuration */
hacl(internet,webServer,tcp,80).
hacl(webServer,database,tcp,3306).
/* configuration information of webServer */
vulExists(webServer,'directAccess',httpd).
vulProperty('directAccess',remoteExploit,privEscalation).
networkServiceInfo(webServer,httpd,tcp,80,apache).
/* vulnerability of the web application */
vulExists(database,'CWE-89',httpd).
vulProperty('CWE-89',remoteExploit,privEscalation).
networkServiceInfo(database,httpd,tcp,3306,user).
```

Figure 6. Prolog predicates for the SQL injection attack.

```
/* initial attack status of being an iaas user and final
   attack status */
attackerLocated(iaas).
attackGoal(execCode(nova,admin)).
/* cloud configuration, "_" represents any protocol
   and port */
hacl(iaas,nova,_,_).
/* vulnerability in nova */
vulExists(nova,'CVE-2015-3241','REST').
vulProperty('CVE-2015-3241',remoteExploit,privEscalation).
networkServiceInfo(nova,'REST',http,_,admin).
```

Figure 7. Prolog predicates for the denial-of-service attack.

chine as the database server (VM1) that launched the denial-of-service attack on the database server.

In order to use the forensic analysis tool, system configurations and the evidence related to the SQL injection and denial-of-service attacks were converted to the Prolog predicates shown in Figures 6 and 7.

Figures 8(a) and 8(b) show the output logical evidence graphs produced by the tool; Tables 3 and 4 provide descriptions of the nodes in the two graphs. The two logical evidence graphs are not grouped together due to distinct locations and privileges of the attacker.

Consider the attack step $3, 7, 8 \rightarrow 2 \rightarrow 1$ in Figure 8(b). Nodes 7 and 8 in the attack step model the pre-attack configurations and vulnerabilities. The consequence fact (Node 1) shows that post-attack evidence is derived by applying a rule (Node 2) to the existing system facts (Nodes 7 and 8) and the consequence fact from a prior step (Node 3).

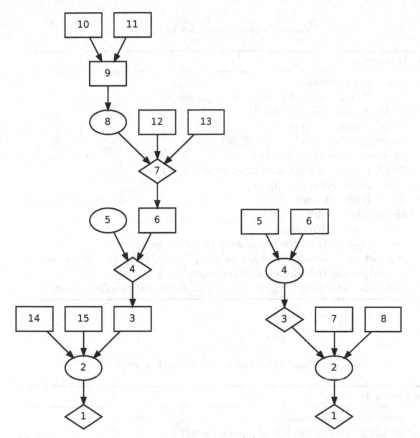

(a) SQL injection attack on database.   (b) DoS attack on database server.

Figure 8. SQL injection attack and DoS database attack LEGs.

```
execve("/home/flush-reload/build_gpg/gnupg-1.4.12/bin/gpg",
    ["/home/flush-reload/buil"..., "- -yes", "- -sign",
    ''message.txt"], [/* 18 vars */]) = 0
...
```

Figure 9. Filtered system calls for the side-channel attack from VM1.

Object Dependency Graph. Due to the lack of intrusion detection system alerts and system logs for the cross-VM side-channel and social engineering attacks, it was not possible to reconstruct the two attack scenarios in the form of logical evidence graphs. Therefore, the system calls captured during the attacks were examined and the method presented above was used to construct object dependency graphs for a forensic analysis.

Table 3.   Descriptions of the nodes in Figure 8(a).

Node	Notation
1	execCode(database,_)
2	RULE 2 (remote exploit of a server program)
3	netAccess(database,tcp,3306)
4	RULE 5 (multi-hop access)
5	hacl(webServer,database,tcp,3306)
6	execCode(webServer,apache)
7	RULE 2 (remote exploit of a server program)
8	netAccess(webServer,tcp,80)
9	RULE 6 (direct network access)
10	hacl(internet,webServer,tcp,80)
11	attackerLocated(internet)
12	networkServiceInfo(webServer,httpd,tcp,80,apache)
13	vulExists(webServer,'directAccess',httpd, remoteExploit,privEscalation)
14	networkServiceInfo(database,httpd,tcp,3306,_)
15	vulExists(database,'CWE-89',httpd,remoteExploit,privEscalation)

Table 4.   Descriptions of the nodes in Figure 8(b).

Node	Notation
1	execCode(nova,admin)
2	RULE 2 (remote exploit of a server program)
3	netAccess(nova,http,_)
4	RULE 6 (direct network access)
5	hacl(cloud,nova,http,_)
6	attackerLocated(cloud)
7	networkServiceInfo(nova,'REST',http,_,admin)
8	vulExists(nova,'CVE-2015-3241','REST',remoteExploit,privEscalation)

Figure 9 shows some system calls captured from VM1 (database server) and VM2 (attacker) during the cross-VM side-channel attack. The system calls show that file **message.txt** in VM1 was encrypted using GnuPG 1.4.12.

The system calls in Figure 10 show that a probe program **bin/probe** in VM2 used **mmap2** to force the system to share memory addresses with the attacker's probing process. This enabled the probing process to read data from the shared memory addresses and write the data to an output file for malicious purposes.

```
execve("bin/probe", ["bin/probe", "/home/flush-reload/buil"...,
    "docs/addr/osx.txt", "out.txt", "200"], [/* 18 vars */]) = 0
...
fstat(3, {st_mode=S_IFREG\0644, st_size=101240,...}) = 0
mmap(NULL, 2206376, PROT_READ|PROT_EXEC, MAP_PRIVATE|
    MAP_DENYWRITE, 3, 0) = 0x7f80b73ec000
read(4, "4\n0x00000000000967c7\n0x000000000" ..., 4096) = 78
write(1, "Probing 4 addresses:\n", 21) = 21
write(1, "0x967c7\n", 8) = 8
write(1, "0x95f5d\n", 8) = 8
write(1, "0x97225\n", 8) = 8
write(1, "0x9757f\n", 8) = 8
...
write(1, "Started spying\n", 15) = 15
...
mmap(NULL, 4096, PROT_READ|PROT_WRITE, MAP_PRIVATE|
    MAP_ANONYMOUS, -1, 0) = 0x7f5e24ab7000
write(5, "0 0 47064\n0 1 6290\n0 2 6246\n0 3"..., 4096) = 4096
write(5, "3 1 279\n113 2 229\n113 3 254\n114" ..., 4096) = 4096
write(5, "9\n215 3 257\n216 0 239\n216 1 279\n" ..., 4096) = 4096
...
```

Figure 10. Filtered system calls for the side-channel attack from VM2.

Figure 11 shows some of the system calls captured from the file server. The read/write system call trace shows that test.txt in the file server was modified. Because the corresponding sshd log in the file server recorded user accesses, it was easy to conclude that the attacker stole the file server administrator's credentials to modify the insurance policy file (the sshd log is omitted for reasons of space).

The system calls and dependency rules listed in Table 1 were used to filter the important system calls. Two object dependency graphs were subsequently constructed. One object dependency graph showed that the attacker in VM2 read the shared cache between VM1 and VM2. The other graph showed that the attacker used the file server administrator's credentials from the Internet to modify an insurance policy file in the file server. The two object dependency graphs were then mapped to the logical evidence graphs in Figure 8.

The resulting integrated logical evidence graphs revealed that:

■ The attacker launched two attacks from the Internet. One attack involved the use of the stolen credentials to modify an insurance policy file and the other, a SQL injection attack, involved the theft of customer medical records.

```
write(9, "v", 1) = 1
read(11, "v", 16384) = 1
write(3, "\0\0\0\20\331\255\275\264c\2173)z2j\32\255n\2007d
    \366m\21\316\2648\240\207\31\211" ..., 36) = 36
read(3, "\0\0\0\20\240\253\341\227\321xU\305\347\226\246\361/316
    \242S=\30\341QT\231\n\343\314\343\307\f\361" ..., 16384) = 36
write(9, "i", 1) = 1
read(11, "i", 16384) = 1
write(3, "\0\0\0\20\177\352\313\332\373yjM\34161\230\215\10\220p
    \252g\375\365\1\f\335\361\r\273\374\357" ..., 36) = 36
read(3, "\0\0\0\20\27\334?\201x\300\16\356\346\0379\32\220\372
    \366\4\v\1=\347\263\311\250k\353" ..., 16384) = 36
write(9, "", 1) = 1
read(11, "", 16384) = 1
write(3, "\0\0\0\20i\321\344\220\313\322\254S\252o\201\225;6v
    \243\205\10gs\253\237\325\375\332v" ..., 36) = 36
read(3, "\0\0\0\20\5\27k;\254\301\24\n\ZN\267\260\336\323\323
    \32\345\2b\226-\271}[B\21" ..., 16384) = 36
write(9, "t", 1) = 1
read(11, "t", 16384) = 1
read(3, "\0\0\0\20\325\261\7\254\211(\201\331\272\344[\355\200u4
    \357G\347\232\276:\201\376\342\202\201" ..., 16384) = 36
write(3, "\0\0\0\20\320\254\#\312\211_\3022\n\227\16I\372\202
    \347\37\252T\257\220\210E\343\222\342\24S" ..., 36) = 36
write(9, "e", 1) = 1
read(11, "e", 16384) = 1
...
write(9, "t", 1) = 1
read(11, "st.txt", 16384) = 7
...
```

Figure 11.   Filtered system calls for the file modification from the file server.

- The attacker launched two other attacks as an infrastructure-as-a-service user. One was a denial-of-service attack and the other was a cross-VM side-channel attack on the database server.

Table 5.   CVSS attack impact scores.

Attack	CVE Entry	Symbol	Attack Impact
SQL Injection Attack	CWE-89	N_1	0.90
Denial-of-Service Attack	CVE-2015-3241	N_1'	0.69
Social Engineering Attack		N_s	0.50
Side-Channel Attack	CVE-2013-4576	N_{sc}	0.29

4.3   Computing Mission Impact

Table 5 lists the impact scores of the reconstructed attacks. The impact scores for CWE-89, CVE-2015-3241 and CVE-2013-4576 were obtained from NIST's National Vulnerability Database – Common Vulnerability Scoring System. The impact score for the social engineering attack was based on expert knowledge. The impact scores, which were originally specified on a [0,10] scale, were converted to the [0,1] scale.

All the reconstructed attacks were associated with the corresponding tasks by mapping object dependency graphs to logical evidence graphs and, eventually, to the business process diagram as shown in Figure 4. Table 6 shows the mission impact scores that were computed using the graph mappings.

Finally, using the attack impact scores for all tasks listed in Table 6 and the business process diagram shown in Figure 4, the cumulative attack impacts on the final missions were computed. Table 7 presents the results of the computations.

4.4 Reducing Attack Risk

In complex infrastructures, enterprise missions rely on combinations of and connections between multiple services. Because each service is supported by software and hardware assets, which are usually the targets of attackers, a tool that relates the infrastructure assets to the final missions can help determine the impacts of cyber attacks on enterprise missions. By correlating the attacks on lower-level assets to the higher-level business process diagram and using mission impact scores of the attacks as listed in Table 5, the proposed graphical model enables the computation of the impacts of attacks on complex missions. This information is valuable to digital forensic investigators and infrastructure risk managers.

The experimental network can be used as an exemplar to demonstrate how the computed mission impacts can be used by managers to reduce the risks of attacks. The cumulative impact scores in Table 7 show that the attacks on the Review Medical Records mission have a higher impact because customer medical records could be stolen via a SQL injection attack. This suggests that input sanitization should be implemented to defeat SQL injection attacks.

Additionally, the attacks and their impact scores in Table 6 reveal that two attacks – the denial-of-service attack and the side-channel attack – exploited cloud service vulnerabilities. Therefore, the services should be moved to a stable cloud that implements countermeasures for attacks launched from the shared hypervisor or physical machine.

Finally, Table 6 shows that, although the mission impact on the health insurance policies stored on the file server might not be as bad as the SQL injection attack on the database server, its score of 0.5 cannot be

Table 6. Mission impact scores.

Pool	Task	Attack	Weight	Mission Impact
Pool 1	Check Username and Password	CWE-89 (N_1)	1.0	$I_1 = 1 \times P(N_1) = 1 \times 0.9 = 0.9$
Pool 2	Data Available	CVE-2015-3241 (N'_1)	0.9	$I_2 = 0.9 \times P(N'_1) = 0.9 \times 0.69 = 0.621$
Pool 2	Request Policy Files	Social Engineering (N_s)	1.0	$I_3 = 1 \times P(N_s) = 1 \times 0.5 = 0.5$
Pool 3	Encrypt Data in VM1	CVE-2013-4576 (N_{sc})	1.0	$I_4 = 1 \times P(N_{sc}) = 1 \times 0.29 = 0.29$

Table 7. Cumulative mission impact.

Pool	Mission	Mission Task Attack	Cumulative Mission Impact
Pool 1	Review Policy File	Social Engineering	$C = \text{Max}(I_3) = \text{Max}(0.5) = 0.5$
Pool 1	Review Medical Records	Check Username and Password; Data Available	$C = \text{Max}(I_1, I_2) = \text{Max}(0.9, 0.621) = 0.9$
Pool 3	Encrypt Data in VM1	Encrypt Data in VM1	$C = \text{Max}(I_4) = \text{Max}(0.29) = 0.29$

ignored. A simple attack countermeasure is to restrict file write/modify rights to administrators with local access.

5.   Conclusions

The three-layer graphical model presented in this chapter is designed to support forensic investigations of attacks on computing infrastructures. It helps reconstruct attack scenarios based on evidence from attack logs and leverages system call sequences when the logs do not have adequate evidence to reconstruct attack steps. NIST's National Vulnerability Database – Common Vulnerability Scoring System scores are used to compute the mission impacts of attacks; attacks that are not included in the NIST database are handled using estimates provided by human experts. The case study involving an experimental network with cloud services demonstrates the utility of the graphical model and its ability to support forensic investigations and risk mitigation efforts.

Future research will investigate applications of the graphical model in advanced networking and cloud infrastructures. Additionally, research will focus on determining how the model can be engaged in a framework that would enable enterprises to measure and manage the security risks to their infrastructures.

This chapter is not subject to copyright in the United States. Commercial products are identified in order to adequately specify certain procedures. In no case does such an identification imply a recommendation or endorsement by the National Institute of Standards and Technology, nor does it imply that the identified products are necessarily the best available for the purpose.

References

[1] L. Herbert, Specification, Verification and Optimization of Business Processes: A Unified Framework, Ph.D. Dissertation, Department of Applied Mathematics and Computer Science, Technical University of Denmark, Kongens Lyngby, Denmark, 2014.

[2] S. Jajodia and S. Noel, Topological vulnerability analysis, in *Cyber Situational Awareness*, S. Jajodia, P. Liu, V. Swarup and C. Wang (Eds.), Springer, Boston, Massachusetts, pp. 139–154, 2010.

[3] C. Liu, A. Singhal and D. Wijesekera, Mapping evidence graphs to attack graphs, *Proceedings of the IEEE International Workshop on Information Forensics and Security*, pp. 121–126, 2012.

[4] C. Liu, A. Singhal and D. Wijesekera, A logic-based network forensic model for evidence analysis, in *Advances in Digital Forensics XI*, G. Peterson and S. Shenoi (Eds.), Springer, Heidelberg, Germany, pp. 129–145, 2015.

[5] C. Liu, A. Singhal and D. Wijesekara, A probabilistic network forensic model for evidence analysis, in *Advances in Digital Forensics XII*, G. Peterson and S. Shenoi (Eds.), Springer, Heidelberg, Germany, pp. 189–210, 2016.

[6] P. Mell and T. Grance, NIST Definition of Cloud Computing, NIST Special Publication 800-145, National Institute of Standards and Technology, Gaithersburg, Maryland, 2011.

[7] S. Musman and A. Temin, A cyber mission impact assessment tool, *Proceedings of the IEEE International Symposium on Technologies for Homeland Security*, 2015.

[8] National Institute of Standards and Technology, National Vulnerability Database, Gaithersburg, Maryland (nvd.nist.gov/vuln-metrics/cvss), 2018.

[9] S. Noel, J. Ludwig, P. Jain, D. Johnson, R. Thomas, J. McFarland, B. King, S. Webster and B. Tello, Analyzing mission impacts of cyber actions (AMICA), *Proceedings of the NATO IST-128 Workshop: Assessing Mission Impact of Cyberattacks*, pp. 80–86, 2015.

[10] OpenStack Foundation, Software, Austin, Texas (www.openstack.org/software), 2018.

[11] X. Ou, S. Govindavajhala and A. Appel, MulVAL: A logic-based network security analyzer, *Proceedings of the Fourteenth USENIX Security Symposium*, 2005.

[12] K. Ruan, J. Carthy, T. Kechadi and M. Crosbie, Cloud forensics, in *Advances in Digital Forensics V*, G. Peterson and S. Shenoi (Eds.), Springer, Heidelberg, Germany, pp. 35–46, 2011.

[13] M. Saudi, An Overview of a Disk Imaging Tool in Computer Forensics, InfoSec Reading Room, SANS Institute, Bethesda, Maryland, 2001.

[14] X. Sun, J. Dai, P. Liu, A. Singhal and J. Yen, Towards probabilistic identification of zero-day attack paths, *Proceedings of the IEEE Conference on Communications and Network Security*, pp. 64–72, 2016.

[15] X. Sun, A. Singhal and P. Liu, Towards actionable mission impact assessment in the context of cloud computing, in *Data and Applications Security and Privacy XXXI*, G. Livraga and S. Zhu (Eds), Springer International, Cham, Switzerland, pp. 259–274, 2017.

[16] Y. Sun, T. Wu, X. Liu and M. Obaidat, Multilayered impact evaluation model for attacking missions, *IEEE Systems Journal*, vol. 10(4), pp. 1304–1315, 2016.

[17] W. Wang and T. Daniels, A graph based approach toward network forensic analysis, *ACM Transactions on Information and Systems Security*, vol. 12(1), article no. 4, 2008.

[18] Y. Yarom and K. Falkner, FLUSH+RELOAD: A high resolution, low noise, L3 cache side-channel attack, *Proceedings of the Twenty-Third USENIX Security Symposium*, pp. 719–732, 2014.

[19] Y. Zhang, A. Juels, M. Reiter and T. Ristenpart, Cross-VM side channels and their use to extract private keys, *Proceedings of the ACM Conference on Computer and Communications Security*, pp. 305–316, 2012.

V

MOBILE AND EMBEDDED DEVICE FORENSICS

Chapter 16

FORENSIC ANALYSIS OF ANDROID STEGANOGRAPHY APPS

Wenhao Chen, Yangxiao Wang, Yong Guan, Jennifer Newman, Li Lin and Stephanie Reinders

Abstract   The processing power of smartphones supports steganographic algorithms that were considered to be too computationally intensive for handheld devices. Several steganography apps are now available on mobile phones to support covert communications using digital photographs.

This chapter focuses on two key questions: How effectively can a steganography app be reverse engineered? How can this knowledge help improve the detection of steganographic images and other related files? Two Android steganography apps, PixelKnot and Da Vinci Secret Image, are analyzed. Experiments demonstrate that they are constructed in very different ways and provide different levels of security for hiding messages. The results of detecting steganography files, including images generated by the apps, using three software packages are presented. The results point to an urgent need for further research on reverse engineering steganography apps and detecting images produced by these apps.

Keywords: Image forensics, steganography, steganalysis, Android apps

1.   Introduction

The field of covert communications has a long history. Message encryption, called cryptography, is a well-known method for secret communications, but its limitation is that the transmission of encrypted messages is not kept secret. Steganography, on the other hand, attempts to send a message while hiding the fact that it is being transmitted, essentially evading the detection of the secret communication itself. The word steganography originates from Greek, meaning "covered writing." The first evidence of steganography dates back to late sixth century BC Greece: Herodotus [11] describes how Histiaeus sent his slave to the Io-

© IFIP International Federation for Information Processing 2018
Published by Springer Nature Switzerland AG 2018. All Rights Reserved
G. Peterson and S. Shenoi (Eds.): Advances in Digital Forensics XIV, IFIP AICT 532, pp. 293–312, 2018.
https://doi.org/10.1007/978-3-319-99277-8_16

nian city of Miletus with a hidden message to incite a revolt against the Persian king. The slave's head was shaved, a message was tattooed on his scalp and his hair was allowed to grow back. After his hair had concealed the message, the slave was sent to Aristagoras, the city's regent. Aristagoras had the slave's head shaved and read the secret message. Modern versions of steganographic communications include invisible ink and microdots. Digital versions of steganographic messaging are now provided by software on computers as well as by smartphone apps.

Digital steganography hides a message or payload in the form of bits in a cover medium, also represented by bits, so as to not arouse suspicion of the hidden content. The cover file is combined with the payload to produce a "stego" file. The stego file is transmitted to the intended recipient, who extracts the hidden payload. A key is sometimes involved in steganographic communications.

The fundamental question is: How can one change the bits of a cover medium, such as a digital photograph, PDF document, digital audio file or video file, to represent the payload bits and then have the recipient successfully extract the payload after the stego version is received?

Hiding a payload in a digital photograph may be accomplished by appending it after the end-of-file (EOF) marker in a JPG image [23, 25, 29], in the color palette of a GIF image [14], in the EXIF header of an image [1, 5], in a PDF file [15], in the lower bits of a non-compressed RGB or grayscale image [8] or in the quantized discrete cosine transform coefficients of a compressed JPG image [12]. Digital audio [6] and video [22] files can also be used to hide payloads, as well as TCP/IP packets [17].

The discovery of stego-related files is called "steg detection." The existence of stego executables and related files on a system may indicate that steganography was used, so steg detection includes the detection of ancillary files that do not contain payloads. Patterns in stego files such as an embedded signature or statistical properties can also be exploited in steganalysis. Signature-based detection of a stego or ancillary file, based on specific characters or, perhaps, locations of added information, requires signatures and computer code that opens the file and searches for signatures. Statistics-based detection employs statistical measures of a suspected stego file and searches for abnormalities that indicate steganography. Another type of steg detection engages machine learning algorithms that do not depend on signatures written explicitly into stego files.

Although a mobile phone app makes steganography very easy to use, the detection of stego images produced by mobile phone apps has not as yet been discussed in the literature. Mobile apps for iOS and Android phones can conceal a text payload in a photograph stored on the phone or acquired using the camera. Certain apps enable another file (e.g., image file) to be hidden in the cover image. However, some of the roughly 30 available steganography apps are unstable and may crash when using certain cover photographs, large payloads or specific mobile phone models.

The code used in the bit embedding process, where the bits of a cover image are changed to capture payload bits, varies according to the apps. In addition, not all apps have open-source code, which makes it difficult to reverse engineer their code. Thus, signature-based investigations of these apps are difficult, if not impossible, when signatures do not exist. Machine-learning-based detection may be more reliable than signature-based detection, but it requires substantial image data for training and classification.

In principle, applying machine learning to detect stego images from a mobile phone camera is no different from the "classical academic setting." In this classical setting, steganography or steganalysis is performed on a known set of image data, where the embedding algorithm is completely known and machine learning detection algorithms can be applied. Many academic steganography algorithms demonstrate the difficulty in detecting new embedding algorithms using known "best detection" algorithms (typically machine learning algorithms). In the case of steganalysis, the goal is to show that a new algorithm has clear performance advantages over existing algorithms. This chapter does not present any steganalysis results involving machine learning applications, although it includes a short description for completeness. The focus is on software that forensic practitioners can use to detect the existence of steganography.

This chapter discusses reverse engineering efforts on two Android apps, PixelKnot [10] and Da Vinci Secret Image [21]. The results underpin a procedure for generating a large quantity of stego images on a computer using PixelKnot code without having a human enter information manually using the mobile phone app. This chapter also presents the results of the first publicly-available evaluation of steg detection tools.

2. Related Work

This section discusses methods for detecting steganography payloads hidden in image files. Also, it discusses tools used for reverse engineering Android apps.

2.1   Steg Detection Approaches

Steg detection has two principal use cases: (i) discrimination of a normal image from a stego image; and (ii) identification of a file that can be associated with a steganographic process. While steganalysis commonly refers to the first use case, the second use case covers the identification of executable files and other non-image files involved in producing stego images. Digital forensic practitioners are interested in both use cases.

There are three basic types of steg detection approaches: (i) signature-based detection; (ii) hash-based detection: and (iii) machine-learning-based detection:

- **Signature-Based Detection:** Signature-based detection identifies possible signatures that a steganography program writes to an output stego image. Following this, stego files are detected using the signatures.

  Stego signatures exist in various forms. A program could embed the same fixed bit string along with a payload; or, the embedding path could visit the same pixel locations in the same order regardless of payload content, leaving a repeated pattern in the stego file.

  The commercial tool, StegoHunt [28], and the academic tool, StegDetect, perform signature-based steg detection. If the signature of the steganography program is known, then a signature-based approach can accurately identify stego images and, possibly, extract the hidden payloads. However, this approach requires continual updating of the detection code. This is because a change to the steganography program produces a different signature from the previous one, resulting in the failure to detect stego files created with the new program.

- **Hash-Based Detection:** Hash-based steg detection involves the identification of a previous, identical stego file, such as an image identified as child pornography. In this scenario, copies of the stego image that hide the payload are available; thus, all the stego images are identical in a bit-by-bit comparison and have identical hashes. This enables comparisons of the hash values of unknown images against a database of hash values of known stego images. New images that need to be analyzed are only required to have their hash values compared against the hash values of known stego images in the database.

- **Machine-Learning-Based Detection:** Machine-learning-based steg detection is a more complex task. In theory, a machine learning classifier can be constructed to identify an unknown stego image, if training data is available along with other caveats. The details of this type of approach are omitted because they are beyond the scope of this research. However, two machine-learning-based classifiers are discussed in [8, 16]. They require large amounts of training data – 700 to 6,000 cover images, the same number of corresponding stego images and a representative feature set and classifier. With these items and enough computing power, it is possible to create a machine classifier that detects stego images.

2.2 Reverse Engineering Android Applications

The approach for detecting stego images produced by an Android app involves the inspection of the app code. This so-called reverse engineering task attempts to understand the logic and other code details with the ultimate goal of exploiting certain characteristics of how the code processes images.

Reverse engineering is commonly used for program analysis. Analyzing an Android app often requires a reverse engineering tool that converts application binaries (APK) to a human-readable format. Android apps are developed in the Java programming language and compiled to Dalvik bytecode [3], which is similar to Java bytecode. The Dalvik bytecode is then encoded and written to a DEX file in the APK.

Several tools are available for extracting and decoding DEX files from an Android APK, and recreating the app code in the source or intermediate code format. Apktool [24] is designed for reverse engineering Android APK files; it decodes a DEX file to an intermediate code format called Smali [9]. The tool can also decode resource XML files, including the graphical interface definition and manifest file. Although Apktool does not translate DEX files into Java code, it provides accurate representations of binaries by avoiding translation loss.

The `dex2jar` tool [18] converts DEX to Java bytecode. Java Decompiler [13] can then be used to decompile the Java bytecode into Java source code, with possible loss of metadata and certain irreversible DEX code blocks. Using `dex2jar` and Java Decompiler in combination makes it possible to recreate the Java source code from an APK file. However, due to inconsistencies in Java Decompiler, the output source code can only be used as a reference for application analysis.

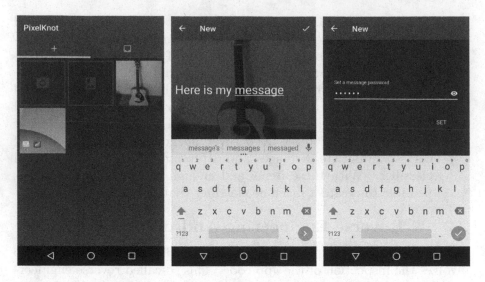

Figure 1. User input sequence for the PixelKnot app.

3.   Android App Reverse Engineering

Steganography apps developed for Android devices have certain common characteristics that can be exploited during the reverse engineering process. These characteristics can be leveraged to reduce the scope of code analysis and provide clues that help locate the core embedding algorithm. This section analyzes the common characteristics of Android steganography apps and describes the technical details involved in reverse engineering the apps.

3.1   Common Characteristics

The first common characteristic of Android steganography apps is the user interface components. At a minimum, a user interface should enable a user to: (i) select a cover image; (ii) input a payload; and (optionally) (iii) input a password. As such, an app must provide the user interface components to enable these interactions. Figures 1 and 2 show the similarities of the user input sequences (select a cover image, input a message to embed and input a password) for the PixelKnot and Da Vinci Secret Image apps, respectively.

Additionally, as shown in Figure 3, in order to enable a user to select an image or take a picture, the app must request the corresponding "permissions" in the program code and manifest file.

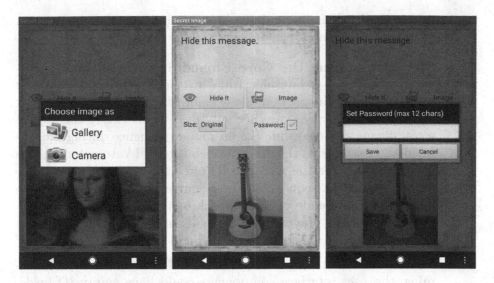

Figure 2.   User input sequence for the Da Vinci app.

```
<uses-permission android:name="android.permission.WRITE_EXTERNAL_STORAGE"/>
<uses-permission android:name="android.permission.READ_EXTERNAL_STORAGE"/>
<uses-permission android:name="android.permission.CAMERA"/>
```

Figure 3.   Permission request code from the Android app manifest.

Another common characteristic is the use of image processing libraries. Although there are several Android image processing libraries, the image pixels are always loaded into a bitmap object that stores all the pixel values. Therefore, the embedding algorithm always has an instruction that instantiates a bitmap object and a method call that accesses the bitmap object, e.g., `Bitmap.getPixel(x,y)`.

3.2   Reverse Engineering Process

Reverse engineering the Android steganography apps involved three steps:

- **Step 1. Extracting the App Code:** In this step, Apktool was used to extract the app code along with the resource files in order to search for the location of the core embedding algorithm. Apktool was selected over other tools because it provides the most accurate representation of binary code. It does not attempt to transform or optimize the original binaries, and increases code readability using a one-to-one mapping from DEX instructions to Smali instructions.

Although Smali is more difficult to read than other instruction formats, it guarantees the integrity of the code.

- **Step 2. Locating the Core Embedding Algorithm:** Locating the core embedding algorithm involved two parts. The first part involved an inspection of the embedding workflow in the user interface domain. This was accomplished by executing the app on a test device and recording the user input sequence during the embedding task. Next, the Android debugger UIAutomator [2] was used to search for the resource ID of each user interface component in the input sequence. The resource IDs were then used to locate the Smali code of the callback method for each user interface component. The callback methods may contain the code for image processing, payload processing and payload embedding.

  However, due to the flexibility of Android user interface programming, the user interface components could have empty ID fields. Since Android enables authors to register the callback methods for user interface components created at runtime, the resource IDs were not required. Therefore, the search for the embedding algorithm employed keywords. As mentioned above, certain libraries and objects would most likely be used during embedding. Keywords such as `BitmapFactory` and `Bitmap.getPixel(x,y)` could be employed to trace the execution flow and eventually locate the entry point of the embedding algorithm.

- **Step 3. Analyzing the Embedding Algorithm:** After the embedding algorithm code was located, it was inspected manually to find the lines of code that perform the embedding. Generally, an embedding algorithm starts by defining the order in which pixels are visited; this is called the embedding path. Next, the payload is divided into bits or bytes that are embedded in a certain manner along the embedding path. Other embedding tasks such as payload encryption and random path generation also must be analyzed. Since almost every steganography app has a unique way of embedding a bit stream, embedded algorithm analysis varies based on the app and relies greatly on the experience of the analyst.

4.   Case Study

This section presents detailed results of the reverse engineering efforts on the PixelKnot and Da Vinci Secret Image Android apps. These two Google Play Store apps have similar user interfaces and functionality. However, they employ very different embedding processes.

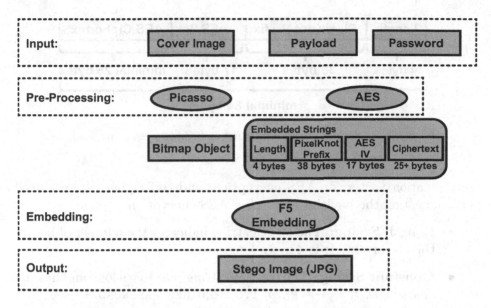

Figure 4. PixelKnot embedding process workflow.

4.1   PixelKnot

PixelKnot [10] is an Android implementation of the F5 steganography algorithm [27] with some modifications. The PixelKnot user interface was examined by running the app on an Android test device (Google Pixel phone). The embedding algorithm code was downloaded from Github [9]. The academic version of F5 is distinguished from the Pixel-Knot version of F5 by calling it standard F5.

Figure 4 shows the workflow of the PixelKnot embedding process. PixelKnot has three user inputs: (i) cover image; (ii) payload (text message); and (iii) password. It produces the stego image in the JPG format. The F5 algorithm uses the quantized discrete cosine transform technique to embed bits.

The PixelKnot algorithm performs two preparatory steps before executing the bit embedding process. First, the input image must be resized by downsampling if its width or height exceed 1,280 pixels. In this case, the larger side is scaled to 1,280 pixels and the other side is scaled in proportion to the original dimensions. For example, a $1,920 \times 1,280$ input image is downsampled to $1,280 \times 853$ pixels. The resized image is then loaded into a bitmap object, which is a matrix array of the pixel values. In the second step, the bit string to be embedded is created by concatenating four strings: (i) length string; (ii) constant string; (iii)

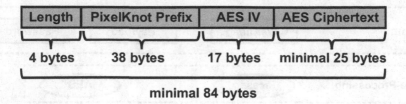

Figure 5. Format of the PixelKnot embedded message payload.

initialization vector for AES encryption; and (iv) ciphertext produced
by encrypting the payload text using AES encryption:

- **Length String:** The length string indicates the number of bits in
  the ciphertext. It is 4 bytes long.

- **Constant String:** The constant string is 38 bytes long and has the
  characters: ''----* PK v 1.0 REQUIRES PASSWORD ----*''.

- **Initialization Vector:** The initialization vector is always 17 bytes
  long. It is a randomly-generated string used by AES to produce
  the ciphertext. The initialization vector is stored in the image so
  that it can be used to extract the message later.

- **AES-Encrypted Payload:** The payload is the AES ciphertext
  of the payload text input by the user.

The ciphertext generated by PixelKnot's AES encryption has a minimum length of 25 bytes. Therefore, the bit string embedded in the input
image has a minimum length of 84 bytes (Figure 5).

The algorithm used by PixelKnot to produce ciphertext adds security
over and above the standard F5 algorithm. First, an AES key is generated using PBKDF2 with HMAC and SHA1, where the first third of
the password is the key and the second third of the password is the salt.
Next, the AES-GCM-NoPadding cipher is used to encrypt the plaintext
with the AES key and a random initialization vector; the initialization
vector is stored in the image because it is needed to decrypt the ciphertext. Finally, a pseudorandom visitation of the pixel sites in the image
is generated using the last third of the password. The random path
through the image visits a pixel and embeds a bit at the site using the
F5 algorithm. The random spreading of the embedded bits around the
image ensures that even if a constant string is embedded, it can only be
found if the password is known. Note that even if the same password,
input image and payload text are used, different ciphertext is generated
each time the app is run. This is because the initialization vector, which

is randomly generated, is different for each execution of the app. Thus, the security of the PixelKnot implementation of F5 depends largely on the strength of the password.

Thousands of stego images had to be generated in order to evaluate the effectiveness of the evaluated stego detection programs. This was accomplished by installing PixelKnot on multiple Android emulators running on a computer to batch-generate stego images. To verify that the emulator environment was identical to a real Android device when running PixelKnot, a test was devised that compared the stego images produced by an emulator with the stego images from a real device. Due to the randomness of the initialization vector, even with the same plaintext message and password, PixelKnot produces different ciphertext in different runs, resulting in different stego images. Therefore, the verification test used a slightly modified version of PixelKnot called PK.v1, which disabled AES encryption to eliminate randomness.

PK.v1 was installed on two Android emulators and a Google Pixel phone. Identical stego images were obtained upon providing identical cover images, payload text and passwords to PK.v1 on the emulators and on the Pixel phone. This test was performed ten times using ten different combinations of images, payloads and passwords.

After it was verified that the emulator exactly mimicked code running on the Pixel phone, a second version of the PixelKnot source code, called PK.v2, was created to efficiently generate large numbers of stego images. PK.v2 removed all the user interface portions from the original app while adding functionality such as saving an intermediate cover image and saving embedding stats, including the embedding rate. PK.v2 read input images from a folder and used different passwords, payloads and predetermined embedding rates to generate the corresponding stego images. This procedure generated more than 4,000 stego images at the rate of about 100 images per minute.

4.2 Da Vinci Secret Image

Da Vinci Secret Image is a steganography application that uses a simpler embedding algorithm than PixelKnot. Because its source code is not available to the public, Smali code was extracted from its APK file using Apktool. The embedding algorithm code was then located using the two-step approach described above. Following this, analysis was performed on the target Smali code.

The Da Vinci Secret Image app provides similar functionality as PixelKnot. It enables a user to select a cover image, input the payload text and, optionally, enter a password. The user can also select one of a fixed

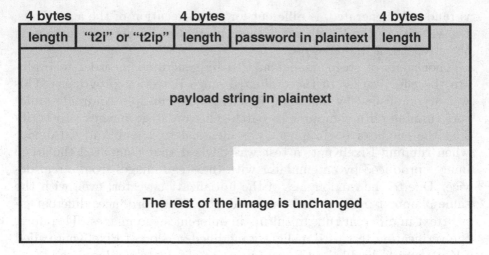

Figure 6. Embedding process of the Da Vinci Secret Image app.

number of image dimensions for the output image, including maintaining the original image size. Depending on the selected size, the input image may be resized before the embedding process. While several different formats are supported for the input image, the stego output is always in the PNG format.

Figure 6 shows the embedding process of the Da Vinci Secret Image app. The embedding is performed in the alpha channel of the PNG image. During the embedding process, pixel sites are visited in a lexicographical manner from top left to bottom right. This is very different from PixelKnot, where the pixel site visitation is random.

The image is first pre-processed to prepare for the embedding. The input image file is decoded and loaded into a bitmap object using the Android API `BitmapFactory.decodeFile(path/to/image)`. If the user selects a size that is different from the original size, the bitmap object is adjusted to match the target size.

Next, a series of six strings are generated:

- **String 1:** This string indicates the number of bits in the string t2i or t2ip, depending on whether or not the user entered a password. The string is always 4 bytes long. If a password was supplied by the user, then the string comprises the bits 100000 preceded by 26 zeros (because there are 32 bits in the length string); otherwise, the string comprises the bits 10100 preceded by 27 zeros.

- **String 2:** This string is the bit representation of t2i or t2ip. If a password was supplied, then the string t2i is embedded; otherwise, t2ip is embedded. This string is always 4 bytes long.

- **String 3:** This string, which is always 4 bytes long, indicates the length of the password.

- **String 4:** This string contains the bit representation of the plaintext password.

- **String 5:** This string, which is always 4 bytes long, indicates the length of the payload.

- **String 6:** This string contains the bit representation of the plaintext payload.

The remaining bits of the image are unchanged should the payload string be shorter than the remaining bits. The six strings are concatenated and then embedded into the alpha channel. The alpha channel can be viewed as the fourth 8-bit plane of the RBG color image in the PNG format. The bit value "zero" of the string to be embedded is given the value 254 in the alpha channel whereas the bit value "one" is given the value 255. If the input image contains information in the alpha channel and the original size is unchanged, then information in the alpha is overwritten. However, changing pixels in the alpha channel does not change the RGB values representing the image content and, thus, the image scene is untouched.

After the embedding process is known, it is relatively straightforward to analyze a PNG image and determine if it was produced by the Da Vinci Secret Image app. First, the alpha channel is inspected for the characters t2i or t2ip in bytes 5–8. This identifies the stego file as being produced by Da Vinci, so the first 64 bits of the alpha channel serves as a signature.

The app uses the password only to verify that the extraction of the payload can proceed, not to encrypt the payload. If an incorrect password is provided, the app does not extract the payload. However, since it is known that information resides in the alpha channel, upon observing the characters t2i or t2ip, the length of the payload can be read and the payload extracted and reconstructed into plaintext.

Despite the similarities in their user interfaces and functionality, Da Vinci and PixelKnot employ very different embedding processes. Da Vinci uses a fixed embedding path whereas PixelKnot uses a random embedding path. Da Vinci embeds bits directly into the alpha channel whereas PixelKnot embeds bits into the quantized discrete cosine transform domain of JPG. Most importantly, Da Vinci neither uses encryption nor randomness. The analysis of the Da Vinci algorithm reveals that its stego images have easily detectable signatures. Due to the embedding of a signature message and absence of encryption and randomness, merely reading the first 64 pixels is enough to identify a Da Vinci stego image.

5.　　　Performance Evaluation

This section presents the results of evaluating three steganography detection programs: (i) StegDetect (from DC3); (ii) StegoHunt [28] (commercially-available); and (iii) StegDetect (by Provos) [20] (freeware). The evaluation sought to assess the effectiveness of the programs at detecting stego images generated by various Android apps.

5.1　　　Experimental Setup

StegDetect from DC3 is a software program that detects stego-related files on a computer. It has a graphical user interface that provides several options, including identifying the programs to be detected. The program can be applied to several types of files, including executable files and stego images. In the experiments, StegDetect was applied to image files and executable files. It uses signatures for detection, and attempts to extract a password, decrypt it and extract the payload. StegDetect was last updated in the mid 2000s, so it does not contain the signatures of new and updated programs.

StegoHunt, commercial software from WetStone [28], is advertised as the "leading software tool for discovering the presence of data hiding activities." It can "generate case specific reports for management or court presentation" and "identify suspect carrier files: program artifacts, program signatures, statistical anomalies." No details are provided, but it appears that the program uses hash tables for lookups and file signatures and statistics to perform its analysis. The software has ten possible detection responses for a given file and the results are provided in a report.

StegDetect by Provos [20] only accepts JPG images as input. It is designed to detect stego images produced by three steganography programs: (i) jsteg [26]; (ii) jphide [26]; and (iii) outguess 0.13b [19]. All three steg embedding programs output JPG images. If a file is detected as containing steganography, then StegDetect proceeds to identify the most likely embedding algorithm used.

In the experiments, the three detection programs were executed on cover and stego images. The images were in the JPG and PNG formats. Since StegDetect cannot handle PNG files, these files were not used when evaluating the program.

Table 1. Image sets used in the evaluation.

	Image Format	Image Type	Image Quantity	Embedding Algorithm
Set 1	PNG	Cover	2,090	None
Set 2	JPG	Cover	1,606	None
Set 3	JPG	Stego	4,818	PixelKnot
Set 4	JPG	Stego	421	Standard FS
Set 5	PNG	Stego	10	Camouflage

5.2   Detection Results

A set of cover images was first created. The images were acquired using a set of mobile phones [4]. The cover images were created in the JPG and PNG formats.

Table 1 describes the image sets used in the evaluation. The test images were grouped into five sets, each indicating a different file type or embedding algorithm.

Table 2. Detection results for cover images.

	Image Quantity	StegoHunt	StegDetect DC3	StegDetect Provos
Set 1	2,090	1,304 Carrier Anomalies	0 Suspicious	N/A
Set 2	1,606	0 Anomalies	0 Suspicious	380 Stegos (24%)

First, the three detection programs were applied to the cover images in Sets 1 and 2. Table 2 presents the detection results. Note that StegoHunt identified more than half of the cover PNG images as having "anomalies," which may be due to the different type of file formatting applied to produce the PNG images. StegDetect by Provos identified 24% of the cover JPGs images as stego images.

Next, the detection programs were tested on the stego images in Sets 3 and 4. The stego images from Set 3 were generated by PixelKnot using scripts executing on Android emulators. Note that this set of stego images was generated using different embedding rates. Generally, a longer payload means that more bits were changed, which makes detection easier; this topic is not discussed further because it outside the scope of this research. The stego images in Set 4 were generated by the standard F5 steganography algorithm executing on a desktop computer [7].

Table 3. Detection results for PixelKnot and Standard F5 stego images.

	Image Quantity	Algorithm	StegoHunt	StegDetect DC3	StegDetect Provos
Set 3	4,818	PixelKnot	0 Anomalies	0 Suspicious	1,160 Stegos (24%)
Set 4	421	Standard F5	399 Carrier Anomalies	421 Marked as F5	223 Stegos (53%)

Table 3 shows the detection results for Sets 3 and 4. Neither Stego-Hunt nor the DC3 StegDetect properly detected a single stego image created using PixelKnot. Note that PixelKnot was created around 2012 and, thus, is not in the DC3 StegDetect database. However, Provos StegDetect correctly identified around 24% of the PixelKnot stego images without, of course, the correct identifying algorithm (because the F5 algorithm was not one of the three labeled algorithms). In the case of the standard F5 stego images in Set 4, StegoHunt identified almost the images as having anomalies, but not as stego. In contrast, DC3 StegDetect properly identified all 421 stego images as being embedded by the standard F5 algorithm. However, Provos StegDetect identified only 53% of the stego images correctly, about the same percentage as random guessing.

Table 4. Detection results for Camouflage stego images.

	Image Quantity	Algorithm	StegoHunt	StegDetect DC3	StegDetect Provos
Set 5	10	Camouflage	0 out of 10 Data added after EOF	10 out of 10 Detected as Camouflage	N/A

For the final set of experiments, the older Camouflage steganography software [25] was used to create ten stego images (Set 5). Table 4 shows the detection results. Both StegoHunt and DC3 StegDetect correctly identified all ten images as stego, with StegoHunt correctly warning that data was appended past the end-of-file marker and DC3 StegDetect recognizing the images as having been created by Camouflage. Additionally, DC3 StegDetect extracted the passwords and payloads for all ten stego images.

5.3 Discussion

In the evaluation, DC3 StegDetect performed better than StegoHunt and Provos StegDetect on the image sets. StegoHunt identified Camouflage stegos and detected anomalies in most standard F5 stegos, but they were not detected correctly as stego images. DC3 StegDetect identified all the F5 stegos, and also identified and extracted the messages in all the Camouflage stegos. Neither StegoHunt nor DC3 StegDetect identified PixelKnot stegos. As shown in Table 2, Provos StegDetect had a high false alarm rate of 24% and a high missed detection rate of 75% (Table 3). Of the 223 stegos in Set 4 that were detected by Provos StegDetect, 219 were correctly identified as standard F5 stegos while the other four were incorrectly identified as Outguess and jphide. Finally, Provos StegDetect identified the tested (cover and stego) images with a rate between 25% and 50%, which is rather poor.

Since StegoHunt and DC3 StegDetect can be employed to identify steganography programs, they were also used to scan the standard F5 and Camouflage executables and the source code of standard F5. However, neither program was able to correctly identify any of the files.

6. Conclusions

This research has analyzed the common characteristics and key features of the well-known PixelKnot and Da Vinci Secret Image apps for Android devices. The analysis has revealed that, despite having similar user interfaces, the two apps have completely different embedding processes. PixelKnot is based on the F5 steganography algorithm that hides payloads in the quantized discrete cosine transform domain and implements anti-analysis measures such as encryption and randomness. Da Vinci Secret Image, on the other hand, is simple and straightforward to analyze. Since it does not employ encryption or randomness, the Da Vinci Secret Image app exhibited a signature that readily identifies its stego images. Other newer stego apps may also have their own signatures.

The evaluation has demonstrated that current steganography detection software is inadequate at identifying stego images created by PixelKnot, which is a relatively recent steganography app. Clearly, detecting steg files created by mobile steg apps is in its infancy, but it is an interesting and most important research area.

Acknowledgements

This research was partially supported by the Center for Statistics and Applications in Forensic Evidence (CSAFE) through Cooperative Agreement No. 70NANB15H176 between NIST and Iowa State University, which includes research conducted at Carnegie Mellon University, University of California Irvine and University of Virginia. The authors are grateful to Yiqiu Qian, Joseph Bingham, Chase Webb and Mingming Yue for their assistance in generating the images used in this research.

References

[1] P. Alvarez, Using extended file information (EXIF) file headers in digital evidence analysis, *International Journal of Digital Evidence*, vol. 2(3), 2004.

[2] Android Developers, UI Automator (`developer.android.com/training/testing/ui-automator.html`), 2018.

[3] Android Open Source Project, Dalvik Bytecode (`source.android.com/devices/tech/dalvik/dalvik-bytecode`), 2018.

[4] Center for Statistics and Applications in Forensic Evidence, StegoDB: An Image Dataset for Benchmarking Steganalysis Algorithms, Final Technical Report, Iowa State University, Ames, Iowa, 2017.

[5] A. Cheddad, J. Condell, K. Curran and P. McKevitt, Digital image steganography: Survey and analysis of current methods, *Signal Processing*, vol. 90(3), pp. 727–752, 2010.

[6] F. Djebbar, B. Ayad, K. Abed Meraim and H. Hamam, Comparative study of digital audio steganography techniques, *EURASIP Journal on Audio, Speech and Music Processing*, vol. 2012, article no. 25, 2012.

[7] F5-Steganography Project, F5 Steganography in Java (`code.google.com/archive/p/f5-steganography`), 2017.

[8] J. Fridrich and J. Kodovsky, Rich models for steganalysis of digital images, *IEEE Transactions on Information Forensics and Security*, vol. 7(3), pp. 868–882, 2012.

[9] B. Gruver, Smali Home (`github.com/JesusFreke/smali/wiki`), 2017.

[10] Guardian Project, Pixelknot: Hidden Messages (`guardianproject.info/apps/pixelknot`), 2017.

[11] Herodotus, *The Histories*, A. Burn (Ed.) and A. de Selincourt (Translator), Penguin Books, Harmondsworth, United Kingdom, 1954.

[12] F. Huang, J. Huang and Y. Shi, New channel selection rule for JPEG steganography, *IEEE Transactions on Information Forensics and Security*, vol. 7(4), pp. 1181–1191, 2012.

[13] JD Project, Java Decompiler – Yet Anther Fast Java Decompiler (jd.benow.ca), 2015.

[14] N. Johnson and S. Jajodia, Exploring steganography: Seeing the unseen, *IEEE Computer*, vol. 31(2), pp. 26–34, 1998.

[15] I. Lee and W. Tsai, A new approach to covert communications via PDF files, *Signal Processing*, vol. 90(2), pp. 557–565, 2010.

[16] S. Lyu and H. Farid, Steganalysis using higher-order image statistics, *IEEE Transactions on Information Forensics and Security*, vol. 1(1), pp. 111–119, 2006.

[17] W. Mazurczyk, P. Szaga and K. Szczypiorski, Using transcoding for hidden communications in IP telephony, *Multimedia Tools and Applications*, vol. 70(3), pp. 2139–2165, 2014.

[18] B. Pan, dex2jar (github.com/pxb1988/dex2jar), 2018.

[19] N. Provos, Outguess (www.outguess.org), 2017.

[20] N. Provos, StegDetect (github.com/abeluck/stegdetect), 2017.

[21] RADJAB, Da Vinci Secret Image (play.google.com/store/apps/details?id=jubatus.android.davinci), 2012.

[22] M. Sadek, A. Khalifa and M. Mostafa, Video steganography: A comprehensive review, *Multimedia Tools and Applications*, vol. 74(17), pp. 7063–7094, 2015.

[23] Sky Juice Software, Data Stash, Singapore (www.skyjuicesoftware.com/software/ds_info.html), 2017.

[24] C. Tumbleson and R. Winsniewski, Apktool: A Tool for Reverse Engineering Android APK Files, version 2.2.0, 2016.

[25] Twisted Pear Productions, Camouflage (camouflage.unfiction.com), 2018.

[26] D. Upham, Steganographic Algorithm Jsteg (zooid.org/paul/crypto/jsteg), 1993.

[27] A. Westfeld, F5 – A steganographic algorithm, in *Information Hiding*, I. Moskowitz (Ed.), Springer-Verlag, Berlin Heidelberg, Germany, pp. 289–302, 2001.

[28] WetStone Technologies, StegoHunt, Cortland, New York (`www.wetstonetech.com/product/stegohunt`), 2018.

[29] Wikibin, Jpegx (www.nerdlogic.org/jpegx/old/jpgx.html), 2017.

Chapter 17

AUTOMATED VULNERABILITY DETECTION IN EMBEDDED DEVICES

Danjun Liu, Yong Tang, Baosheng Wang, Wei Xie and Bo Yu

Abstract   Embedded devices are widely used today and are rapidly being incorporated in the Internet of Things that will permeate every aspect of society. However, embedded devices have vulnerabilities such as buffer overflows, command injections and backdoors that are often undocumented. Malicious entities who discover these vulnerabilities could exploit them to gain control of embedded devices and conduct a variety of criminal activities.

Due to the large number of embedded devices, non-standard codebases and complex control flows, it is extremely difficult to discover vulnerabilities using manual techniques. Current automated vulnerability detection tools typically use static analysis, but the detection accuracy is not high. Some tools employ code execution; however, this approach is inefficient, detects limited types of vulnerabilities and is restricted to specific architectures. Other tools use symbolic execution, but the level of automation is not high and the types of vulnerabilities they uncover are limited. This chapter evaluates several advanced vulnerability detection techniques used by current tools, especially those involving automated program analysis. These techniques are leveraged in a new automated vulnerability detection methodology for embedded devices.

Keywords: Embedded devices, automated vulnerability detection, binary analysis

1.   Introduction

As the Internet of Things becomes more popular, massive numbers of embedded devices will permeate our lives. These devices include smart locks, smart utility meters, network routers, printers, surveillance systems, smart TVs, medical implants and automobiles. The tremendous growth of embedded devices has been spurred by advances in telecommunications and microelectronics. As far back as 2012, the Wi-Fi penetra-

G. Peterson and S. Shenoi (Eds.): Advances in Digital Forensics XIV, IFIP AICT 532, pp. 313–329, 2018.
https://doi.org/10.1007/978-3-319-99277-8_17

tion in South Korea reached 80% and nearly two-thirds of U.S. families had network routers; by 2020, the smart meter coverage in the United States will be close to 100% [16].

Firmware is the software that runs on embedded devices. It initiates the operating system, performs computations and realizes input/output operations. Just like general software, firmware may have vulnerabilities whose consequences can be very serious. For example, a home router is the only line of defense between a user's networked device and the Internet. Unfortunately, most vendors do not enhance home router security via updates. Therefore, once a router vulnerability is known, a malicious entity could, for example, modify router configurations and hijack network traffic [13, 18].

Embedded device analysis typically focuses on a specific version of firmware [10, 15, 22]. Although manual analysis can identify vulnerabilities in the firmware of an embedded device, it is a long and tedious process. Manual analysis does not scale – in the real-world, there are thousands of firmware images to be analyzed, and their underlying architectures, instruction sets and execution environments are diverse and complicated.

For these reasons, it is prudent to focus on the development of automated vulnerability detection techniques. Costin et al. [8, 9] have proposed automated analysis techniques, but the techniques have limited levels of automation and are unable to identify vulnerabilities in unknown firmware. Other researchers [22, 24] have also proposed automated firmware analysis techniques, but the automation is limited and only specific types of firmware vulnerabilities can be discovered.

Fortunately, several automated analysis tools have been developed for general programs based on source code, binary files, static analysis or dynamic execution. The techniques underlying these tools can be engaged in automating vulnerability detection in embedded devices. This chapter analyzes and evaluates the principal automated analysis techniques and leverages them in a new automated vulnerability detection methodology for embedded devices.

2.   Vulnerability Detection Techniques

Several techniques have been proposed for program vulnerability detection. Some techniques have attracted considerable attention due to their good test results. However, even techniques that produce ordinary results have excellent underlying concepts that can be employed in developing enhanced techniques. This section discusses influential vulnerability detection techniques. In order to provide clarity, the techniques

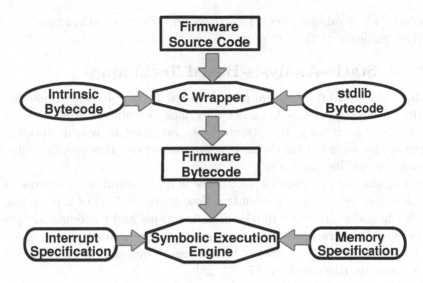

Figure 1. FIE workflow.

are divided into four categories: (i) source-code-based techniques; (ii) static-analysis-based techniques; (iii) actual-execution-based techniques; and (iv) symbolic-execution-based techniques.

2.1   Source-Code-Based Techniques

The FIE platform [11] is designed to detect vulnerabilities in firmware running on the MSP430 family of microcontrollers, primarily focusing on memory safety issues. Although FIE supports a specific architecture and relies on source code written in C, it provides a useful and effective framework for analyzing programs.

Figure 1 presents the FIE workflow. The source code of a target program is translated to LLVM bytecode and symbolic execution based on KLEE [3] is employed to analyze the bytecode. The symbolic engine supports 16-bit architectures and has a special memory structure that makes it easy to access program memory and hardware. It allows interrupts at any program statement and at any time during program execution. FIE performs an analysis of the entire firmware, but the symbolic execution can suffer from path explosion for certain loops, resulting in non-termination. However, this problem can be mitigated by state pruning, removing redundant (equivalent) states from the list of states to explore and performing "memory smudging" to concretize variables with respect to a finite set of values.

From the perspective of automating vulnerability discovery, FIE incorporates two key features. First, source code is translated to LLVM bytecode for symbolic execution. Second, effective techniques are applied to mitigate path explosion.

2.2   Static-Analysis-Based Techniques

Most static analysis techniques are used to supplement dynamic execution analysis; this is because they lack semantic understanding of programs. Specifically, these techniques are used to reason about programs without executing them, helping make proactive preparations for dynamic execution analysis.

Static analysis can provide assistance in understanding programs. The creation (i.e., recovery) of a control-flow graph (CFG) of a program, in which the nodes are basic blocks of instructions and the edges are possible control flow transfers between them, is a prerequisite for practically all static vulnerability discovery techniques. Control-flow graph recovery techniques are discussed in [17, 23, 28].

Another approach relies on the fact that certain kinds of program vulnerabilities have regular patterns. By analyzing graphs that embody program properties (e.g., control-flow graphs, data-flow graphs and control-dependence graphs), it is possible to construct vulnerability models that comprise sets of nodes in the graphs. Thus, finding program vulnerabilities is transformed to the problem of identifying vulnerability models in a program graph [19].

Yet another static analysis technique is value-set analysis [1]. This technique creates a value-flow graph (VFG), which provides an understanding of the possible targets of indirect jumps and memory write operations. It can detect buffer overflow vulnerabilities by analyzing overlapping buffers.

Costin et al. [8] have developed a framework that performs firmware collection, filtering, unpacking and analysis at a large scale (more than 30,000 firmware samples). They also proposed a correlation technique that propagates vulnerability information to similar firmware images. They discovered that one type of vulnerability affected 693 firmware images and reported 38 new common vulnerabilities and exposures (CVEs). Additionally, they searched for private encryption keys and known-bad strings to discover backdoors in devices whose firmware shared the same codebase with devices with known backdoors.

Wysopal et al. [27] have proposed a pattern-based, static analysis approach for detecting software backdoors. However, their approach requires the potential backdoors to be specified in advance. The corresponding patterns are used to perform the analysis. However, the search for pivotal strings needs to be improved. For example, a static ASCII string is more likely to represent a static password when it is referenced by or is located near a function that is known to be involved in the authentication process of an application.

2.3   Actual-Execution-Based Techniques

Fuzzing is the most practical vulnerability detection technique. It involves the creation and injection of mutated inputs to crash a target program.

Coverage-based fuzzing produces inputs that maximize the amount of code executed in a target application based on the insight that the greater the amount of code executed, the greater the possibility of executing vulnerable code. American Fuzzy Lop [30] is a security-oriented fuzzer that employs novel compile-time instrumentation and genetic algorithms to automatically discover clean, interesting test cases that trigger new internal states in a targeted binary. This substantially improves the functional coverage of the fuzzed code. The compact synthesized corpora produced by the tool are also useful for seeding other more labor- or resource-intensive testing regimes.

The second type of fuzzing is taint-based fuzzing [2]. It enhances the semantic understanding of target programs. Specifically, it helps understand which portions of the input must be mutated to execute new portion of the code.

Other techniques use actual execution to find specific types of vulnerabilities. An interesting example is PinTools, whose source code is available at GitHub (`github.com/JonathanSalwan/PinTools`). It performs actual execution using Pin, a dynamic binary instrumentation framework for the IA-32, x86-64 and MIC instruction-set architectures that enables the creation of dynamic program analysis tools [21]. PinTools uses behavior pattern matching to detect stack and heap overflows. It checks load and store instructions to determine the instructions that are outside the permitted area.

Schuster et al. [21] have proposed an approach for automatically identifying software backdoors in binary applications running on x86, x64 and MIPS32 architectures. They identify the specific regions in a binary that are prone to attacks and leverage this knowledge to determine suspicious components in an application.

Zaddach et al. [29] have developed the Avatar framework, which serves as an orchestration engine between a physical device and an external emulator based on S2E [27]. By injecting a special software proxy in the embedded device under test, Avatar can execute the firmware instructions in the emulator while channeling I/O operations to the physical

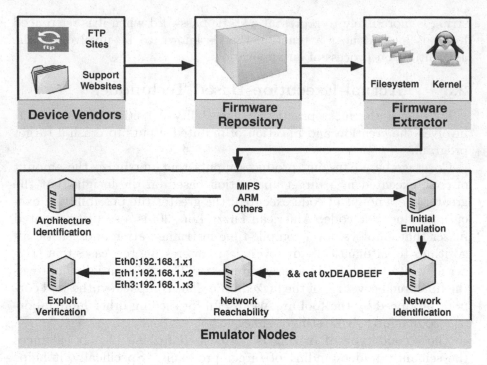

Figure 2.   FIRMADYNE workflow.

hardware. The Avatar framework is able to detect vulnerabilities and backdoors.

FIRMADYNE [6] employs the most typical form of actual code execution. The tool uses an automated and scalable dynamic analysis technique to accurately identify vulnerabilities in Linux-based embedded firmware. Figure 2 presents the FIRMADYNE workflow. The tool automatically downloads firmware images from vendor websites. Next, it uses a custom extraction utility built around the `binwalk` API to extract the kernel (optional) and root filesystem contained in a firmware image. After it identities the architecture, the environment is dynamically reconfigured to match the expectations of the firmware image. Finally, the tool performs dynamic analysis.

2.4   Symbolic-Execution-Based Techniques

Symbolic execution techniques are generally used to determine the inputs that cause each portion of a program to execute. An interpreter follows the program, assuming symbolic values for inputs instead of obtaining actual inputs as a program would during normal execution; this

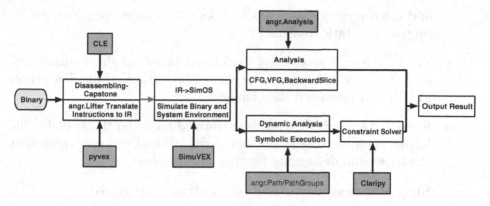

Figure 3. **angr** workflow.

approach is referred to as abstract interpretation. The interpreter produces expressions in terms of the symbolic values of program expressions and variables, and the possible outcomes of each conditional branch.

The most complete and powerful symbolic execution platform is Mayhem [5]. Its hybrid symbolic execution technique supports execution alternatives between online and offline symbolic execution runs; this speeds up the execution of multiple paths. Index-based memory modeling helps deal with code blocks in binaries.

Traditional dynamic symbolic execution requires considerable time, and loops and iterative constructs induce path explosion. To address these problems, Stephens et al. [26] developed the Driller tool, which leverages selective symbolic execution when performing fuzzing [4, 14]. The fuzzer is employed to explore the initial compartments of a program. When the fuzzer cannot go any further, concolic (i.e., concrete-symbolic) execution is employed to explore new compartments. Concolic execution, which involves under-constrained symbolic execution [20], can handle parts of programs without any function context.

The **angr** tool [25] implements all of the above symbolic execution techniques – binary and system state simulation, static analysis, dynamic analysis and constraint solving. Figure 3 presents the **angr** workflow. The tool performs the following steps:

- **Step 1:** The CLE module loads everything. The input binary is loaded, disassembled and converted to an intermediate representation IR [12].

- **Step 2:** Based on the generated intermediate language basic block, the binary with the system environment parameters is simulated and the corresponding class and data structures are generated to prepare for static analysis.

- **Step 3:** Static analysis is performed based on the available information, including from the control-flow graph, value-flow graph (VFG) and backward slice analysis.

- **Step 4:** Dynamic analysis is performed based on the available information (primarily symbolic execution), and various exploration strategies and debugging functions are applied.

- **Step 5:** The symbol execution constraints are solved.

- **Step 6:** The results are output.

3.   Evaluation of Techniques

Vulnerability detection based on source code has a high degree of automation and good detection speed. Because the source code is available (instead of assembly code corresponding to a specific architecture), the technique has low dependence on architecture. The vulnerability detection efficiency is high, but its accuracy is average at best.

In order to enhance vulnerability detection, source code may be translated to an intermediate representation, whose execution is then simulated. The major limitation is the reliance on source code, which is often not available in the case of embedded devices; vendors typically provide compiled programs and updated firmware. Another limitation is that source code may not have vulnerabilities and vulnerabilities could be introduced during compilation. This also means that the same source code could manifest different vulnerabilities in different architectures. Additionally, even if vulnerabilities are found in source code, the compiler may add mechanisms that eliminate or exacerbate the vulnerabilities in the compiled code.

Vulnerability detection based on static analysis has a high degree of automation and the detection speed depends on the technique. This method can detect known types of vulnerabilities according to the established models. The goal is to derive a grammatical or semantic description of a vulnerability via grammatical or semantic level analysis of the program source code or binary. Static analysis is better suited to determining that a program does not contain certain errors.

A limitation is that static analysis cannot provide accurate run-time information. Additionally, if a target binary contains infeasible paths, false positives and omissions may result. Static analysis can find suspicious vulnerabilities, but it is difficult to reproduce an input that causes a crash; also, the replayability is poor. The most significant limitation is that static analysis is semantically poor. Although static analysis can tell what a program is, it cannot tell what the program is doing. This is why static analysis is often used to support dynamic execution.

Vulnerability detection based on actual execution has a low degree of automation and low detection speed. The detection efficiency is relatively low, but some unknown vulnerabilities can be discovered based on crash behavior. Dynamic analysis executes a test program to determine its run-time semantics. Dynamic information is accurate due to actual code execution, so there are no false positives. However, some omissions may occur because it is difficult to fully enumerate all the execution paths. The major difficulty with actual program execution is the proper configuration of the operating environment. As mentioned above, embedded devices have diverse architectures and complex library environments; this significantly complicates the task of automating the configuration process. For example, the FIRMADYNE tool [6] was able to simulate 96.6% of the firmware images it collected, but the network configuration of only 32.3% of the images could be inferred successfully. This causes the tool to be very unstable.

Vulnerability detection based on symbolic execution has a higher degree of automation than actual execution. The vulnerability detection efficiency is low, but unknown vulnerabilities can be discovered. The detection ability depends entirely on the prevailing constraints and the power of the constraint solver. Although the detection time is longer that for other methods, the detection accuracy is higher. Many wispy logic program errors can be identified, rendering symbolic execution appropriate for detecting specific problems. Branch statements are problematic because the number of paths grows exponentially relative to the size of the program. Additionally, loops and recursive structures can cause the number of paths to increase without bound. Indeed, path explosion is the major limitation of symbolic execution. Nevertheless, symbolic execution is attractive because assembly code for various architectures can be converted to a common intermediate code, following which the memory and running processes can be fully simulated; thus, multiple architectures are supported without the problems imposed by environmental configuration.

Table 1 summarizes the comparison results for the four program analysis techniques.

Table 1.   Comparison of program analysis techniques.

	Source Code Analysis	Static Analysis	Actual Execution	Symbolic Execution
Vulnerabilities	Specific	Specific	Any	Anye
Replayable	No	No	Yes	Yes
Semantic Insight	Low	Low	High	High
Automation	High	High	Low	High
Architecture	Any	Specific	Partial	Any
Speed	Fast	Fast/Slow	Slow	Slow
Communication with Environment	No	No	Yes	No

4.   Proposed Methodology

This section proposes a more comprehensive and efficient solution for detecting vulnerabilities in embedded devices. The proposed methodology leverages the advantages of the four program analysis techniques discussed above.

4.1   Design

Vendors typically do not release source code for their embedded devices; instead, they provide packaged firmware. This means that vulnerability detection methods based on source code are inappropriate. Additionally, as discussed above, there are numerous embedded devices with different architectures, reference libraries and operating environments. Embedded devices also differ in their endianness. As a result, environment configuration is a big problem. Since large-scale, automated analysis is desired, vulnerability detection techniques based on actual execution are inappropriate.

All things considered, an ideal methodology should apply static analysis followed by symbolic execution to support large-scale, automatic analysis. Thus, the proposed detection methodology is based on the `angr` framework. The analysis target is based on FIRMADYNE [6], which collects and unpacks a number of firmware images.

Figure 4 shows the workflow of the proposed vulnerability detection methodology.

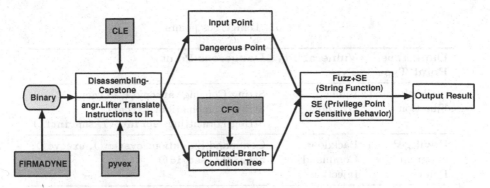

Figure 4. Proposed vulnerability detection methodology workflow.

4.2   Static Analysis Stage

The static analysis stage involves two main tasks that automatically identify the binary input points and program execution points that are likely to induce vulnerabilities.

Table 2. Input points.

Type	Function
Command Line Arguments	argv operation
Environment Variable	getenv()
File Data	read(), fscanf(), getc(), fgetc(), fgets(), vfscanf()
Keyboard Input/stdin	read(), scanf(), getchar(), gets()
Network Data	read(), recv(), recvfrom()

- **Input Points:** The library functions in Table 2 may be invoked to obtain inputs. Due to the specificity of embedded devices, their binaries rarely receive inputs from such obvious library functions. However, the common gateway interface (CGI) for embedded devices can parse user requests and send the parsed requests to other binaries. This method is used by the proposed methodology to provide inputs to a target binary.

  Real embedded devices have complex firmware, which makes it very difficult to identify input points. One approach is to search for the memory addresses of input values based on the parameter-passing convention used by a function call. Additionally, there is

Table 3. Dangerous points.

Dangerous Point Type	Vulnerability Type	Dangerous Points
String-Related Function	Buffer Overflow	String Copying: `strcpy()`, `strncpy()`; String Combination: `strcat()`; String Formatting: `sprintf()`, `snprintf()`
Privileged Program Points	Backdoor, Command Injection	Command Execution: `system()`, `execve()`, `setuid()`, `setgid()`
Sensitive Behavior	Backdoor, Command Injection	Peripheral Device Access; Suspicious String Output; Sensitive Memory Access

always a binary program in firmware – called the initial binary – that calls a library function to handle a user request. The initial binary acts as the input point to multiple binaries, enabling all the binaries to be analyzed at the same time.

- **Dangerous Points:** A dangerous point is a program execution point that could cause a vulnerability. A dangerous point can be a specific statement that a program executes or it can be a certain type of behavior exhibited by the program. Table 3 provides information about the three types of dangerous points.

4.3 Execution Preparation Stage

The execution preparation stage uses `pyvex` to translate assembly code for different architectures to the intermediate language IR, which is used to simulate execution. This feature supports multi-architecture vulnerability detection. During this stage, a control-flow graph created by `angr` is employed to construct the optimized-branch-condition tree. The condition tree expresses the constraint that an input should satisfy at an arbitrary point in the program; therefore, it contains the input constraint to a dangerous point in the program. The conditional tree is used in subsequent executions.

Unlike the condition tree employed by `angr`, the optimized-branch-condition tree used in the proposed methodology assumes that every part of the input value has no multiple or crossed meanings. Thus, before the execution flow reaches a point, there is no effect on the program if the input condition changes its evaluation order. For exam-

```
1    int main(void) {
2        char user_command[10];
3        int user_hash;
4
5        read(0, user_command, 10);
6        read(0, user_hash, sizeof(int));
7
8        if (user_hash != hash(user_command)) {
9            puts("Hash mismatch!");
10           return 1;
11       }
12
13       if (strncmp("CRASH", user_command, 5) == 0) {
14           puts ("Welcome to compartment 3!");
15           if (user_command[5] == '!') {
16               path_explosion_function();
17               if (user_command[6] == '!') {
18                   puts ("CRASHING!");
19                   abort();
20               }
21           }
22       }
23
24       return 0;
25   }
```

Figure 5. Code example from Driller [26].

ple, a user may submit a request using a URL with format `http://[router-address]/cgi-bin/;uname\$IFS-a`. Each word has a unique meaning and mutual evaluation has no effects. Therefore, when constructing the condition tree, the order of conditional evaluation can be changed appropriately.

The optimized-branch-condition tree facilitates the understanding of complex conditional evaluations. Figure 5 shows a code example from Driller [26]. The program has a generic input and a specific input at the same time. A generic input has a wide range of valid values (e.g., user name) whereas a specific input has a limited set of valid values (e.g., name hash). In the program, the **user_command** parameter is treated as a generic input (Line 8) and as a specific input (Line 13), causing Driller to switch between the fuzzer and concolic execution engine. At this point, Driller gets stuck. The optimized-branch-condition tree can change the order of evaluation of **user_command**, preventing the analysis from getting stuck.

4.4   Symbolic Execution Stage

The performance of the symbolic execution step depends on the type of vulnerability to be detected. For example, if the dangerous point is a function involving string manipulation (i.e., where a buffer overflow may occur), then a smart fuzzing method is applied. The fuzzer mutates the inputs in an intelligent manner based on the input constraints for the string manipulation function, where the constraints are embodied in the optimized-branch-condition tree.

Next, mutated values are used as input values and the execution of the program is simulated. During the execution, crashes are recorded. Moreover, the behavior of the program is monitored to check if the string manipulation function goes out of bounds or if load and/or store instructions in an assignment loop are out of bounds. A program crash or cross-border operation may indicate a buffer overflow vulnerability.

The simulation method may be applied directly if the dangerous point is a privileged program point or exhibits sensitive behavior, where a backdoor or command injection vulnerability may occur. The actual input value of the target program is replaced with a symbolic value that satisfies the input constraints to a privileged program point, following which the simulation is executed. A backdoor or command injection vulnerability may exist if the program can reach the privilege point or generate sensitive behavior.

Optimizations should be performed during concolic execution to avoid path explosion. In this context, the `angr` tool incorporates two interesting strategies, function summarization and path exploration. Function summarization replaces irrelevant library function calls for which there is no need to detect internal errors. Path exploration is good for path pruning. For example, if execution falls into a loop, the loop is only executed three times. Other innovative approaches may also be applied as long as the final results are not affected.

5.   Conclusions

Vulnerabilities in embedded devices can be exploited to conduct any number of criminal activities. However, due to the large number of embedded devices, non-standard codebases and complex control flows, it is extremely difficult to discover vulnerabilities using manual techniques. The evaluation of automated program analysis techniques – source-code-based analysis, static analysis, actual execution and symbolic execution – has revealed various advantages and limitations. The proposed methodology for vulnerability detection leverages the advantages of existing program analysis techniques. Nevertheless, numerous opportunities are available for enhancing the methodology by incorporating innovative strategies and tactics, including artificial intelligence and machine learning techniques.

References

[1] G. Balakrishnan and T. Reps, WYSINWYX: What you see is not what you execute, *ACM Transactions on Programming Languages and Systems*, vol. 32(6), article no. 23, 2010.

[2] S. Bekrar, C. Bekrar, R. Groz and L. Mounier, A taint-based approach for smart fuzzing, *Proceedings of the Fifth IEEE International Conference on Software Testing, Verification and Validation*, pp. 818–825, 2012.

[3] C. Cadar, D. Dunbar and D. Engler, KLEE: Unassisted and automatic generation of high-coverage tests for complex system programs, *Proceedings of the Eighth USENIX Conference on Operating Systems Design and Implementation*, pp. 209–224, 2008.

[4] D. Caselden, A. Bazhanyuk, M. Payer, L. Szekeres, S. McCamant and D. Song, Transformation-Aware Exploit Generation using a III-CFG, Technical Report No. UCB/EECS-2013-85, Department of Electrical Engineering and Computer Sciences, University of California at Berkeley, Berkeley, California, 2013.

[5] S. Cha, T. Avgerinos, A. Rebert and D. Brumley, Unleashing Mayhem on binary code, *Proceedings of the IEEE Symposium on Security and Privacy*, pp. 380–394, 2012.

[6] D. Chen, M. Egele, M. Woo and D. Brumley, Towards automated dynamic analysis for Linux-based embedded firmware, *Proceedings of the Twenty-Third Annual Network and Distributed System Security Symposium*, 2016.

[7] V. Chipounov, V. Kuznetsov and G. Candea, S2E: A platform for in-vivo multi-path analysis of software systems, *ACM SIGPLAN Notices*, vol. 46(3), pp. 265–278, 2011.

[8] A. Costin, J. Zaddach, A. Francillon and D. Balzarotti, A large-scale analysis of the security of embedded firmware, *Proceedings of the Twenty-Third USENIX Security Symposium*, pp. 95–110, 2014.

[9] A. Costin, A. Zarras and A. Francillon, Automated dynamic firmware analysis at scale: A case study on embedded web interfaces, *Proceedings of the Eleventh ACM Asia Conference on Computer and Communications Security*, pp. 437–448, 2016.

[10] A. Cui, M. Costello and S. Stolfo, When firmware modifications attack: A case study of embedded exploitation, *Proceedings of the Twentieth Annual Network and Distributed System Security Symposium*, 2013.

[11] D. Davidson, B. Moench, S. Jha and T. Ristenpart, FIE on firmware: Finding vulnerabilities in embedded systems using symbolic execution, *Proceedings of the Twenty-Second USENIX Security Symposium*, pp. 463–478, 2013.

[12] T. Dullien and S. Porst, REIL: A platform-independent intermediate representation of disassembled code for static code analysis, *Proceedings of the Ninth CanSecWest Applied Security Conference*, 2009

[13] A. Fournaris, L. Pocero Fraile and O. Koufopavlou, Exploiting hardware vulnerabilities to attack embedded system devices: A survey of potent microarchitectural attacks, *Electronics*, vol. 6(3), article no. 52, 2017.

[14] P. Godefroid, N. Klarlund and K. Sen, DART: Directed automated random testing, *Proceedings of the ACM SIGPLAN Conference on Programming Language Design and Implementation*, pp. 213–223, 2005.

[15] B. Gourdin, C. Soman, H. Bojinov and E. Bursztein, Toward secure embedded web interfaces, *Proceedings of the Twentieth USENIX Security Symposium*, 2011.

[16] M. Hachman, U.S. barely cracks list of countries with top Wi-Fi penetration, *PC Magazine*, April 5, 2012.

[17] J. Kinder and H. Veith, Jakstab: A static analysis platform for binaries, *Proceedings of the Twentieth International Conference on Computer Aided Verification*, pp. 423–427, 2008.

[18] D. Papp, Z. Ma and L. Buttyan, Embedded systems security: Threats, vulnerabilities and attack taxonomy, *Proceedings of the Thirteenth Annual Conference on Privacy, Security and Trust*, pp. 145–152, 2015.

[19] J. Pewny, B. Garmany, R. Gawlik, C. Rossow and T. Holz, Cross-architecture bug search in binary executables, *Proceedings of the IEEE Symposium on Security and Privacy*, pp. 709–724, 2015.

[20] D. Ramos and D. Engler, Under-constrained symbolic execution: Correctness checking for real code, *Proceedings of the Twenty-Fourth USENIX Security Symposium*, pp. 49–64, 2015.

[21] J. Salwan, Stack and heap overflow detection at runtime via behavior analysis and Pin (`shell-storm.org/blog/Stack-and -heap-overflow-detection-at-runtime-via-behavior-analys is-and-PIN`), October 14, 2010.

[22] F. Schuster and T. Holz, Towards reducing the attack surface of software backdoors, *Proceedings of the ACM Conference on Computer and Communications Security*, pp. 851–862, 2013.

[23] B. Schwarz, S. Debray and G. Andrews, Disassembly of executable code revisited, *Proceedings of the Ninth Working Conference on Reverse Engineering*, pp. 45–54, 2002.

[24] Y. Shoshitaishvili, R. Wang, C. Hauser, C. Kruegel and G. Vigna, Firmalice – Automatic detection of authentication bypass vulnerabilities in binary firmware, *Proceedings of the Twenty-Second Annual Network and Distributed System Security Symposium*, 2015.

[25] Y. Shoshitaishvili, R. Wang, C. Salls, N. Stephens, M. Polino, A. Dutcher, J. Grosen, S. Feng, C. Hauser, C. Kruegel and G. Vigna, SOK: (State of) The art of war: Offensive techniques in binary analysis, *Proceedings of the IEEE Symposium on Security and Privacy*, pp. 138–157, 2016.

[26] N. Stephens, J. Grosen, C. Salls, A. Dutcher, R. Wang, J. Corbetta, Y. Shoshitaishvili, C. Kruegel and G. Vigna, Driller: Augmenting fuzzing through selective symbolic execution, *Proceedings of the Twenty-Third Annual Network and Distributed System Security Symposium*, 2016.

[27] C. Wysopal, C. Eng and T. Shields, Static detection of application backdoors, *Datenschutz und Datensicherheit*, vol. 34(3), pp. 149–155, 2010.

[28] L. Xu, F. Sun and Z. Su, Constructing Precise Control Flow Graphs from Binaries, Technical Report, Department of Computer Science, University of California, Davis, Davis, California, 2009.

[29] J. Zaddach, L. Bruno, A. Francillon and D. Balzarotti, Avatar: A framework to support dynamic security analysis of embedded system firmware, *Proceedings of the Twenty-First Annual Network and Distributed System Security Symposium*, 2014.

[30] M. Zalewski, American Fuzzy Lop (`lcamtuf.coredump.cx/afl`), 2017.

Chapter 18

A FORENSIC LOGGING SYSTEM FOR SIEMENS PROGRAMMABLE LOGIC CONTROLLERS

Ken Yau, Kam-Pui Chow and Siu-Ming Yiu

Abstract   Critical infrastructure assets are monitored and managed by industrial control systems. In recent years, these systems have evolved to adopt common networking standards that expose them to cyber attacks. Since programmable logic controllers are core components of industrial control systems, forensic examinations of these devices are vital during responses to security incidents. However, programmable logic controller forensics is a challenging task because of the lack of effective logging systems.

This chapter describes the design and implementation of a novel programmable logic controller logging system. Several tools are available for generating programmable logic controller audit logs; these tools monitor and record the values of programmable logic controller memory variables for diagnostic purposes. However, the logged information is inadequate for forensic investigations. To address this limitation, the logging system extracts data from Siemens S7 communications protocol traffic for forensic purposes. The extracted data is saved in an audit log file in an easy-to-read format that enables a forensic investigator to efficiently examine the activity of a programmable logic controller.

Keywords: Programmable logic controllers, forensics, logging system

1.   Introduction

Critical infrastructure assets such as electricity generation plants, transportation systems and manufacturing facilities are monitored and controlled by industrial control systems [4]. Historically, industrial control systems were operated as isolated, proprietary systems with no external network connections. Thus, these systems and the critical infrastructure assets they managed were primarily exposed to internal as op-

© IFIP International Federation for Information Processing 2018
Published by Springer Nature Switzerland AG 2018. All Rights Reserved
G. Peterson and S. Shenoi (Eds.): Advances in Digital Forensics XIV, IFIP AICT 532, pp. 331–349, 2018.
https://doi.org/10.1007/978-3-319-99277-8_18

posed to external threats. However, for reasons of convenience, modern industrial control systems use TCP/IP and wireless protocols that connect to corporate networks, vendor networks and even the Internet [12]. Additionally, industrial control systems increasingly use common embedded system platforms and commercial off-the-shelf software [4]. As a result, modern industrial control systems and the infrastructures they manage are exposed to numerous external threats, including over the Internet. Digital forensics is an important component of incident investigations involving industrial control systems. The forensic investigations provide insights to the root causes of incidents, enable the identification and prosecution of attackers, and help design appropriate security controls.

Programmable logic controllers (PLCs), which are used to automate industrial systems and processes, are important components of industrial control systems. Modern programmable logic controllers have evolved to utilize common networking standards such as IEEE 802.3 Ethernet and IEEE 802.11 Wi-Fi [1]. As a result, communicating with a programmable logic controller is similar to communicating with a commodity computer. In addition, communications suites such as libnodave and Snap7 for interfacing and exchanging data with Siemens S7 programmable logic controllers are readily available for download on the Internet. The libnodave library provides the functions needed to connect to and exchange data with Siemens S7 300/400 programmable logic controllers (it partially supports Siemens S7 1200/1500 programmable logic controllers) [5]. Snap 7 is an open source, 32/64 bit, multi-platform Ethernet communications suite for interfacing natively with Siemens S7 programmable logic controllers [8].

The popular Shodan search engine has discovered numerous industrial control systems around the world that can be accessed directly over the Internet [6]. Such a tool enables an attacker to identify a vulnerable programmable logic controller, following which the attacker could directly manipulate its logic code over the Internet. The attacker can then leverage the programmable logic controller to reach other control and network devices [6]. The likelihood of such attacks on industrial control systems makes digital forensic readiness of programmable logic controllers an important part of the security posture of critical infrastructure owners and operators.

A key challenge is that the proprietary architectures, operating systems, filesystems and data formats of programmable logic controllers make it difficult to apply traditional digital forensic tools and techniques in investigations of industrial control system incidents. Additionally,

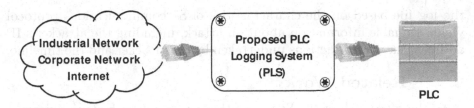

Figure 1. Programmable logic controller logging system.

programmable logic controllers operate vital industrial processes and systems that cannot be stopped for data collection and examination.

Another key challenge is inadequate logging. Several tools have been developed for generating audit logs for programmable logic controllers, but the logged information is often insufficient for forensic investigations. In general, these tools (e.g., PLC Logger [9]) monitor and capture the values of programmable logic controller memory variables, and also access programmable logic controller memory regions to record changes of memory values along with timestamps for diagnostic purposes such as tracing faults in machinery and improving system efficiency [15]. However, they do not capture crucial forensic information such as the IP address of the device that connected to a programmable logic controller, the commands sent to the programmable logic controller and the duration of the connection to the programmable logic controller.

This chapter describes a novel programmable logic controller logging system that captures information required for digital forensic investigations. Figure 1 shows a schematic diagram of the programmable logic controller logging system. The logging system is a lightweight computer installed with a network packet analyzer that captures network traffic between a programmable logic controller and other network devices. The logging system dissects network packets and extracts potential forensic information, which it logs in the form of timestamped records. The log provides documentary evidence of the sequence of activities related to commands and data transmitted between the programmable logic controller and other network devices.

A case study involving a Siemens Simatic S7-1212C programmable logic controller is presented. The decision to focus on a Siemens Simatic S7 programmable logic controller was motivated by their widespread use around the world [1] and the fact that they were targeted successfully by the powerful and insidious Stuxnet malware. The case study uses the Siemens programmable logic controller to create two simulated control systems, a traffic light control system and a liquid mixing control system. The case study demonstrates that the analysis of packet details in the log file based on the characteristics of S7 communications protocol yields valuable information about an attack, including the attacker's IP address, the specific actions undertaken by the attacker and the timeline.

2.   Related Work

In the aftermath of the Stuxnet attack, researchers have significantly increased their efforts to discover and mitigate the vulnerabilities existing in programmable logic controllers. However, limited research has been conducted in the area of programmable logic controller forensics. An example is the work of Chan et al. [2], which focuses on the logging mechanisms of a Siemens programmable logic controller, specifically the Siemens Total Integrated Automation Portal V13 (Siemens TIA Portal). Chan and colleagues demonstrated that the Siemens logging system provides detailed information about event activities for forensic investigations. However, the system only works under two conditions. First, the incidents must be created by the workstation that runs Siemens TIA Portal. Second, the workstation with Siemens TIA Portal must not be compromised; otherwise, the logging system cannot be trusted.

Wu and Nance [15] have shown that attacks on programmable logic controllers can be determined by monitoring the memory addresses of user control programs. In particular, they identified the memory addresses used by program code, and monitored and logged the memory values to capture normal programmable logic controller behavior. The logged behavior was used to determine whether the programmable logic controller was running normally or was under attack.

Yau et al. [16] have proposed forensic solutions for programmable logic controllers. One solution involves control program logic change detection that employs user-defined rules to detect and record anomalous programmable logic controller operations. Another solution captures the values of relevant memory addresses used by a programmable logic controller in a log file [2, 13]. Machine learning techniques were applied to the logged file to identify anomalous programmable logic controller behavior.

Wu and Nance [15] and Yau et al. [16] have demonstrated that it is possible to detect anomalous programmable logic controller behavior. However, they do not capture forensic information such as the IP address of a device that connected to a programmable logic controller, the commands sent to the programmable logic controller and the duration of the connection to the programmable logic controller. The logging system described in this chapter captures vital information that enable

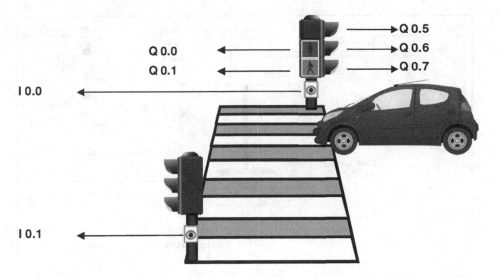

Figure 2. Input/output connections for the traffic light control system.

forensic investigators to reconstruct events and identify anomalous programmable logic controller behavior.

3. PLC Architecture and Programming

A programmable logic controller is a solid state industrial control computer with a central processor unit (CPU), memory, input/output interface and programming functionality. It can be programmed to implement functions such as control logic, sequencing, timing, arithmetic data manipulations and counting in order to monitor and control machines and processes. It accepts data and status information from devices such as switches and temperature sensors, and executes a control program stored in its memory to provide appropriate commands to devices such as valves, lights and motors [3].

Two simulated control systems, a traffic light control system [10] and a liquid mixing control system [11], were set up to demonstrate the proposed programmable logic controller logging system.

The traffic light control system controls vehicular and pedestrian traffic at an intersection. In order to simulate the hardware configuration of the traffic light control system, the Siemens Simatic S7 programmable logic controller inputs I0.0 and I0.1 were connected to switches and the programmable logic controller outputs Q0.0, Q0.1, Q0.5, Q0.6 and Q0.7 were connected to LEDs (Figure 2).

The liquid mixing control system mixes two ingredients, such different colored paints. Two pipes at the top of the mixing tank supply the

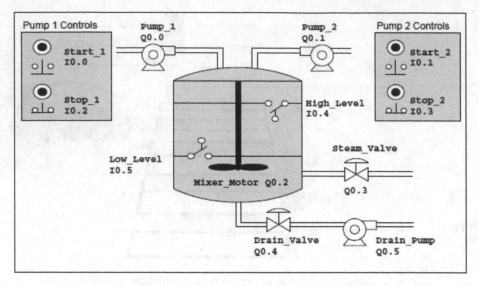

Figure 3.   Input/output connections for the liquid mixing control system [11].

two ingredients. A single pipe at the bottom of the tank drains the mixture. In order to simulate the hardware configuration of the system, the Siemens Simatic S7 programmable logic controller inputs were connected to switches for the pumps and liquid level sensors. The outputs were connected to LEDs corresponding to the motor, steam/drain valves and pumps (Figure 3).

Table 1 presents the program instructions (inputs, outputs and memory bits) used by the Siemens Simatic S7 control programs for the traffic light and liquid mixing control systems.

4.   Proposed Logging System

The proposed programmable logic controller logging system is implemented as a transparent proxy between an Ethernet network and the programmable logic controller. The transparency ensures that the existing network configurations are maintained. The logging system forwards all traffic except for S7 communications traffic [7].

The logging system has two processes. The first process is initiated when the logging system detects a connection request to the programmable logic controller on TCP port 102. The process captures the communications and filters potential forensic information such as IP addresses, commands and timestamps. The second process then translates and stores the information in an audit log file that is easily read and understood for forensic investigators. Table 2 shows a sample log file.

Table 1. Program instructions for the traffic light and liquid mixing control systems.

Digital Input Address	Traffic Light Control System	Liquid Mixing Control System
I0.0	Switch on right-hand side of street	Start switch for paint ingredient 1
I0.1	Switch on left-hand side of street	Start switch for paint ingredient 2
I0.2	N/A	Stop switch for paint ingredient 1
I0.3	N/A	Stop switch for paint ingredient 2
I0.4	N/A	Limit switch for maximum level
I0.5	N/A	Limit switch for minimum level

Digital Output Address	Traffic Light Control System	Liquid Mixing Control System
Q0.0	Pedestrian red light	Pump for paint ingredient 1
Q0.1	Pedestrian green light	Pump for paint ingredient 2
Q0.2	N/A	Motor for mixing paint ingredients
Q0.3	N/A	Steam for heating mixture in tank
Q0.4	N/A	Valve for draining mixture out of tank
Q0.5	Vehicle red light	Pump for draining mixture out of tank
Q0.6	Vehicle yellow light	N/A
Q0.7	Vehicle green light	N/A

Memory Bit	Traffic Light Control System	Liquid Mixing Control System
M0.0	Memory bit for switching signal after green light request from pedestrian	Memory bit for high level reached

The logging system must be trusted because it is used for evidence collection. It is vital that the system is not hacked and the data log is not altered. Therefore, the logging system should be made hacker-proof and tamper-resistant to the extent possible.

5. S7 Communications Protocol

The S7 communications protocol (S7comm) is a proprietary protocol used by the Siemens S7-300/400 family of programmable logic controllers [13]. The protocol is also partially supported by the Siemens S7-1200/1500 family of programmable logic controllers [8]. It is used for programmable logic controller programming, data exchange with programmable logic controllers, programmable logic controller data access by SCADA systems and diagnostics [13].

Table 2.   Log file structure.

Date/Time	Source IP Address	Protocol	PLC Command	PLC Memory Value Change
01 Jan 2017 10:05pm	192.168.0.10	TCP	Establish connection	N/A
01 Jan 2017 10:10pm	192.168.0.10	S7comm	WRITE	Set Output Q0.7 to TRUE from FALSE
01 Jan 2017 11:00pm	192.168.0.10	S7comm	CPU STOP	N/A
01 Jan 2017 11:30pm	192.168.0.10	TCP	Close connection	N/A

Table 3.   S7comm commands.

No.	Command
1	Data Read/Write
2	Cyclic Data Read/Write
3	Directory Information
4	System Information
5	Block Move
6	PLC Control
7	Date and Time
8	Security
9	Programming

The Ethernet implementation of S7comm is based on ISO TCP (RFC 1006), which is block-oriented. Each block is called a protocol data unit (PDU). The S7comm protocol is function-oriented or command-oriented, i.e., each transmission contains a command or a reply to a command. If a command or reply does not fit inside a single protocol data unit, it is split across multiple protocol data units [8].

Table 3 shows the nine categories of S7comm commands. Each command has four components: (i) header; (ii) parameters; (iii) parameter data; and (iv) data block.

The first two components of an S7comm command (header and parameters) are mandatory; the other components are optional. Figure 4 presents the protocol encapsulation structure followed by S7 Telegram, ISO on TCP and TCP/IP.

S7comm data is inserted in the payloads of connection-oriented transport protocol (COTP) packets. As shown in Figure 5, the first byte is always 0x32, which corresponds to the protocol identifier [13].

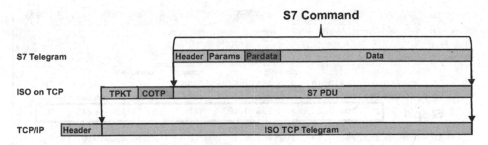

Figure 4. Protocol encapsulation [8].

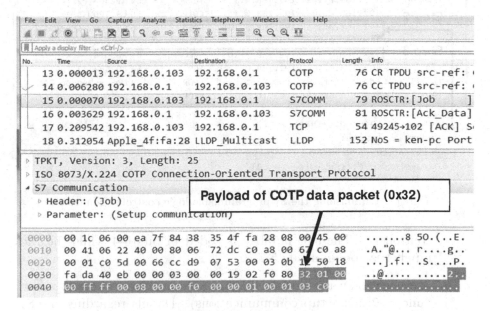

Figure 5. Data packets.

A programmable logic controller connection had to be established in order to collect S7comm protocol traffic. The following steps were involved in establishing a connection to the S7 programmable logic controller [13]:

- A connection was established to the programmable logic controller using its IP address and TCP port 102.

- A connection was established at the ISO layer (COTP connect request). The destination transport services activity point (TSAP) data has two bytes. The first byte of the destination TSAP data specifies the communications type (1 = PG (programming console); 2 = OP (Siemens HMI panel)). The second byte specifies the slot and rack numbers (position of the programmable logic

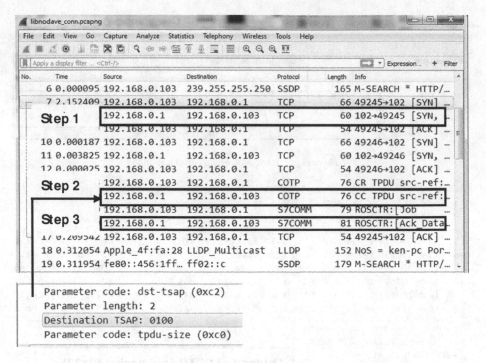

Figure 6. Establishing the S7 programmable logic controller connection.

controller). The slot number is coded in bits 0-4 while the rack number is coded in bits 5-7.

- A connection was established at the S7comm layer (`s7comm.param. func = 0xf0`; setup communications). Details regarding the S7-comm protocol (e.g., protocol data unit size) were negotiated.

Figure 6 shows a Wireshark capture of the S7 programmable logic controller connection steps.

6.   Creating Audit Log Records

To demonstrate the data logging methodology, a Siemens Simatic S7 1212C programmable logic controller was used to set up two simulated control systems. A computer was installed with the Snap7 software to create anomalous programmable logic controller behavior. Another computer was installed with Wireshark and the S7comm Wireshark dissector plugin [14] to capture programmable logic controller activities. Figure 7 shows the experimental setup.

The experiments involved two parts. In the first part, the traffic light control system was connected to a wireless access point. In the second

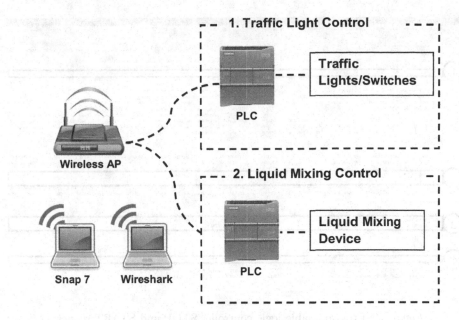

Figure 7. Experimental setup.

part, the traffic light control system was replaced with the liquid mixing control system. Four common programmable logic controller requests were employed: (i) CPU START; (ii) CPU STOP; (iii) READ; and (iv) WRITE.

6.1 Traffic Light Control System

The following steps were involved in sending CPU STOP/START requests to the programmable logic controller:

- Wireshark was started to capture network packets.

- Snap7 established a connection to the programmable logic controller.

- Snap7 sent the CPU STOP request to the programmable logic controller.

- Snap7 sent the CPU START request to the programmable logic controller.

- Snap7 closed its connection to the programmable logic controller.

- Wireshark was stopped and the captured packets were saved in a log file.

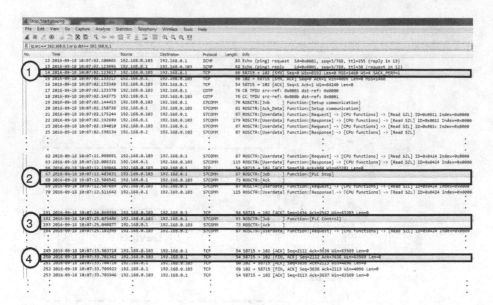

Figure 8. Programmable logic controller STOP and START requests.

- The packets with the programmable logic controller IP address [192.168.0.1] were filtered for analysis.

Figure 8 shows the captured log file associated with the programmable logic controller STOP and START requests. Analysis of the log file yields the following reconstruction of programmable logic controller activities:

- 10:07:02am, 18 Sep 2016: A computer [192.168.0.103] established a connection to the programmable logic controller [192.168.0.1].

- 10:07:12am, 18 Sep 2016: The computer sent a CPU STOP request to the programmable logic controller to stop the traffic light system.

- 10:07:25am, 18 Sep 2016: The computer sent a CPU START request to the programmable logic controller to re-start the traffic light system.

- 12:07:46pm, 18 Sep 2016: The computer closed its connection to the programmable logic controller.

Based on the data in Table 1, the memory values of the programmable logic controller outputs at 12:07:46pm, 18 Sep 2016 indicate that all the pedestrian and vehicle lights were turned on. The programmable logic controller operation appears to be anomalous because an attempt was made to turn on all the traffic lights at the same time.

The following steps were involved in sending READ and WRITE requests to the programmable logic controller:

- Wireshark was started to capture network packets.

- Snap7 established a connection to the programmable logic controller.

- Snap7 read the values of inputs (I0.0 to I0.7), outputs (Q0.0 to Q0.7) and memory bits (M0.0 to M0.7) from the programmable logic controller.

- Snap7 wrote the value 1 to inputs (I0.0 to I07), outputs (O0.0 to 0.7) and memory bits (M0.0 to M0.7) of the programmable logic controller.

- Snap7 closed its connection to the programmable logic controller.

- Wireshark was stopped and the captured packets were saved in a log file.

- The packets with the programmable logic controller IP address [192.168.0.1] were filtered for analysis.

Figure 9 shows the captured log file associated with the programmable logic controller READ and WRITE requests. The following controller activities can be reconstructed in time sequence upon analyzing the log file:

- 12:07:28pm, 18 Sep 2016: A computer [192.168.0.103] established a connection to the programmable logic controller [192. 168.0.1].

- 12:07:31pm, 18 Sep 2016: The log reveals that the computer read memory values from the programmable logic controller (shown in Figure 9):

  - I0.7 to I0.0: 0x03 [0000 0011]

  - Q0.7 to Q0.0: 0x03 [0000 0011]

  - M0.7 to M0.0: 0x00 [0000 0000]

- 12:07:44pm, 18 Sep 2016: The log reveals that the programmable logic controller memory values were altered as follows (shown in Figure 9):

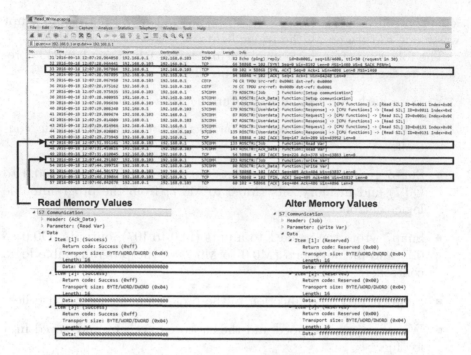

Figure 9. Programmable logic controller READ and WRITE requests.

- I0.7 to I0.0: `0xff [1111 1111]`
- Q0.7 to Q0.0: `0xff [1111 1111]`
- M0.7 to M0.0: `0xff [1111 1111]`

- **12:07:46pm, 18 Sep 2016:** The computer closed its connection to the programmable logic controller.

Based on the data in Table 1, the memory values of the programmable logic controller outputs at `12:07:44pm, 18 Sep 2016` indicate that all the pedestrian and vehicle lights were turned on. The programmable logic controller operation appears to be anomalous because an attempt was made to turn on all the traffic lights at the same time.

6.2 Liquid Mixing Control System

The following steps were involved in sending CPU WRITE requests to the programmable logic controller.

- Wireshark was started to capture network packets.

- Snap7 established a connection to the programmable logic controller.

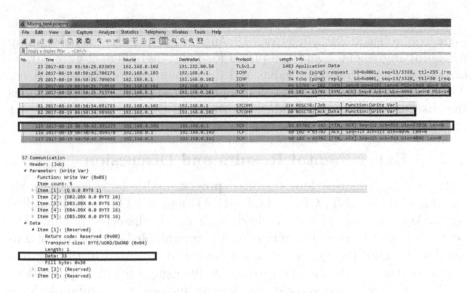

Figure 10. Programmable logic controller WRITE requests.

- Snap7 wrote the value 1 to outputs (O0.0 to 0.7) of the programmable logic controller.

- Snap7 closed its connection to the programmable logic controller.

- Wireshark was stopped and the captured packets were saved in a log file.

- The packets with the programmable logic controller IP address [192.168.0.1] were filtered for analysis.

Figure 10 shows the captured log file associated with the programmable logic controller WRITE requests. The following controller activities can be reconstructed in time sequence upon analyzing the log file:

- 08:50:25pm, 19 Aug 2017: A computer [192.168.0.102] established a connection to the programmable logic controller [192.168.0.1].

- 08:50:34pm, 19 Aug 2017: The log reveals that the programmable logic controller memory values were altered as follows (shown in Figure 10):

    Q0.7 to Q0.0: 0x33 [0011 0011]

- 12:07:42pm, 19 Aug 2017: The computer closed its connection to the programmable logic controller.

Based on the data in Table 1, the memory values of the programmable logic controller at 08:50:34pm, 19 Aug 2017 indicate that the pump for paint ingredient 1 and the pump for paint ingredient 2 were turned on; meanwhile, the drain valve and drain pump were also turned on. The programmable logic controller operation appears to be anomalous because an attempt was made to turn on all the valves and pumps at the same time.

7.   Experimental Results and Discussion

In the experiments, four common programmable logic controller requests, CPU START, CPU STOP, READ and WRITE were identified by packet analysis using Wireshark with the S7 dissector plugin. The sequences with timestamps related to programmable logic controller connection establishments and requests were also captured in the log file. Based on the log file and the programmable logic controller application, an investigator could reconstruct the anomalous programmable logic controller operations. In addition to the four programmable logic controller requests, other programmable logic controller activities were also be revealed via packet analysis, including programmable logic controller program uploads and downloads. The upload and download commands have the S7comm function parameter (first parameter byte) of 0x1A [7]. The download commands provide valuable information about the timeline of programmable logic controller program updates.

The experiments used Wireshark with the S7 dissector plugin to capture and analyze S7 packets for forensic purposes. However, due to the large volume of packets, it is infeasible to capture all the information related to the packets for analysis. Therefore, the proposed programmable logic controller logging system uses Wireshark with the S7 dissector plugin and an add-on feature to capture packets selectively. When the logging system detects a connection request sent to the programmable logic controller on TCP port 102, it starts capturing the communications. Likewise, when the logging system detects a disconnection request sent to programmable logic controller on TCP port 102, it stops capturing the communications.

Since the raw data capture is disorganized, a logging system process converts the captured packet information to a human-readable format that is stored in an audit file. Thus, a forensic investigator would only have to examine the audit file. This reduces the effort required by the investigator, who would not be expected to be a control system expert.

Since the ISO-TSAP packets that encapsulate the proprietary Siemens S7comm protocol are sent in plaintext, it is relatively simple to reverse engineer them and make modifications as needed. This characteristic of ISO-TSAP packets enables attackers to replicate operator activities involving programming and management, including turning off the CPU, disabling memory protection and uploading new project files to the programmable logic controller [1]. On one hand, attackers leverage ISO-TSAP to monitor and interfere with programmable logic controller operations. On the other hand, the proposed logging system leverages ISO-TSAP to capture valuable information about attacker activities for forensic investigations.

Several tools are available for creating audit logs for programmable logic controllers, but the information they capture is insufficient in forensics investigations. Specifically, the audit logs usually capture the values of relevant memory addresses used by programmable logic controller programs to support debugging and troubleshooting. Crucial forensic information is always missing, including the IP address of the device that connected to the programmable logic controller, the commands (e.g., READ data, WRITE data and DOWNLOAD program) sent to the programmable logic controller and the duration of the connection to the programmable logic controller.

Finally, the logging system incorporate two processes in order to minimize its impact on programmable logic controller operations. The first process is responsible for capturing packets. The second process analyzes the captured packets and stores forensically-relevant data in a human-readable format in the audit log file. Because this process is time consuming, it is executed as a batch process instead of a real-time process to enhance the efficiency of the logging system.

8. Conclusions

Current programmable logic controller logging tools provide insufficient information for digital forensic investigations. To address this limitation, the logging system described in this chapter analyzes network traffic between a Siemens Simatic S7 programmable logic controller and network devices based on the Siemens S7 communications protocol to record evidence of the sequence of activities related to commands and data exchanged between the programmable logic controller and other network devices. The log provides valuable information about attacks, including the attacker IP addresses, specific actions and timelines. The decision to focus on a Siemens Simatic S7 programmable logic controller was motivated by their widespread use [1] and the fact that they were targeted successfully by the insidious Stuxnet malware.

Future research will focus on developing a production logging system for industrial control system environments. Attempts will also be made to expand the logging capabilities to handle other popular industrial control protocols such as Modbus and DNP3 for various programmable logic controller models.

References

[1] D. Beresford, Exploiting Siemens Simatic S7 PLCs, presented at *Black Hat USA*, 2011.

[2] R. Chan and K. Chow, Forensic analysis of a Siemens programmable logic controller, in *Critical Infrastructure Protection X*, M. Rice and S. Shenoi (Eds.), Springer, Heidelberg, Germany, pp. 117–130, 2016.

[3] T. Cruz, J. Barrigas, J. Proenca, A. Graziano, S. Panzieri, L. Lev and P. Simoes, Improving network security monitoring for industrial control systems, *Proceedings of the IFIP/IEEE International Symposium on Integrated Network Management*, pp. 878–881, 2015.

[4] European Union Agency for Network and Information Security, Critical Infrastructures and Services, Heraklion, Greece (`enisa.europa.eu/topics/critical-information-infrastructures-and-services`), 2017.

[5] T. Hergenhahn, libnodave (`sourceforge.net/projects/libnodave`), 2014.

[6] J. Klick, S. Lau, D. Marzin, J. Malchow and V. Roth, Internet-facing PLCs – A new back orifice, presented at *Blackhat USA*, 2015.

[7] J. Malchow, D. Marzin, J. Klick, R. Kovacs and V. Roth, PLC Guard: A practical defense against attacks on cyber-physical systems, *Proceedings of the IEEE Conference on Communications and Network Security*, pp. 326–334, 2015.

[8] D. Nardella, Step 7 Open Source Ethernet Communications Suite, Bari, Italy (`snap7.sourceforge.net`), 2016.

[9] PLC-Logger Project, PLC-Logger and Analyzer (`sourceforge.net/projects/plclogger`), 2014.

[10] Siemens, SIMATIC S7-300 Programmable Controller Quick Start, Primer, Preface, C79000-G7076-C500-01, Nuremberg, Germany, 1996.

[11] Siemens, SIMATIC S7-200 Programmable Controller System Manual, 6ES7298-8FA01-8BH0, Edition 08/2005, Nuremberg, Germany, 2005.

[12] T. Spyridopoulos, T. Tryfonas and J. May, Incident analysis and digital forensics of SCADA and industrial control systems, *Proceedings of the Eighth IET International System Safety Conference Incorporating the Cyber Security Conference*, 2013.

[13] T. Wiens, S7 Communications (s7comm), *Wireshark Wiki* (`wiki.wireshark.org/S7comm`), 2016.

[14] T. Wiens, S7comm Wireshark Dissector Plugin (`sourceforge.net/projects/s7commwireshark`), 2017.

[15] T. Wu and J. Nurse, Exploring the use of PLC debugging tools for digital forensic investigations of SCADA systems, *Journal of Digital Forensics, Security and Law*, vol. 10(4), pp. 79–96, 2015.

[16] K. Yau and K. Chow, PLC forensics based on control program logic change detection, *Journal of Digital Forensics, Security and Law*, vol. 10(4), pp. 59–68, 2015.

[17] K. Yau and K. Chow, Detecting anomalous programmable logic controller events using machine learning, in *Advances in Digital Forensics XIII*, G. Peterson and S. Shenoi (Eds.), Springer, Heidelberg, Germany, pp. 81–94, 2017.

[18] K. Yau, K. Chow, S. Yiu and C. Chan, Detecting anomalous behavior of a PLC using semi-supervised machine learning, *Proceedings of the IEEE Conference on Communications and Network Security*, pp. 580–585, 2017.

Chapter 19

ENHANCING THE SECURITY AND FORENSIC CAPABILITIES OF PROGRAMMABLE LOGIC CONTROLLERS

Chun-Fai Chan, Kam-Pui Chow, Siu-Ming Yiu and Ken Yau

Abstract   Industrial control systems are used to monitor and operate critical infrastructures. For decades, the security of industrial control systems was preserved by their use of proprietary hardware and software, and their physical separation from other networks. However, to reduce costs and enhance interconnectivity, modern industrial control systems increasingly use commodity hardware and software, and are connected to vendor and corporate networks, and even the Internet. These trends expose industrial control systems to risks that they were not designed to handle.

This chapter describes a novel approach for enhancing industrial control system security and forensics by adding monitoring and logging mechanisms to programmable logic controllers, key components of industrial control systems. A proof-of-concept implementation is presented using a popular Siemens programmable logic controller. Experiments were conducted to compare the accuracy and performance impact of the proposed method versus the conventional programmable logic controller polling method. The experimental results demonstrate that the new method yields increased anomaly detection coverage and accuracy with only a small performance impact. Additionally, the new method increases the speed of anomaly detection and reduces network overhead, enabling forensic investigations of programmable logic controllers to be conducted more efficiently and effectively.

Keywords: Programmable logic controllers, anomaly detection, forensics

© IFIP International Federation for Information Processing 2018
Published by Springer Nature Switzerland AG 2018. All Rights Reserved
G. Peterson and S. Shenoi (Eds.): Advances in Digital Forensics XIV, IFIP AICT 532, pp. 351–367, 2018.
https://doi.org/10.1007/978-3-319-99277-8_19

1.   Introduction

Industrial control systems are commonly used to manage critical infrastructure assets. In the past, industrial control systems utilized proprietary hardware and software, and were separated from other networks. Thus, the vast majority of attacks required physical assess to the systems or internal network access.

Modern industrial control systems increasingly use commodity hardware, software and networking technologies to reduce costs and enhance connectivity. In fact, most industrial control systems are now connected to vendor and corporate networks, and even the Internet. This makes them highly vulnerable to remote cyber attacks.

Attempts have been made to apply security controls and mechanisms developed for information technology (IT) infrastructures to secure and isolate industrial control systems. However, a limited number of intrusion detection systems and firewalls understand industrial control protocols. Moreover, these protection systems may not be deployable because of the limited computational resources, tight timing constraints and harsh conditions encountered in industrial control environments.

This chapter describes a novel approach for enhancing industrial control system security by adding monitoring and logging mechanisms to a programmable logic controller (PLC). A proof-of-concept implementation is presented using the popular Siemens S7 programmable logic controller with a traffic light control simulation system. Several new attacks targeting the Siemens S7 model have been released recently [3], increasing the urgency of incorporating security and forensic capabilities in the popular programmable logic controller. The experimental results demonstrate that the proposed approach provides good anomaly detection accuracy with limited impact on performance. Additionally, the implementation increases the anomaly detection speed and reduces network overhead, enabling forensic investigations of programmable logic controllers to be conducted more efficiently and effectively.

2.   Programmable Logic Controllers

A programmable logic controller is a microprocessor-based system that uses programmable memory to store user-defined control programs. It is designed to operate reliably even in harsh industrial control environments. It has strict real-time constraints that mandate each execution cycle not exceed the predefined execution time. The program in a Siemens programmable logic controller is structured in the form of program blocks. The following blocks were used in the experiments conducted in this research [11]:

- **Organization Block (OB):** This type of block serves as an interface between the S7 operating system and a user program. Each organization block has a block number that indicates when it is called by the operating system. For example, OB1 is essentially the main loop of the program and is called during every execution cycle. OB100 to OB102 are called at CPU start-up to process user-defined initialization procedures prior to calling OB1. Aside from specific organization blocks that are called by the operating system, other organization blocks are executed in sequence.

- **Data Block (DB):** This type of block stores memory addresses that are shared by other program blocks and functions.

Other block structures, such as function code blocks, function blocks and system data blocks, are also components of programmable logic controller programs. However, these structures are omitted because they are not related to the experiments described in this chapter.

A Siemens programmable logic controller has a real-time operating system that controls the sequence of user programs and interrupt handlers to be executed. After the CPU boots up, the operating system calls organization blocks OB100 through OB102 if they are defined. When the programmable logic controller is in the run mode, the operating system first reads the inputs from the connected devices and updates its process image input (PII) memory addresses. Following this, the programmable logic controller calls organization block OB1 as the main entry point of the user program. If an interrupt occurs during the cycle, the organization block OB1 pauses and transfers execution flow to a predefined organization block that handles the interrupt. After all the user-defined organization blocks are executed, the operating system reads the process image output (PIQ) memory addresses and send the corresponding signals to the connected devices. Figure 1 summarizes the program execution cycle of a Siemens programmable logic controller.

3. Related Work

The intensity of research in industrial control system security and forensics has increased significantly since the Stuxnet malware was discovered in 2010. Stuxnet targeted Siemens industrial control software at Iran's uranium hexafluoride centrifuge facility in Natanz, specifically, the Siemens Total Integrated Automation (TIA) Step 7 software running on Windows. The malware was able to alter the logic flow of the industrial control system by modifying its memory and hiding the changes from equipment operators [5].

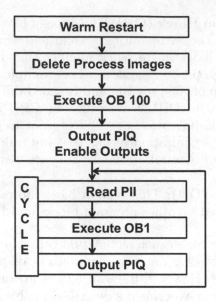

Figure 1. Program execution cycle (from [17]).

Spenneberg et al. [19] and Klick et al. [13] have demonstrated the feasibility of programmable logic controller worms and backdoors. Their malware code can infect other programmable logic controllers without leveraging personal computers and proprietary software.

The first step in programmable logic controller anomaly detection and forensics is data acquisition. Most researchers have focused on extracting data via network traffic analysis, computer and network device imaging, and remote programmable logic controller memory variable monitoring. Spyridopoulos et al. [20] and van Vliet et al. [21] have discussed the challenges of conducting forensic investigations of industrial control systems and programmable logic controllers due to the lack of security-oriented logging mechanisms that could provide valuable evidence of attacks.

Chan and Chow [4] have proposed a forensic analysis methodology that collects programmable logic controller diagnostic buffer data and metadata used in the Siemens Total Integrated Automation software [18]. However, their approach is focused on static data collection and the limited size of the diagnostic buffer may not provide complete information about an incident.

Garitano et al. [7] have reviewed various anomaly detection methodologies for industrial control systems. They argue that a network intrusion detection system may not be able to detect attacks on an industrial control system in an effective manner. Moreover, due to the limited computing resources provided by control system components, host-based intrusion detection is limited at best. Hadziosmanovic et al. [8] also argue that conventional security countermeasures such as network intrusion detection can barely identify process-related attacks involving execution code injection. This shortcoming is mainly due to the fact that network traffic generated by process-related attacks is similar to regular traffic, thereby evading common pattern-matching-based and statistics-based intrusion detection.

Wu and Nurse [22] have demonstrated that memory address monitoring can help determine if a programmable logic controller is running normally or is under attack. They also evaluated the use of a programmable logic controller as a forensic tool that continuously polls memory variables of industrial control devices and logs their values. However, remote monitoring via active polling imposes network overhead that cannot be handled in many industrial control environments.

Yau and Chow [23] have proposed two solutions for programmable logic controller anomaly detection. The first solution uses a control program logic change detector that engages a set of rules to detect and record anomalous memory address value changes. The second solution captures the values of memory addresses of interest in a log file; machine learning techniques are used to analyze the logged data and identify anomalous programmable logic controller operations [24].

Lerner et al. [15] have developed a trusted hardware system with a software simulator that predicts the output signals of a production programmable logic controller. If inconsistencies are observed between the predicted and actual outputs of the programmable logic controller, the trusted system takes over and produces the correct output signals. However, this solution is expensive due to the additional hardware and the need to reconfigure the industrial control system infrastructure.

Researchers often assume that industrial control environments are isolated and have strong physical security protection mechanisms, implying that common attack paths would start from computers in the internal network and terminate at programmable logic controllers [2]. However, many real-world infrastructures do not have such architectures. For example, it is relatively common for remote sites to have multiple programmable logic controllers that are connected to a master station over a wireless network. Moreover, remote sites are often constrained by limited space, high humidity and extreme temperatures. Therefore, standard information technology solutions such as firewalls, intrusion detection systems and network monitoring devices may be impractical, perhaps even impossible, to implement.

4. Security and Forensic Challenges

Conventional security tools and techniques are not directly applicable to programmable logic controllers because of their unique architectures, custom operating systems, and limited memory and processing power. Ahmed et al. [1] and Folkerth [6] identify the following common security and forensic challenges facing programmable logic controllers:

- **Lack of Documentation:** Inadequate low-level documentation for programmable logic controllers adversely impacts security assessments and forensic investigations.

- **Lack of Tools:** Inadequate security and forensic tools (e.g., logging systems) are available for programmable logic controllers. Many programmable logic controllers use non-routable and proprietary serial protocols for communications that are not supported by modern security and forensic tools.

- **Availability/Always-On Requirement:** Programmable logic controller availability is always the top priority in an industrial control environment. It may be infeasible to shut down a programmable logic controller to conduct an incident response or forensic investigation.

- **Limited Computing Resources:** Limited memory and processor power make it difficult to add security functionality such as encryption, authentication and intrusion/anomaly detection. Incorporating logging functionality is also difficult; this significantly hinders security analyses and forensic investigations of incidents.

- **Large Distributed Architecture:** An infrastructure often has a large number of control devices that are dispersed over a large geographical area. Acquiring timely data for implementing security functionality may not be possible due to limited bandwidth and delays.

- **Lack of Expertise:** Limited expertise exists with regard to performing programmable logic controller forensics.

5. Proposed Solution

The proposed solution for addressing the security and forensic challenges involves the implementation of active programmable logic controller monitoring. This is accomplished by incorporating a security block in a programmable logic controller. The security block monitors

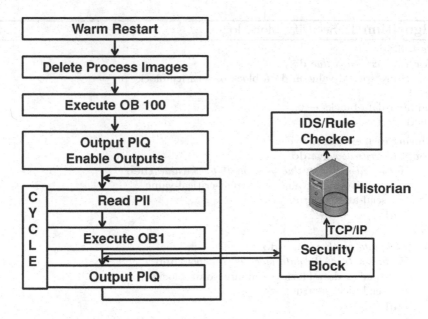

Figure 2. Program execution cycle with a security block.

critical information and system integrity, and timestamps and logs events with minimal impact on the program execution cycle of the programmable logic controller.

Figure 2 shows the new program execution cycle with the added security block. The security block is executed at the end of each scan cycle and/or before any external network communications.

Algorithm 1 specifies the security block logic. The security block implements the following three actions:

- **Critical Information Monitoring:** Lines 8–13 of the algorithm monitor the critical variables before sending information to the historian. All the digital inputs and outputs (total sixteen memory addresses) were selected as critical variables to monitor. Other memory addresses and data block variables may also be monitored.

- **System Integrity Monitoring:** Lines 14–19 of the algorithm monitor system integrity by tracking the number of installed data blocks. Monitoring the number of data blocks is necessary because modern malware is capable of spreading to programmable logic controllers without the use of conventional computer workstations or laptops. The proof-of-concept malware implementations described in [3, 19] require additional data blocks for network communications and malware program code storage. By checking the

---

Algorithm 1: Security block logic.

---

1 Initialize:
2 **for** *each critical-value* **do**
3   Store critical-value in data block of security block
4 **end**
5 number-data-blocks ← 0
6 send-alert ← false

7 During each execution cycle:
8 **for** *each critical-value* **do**
9   **if** *current-critical-value ≠ security-block-value* **then**
10   security-block-value ← current-critical-value
11   send-alert ← true
12   **end**
13 **end**
14 **for** *each data-block-address* **do**
15   **if** *first-byte of the data-block is readable* **then**
16   number-data-blocks ← number-data-blocks + 1
17   send-alert ← true
18   **end**
19 **end**
20 **if** *send-alert = true* **then**
21   Query current-system-time
22   Format current-system-time to byte stream
23   Invoke network system call to send current-system-time
24   and every security-block-value to historian
25 **end**

---

number of data blocks, it is possible to detect unauthorized modifications to the programmable logic controller structure.

- **Event Logging:** Lines 20–24 of the algorithm query the system for the time and format the timestamp to a byte stream. The monitored information is timestamped and sent via TCP/IP to a historian for long-term storage.

6.   Experimental Methodology and Results

This section describes the experiments undertaken to evaluate the proposed security and forensic solution for programmable logic controllers.

6.1   Experimental Setup

The experiments employed a Siemens S7-1200 model programmable logic controller with the 1214C CPU and firmware version v4.0. The

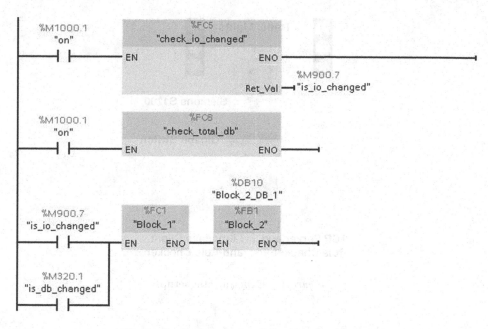

Figure 3. Ladder logic of the security block.

programmable logic controller was loaded with a traffic light control simulation program.

The security block in the programmable logic controller was implemented using the structured control language (SCL) and ladder diagram (ladder logic) language. The Total Integrated Automation Portal v13 was used to add the security block (organization block OB32767), the last organization block in the programmable logic controller. Figure 3 shows the ladder logic of the security block. The security block only executes after all the other organization blocks have executed.

A computer workstation with Netcat as a TCP server was deployed as the historian. The received data was multiplexed to a rule checker program written in Python. The rule checker parsed the data and applied the detection rules suggested by Yau and Chow [23].

Another computer workstation was used for performance benchmarking. It employed the conventional approach to poll the relevant memory address values of the programmable logic controller using the libnodave open source library [10]. The libnodave client, written in C, connected to the programmable logic controller via ISO-TSAP-over-TCP/IP. All the collected information was timestamped according to the clock on the computer workstation.

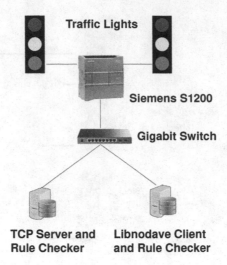

Figure 4. Experimental setup.

Figure 4 shows the experimental setup. The programmable logic controller and the two computer workstations were connected using a gigabit switch.

6.2   Attacks

The following attacks were executed to compare the detection accuracy of the security block implementation versus the conventional monitoring method:

- **Memory Read/Write Logic Attack:** This attack attempted to read and alter the values of memory variables in the running programmable logic controller.

  A conventional method for monitoring the attack is to poll the memory address values and compare them with the expected values. The libnodave client was employed to implement the conventional method as a benchmark. It sent about 180 packets per second to query the current value of a memory variable. The current value was compared against the previous value to determine if there was an unexpected change to the memory variable. The conventional method was able to detect a change to a single variable within 100 ms. In contrast, the security block could detect changes to multiple variables within just 10 ms and it sent just one packet after a change was detected.

■ **Malware Worm Attack:** This attack simulated the injection of a programmable logic controller worm as in [3, 19] by pushing one or more data blocks and an organization block to the programmable logic controller.

In order to detect if an additional data block had been added to the programmable logic controller, the total number of installed data blocks was counted and compared against the expected number of data blocks. The maximum number of data blocks available in the test device is 60,000. Unfortunately, the S7-1200 device does not provide an API or a system function call to identify the number of installed data blocks as in the case of the earlier S7-300 model. As a workaround, the first byte of every possible data block was examined and the number of times a value could be successfully read was counted.

In the conventional monitoring method, libnodave was used to send a probe message to query for the first byte in a data block. If the data could be read, then it was possible to infer that the specific data block was installed. This process was repeated for all possible data blocks from DB0 to DB59999. Finally, the total number of installed blocks was compared against the expected number of blocks to determine if there was a change in the number of data blocks installed.

In the case of the security block method, a problem was encountered because examining all the data blocks in one execution cycle exceeded the hard execution time constraint of 150 ms. Therefore, the workaround checked a fixed number of data blocks in a single execution cycle and the remaining checks were performed in subsequent cycles until all 60,000 data blocks were checked. This implementation satisfies the execution time constraint and also enables the performance impact imposed by the security block to be controlled.

■ **Time Bomb Attack:** This attack inserted malware that triggered at a particular time. Upon being triggered, the malware sent an output signal and reverted to its normal state during the next scan cycle. This attack was difficult to detect because the anomalous output signal was active for a very short period of time. Moreover, the program was not changed in any other way. No additional network traffic was generated because the output device was not connected to the monitoring network (so network sniffing would not capture any anomalous traffic).

In the conventional and proposed methods, a particular output address was monitored as in the case of the memory read/write logic attack. The time bomb was set to trigger every five seconds and change an output address value for exactly one cycle. In the next cycle, the time bomb changed the output address value back to its original value.

The monitoring was conducted for five hours and the number of alerts triggered by each method was recorded. The conventional monitoring method using libnodave triggered around 850 alerts whereas the security block method triggered 3,600 alerts. Thus, the sensitivity of the security block method is four times better than conventional active polling using libnodave.

6.3   Performance Impact

The performance impact of the security block was tested using the Siemens Total Integrated Automation Professional software v13 SP1. The software was executed on a computer workstation that was connected to the programmable logic controller via TCP/IP using a Profinet interface. The online and diagnostics feature of the software was employed to capture the shortest, current and longest cycle times for the following test cases:

- **Test Case 1:** This test case involved a control benchmark without the security block.

- **Test Case 2:** This test case employed the security block, but without a status change.

- **Test Case 3:** This test case involved frequent manual status changes by modifying the input signal rapidly (more than fifteen status changes per second).

- **Test Case 4:** This (stress) test case changed the input signal every cycle (approximately 150 updates per second).

- **Test Case 5:** This test case employed an optimized security block that did not perform timestamp and I/O string conversions.

Table 1 shows the performance impacts introduced by the security block for the five test cases. The security block added about 5 ms performance impact to the existing program under normal usage (Test Cases 2 and 3) and about 10 ms under stress testing (Test Case 4). The experimental results are consistent with the performance benchmarking performed by Klick et al. [13]. Most of the cycle time (80%) used by the

Table 1. Performance impacts introduced by the security block.

Test Case	Shortest Cycle Time (ms)	Current Cycle Time (ms)	Longest Cycle Time (ms)
1	1	1	5
2	3	6	7
3	3	6	7
4	3	9	12
5	3	6	8

security block was employed to check for new data blocks. The performance impact can be optimized by adjusting the number of data blocks checked per cycle.

7. Discussion

The incorporation of a security block in the programmable logic controller offers several advantages over conventional passive or external monitoring:

- The security block provides access to internal programmable logic controller information, functions and addresses; some of this information is not accessible using a network protocol. For example, there is no easy way to access the internal system clock at a certain point in execution, or intermediate execution states or interrupts during an execution cycle.

- The performance impact of the security block can be adjusted. This is because the number of steps required can be computed and the time required can be measured like other programmable logic controller functions; the steps can then be distributed over multiple execution cycles to adjust the performance impact. In contrast, the conventional polling approach is handled by the programmable logic controller operating system with undocumented time requirements.

- The security block method has a higher detection accuracy rate than the conventional polling method. For example, in the case of the time bomb attack, some memory addresses changes were missed by the conventional method. The security block method provides more complete data, which facilitates the implementation of additional anomaly detection functionality.

- Events identified by the security block method can be crafted like syslog messages and matched against simple regular expressions. These messages can be parsed by intrusion detection or situational awareness and event management systems to trigger alerts.

- Compared with the conventional memory variable polling method, the security block method only sends traffic when certain conditions are met, avoiding the network overhead incurred by continuous monitoring.

- The security block method does not require network traffic captures and network traffic analysis. Neither special network equipment nor the reconfiguration of a mirror port to redirect network traffic for sniffing are required.

- The security block method is well suited to programmable logic controllers that are deployed individually in remote locations. Accurate timestamps provided by the programmable logic controllers facilitate the creation of event timelines in forensic investigations.

- The security block method facilitates the implementation of security and forensic functionality. For example, the security block could be enhanced to configure the reading of memory address values on the fly and to report when changes are detected.

However, the security block method has certain limitations. Cases exist were this solution may not be appropriate or may require careful consideration before being applied. One example is when a programmable logic controller must operate continuously and cannot be taken down to introduce the security block. Other examples are when the programmable logic controller program is developed by a third-party and modifications to the main program block are not allowed. Finally, selecting the information to be monitored requires domain-specific expertise; too much monitoring can negatively impact performance.

Another drawback of the security block method is that additional information is sent to the network. This information is exposed to passive network sniffing attacks as in the case of the conventional method that polls memory variables.

This research has focused exclusively on the Siemens S7-1200 programmable logic controller. Other programmable logic controller models have different instruction sets. For example, the S7-300 series uses TEST_DB to detect the creation of a new data block; this may, in fact, improve the performance impact of the security block.

The current security block method is unable to combat malware that injects code in organization block OB1 without using a data block [14].

Fortunately, the programmable logic controller used in this research employs the S7-Comm Plus v3.0 protocol, which is equipped with additional digest checking. Thus, it appears that the programmable logic controller is not vulnerable to the code injection attack, unless the latest protocol has been hacked [9].

8.   Conclusions

This chapter has presented a novel security block method for detecting memory variable changes that may affect programmable logic controller integrity, and for supporting incident response and forensic investigations. Experiments that evaluated the proposed method against the conventional programmable logic controller polling method reveal that it provides increased accuracy and reduced (and adjustable) performance impact. Additionally, the proposed method introduces minimal network traffic overhead and detects attacks that are rarely identified by other approaches. However, although the method offers promising anomaly detection and forensic functionality, implementing it in a production environment requires careful study to prevent disruptions to the industrial control system and the infrastructure assets it operates.

Future research will focus on applying the proposed method to other programmable logic controller models. Research will also concentrate on detecting program code changes caused by worm and code injection attacks. Furthermore, machine learning techniques will be employed to enhance the coverage and accuracy of attack detection.

References

[1] I. Ahmed, S. Obermeier, M. Naedele and G. Richard, SCADA systems: Challenges for forensic investigators, *IEEE Computer*, vol. 45(12), pp. 44–51, 2012.

[2] B. Akyol, H. Kirkham, S. Clements and M. Hadley, A Survey of Wireless Communications for the Electric Power System, Technical Report PNNL-19084, Pacific Northwest National Laboratory, Richland, Washington, 2010.

[3] D. Beresford, Exploiting Siemens Simatic S7 PLCs, presented at *Black Hat USA*, 2011.

[4] R. Chan and K. Chow, Forensic analysis of a Siemens programmable logic controller, in *Critical Infrastructure Protection X*, M. Rice and S. Shenoi (Eds.), Springer, Heidelberg, Germany, pp. 117–130, 2016.

[5] N. Falliere, L. O'Murchu and E. Chien, W32.Stuxnet Dossier, Version 1.4, Symantec, Mountain View, California, 2011.

[6] L. Folkerth, Forensic Analysis of Industrial Control Systems, InfoSec Reading Room, SANS Institute, Bethesda, Maryland, 2015.

[7] I. Garitano, R. Uribeetxeberria and U. Zurutuza, A review of SCADA anomaly detection systems, *Proceedings of the Sixth International Conference on Soft Computing Models in Industrial and Environmental Applications*, pp. 357–366, 2011.

[8] D. Hadziosmanovic, D. Bolzoni and P. Hartel, A log mining approach for process monitoring in SCADA, *International Journal of Information Security*, vol. 11(4), pp. 231–251, 2012.

[9] C. Hao, New PLC worm virus and its countermeasures (in Chinese), NSFOCUS, Santa Clara, California (`blog.nsfocus.net/worm-plc-strategy`), September 12, 2016.

[10] T. Hergenhahn, libnodave (`sourceforge.net/projects/libnodave`), 2014.

[11] C. Jones, *STEP 7 Programming Made Easy in LAD, FBD and STL: A Practical Guide to Programming S7300/S7-400 Programmable Logic Controllers*, Patrick-Turner Publishing, Atlanta, Georgia, 2013.

[12] S. Karnouskos, Stuxnet worm impact on industrial cyber-physical system security, *Proceedings of the Thirty-Seventh Annual Conference of the IEEE Industrial Electronics Society*, pp. 4490–4494, 2011.

[13] J. Klick, S. Lau, D. Marzin, J. Malchow and V. Roth, Internet-facing PLCs as a network backdoor, *Proceedings of the IEEE Conference on Communications and Network Security*, pp. 524–532, 2015.

[14] Langner, A time bomb with fourteen bytes, Dover, Delaware (`www.langner.com/2011/07/a-time-bomb-with-fourteen-bytes`), July 21, 2011.

[15] L. Lerner, Z. Franklin, W. Baumann and C. Patterson, Application-level autonomic hardware to predict and preempt software attacks on industrial control systems, *Proceedings of the Forty-Fourth Annual IEEE/IFIP International Conference on Dependable Systems and Networks*, pp. 136–147, 2014.

[16] Mice Engineering, Yuen Long Sewage Treatment Works System, Hong Kong, China (`www.miceeng.com/eng/project_id=yuenlong.htm`), 2008.

[17] Siemens, SITRAIN – Training for Industry Worldwide, Nuremberg, Germany (`www.sitrain-learning.siemens.com`), 2018.

[18] Siemens, Totally Integrated Automation Portal, Nuremberg, Germany (`www.siemens.com/global/en/home/products/autom ation/industry-software/automation-software/tia-portal. html`), 2018.

[19] R. Spenneberg, M. Bruggemann and H. Schwartke, PLC-blaster: A worm living solely in the PLC, presented at *Black Hat USA*, 2016.

[20] T. Spyridopoulos, T. Tryfonas and J. May, Incident analysis and digital forensics of SCADA and industrial control systems, *Proceedings of the Eighth IET International System Safety Conference Incorporating the Cyber Security Conference*, 2013.

[21] P. van Vliet, M. Kechadi and N. Le-Khac, Forensics in industrial control systems: A case study, *Proceedings of the Workshop on the Security of Cyber-Physical Systems; Conference on Cybersecurity of Industrial Control Systems*, pp. 147–156, 2016.

[22] T. Wu and J. Nurse, Exploring the use of PLC debugging tools for digital forensic investigations of SCADA systems, *Journal of Digital Forensics, Security and Law*, vol. 10(4), pp. 79–96, 2015.

[23] K. Yau and K. Chow, PLC forensics based on control program logic change detection, *Journal of Digital Forensics, Security and Law*, vol. 10(4), pp. 59–68, 2015.

[24] K. Yau and K. Chow, Detecting anomalous programmable logic controller events using machine learning, in *Advances in Digital Forensics XIII*, G. Peterson and S. Shenoi (Eds.), Springer, Heidelberg, Germany, pp. 81–94, 2017.

Printed in the United States
By Bookmasters